Robert Browning

Selections from the poetical Works of Robert Browning

Robert Browning

Selections from the poetical Works of Robert Browning

ISBN/EAN: 9783337140274

Printed in Europe, USA, Canada, Australia, Japan

Cover: Foto ©ninafisch / pixelio.de

More available books at **www.hansebooks.com**

SELECTIONS

FROM

THE POETICAL WORKS

OF

ROBERT BROWNING.

FROM THE SIXTH LONDON EDITION.
(FIRST AND SECOND SERIES.)

NEW YORK:
THOMAS Y. CROWELL & CO.,

Press of Berwick & Smith,

Boston, Mass.

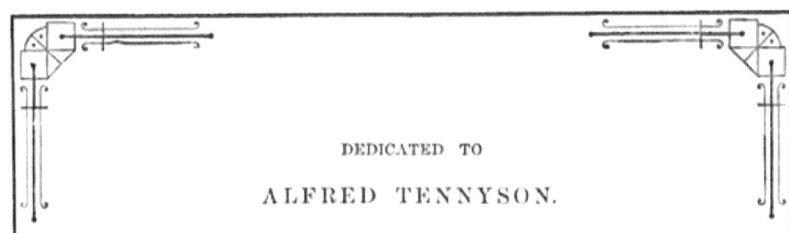

DEDICATED TO

ALFRED TENNYSON.

IN POETRY — ILLUSTRIOUS AND CONSUMMATE;

IN FRIENDSHIP — NOBLE AND SINCERE.

IN the present selection from my poetry, there is an attempt to escape from the embarrassment of appearing to pronounce upon what myself may consider the best of it. I adopt another principle; and by simply stringing together certain pieces on the thread of an imaginary personality, I present them in succession, rather as the natural development of a particular experience than because I account them the most noteworthy portion of my work. Such an attempt was made in the volume of selections from the poetry of Elizabeth Barrett Browning : to which — in outward uniformity at least — my own would venture to become a companion.

A few years ago, had such an opportunity presented itself, I might have been tempted to say a word in reply to the objections my poetry was used to encounter. Time has kindly co-operated with my disinclination to write the poetry and the criticism besides. The readers I am at last privileged to expect, meet me fully half-way; and if, from the fitting stand-point, they must still "censure me in their wisdom," they have previously "awakened their senses that they may the better judge." Nor do I apprehend any more charges of being wilfully obscure, unconscientiously careless, or perversely harsh. Having hitherto done my utmost in the art to which my life is a devotion, I cannot engage to increase the effort; but I conceive that there may be helpful light, as well as re-assuring warmth, in the attention and sympathy I gratefully acknowledge.

R. B.

LONDON, May 14, 1872.

iii

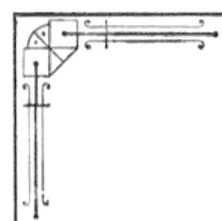
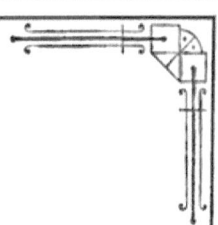

CONTENTS.

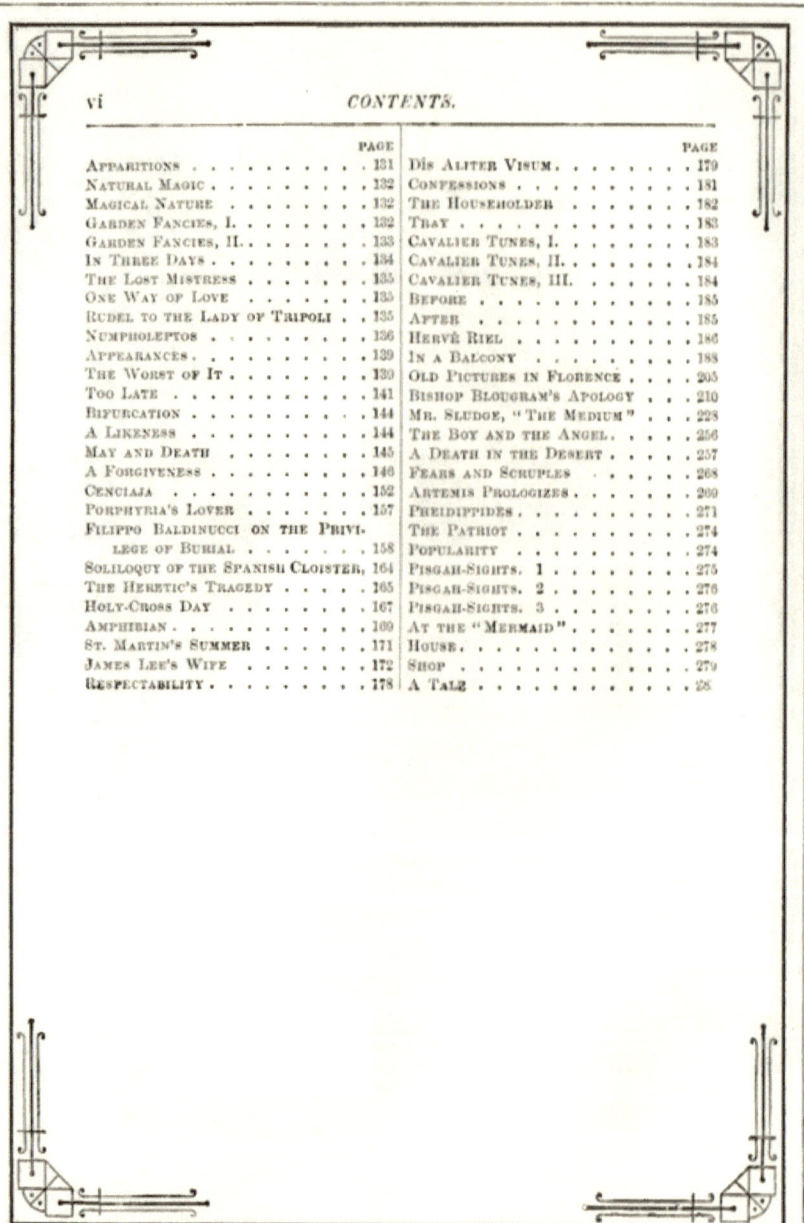

vi CONTENTS.

A Face. — Page 1.

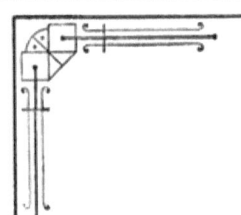
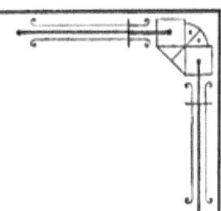

SELECTIONS FROM ROBERT BROWNING.

MY STAR.

ALL that I know
　Of a certain star
Is, it can throw
　(Like the angled spar)
Now a dart of red,
　Now a dart of blue ;
Till my friends have said
　They would fain see, too,
My star that dartles the red and the
　blue !
Then it stops like a bird ; like a
　flower, hangs furled :
　They must solace themselves with
　the Saturn above it.
What matter to me if their star is a
　world ?
　Mine has opened its soul to me ;
　therefore I love it.

A FACE.

IF one could have that little head of
　hers
Painted upon a background of pale
　gold,
Such as the Tuscan's early art prefers !
No shade encroaching on the match-
　less mould
Of those two lips, which should be
　opening soft
In the pure profile ; not as when she
　laughs,
For that spoils all : but rather as if
　aloft
Yon hyacinth, she loves so, leaned its
　staff's
Burthen of honey-colored buds, to
　kiss
And capture 'twixt the lips apart for
　this.

Then her lithe neck, three fingers
　might surround.
How it should waver, on the pale gold
　ground,
Up to the fruit-shaped, perfect chin it
　lifts !
I know, Correggio loves to mass, in
　rifts
Of heaven, his angel faces, orb on orb
Breaking its outline, burning shades
　absorb ;
But these are only massed there, I
　should think,
Waiting to see some wonder momently
Grow out, stand full, fade slow against
　the sky
(That's the pale ground you'd see this
　sweet face by),
All heaven, meanwhile, condensed
　into one eye
Which fears to lose the wonder,
　should it wink.

MY LAST DUCHESS.

FERRARA.

THAT's my last Duchess painted on
　the wall,
Looking as if she were alive.　I call
That piece a wonder, now : Frà Pan-
　dolf's hands
Worked busily a day, and there she
　stands.
Will't please you sit and look at her ?
　I said
" Frà Pandolf " by design : for never
　read
Strangers like you that pictured coun-
　tenance,
The depth and passion of its earnest
　glance,

1

But to myself they turned (since none puts by
The curtain I have drawn for you, but I),
And seemed as they would ask me, if they durst,
How such a glance came there; so, not the first
Are you to turn and ask thus. Sir, 'twas not
Her husband's presence only, called that spot
Of joy into the Duchess' cheek: perhaps
Frà Pandolf chanced to say, "Her mantle laps
Over my lady's wrist too much," or "Paint
Must never hope to reproduce the faint
Half-flush that dies along her throat;" such stuff
Was courtesy, she thought, and cause enough
For calling up that spot of joy. She had
A heart — how shall I say? — too soon made glad,
Too easily impressed; she liked whate'er
She looked on, and her looks went everywhere.
Sir, 'twas all one! My favor at her breast,
The dropping of the daylight in the West,
The bough of cherries some officious fool
Broke in the orchard for her, the white mule
She rode with round the terrace, — all and each
Would draw from her alike the approving speech,
Or blush, at least. She thanked men, — good! but thanked
Somehow — I know not how — as if she ranked
My gift of a nine-hundred-years-old name
With anybody's gift. Who'd stoop to blame
This sort of trifling? Even had you skill
In speech — (which I have not) — to make your will
Quite clear to such an one, and say, "Just this
Or that in you disgusts me; here you miss,
Or there exceed the mark" — and if she let
Herself be lessoned so, nor plainly set
Her wits to yours, forsooth, and made excuse,
— E'en then would be some stooping; and I choose
Never to stoop. O sir! she smiled, no doubt,
Whene'er I passed her; but who passed without
Much the same smile? This grew; I gave commands;
Then all smiles stopped together. There she stands
As if alive. Will't please you rise? We'll meet
The company below, then. I repeat,
The Count your master's known munificence
Is ample warrant that no just pretence
Of mine for dowry will be disallowed;
Though his fair daughter's self, as I avowed
At starting, is my object. Nay, we'll go
Together down, sir. Notice Neptune, though,
Taming a sea-horse, thought a rarity,
Which Claus of Innsbruck cast in bronze for me!

SONG FROM "PIPPA PASSES."

I.

GIVE her but a least excuse to love me!
  When — where —
How — can this arm establish her above me,
  If fortune fixed her as my lady there,
There already, to eternally reprove me?
  ("Hist!" said Kate the queen;
But "Oh," cried the maiden, binding her tresses,
  "'Tis only a page that carols unseen,
Crumbling your hounds their messes!")

II.

Is she wronged? — To the rescue of
  her honor,
  My heart!
Is she poor? — What costs it to be-
  come a donor?
  Merely an earth to cleave, a sea to
  part.
But that fortune should have thrust
  all this upon her!
("Nay, list!" bade Kate the queen;
And still cried the maiden, binding
  her tresses,
  "'Tis only a page that carols un-
  seen,
Fitting your hawks their jesses!")

CRISTINA.

I.

SHE should never have looked at me
  if she meant I should not love
  her!
There are plenty . . . men, you call
  such, I suppose . . . she may
  discover
All her soul to, if she pleases, and yet
  leave much as she found them:
But I'm not so; and she knew it when
  she fixed me, glancing round
  them.

II.

What? To fix me thus meant noth-
  ing? But I can't tell (there's
  my weakness)
What her look said! — no vile cant,
  sure, about "need to strew the
  bleakness
Of some lone shore with its pearl-seed,
  that the sea feels" — no "strange
  yearning
That such souls have, most to lavish
  where there's chance of least
  returning."

III.

Oh! we're sunk enough here, God
  knows! but not quite so sunk
  that moments,
Sure though seldom, are denied us,
  when the spirit's true endow-
  ments
Stand out plainly from its false ones,
  and apprise it if pursuing
Or the right way or the wrong way,
  to its triumph or undoing.

IV.

There are flashes struck from mid-
  nights, there are fire-flames
  noondays kindle,
Whereby piled-up honors perish,
  whereby swollen ambitions
  dwindle;
While just this or that poor impulse,
  which for once had play unsti-
  fled,
Seems the sole work of a lifetime
  that away the rest have trifled.

V.

Doubt you if, in some such moment,
  as she fixed me, she felt clearly,
Ages past the soul existed, here an
  age 'tis resting merely,
And hence fleets again for ages; while
  the true end, sole and single,
It stops here for is, this love way,
  with some other soul to mingle?

VI.

Else it loses what it lived for, and
  eternally must lose it;
Better ends may be in prospect,
  deeper blisses (if you choose it),
But this life's end and this love-bliss
  have been lost here. Doubt you
  whether
This she felt as, looking at me, mine
  and her souls rushed together?

VII.

Oh, observe! Of course, next moment,
  the world's honors, in derision,
Trampled out the light forever.
  Never fear but there's provision
Of the Devil's to quench knowledge,
  lest we walk the earth in rap-
  ture!
—Making those who catch God's se-
  cret, just so much more prize
  their capture!

VIII.

Such am I: the secret's mine now!
  She has lost me, I have gained
  her;
Her soul's mine: and thus, grown
  perfect, I shall pass my life's
  remainder.
Life will just hold out the proving both
  our powers, alone and blended;
And then, come next life quickly!
  This world's use will have
  been ended.

COUNT GISMOND.

AIX IN PROVENCE.

I.

CHRIST God who savest man, save most
  Of men Count Gismond who saved me!
Count Gauthier, when he chose his post,
  Chose time and place and company
To suit it: when he struck at length
My honor, 'twas with all his strength.

II.

And doubtlessly, ere he could draw
  All points to one, he must have schemed!
That miserable morning saw
  Few half so happy as I seemed,
While being dressed in queen's array
To give our tourney prize away.

III.

I thought they loved me, did me grace
  To please themselves: 'twas all their deed.
God makes, or fair or foul, our face:
  If showing mine so caused to bleed
My cousins' hearts, they should have dropped
  A word, and straight the play had stopped.

IV.

They, too, so beauteous! Each a queen
  By virtue of her brow and breast;
Not needing to be crowned, I mean,
  As I do. E'en when I was dressed,
Had either of them spoke, instead
Of glancing sideways with still head!

V.

But no: they let me laugh, and sing
  My birthday song quite through, adjust
The last rose in my garland, fling
  A last look on the mirror, trust
My arms to each an arm of theirs,
And so descend the castle-stairs —

VI.

And come out on the morning troop
  Of merry friends who kissed my cheek,

And called me queen, and made me stoop
  Under the canopy — (a streak
That pierced it, of the outside sun,
Powdered with gold its gloom's soft dun) —

VII.

And they could let me take my state
  And foolish throne amid applause
Of all come there to celebrate
  My queen's-day — Oh, I think the cause
Of much was, they forgot no crowd
Makes up for parents in their shroud!

VIII.

However that be, all eyes were bent
  Upon me, when my cousins cast
Theirs down; 'twas time I should present
  The victor's crown, but . . . there, 'twill last
No long time . . . the old mist again
Blinds me as then it did. How vain!

IX.

See! Gismond's at the gate, in talk
  With his two boys: I can proceed.
Well, at that moment, who should stalk
  Forth boldly — to my face, indeed —
But Gauthier? and he thundered "Stay!"
And all staid. "Bring no crowns, I say!

X.

"Bring torches! Wind the penance-sheet
  About her! Let her shun the chaste,
Or lay herself before their feet!
  Shall she, whose body I embraced
A night long, queen it in the day?
For honor's sake no crowns, I say!"

XI.

I? What I answered? As I live,
  I never fancied such a thing
As answer possible to give.
  What says the body when they spring
Some monstrous torture-engine's whole
Strength on it? No more says the soul.

XII.

Till out strode Gismond: then I knew
  That I was saved. I never met
His face before; but, at first view,
  I felt quite sure that God had set
Himself to Satan: who would spend
A minute's mistrust on the end?

XIII.

He strode to Gauthier, in his throat
  Gave him the lie, then struck his
    mouth
With one back-handed blow that
    wrote
  In blood men's verdict then. North,
    South,
East, West, I looked. The lie was
    dead
And damned, and truth stood up in-
    stead.

XIV.

This glads me most, that I enjoyed
  The heart o' the joy, with my con-
    tent
In watching Gismond unalloyed
  By any doubt of the event;
God took that on him — I was bid
Watch Gismond for my part: I did.

XV.

Did I not watch him while he let
  His armorer just brace his greaves,
Rivet his hauberk, on the fret
  The while! His foot . . . my mem-
    ory leaves
No least stamp out, nor how anon
He pulled his ringing gauntlets on.

XVI.

And e'en before the trumpet's sound
  Was finished, prone lay the false
    knight,
Prone as his lie, upon the ground:
  Gismond flew at him, used no
    sleight
O' the sword, but open-breasted
    drove,
Cleaving till out the truth he clove.

XVII.

Which done, he dragged him to my
    feet,
  And said, "Here die, but end thy
    breath
In full confession, lest thou fleet
  From my first to God's second
    death!

Say, hast thou lied?" And, "I have
    lied
To God and her," he said, and died.

XVIII.

Then Gismond, kneeling to me, asked
  — What safe my heart holds, though
    no word
Could I repeat now, if I tasked
  My powers forever, to a third,
Dear even as you are. Pass the rest
Until I sank upon his breast.

XIX.

Over my head his arm he flung
  Against the world; and scarce I
    felt
His sword (that dripped by me and
    swung)
  A little shifted in its belt,
For he began to say the while
How South our home lay many a
    mile.

XX.

So 'mid the shouting multitude
  We two walked forth to never more
Return. My cousins have pursued
  Their life, untroubled as before
I vexed them. Gauthier's dwelling-
    place
God lighten! May his soul find
    grace!

XXI.

Our elder boy has got the clear
  Great brow; though when his broth-
    er's black
Full eye shows scorn, it . . . Gismond
    here?
  And have you brought my tercel
    back?
I was just telling Adela
How many birds it struck since May.

EURYDICE TO ORPHEUS.

A PICTURE BY FREDERICK LEIGH-
TON, R.A.

But give them me, the mouth, the
    eyes, the brow!
Let them once more absorb me! One
    look now

Will lap me round forever, not to pass
Out of its light, though darkness lie beyond:
Hold me but safe again within the bond
Of one immortal look! All woe that was,
Forgotten, and all terror that may be,
Defied, — no past is mine, no future: look at me!

THE GLOVE.

(PETER RONSARD *loquitur.*)

"HEIGHO," yawned one day King Francis,
"Distance all value enhances!
When a man's busy, why, leisure
Strikes him as wonderful pleasure:
'Faith, and at leisure once is he?
Straightway he wants to be busy.
Here we've got peace; and aghast I'm
Caught thinking war the true pastime.
Is there a reason in metre?
Give us your speech, master Peter!"
I who, if mortal dare say so,
Ne'er am at loss with my Naso,
"Sire," I replied, "joys prove cloudlets:
Men are the merest Ixions" —
Here the King whistled aloud, "Let's
. . . Heigho . . . go look at our lions!"
Such are the sorrowful chances
If you talk fine to King Francis.

And so, to the court-yard proceeding,
Our company, Francis was leading,
Increased by new followers tenfold
Before he arrived at the penfold;
Lords, ladies, like clouds which bedizen
At sunset the western horizon.
And Sir de Lorge pressed 'mid the foremost
With the dame he professed to adore most —
Oh, what a face! One by fits eyed
Her, and the horrible pitside;

For the penfold surrounded a hollow
Which led where the eye scarce dared follow,
And shelved to the chamber secluded
Where Bluebeard, the great lion, brooded.
The king hailed his keeper, an Arab
As glossy and black as a scarab,
And bade him make sport, and at once stir
Up and out of his den the old monster.
They opened a hole in the wire-work
Across it, and dropped there a firework,
And fled: one's heart's beating redoubled;
A pause, while the pit's mouth was troubled,
The blackness and silence so utter,
By the firework's slow sparkling and sputter;
Then earth in a sudden contortion
Gave out to our gaze her abortion.
Such a brute! Were I friend Clement Marot
(Whose experience of nature's but narrow,
And whose faculties move in no small mist
When he versifies David the Psalmist)
I should study that brute to describe you
Illum Juda Leonem de Tribu.
One's whole blood grew curdling and creepy
To see the black mane, vast and heapy,
The tail in the air stiff and straining,
The wide eyes, nor waxing nor waning,
As over the barrier which bounded
His platform, and us who surrounded
The barrier, they reached and they rested
On space that might stand him in best stead;
For who knew, he thought, what the amazement,
The eruption of clatter and blaze meant,
And if, in this minute of wonder,
No outlet, 'mid lightning and thunder,
Lay broad, and, his shackles all shivered,
The lion at last was delivered?

Ay, that was the open sky o'erhead!
And you saw by the flash on his fore-
  head,
By the hope in those eyes wide and
  steady,
He was leagues in the desert already,
Driving the flocks up the mountain,
Or catlike couched hard by the foun-
  tain
To waylay the date-gathering negress:
So guarded he entrance or egress.
  "How he stands!" quoth the king:
  "we may well swear
(No novice, we've won our spurs else-
  where,
And so can afford the confession),
We exercise wholesome discretion
In keeping aloof from his threshold;
Once hold you, those jaws want no
  fresh hold,
Their first would too pleasantly pur-
  loin
The visitor's brisket or sirloin:
But who's he would prove so fool-
  hardy?
Not the best man of Marignan, par-
  die!"

The sentence no sooner was uttered,
Than over the rails a glove fluttered,
Fell close to the lion, and rested:
The dame 'twas, who flung it and
  jested
With life so, De Lorge had been
  wooing
For months past; he sat there pursu-
  ing
His suit, weighing out with noncha-
  lance
Fine speeches like gold from a bal-
  ance.

Sound the trumpet, no true knight's
  a tarrier!
De Lorge made one leap at the bar-
  rier,
Walked straight to the glove, — while
  the lion
Ne'er moved, kept his far-reaching
  eye on
The palm-tree-edged desert-spring's
  sapphire,
And the musky oiled skin of the Kaf-
  fir, —
Picked it up, and as calmly retreated,
Leaped back where the lady was
  seated,
And full in the face of its owner
Flung the glove.

"Your heart's queen,
  you dethrone her?
So should I!" — cried the King —
  "'twas mere vanity,
Not love, set that task to humanity!"
Lords and ladies alike turned with
  loathing
From such a proved wolf in sheep's
  clothing.

Not so, I; for I caught an expression
In her brow's undisturbed self-posses-
  sion
Amid the Court's scoffing and merri-
  ment, —
As if from no pleasing experiment
She rose, yet of pain not much heed-
  ful
So long as the process was needful, —
As if she had tried, in a crucible,
To what "speeches like gold" were
  reducible,
And, finding the finest prove copper,
Felt smoke in her face was but proper;
To know what she had *not* to trust
  to,
Was worth all the ashes and dust
  too.
She went out 'mid hooting and laugh-
  ter;
Clement Marot staid; I followed
  after,
And asked, as a grace, what it all
  meant?
If she wished not the rash deed's re-
  calment?
"For I" — so I spoke — "am a poet,
Human nature, — behooves that I
  know it!"

She told me, "Too long had I heard
Of the deed proved alone by the
  word:
For my love — what De Lorge would
  not dare!
With my scorn — what De Lorge could
  compare!
And the endless descriptions of death
He would brave when my lip formed
  a breath,
I must reckon as braved, or, of course,
Doubt his word — and moreover, per-
  force,
For such gifts as no lady could spurn,
Must offer my love in return.
When I looked on your lion, it brought
All the dangers at once to my thought,
Encountered by all sorts of men,
Before he was lodged in his den, —

From the poor slave whose club or
  bare hands
Dug the trap, set the snare on the
  sands,
With no King and no Court to ap-
  plaud,
By no shame, should he shrink, over-
  awed,
Yet to capture the creature made
  shift,
That his rude boys might laugh at
  the gift,
— To the page who last leaped o'er
  the fence
Of the pit, on no greater pretence
Than to get back the bonnet he
  dropped,
Lest his pay for a week should be
  stopped.
So, wiser I judged it to make
One trial what ' death for my sake '
Really meant, while the power was
  yet mine,
Than to wait until time should de-
  fine
Such a phrase not so simply as I,
Who took it to mean just 'to die.'
The blow a glove gives is but weak:
Does the mark yet discolor my cheek?
But, when the heart suffers a blow,
Will the pain pass so soon, do you
  know?"

I looked, as away she was sweeping,
And saw a youth eagerly keeping
As close as he dared to the doorway.
No doubt that a noble should more
  weigh
His life than befits a plebeian;
And yet, had our brute been Ne-
  mean —
(I judge by a certain calm fervor
The youth stepped with, forward to
  serve her)
— He'd have scarce thought you did
  him the worst turn
If you whispered, "Friend, what you'd
  get, first earn!"
And when, shortly after, she carried
Her shame from the Court, and they
  married,
To that marriage some happiness,
  inaugre
The voice of the Court, I dared augur.

For De Lorge, he made women with
  men vie,
Those in wonder and praise, these in
  envy:

And, in short, stood so plain a head
  taller
That he wooed and won . . . how do
  you call her?
The beauty, that rose in the sequel
To the King's love, who loved her a
  week well.
And 'twas noticed he never would
  honor
De Lorge (who looked daggers upon
  her)
With the easy commission of stretch-
  ing
His legs in the service, and fetching
His wife, from her chamber, those
  straying
Sad gloves she was always mislaying,
While the King took the closet to chat
  in, —
But of course this adventure came
  pat in.
And never the King told the story,
How bringing a glove brought such
  glory,
But the wife smiled — "His nerves
  are grown firmer:
Mine he brings now and utters no
  murmur."

Venienti occurrite morbo!
With which moral I drop my theorbo.

SONG.

I.

NAY but you, who do not love her,
  Is she not pure gold, my mistress?
Holds earth aught — speak truth —
  above her?
  Aught like this tress, see, and this
  tress,
And this last fairest tress of all,
So fair, see, ere I let it fall!

II.

Because, you spend your lives in
  praising;
  To praise, you search the wide world
  over:
Then why not witness, calmly gazing,
  If earth holds aught — speak truth
  — above her?
Above this tress, and this, I touch
But cannot praise, I love so much:

A SERENADE AT THE VILLA.

I.

THAT was I, you heard last night,
  When there rose no moon at all,
Nor, to pierce the strained and tight
  Tent of heaven, a planet small:
Life was dead, and so was light.

II.

Not a twinkle from the fly,
  Not a glimmer from the worm.
When the crickets stopped their cry,
  When the owls forbore a term,
You heard music; that was I.

III.

Earth turned in her sleep with pain,
  Sultrily suspired for proof:
In at heaven and out again,
  Lightning! — where it broke the roof,
Bloodlike, some few drops of rain.

IV.

What they could my words expressed,
  O my love, my all, my one!
Singing helped the verses best;
  And, when singing's best was done,
To my lute I left the rest.

V.

So wore night; the east was gray,
  White the broad-faced hemlock-flowers;
There would be another day;
  Ere its first of heavy hours
Found me, I had passed away.

VI.

What became of all the hopes,
  Words and song and lute as well?
Say, this struck you — "When life gropes
  Feebly for the path where fell
Light last on the evening slopes,

VII.

"One friend in that path shall be,
  To secure my step from wrong;
One to count night day for me,
  Patient through the watches long,
Serving most with none to see."

VIII.

Never say — as something bodes —
  "So, the worst has yet a worse!
When life halts 'neath double loads,
  Better the task-master's curse
Than such music on the roads!

IX.

"When no moon succeeds the sun,
  Nor can pierce the midnight's tent,
Any star, the smallest one,
  While some drops, where lightning rent,
Show the final storm begun —

X.

"When the fire-fly hides its spot,
  When the garden-voices fail
In the darkness thick and hot, —
  Shall another voice avail,
That shape be where these are not?

XI.

"Has some plague a longer lease,
  Proffering its help uncouth?
Can't one even die in peace?
  As one shuts one's eyes on youth,
Is that face the last one sees?"

XII.

Oh, how dark your villa was,
  Windows fast and obdurate!
How the garden grudged me grass
  Where I stood — the iron gate
Ground its teeth to let me pass!

YOUTH AND ART.

I.

IT once might have been, once only:
  We lodged in a street together,
You, a sparrow on the housetop lonely,
  I, a lone she-bird of his feather.

II.

Your trade was with sticks and clay,
  You thumbed, thrust, patted, and polished,
Then laughed, "They will see, some day,
  Smith made, and Gibson demolished."

III.

My business was song, song, song:
  I chirped, cheeped, trilled, and
    twittered,
"Kate Brown's on the boards ere
    long,
  And Grisi's existence embittered!"

IV.

I earned no more by a warble
  Than you by a sketch in plaster:
You wanted a piece of marble,
  I needed a music-master.

V.

We studied hard in our styles,
  Chipped each at a crust like Hin-
    doos,
For air, looked out on the tiles,
  For fun, watched each other's win-
    dows.

VI.

You lounged, like a boy of the South,
  Cap and blouse — nay, a bit of beard
    too;
Or you got it, rubbing your mouth
  With fingers the clay adhered to.

VII.

And I — soon managed to find
  Weak points in the flower-fence fa-
    cing,
Was forced to put up a blind
  And be safe in my corset-lacing.

VIII.

No harm! It was not my fault
  If you never turned your eye's tall
    up
As I shook upon E *in alt.*,
  Or ran the chromatic scale up;

IX.

For spring bade the sparrows pair,
  And the boys and girls gave guesses,
And stalls in our street looked rare
  With bulrush and watercresses.

X.

Why did not you pinch a flower
  In a pellet of clay and fling it?

Why did not I put a power
  Of thanks in a look, or sing it?

XI.

I did look, sharp as a lynx
  (And yet the memory rankles),
When models arrived, some minx
  Tripped up stairs, she and her
    ankles.

XII.

But I think I gave you as good!
  "That foreign fellow, — who can
    know
How she pays, in a playful mood,
  For his tuning her that piano?"

XIII.

Could you say so, and never say,
  "Suppose we join hands and for-
    tunes,
And I fetch her from over the way,
  Her, piano, and long tunes and short
    tunes?"

XIV.

No, no; you would not be rash,
  Nor I rasher and something over:
You've to settle yet Gibson's hash,
  And Grisi yet lives in clover.

XV.

But you meet the Prince at the
    Board,
  I'm queen myself at *bals-paré*,
I've married a rich old lord,
  And you're dubbed knight and an
    R.A.

XVI.

Each life's unfulfilled, you see;
  It hangs still, patchy and scrappy:
We have not sighed deep, laughed
    free,
  Starved, feasted, despaired, — been
    happy.

XVII.

And nobody calls you a dunce,
  And people suppose me clever:
This could but have happened once,
  And we missed it, lost it forever.

THE FLIGHT OF THE DUCHESS.

I.

You're my friend:
I was the man the Duke spoke to;
I helped the Duchess to cast off his
    yoke, too:
So, here's the tale from beginning to
    end,
My friend!

II.

Ours is a great wild country:
If you climb to our castle's top,
I don't see where your eye can stop;
For when you've passed the corn-field
    country,
Where vineyards leave off, flocks are
    packed,
And sheep-range leads to cattle-tract,
And cattle-tract to open-chase,
And open-chase to the very base
O' the mountain where, at a funeral
    pace,
Round about, solemn and slow,
One by one, row after row,
Up and up the pine-trees go,
So, like black priests up, and so
Down the other side again
To another greater, wilder country,
That's one vast red drear burnt-up
    plain,
Branched through and through with
    many a vein
Whence iron's dug, and copper's
    dealt;
Look right, look left, look straight
    before,—
Beneath they mine, above they smelt,
Copper-ore and iron-ore,
And forge and furnace mould and
    melt,
And so on, more and ever more,
Till at the last, for a bounding belt,
Comes the salt sand hoar of the great
    seashore,
— And the whole is our Duke's coun-
    try.

III.

I was born the day this present Duke
    was —
(And O, says the song, ere I was old!)
In the castle where the other Duke
    was —
(When I was happy and young, not
    old!)

I in the kennel, he in the bower:
We are of like age to an hour.
My father was huntsman in that day;
Who has not heard my father say,
That, when a boar was brought to
    bay,
Three times, four times out of five,
With his huntspear he'd contrive
To get the killing-place transfixed,
And pin him true, both eyes betwixt?
And that's why the old Duke would
    rather
He lost a salt-pit than my father,
And loved to have him ever in call;
That's why my father stood in the
    hall
When the old Duke brought his in-
    fant out
To show the people, and while they
    passed
The wondrous bantling round about,
Was first to start at the outside blast
As the Kaiser's courier blew his horn,
Just a month after the babe was born.
"And," quoth the Kaiser's courier,
    "since
The Duke has got an heir, our Prince
Needs the Duke's self at his side:"
The Duke looked down and seemed
    to wince,
But he thought of wars o'er the world
    wide,
Castles a-fire, men on their march,
The toppling tower, the crashing arch;
And up he looked, and a while he
    eyed
The row of crests and shields and
    banners
Of all achievements after all manners,
And "Ay," said the Duke with a
    surly pride.
The more was his comfort when he
    died
At next year's end, in a velvet suit,
With a gilt glove on his hand, his foot
In a silken shoe for a leather boot,
Petticoated like a herald,
In a chamber next to an ante-room,
Where he breathed the breath of page
    and groom,
What he called stink, and they, per-
    fume:
— They should have set him on red
    Berold
Mad with pride, like fire to manage!
They should have got his cheek fresh
    tannage
Such a day as to-day in the merry
    sunshine!

Had they stuck on his fist a rough-foot merlin !
(Hark, the wind's on the heath at its game !)
Oh for a noble falcon-lanner
To flap each broad wing like a banner,
And turn in the wind, and dance like flame !)
Had they broached a cask of white beer from Berlin !
— Or if you incline to prescribe mere wine,
Put to his lips when they saw him pine,
A cup of our own Moldavia fine,
Cotnar for instance, green as May sorrel
And ropy with sweet, — we shall not quarrel.

IV.

So, at home, the sick tall yellow Duchess
Was left with the infant in her clutches,
She being the daughter of God knows who;
And now was the time to revisit her tribe.
Abroad and afar they went, the two,
And let our people rail and gibe
At the empty hall and extinguished fire,
As loud as we liked, but ever in vain,
Till after long years we had our desire,
And back came the Duke and his mother again.

V.

And he came back the pertest little ape
That ever affronted human shape;
Full of his travel, struck at himself.
You'd say, he despised our bluff old ways?
— Not he! For in Paris they told the elf
That our rough North land was the Land of Lays,
The one good thing left in evil days;
Since the Mid-Age was the Heroic Time,
And only in wild nooks like ours
Could you taste of it yet as in its prime,
And see true castles with proper towers,

Young-hearted women, old-minded men,
And manners now as manners were then,
So, all that the old Dukes had been, without knowing it,
This Duke would fain know he was, without being it;
'Twas not for the joy's self, but the joy of his showing it,
Nor for the pride's self, but the pride of our seeing it,
He revived all usages thoroughly worn-out,
The souls of them fumed-forth, the hearts of them torn-out:
And chief in the chase his neck he perilled,
On a lathy horse, all legs and length, With blood for bone, all speed, no strength;
— They should have set him on red Berold
With the red eye slow consuming in fire,
And the thin stiff ear like an abbey spire!

VI.

Well, such as he was, he must marry, we heard;
And out of a convent, at the word,
Came the lady, in time of spring.
— Oh, old thoughts they cling, they cling!
That day, I know, with a dozen oaths
I clad myself in thick hunting-clothes
Fit for the chase of urox or buffle
In winter-time when you need to muffle.
But the Duke had a mind we should cut a figure,
And so we saw the lady arrive:
My friend, I have seen a white crane bigger!
She was the smallest lady alive,
Made in a piece of nature's madness,
Too small, almost, for the life and gladness
That over-filled her, as some hive
Out of the bears' reach on the high trees
Is crowded with its safe merry bees:
In truth, she was not hard to please!
Up she looked, down she looked, round at the mead,
Straight at the castle, that's best indeed

The Flight of the Duchess. — Page 13.

To look at from outside the walls:
As for us, styled the "serfs and
    thralls,"
She as much thanked me as if she had
    said it,
(With her eyes, do you understand?)
Because I patted her horse while I
    led it;
And Max, who rode on her other
    hand,
Said, no bird flew past but she in-
    quired
What its true name was, nor ever
    seemed tired —
If that was an eagle she saw hover,
And the green and gray bird on the
    field was the plover,
When suddenly appeared the Duke:
And as down she sprung, the small
    foot pointed
On to my hand, — as with a rebuke,
And as if his backbone were not
    jointed,
The Duke stepped rather aside than
    forward,
And welcomed her with his grandest
    smile;
And, mind you, his mother all the
    while
Chilled in the rear, like a wind to
    nor'ward;
And up, like a weary yawn, with its
    pulleys
Went, in a shriek, the rusty portcul-
    lis;
And, like a glad sky the north-wind
    sullies,
The lady's face stopped its play,
As if her first hair had grown gray;
For such things must begin some one
    day.

VII.

In a day or two she was well again;
As who should say, "You labor in
    vain!
"This is all a jest against God, who
    meant
I should ever be, as I am, content
And glad in his sight; therefore, glad
    I will be."
So, smiling as at first went she.

VIII.

She was active, stirring, all fire —
Could not rest, could not tire —
To a stone she might have given life!
(I myself loved once, in my day)

— For a shepherd's, miner's, hunts-
    man's wife,
(I had a wife, I know what I say)
Never in all the world such an one!
And here was plenty to be done,
And she that could do it, great or
    small,
She was to do nothing at all.
There was already this man in his
    post,
This in his station, and that in his
    office,
And the Duke's plan admitted a wife,
    at most,
To meet his eye, with the other tro-
    phies,
Now outside the hall, now in it,
To sit thus, stand thus, see and be
    seen,
At the proper place in the proper
    minute,
And die away the life between.
And it was amusing enough, each in-
    fraction
Of rule — (but for after-sadness that
    came)
To hear the consummate self-satisfac-
    tion
With which the young Duke and the
    old dame
Would let her advise, and criticise,
And, being a fool, instruct the
    wise,
And, childlike, parcel out praise or
    blame:
They bore it all in complacent guise,
As though an artificer, after contriv-
    ing
A wheel-work image as if it were
    living,
Should find with delight it could mo-
    tion to strike him!
So found the Duke, and his mother
    like him:
The lady hardly got a rebuff —
That had not been contemptuous
    enough,
With his cursed smirk, as he nodded
    applause,
And kept off the old mother-cat's
    claws.

IX.

So, the little lady grew silent and
    thin,
    Paling and ever paling,
As the way is with a hid chagrin;
    And the Duke perceived that she
    was ailing,

And said in his heart, " 'Tis done to
    spite me,
" But I shall find in my power to
    right me ! "
Don't swear, friend ! The old one,
    many a year,
Is in hell; and the Duke's self . . .
    you shall hear.

X.

Well, early in autumn, at first winter-
    warning,
When the stag had to break with his
    foot, of a morning,
A drinking-hole out of the fresh ten-
    der ice,
That covered the pond till the sun, in
    a trice,
Loosening it, let out a ripple of gold,
And another and another, and faster
    and faster,
Till, dimpling to blindness, the wide
    water rolled,
Then it so chanced that the Duke our
    master
Asked himself what were the pleas-
    ures in season,
And found, since the calendar bade
    him be hearty,
He should do the Middle Age no trea-
    son
In resolving on a hunting-party.
Always provided, old books showed
    the way of it !
What meant old poets by their stric-
    tures ?
And when old poets had said their
    say of it,
How taught old painters in their pic-
    tures ?
We must revert to the proper chan-
    nels,
Workings in tapestry, paintings on
    panels,
And gather up woodcraft's authentic
    traditions :
Here was food for our various ambi-
    tions,
As on each case, exactly stated —
To encourage your dog, now, the prop-
    erest chirrup,
Or best prayer to St. Hubert on
    mounting your stirrup —
We of the household took thought
    and debated.
Blessed was he whose back ached
    with the jerkin
His sire was wont to do forest-work in;

Blesseder he who nobly sunk " ohs "
And "ahs" while he tugged on his
    grandsire's trunk-hose ;
What signified hats if they had no
    rims on,
Each slouching before and behind like
    the scallop,
And able to serve at sea for a shallop,
Loaded with lacquer and looped with
    crimson ?
So that the deer now, to make a short
    rhyme on't,
What with our Venerers, Prickers,
    and Verderers,
Might hope for real hunters at length
    and not murderers,
And oh the Duke's tailor, he had a
    hot time on't !

XI.

Now you must know that when the
    first dizziness
Of flap-hats and buff-coats and jack-
    boots subsided,
The Duke put this question, " The
    Duke's part provided,
Had not the Duchess some share in
    the business ? "
For out of the mouth of two or three
    witnesses
Did he establish all fit-or-unfitnesses;
And, after much laying of heads to-
    gether,
Somebody's cap got a notable feather
By the announcement with proper
    unction
That he had discovered the lady's
    function;
Since ancient authors gave this tenet,
" When horns wind a mort and the
    deer is at siege,
Let the dame of the castle prick forth
    on her jennet,
And with water to wash the hands of
    her liege
In a clean ewer with a fair towelling,
Let her preside at the disembowel-
    ling."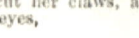
Now, my friend, if you had so little
    religion
As to catch a hawk, some falcon-
    lanner,
And thrust her broad wings like a
    banner
Into a coop for a vulgar pigeon ;
And if day by day and week by week
You cut her claws, and scaled her
    eyes,

And clipped her wings, and tied her
  beak,
Would it cause you any great sur-
  prise,
If, when you decided to give her an
  airing,
You found she needed a little pre-
  paring?
— I say, should you be such a cur-
  mudgeon,
If she clung to the perch, as to take it
  in dudgeon?
Yet when the Duke to his lady signi-
  fied,
Just a day before, as he judged most
  dignified,
In what a pleasure she was to partici-
  pate,—
And, instead of leaping wide in
  flashes,
Her eyes just lifted their long
  lashes,
As if pressed by fatigue even he could
  not dissipate,
And duly acknowledged the Duke's
  forethought,
But spoke of her health, if her health
  were worth aught,
Of the weight by day and the watch
  by night,
And much wrong now that used to be
  right,
So, thanking him, declined the hunt-
  ing,—
Was conduct ever more affronting?
With all the ceremony settled —
With the towel ready, and the sewer
Polishing up his oldest ewer,
And the jennet pitched upon, a pie-
  bald,
Black-barred, cream-coated, and pink
  eye-balled,—
No wonder if the Duke was nettled!
And when she persisted neverthe-
  less,
Well, I suppose here's the time to
  confess
That there ran half round our lady's
  chamber
A balcony none of the hardest to
  clamber;
And that Jacynth the tire-woman,
  ready in waiting,
Staid in call outside, what need of
  relating?
And since Jacynth was like a Jane
  . rose, why, a fervent .
Adorer of Jacynth of course was
  your servant;

And if she had the habit to peep
  through the casement,
How could I keep at any vast dis-
  tance?
And so, as I say, on the lady's per-
  sistence,
The Duke, dumb stricken with
  amazement,
Stood for a while in a sultry smother,
And then, with a smile that partook
  of the awful,
Turned her over to his yellow mother
To learn what was decorous and law-
  ful;
And the mother smelt blood with a
  cat-like instinct,
As her cheek quick whitened through
  all its quince-tinct.
Oh, but the lady heard the whole
  truth at once!
What meant she? — Who was she?
  — Her duty and station,
The wisdom of age and the folly of
  youth, at once,
Its decent regard and its flitting rela-
  tion —
In brief, my friends, set all the devils
  in hell free
And turn them out to carouse in a
  belfry
And treat the priests to a fifty-part
  canon,
And then you may guess how that
  tongue of hers ran on!
Well, somehow or other it ended at
  last,
And, licking her whiskers, out she
  passed;
And after her, — making (he hoped) a
  face
Like Emperor Nero or Sultan Sa-
  ladin,
Stalked the Duke's self with the au-
  stere grace
Of ancient hero or modern paladin,
From door to staircase—oh such a
  solemn
Unbending of the vertebral column!

XII.

However, at sunrise our company
  mustered;
And here was the huntsman bidding
  unkennel,
And there 'neath his bonnet the prick-
  er blustered,
With feather dank as a bough of wet
  fennel;

For the court-yard walls were filled
    with fog
You might cut as an axe chops a log—
Like so much wool for color and bulk-
    iness:
And out rode the Duke in a perfect
    sulkiness ;
Since, before breakfast, a man feels
    but queasily,
And a sinking at the lower abdomen
Begins the day with indifferent
    omen.
And lo! as he looked around un-
    easily,
The sun ploughed the fog up and
    drove it asunder,
This way and that, from the valley
    under ;
And, looking through the court-yard
    arch,
Down in the valley, what should meet
    him
But a troop of gypsies on their march ?
No doubt with the annual gifts to
    greet him.

XIII.

Now, in your land, gypsies reach you,
    only
After reaching all lands beside :
North they go, South they go, troop-
    ing or lonely,
And still, as they travel far and wide,
Catch they and keep now a trace here,
    a trace there,
That puts you in mind of a place here,
    a place there.
But with us, I believe they rise out of
    the ground,
And nowhere else, I take it, are found
With the earth-tint yet so freshly em-
    browned ;
Born, no doubt, like insects which
    breed on
The very fruit they are meant to feed
    on.
For the earth—not a use to which
    they don't turn it,
The ore that grows in the mountain's
    womb,
Or the sand in the pits like a honey-
    comb,
They sift and soften it, bake it and
    burn it—
Whether they weld you, for instance,
    a snaffle
With side-bars never a brute can
    baffle ;

Or a lock that's a puzzle of wards
    within wards ;
Or, if your colt's fore foot inclines to
    curve inwards,
Horseshoes they hammer which turn
    on a swivel
And won't allow the hoof to shrivel.
Then they cast bells like the shell
    of the winkle
That keep a stout heart in the ram
    with their tinkle ;
But the sand—they pinch and pound
    it like otters ;
Commend me to gypsy glass-makers
    and potters !
Glasses they'll blow you, crystal,
    clear,
Where just a faint cloud of rose shall
    appear,
As if in pure water you dropped and
    let die
A bruised black-blooded mulberry ;
And that other sort, their crowning
    pride,
With long white threads distinct in-
    side,
Like the lake-flower's fibrous roots
    which dangle
Loose such a length and never tangle,
Where the bold sword-lily cuts the
    clear waters,
And the cup-lily couches with all the
    white daughters :
Such are the works they put their
    hand to,
The uses they turn and twist iron and
    sand to.
And these made the troop, which our
    Duke saw sally
Toward his castle from out of the
    valley,
Men and women, like new-hatched
    spiders,
Come out with the morning to greet
    our riders.
And up they wound till they reached
    the ditch,
Whereat all stopped save one, a
    witch
That I knew, as she hobbled from the
    group,
By her gait directly and her stoop,
I, whom Jacynth was used to impor-
    tune
To let that same witch tell us our for-
    tune.
The oldest gypsy then above ground ;
And, sure as the autumn season came
    round,

She paid us a visit for profit or pas-
 time,
And every time, as she swore, for the
 last time,
And presently she was seen to sidle
Up to the Duke till she touched his
 bridle,
So that the horse of a sudden reared
 up
As under its nose the old witch peered
 up
With her worn-out eyes, or rather eye-
 holes,
Of no use now but to gather brine,
And began a kind of level whine
Such as they used to sing to their
 viols
When their ditties they go grinding
Up and down with nobody minding ;
And then, as of old, at the end of the
 humming
Her usual presents were forthcoming
— A dog-whistle blowing the fiercest
 of trebles
(Just a seashore stone holding a doz-
 en fine pebbles),
Or a porcelain mouth-piece to screw
 on a pipe-end, —
And so she awaited her annual sti-
 pend.
But this time the Duke would scarcely
 vouchsafe
A word in reply ; and in vain she
 felt
With twitching fingers at her belt
For the purse of sleek pine-martin
 pelt,
Ready to put what he gave in her
 pouch safe, —
Till, either to quicken his apprehen-
 sion,
Or possibly with an after-intention,
She was come, she said, to pay her
 duty
To the new Duchess, the youthful
 beauty.
No sooner had she named his lady,
Than a shine lit up the face so shady,
And its smirk returned with a novel
 meaning —
For it struck him, the babe just want-
 ed weaning ;
If one gave her a taste of what life
 was and sorrow,
She, foolish to-day, would be wiser
 to-morrow ;
And who so fit a teacher of trouble
As this sordid crone bent well-nigh
 double ?

So, glancing at her wolf-skin vesture
(If such it was, for they grow so hir-
 sute
That their own fleece serves for nat-
 ural fur-suit)
He was contrasting, 'twas plain from
 his gesture,
The life of the lady so flower-like and
 delicate
With the loathsome squalor of this
 helicat.
I, in brief, was the man the Duke
 beckoned
From out of the throng ; and while I
 drew near
He told the crone — as I since have
 reckoned
By the way he bent and spoke into
 her ear
With circumspection and mystery —
The main of the lady's history,
Her frowardness and ingratitude ;
And for all the crone's submissive
 attitude
I could see round her mouth the loose
 plaits tightening.
And her brow with assenting intelli-
 gence brightening,
As though she engaged with hearty
 good will
Whatever he now might enjoin to
 fulfil,
And promised the lady a thorough
 frightening.
And so, just giving her a glimpse
Of a purse, with the air of a man who
 imps
The wing of the hawk that shall fetch
 the hernshaw,
He bade me take the gypsy mother
And set her telling some story or
 other
Of hill or dale, oak-wood or fernshaw,
To while away a weary hour
For the lady left alone in her bower,
Whose mind and body craved exer-
 tion
And yet shrank from all better diver-
 sion.

XIV.

Then clapping heel to his horse, the
 mere curveter,
Out rode the Duke, and after his
 hollo
Horses and hounds swept, huntsman
 and servitor,
And back I turned and bade the crone
 follow.

And what makes me confident what's to be told you
Had all along been of this crone's devising,
Is, that, on looking round sharply, behold you,
There was a novelty quick as surprising:
For first, she had shot up a full head in stature,
And her step kept pace with mine nor faltered,
As if age had foregone its usurpature,
And the ignoble mien was wholly altered,
And the face looked quite of another nature,
And the change reached too, whatever the change meant,
Her shaggy wolf-skin cloak's arrangement:
For where its tatters hung loose like sedges,
Gold coins were glittering on the edges,
Like the band-roll strung with tomans
Which proves the veil a Persian woman's:
And under her brow, like a snail's horns newly
Come out as after the rain he paces,
Two unmistakable eye-points duly
Live and aware looked out of their places.
So, we went and found Jacynth at the entry
Of the lady's chamber standing sentry;
I told the command and produced my companion,
And Jacynth rejoiced to admit any one,
For since last night, by the same token,
Not a single word had the lady spoken:
They went in both to the presence together,
While I in the balcony watched the weather.

XV.

And now, what took place at the very first of all,
I cannot tell, as I never could learn it:
Jacynth constantly wished a curse to fall
On that little head of hers and burn it

If she knew how she came to drop so soundly
Asleep of a sudden, and there continue
The whole time, sleeping as profoundly
As one of the boars my father would pin you
'Twixt the eyes where life holds garrison,
— Jacynth forgive me the comparison!
But where I begin my own narration
Is a little after I took my station
To breathe the fresh air from the balcony,
And, having in those days a falcon eye,
To follow the hunt through the open country,
From where the bushes thinlier crested
The hillocks, to a plain where's not one tree.
When, in a moment, my ear was arrested
By — was it singing, or was it saying,
Or a strange musical instrument playing
In the chamber? — and to be certain
I pushed the lattice, pulled the curtain,
And there lay Jacynth asleep,
Yet as if a watch she tried to keep,
In a rosy sleep along the floor
With her head against the door;
While in the midst, on the seat of state,
Was a queen — the gypsy woman late,
With head and face downbent
On the lady's head and face intent:
For, coiled at her feet like a child at ease,
The lady sat between her knees,
And o'er them the lady's clasped hands met,
And on those hands her chin was set,
And her upturned face met the face of the crone
Wherein the eyes had grown and grown
As if she could double and quadruple
At pleasure the play of either pupil
— Very like, by her hands' slow fanning,
As up and down like a gor-crow's flappers
They moved to measure, or bell-clappers,
I said, " Is it blessing, is it banning,

Do they applaud you or burlesque
   you —
Those hands and fingers with no flesh
   on?"
But, just as I thought to spring in to
   the rescue,
At once I was stopped by the lady's
   expression:
For it was life her eyes were drinking
From the crone's wide pair above un-
   winking,
— Life's pure fire, received without
   shrinking,
Into the heart and breast whose heav-
   ing
Told you no single drop they were
   leaving,
— Life, that filling her, passed re-
   dundant
Into her very hair, back swerving
Over each shoulder, loose and abun-
   dant,
As her head thrown back showed the
   white throat curving;
And the very tresses shared in the
   pleasure,
Moving to the mystic measure,
Bounding as the bosom bounded.
I stopped short, more and more con-
   founded,
As still her cheeks burned and eyes
   glistened,
As she listened and she listened:
When all at once a hand detained
   me,
The selfsame contagion gained me,
And I kept time to the wondrous
   chime,
Making out words and prose and
   rhyme,
Till it seemed that the music furled
Its wings like a task fulfilled, and
   dropped
From under the words it first had
   propped,
And left them midway in the world,
Word took word as hand takes
   hand,
I could hear at last, and understand,
And when I held the unbroken thread,
The gypsy said, —

"And so at last we find my tribe.
And so I set thee in the midst,
And to one and all of them describe
What thou saidst and what thou
   didst,
Our long and terrible journey through,
And all thou art ready to say and do

In the trials that remain:
I trace them the vein and the other
   vein
That meet on thy brow and part again,
Making our rapid mystic mark;
And I bid my people prove and probe
Each eye's profound and glorious
   globe,
Till they detect the kindred spark
In those depths so dear and dark,
Like the spots that snap and burst
   and flee,
Circling over the midnight sea.
And on that round young cheek of
   thine
I make them recognize the tinge,
As when of the costly scarlet wine
They drip so much as will impinge
And spread in a thinnest scale afloat
One thick gold drop from the olive's
   coat
Over a silver plate whose sheen
Still through the mixture shall be seen.
For so I prove thee, to one and all,
Fit, when my people ope their breast,
To see the sign, and hear the call,
And take the vow, and stand the test
Which adds one more child to the
   rest —
When the breast is bare and the arms
   are wide,
And the world is left outside.
For there is probation to decree,
And many and long must the trials be
Thou shalt victoriously endure,
If that brow is true and those eyes
   are sure;
Like a jewel-finder's fierce assay
Of the prize he dug from its moun-
   tain tomb, —
Let once the vindicating ray
Leap out amid the anxious gloom,
And steel and fire have done their
   part,
And the prize falls on its finder's
   heart;
So, trial after trial past,
Wilt thou fall at the very last
Breathless, half in trance
With the thrill of the great deliver-
   ance,
Into our arms for evermore;
And thou shalt know, those arms
   once curled
About thee, what we knew before,
How love is the only good in the
   world.
Henceforth be loved as heart can love,
Or brain devise, or hand approve!

Stand up, look below,
It is our life at thy feet we throw
To step with into light and joy ;
Not a power of life but we employ
To satisfy thy nature's want ;
Art thou the tree that props the
    plant,
Or the climbing plant that seeks the
    tree —
Canst thou help us, must we help
    thee ?
If any two creatures grew into one,
They would do more than the world
    has done ;
Though each apart were never so
    weak,
Ye vainly through the world should
    seek
For the knowledge and the might
Which in such union grew their right :
So, to approach at least that end,
And blend, — as much as may be,
    blend
Thee with us or us with thee, —
As climbing plant or propping tree,
Shall some one deck thee over and
    down,
Up and about, with blossoms and
    leaves ?
Fix his heart's fruit for thy garland
    crown,
Cling with his soul as the gourd-vine
    cleaves,
Die on thy boughs and disappear
While not a leaf of thine is sere ?
Or is the other fate in store,
And art thou fitted to adore,
To give thy wondrous self away,
And take a stronger nature's sway ?
I foresee and could foretell
Thy future portion, sure and well :
But those passionate eyes speak true,
    speak true,
Let them say what thou shalt do !
Only be sure thy daily life,
In its peace or in its strife,
Never shall be unobserved ;
We pursue thy whole career,
And hope for it, or doubt, or fear, —
Lo, hast thou kept thy path or
    swerved,
We are beside thee in all thy ways,
With our blame, with our praise,
Our shame to feel, our pride to show,
Glad, angry — but indifferent, no !
Whether it be thy lot to go,
For the good of us all, where the
    haters meet
In the crowded city's horrible street ;

Or thou step alone through the morass
Where never sound yet was
Save the dry quick clap of the stork's
    bill,
For the air is still, and the water
    still,
When the blue breast of the dipping
    coot
Dives under, and all is mute,
So at the last shall come old age,
Decrepit as befits that stage ;
How else wouldst thou retire apart
With the hoarded memories of thy
    heart,
And gather all to the very least
Of the fragments of life's earlier feast,
Let fall through eagerness to find
The crowning dainties yet behind ?
Ponder on the entire past
Laid together thus at last,
When the twilight helps to fuse
The first fresh with the faded hues,
And the outline of the whole,
As round eve's shades their frame-
    work roll,
Grandly fronts for once thy soul.
And then as, 'mid the dark, a gleam
Of yet another morning breaks,
And like the hand which ends a
    dream,
Death, with the might of his sun-
    beam,
Touches the flesh and the soul
    awakes,
Then " —
        Ay, then indeed something
    would happen !
But what ? For here her voice
    changed like a bird's ;
There grew more of the music and
    less of the words ;
Had Jacynth only been by me to clap
    pen
To paper and put you down every
    syllable
With those clever clerkly fingers,
All I've forgotten as well as what
    lingers
In this old brain of mine that's but ill
    able
To give you even this poor version
Of the speech I spoil, as it were, with
    stammering !
— More fault of those who had the
    hammering
Of prosody into me and syntax,
And did it, not with hobnails but tin-
    tacks !
But to return from this excursion, —

Just, do you mark, when the song
was sweetest,
The peace most deep and the charm
completest,
There came, shall I say, a snap —
And the charm vanished !
And my sense returned, so strangely
banished,
And, starting as from a nap,
I knew the crone was bewitching my
lady,
With Jacynth asleep; and but one
spring made I
Down from the casement, round to
the portal,
Another minute and I had entered, —
When the door opened, and more
than mortal
Stood, with a face where to my mind
centred
All beauties I ever saw or shall see,
The Duchess : I stopped as if struck
by palsy.
She was so different, happy and beau-
tiful,
I felt at once that all was best,
And that I had nothing to do, for the
rest,
But wait her commands, obey and be
dutiful.
Not that, in fact, there was any com-
manding ;
I saw the glory of her eye,
And the brow's height and the
breast's expanding.
And I was hers to live or to die.
As for finding what she wanted,
You know God Almighty granted
Such little signs should serve wild
creatures
To tell one another all their desires,
So that each knows what his friend
requires,
And does its bidding without teach-
ers.
I preceded her ; the crone
Followed silent and alone ;
I spoke to her, but she merely jab-
bered
In the old style ; both her eyes had
slunk
Back to their pits ; her stature
shrunk ;
In short, the soul in its body sunk
Like a blade sent home to its scab-
bard.
We descended, I preceding ;
Crossed the court with nobody heed-
ing :

All the world was at the chase,
The court-yard like a desert-place,
The stable emptied of its small fry ;
I saddled myself the very palfry
I remember patting while it carried
her,
The day she arrived and the Duke
married her.
And, do you know, though it 's easy
deceiving
One's self in such matters, I can't help
believing
The lady had not forgotten it either,
And knew the poor devil so much
beneath her
Would have been only too glad, for
her service,
To dance on hot ploughshares like a
Turk dervise,
But, unable to pay proper duty where
owing it,
Was reduced to that pitiful method
of showing it.
For though, the moment I began set-
ting
His saddle on my own nag of Be-
rold's begetting
(Not that I meant to be obtrusive),
She stopped me, while his rug was
shitting,
By a single rapid finger's lifting,
And, with a gesture kind but conclu-
sive,
And a little shake of the head, re-
fused me, —
I say, although she never used me,
Yet when she was mounted, the
gypsy behind her,
And I ventured to remind her,
I suppose with a voice of less steadi-
ness
Than usual, for my feeling exceeded
me,
— Something to the effect that I was
in readiness
Whenever God should please she
needed me, —
Then, do you know, her face looked
down on me
With a look that placed a crown on
me,
And she felt in her bosom, — mark,
her bosom —
And, as a flower-tree drops its
blossom,
Dropped me . . . ah! had it been a
purse
Of silver, my friend, or gold that's
worse,

Why, you see, as soon as I found my-
   self
So understood, — that a true heart so
   may gain
Such a reward, — I should have gone
   home again,
Kissed Jacynth, and soberly drowned
   myself!
It was a little plait of hair
Such as friends in a convent make
To wear, each for the other's sake, —
This, see, which at my breast I wear,
Ever did (rather to Jacynth's grudg-
   ment),
And ever shall till the Day of Judg-
   ment.
And then, — and then, — to cut short,
   — this is idle,
These are feelings it is not good to
   foster, —
I pushed the gate wide, she shook the
   bridle,
And the palfrey bounded, — and so
   we lost her.

XVI.

When the liquor's out why clink the
   cannikin?
I did think to describe you the panic in
The redoubtable breast of our master
   the manikin,
And what was the pitch of his moth-
   er's yellowness,
How she turned as a shark to snap
   the spare-rib
Clean off, sailors say, from a pearl-
   diving Carib,
When she heard, what she called the
   flight of the feloness
— But it seems such child's play,
What they said and did with the lady
   away!
And to dance on, when we've lost the
   music,
Always made me — and no doubt
   makes you — sick.
Nay, to my mind, the world's face
   looked so stern
As that sweet form disappeared
   through the postern,
She that kept it in constant good-
   humor,
It ought to have stopped; there
   seemed nothing to do more.
But the world thought otherwise and
   went on,
And my head's one that its spite was
   spent on:

Thirty years are fled since that morn-
   ing,
And with them all my head's adorn-
   ing.
Nor did the old Duchess die outright,
As you expect, of suppressed spite,
The natural end of every adder
Not suffered to empty its poison-
   bladder:
But she and her son agreed, I take
   it,
That no one should touch on the story
   to wake it,
For the wound in the Duke's pride
   rankled fiery;
So, they made no search and small
   inquiry:
And when fresh gypsies have paid us
   a visit, I've
Noticed the couple were never in-
   quisitive,
But told them they're folks the Duke
   don't want here,
And bade them make haste and cross
   the frontier.
Brief, the Duchess was gone and the
   Duke was glad of it,
And the old one was in the young
   one's stead,
And took, in her place, the household's
   head,
And a blessed time the household had
   of it!
And were I not, as a man may say,
   cautious
How I trench, more than needs, on
   the nauseous,
I could favor you with sundry touches
Of the paint-smutches with which the
   Duchess
Heightened the mellowness of her
   cheek's yellowness
(To get on faster) until at last her
Cheek grew to be one master-plaster
Of mucus and fucus from mere use of
   ceruse:
In short, she grew from scalp to
   udder
Just the object to make you shudder.

XVII.

You're my friend —
What a thing friendship is, world
   without end!
How it gives the heart and soul a stir-
   up
As if somebody broached you a glori-
   ous runlet,

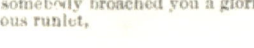

And poured out, all lovelily, spark-
   lingly, sunlit,
Our green Moldavia, the streaky
   sirup,
Cotnar as old as the time of the
   Druids —
Friendship may match with that mon-
   arch of fluids ;
Each supples a dry brain, fills you its
   ins-and-outs,
Gives your life's hour-glass a shake
   when the thin sand doubts
Whether to run on or stop short, and
   guarantees
Age is not all made of stark sloth and
   arrant ease.
I have seen my little lady once more,
Jacynth, the gypsy, Berold, and the
   rest of it,
For to me spoke the Duke, as I told
   you before ;
I always wanted to make a clean
   breast of it :
And now it is made — why, my heart's
   blood, that went trickle,
Trickle, but anon, in such muddy
   driblets,
Is pumped up brisk now, through the
   main ventricle,
And genially floats me about the gib-
   lets.
I'll tell you what I intend to do ;
I must see this fellow his sad life
   through —
He is our Duke, after all,
And I, as he says, but a serf and thrall.
My father was born here, and I in-
   herit
His fame, a chain he bound his son
   with ;
Could I pay in a lump I should pre-
   fer it,
But there's no mine to blow up and
   get done with :
So, I must stay till the end of the
   chapter.
For, as to our middle-age-manners-
   adapter,
Be it a thing to be glad on or sorry on,
Some day or other, his head in a mo-
   rion
And breast in a hauberk, his heels
   he'll kick up,
Slain by an onslaught fierce of hic-
   cup.
And then, when red doth the sword
   of our Duke rust,
And its leathern sheath lie o'ergrown
   with a blue crust,

Then I shall scrape together my earn-
   ings ;
For, you see, in the churchyard Ja-
   cynth reposes,
And our children all went the way of
   the roses :
It's a long lane that knows no turn-
   ings.
One needs but little tackle to travel
   in ;
So, just one stout cloak shall I indue :
And for a staff, what beats the jave-
   lin
With which his boars my father
   pinned you ?
And then, for a purpose you shall
   hear presently,
Taking some Cotnar, a tight plump
   skinful,
I shall go journeying, who but I,
   pleasantly !
Sorrow is vain and despondency sin-
   ful.
What's a man's age ? He must hurry
   more, that's all ;
Cram in a day, what his youth took a
   year to hold :
When we mind labor, then only,
   we're too old —
What age had Methusalem when he
   begat Saul ?
And at last, as its haven some buffeted
   ship sees
(Come all the way from the north-
   parts with sperm oil),
I hope to get safely out of the tur-
   moil
And arrive one day at the land of the
   gypsies,
And find my lady, or hear the last
   news of her
From some old thief and son of Luci-
   fer,
His forehead chapleted green with
   wreathy hop,
Sunburned all over like an Æthiop.
And when my Cotnar begins to oper-
   ate,
And the tongue of the rogue to run at
   a proper rate,
And our wine-skin, tight once, shows
   each flaccid dent,
I shall drop in with — as if by acci-
   dent —
" You never knew, then, how it all
   ended,
What fortune good or bad attended
The little lady your Queen be-
   friended ? "

—And when that's told me, what's remaining?

This world's too hard for my explaining.

The same wise judge of matters equine

Who still preferred some slim four-year-old

To the big-boned stock of mighty Berold,

And, for strong Cotnar, drank French weak wine,

He also must be such a lady's scorner!

Smooth Jacob still robs homely Esau:

Now up, now down, the world's one seesaw.

— So, I shall find out some snug corner

Under a hedge, like Orson the wood-knight,

Turn myself round and bid the world good-night,

And sleep a sound sleep till the trumpet's blowing

Wakes me (unless priests cheat us laymen)

To a world where will be no further throwing

Pearls before swine that can't value them. Amen!

SONG FROM "PIPPA PASSES."

THE year's at the spring,
And day's at the morn;
Morning's at seven;
The hill-side's dew-pearled;
The lark's on the wing;
The snail's on the thorn;
God's in his heaven—
All's right with the world.

"HOW THEY BROUGHT THE GOOD NEWS FROM GHENT TO AIX."

[16—.]

I.

I SPRANG to the stirrup, and Joris, and he;

I galloped, Dirck galloped, we galloped all three;

"Good speed!" cried the watch, as the gate-bolts undrew;

"Speed!" echoed the wall to us galloping through;

Behind shut the postern, the lights sank to rest,

And into the midnight we galloped abreast.

II.

Not a word to each other; we kept the great pace

Neck by neck, stride by stride, never changing our place;

I turned in my saddle and made its girths tight,

Then shortened each stirrup, and set the pique right,

Rebuckled the cheek-strap, chained slacker the bit,

Nor galloped less steadily Roland a whit.

III.

'Twas moonset at starting; but, while we drew near

Lokeren, the cocks crew, and twilight dawned clear;

At Boom, a great yellow star came out to see;

At Düffeld, 'twas morning as plain as could be;

And from Mecheln church-steeple we heard the half-chime.

So, Joris broke silence with, "Yet there is time!"

IV.

At Aershot, up leaped of a sudden the sun,

And against him the cattle stood black every one,

To stare through the mist at us galloping past;

And I saw my stout galloper Roland at last,

With resolute shoulders, each butting away

The haze, as some bluff river headland its spray:

V.

And his low head and crest, just one sharp ear bent back

For my voice, and the other pricked out on his track;

And one eye's black intelligence,—ever that glance

O'er its white edge at me, his own master, askance!

"Stood up in the stirrup, leaned, patted his ear.
Called my Roland his pet-name, my horse without peer." — Page 25.

And the thick heavy spume-flakes
    which aye and anon
His fierce lips shook upwards in gal-
    loping on.

VI.

By Hasselt, Dirck groaned ; and cried
    Joris, "Stay spur !
Your Roos galloped bravely, the
    fault's not in her,
We'll remember at Aix" — for one
    heard the quick wheeze
Of her chest, saw the stretched neck
    and staggering knees,
And sunk tail, and horrible heave of
    the flank,
As down on her haunches she shud-
    dered and sank.

VII.

So, we were left galloping, Joris and
    I,
Past Looz and past Tongres, no cloud
    in the sky ;
The broad sun above laughed a piti-
    less laugh,
'Neath our feet broke the brittle bright
    stubble like chaff ;
Till over by Dalhem a dome-spire
    sprang white,
And "Gallop," gasped Joris, "for
    Aix is in sight !

VIII.

"How they'll greet us !" — and all in
    a moment his roan
Rolled neck and croup over, lay dead
    as a stone ;
And there was my Roland to bear the
    whole weight
Of the news which alone could save
    Aix from her fate,
With his nostrils like pits full of
    blood to the brim,
And with circles of red for his eye-
    sockets' rim.

IX.

Then I cast loose my buffcoat, each
    holster let fall,
Shook off both my jack-boots, let go
    belt and all,
Stood up in the stirrup, leaned, patted
    his ear,
Called my Roland his pet-name, my
    horse without peer ;

Clapped my hands, laughed and sang,
    any noise, bad or good,
Till at length into Aix Roland gal-
    loped and stood.

X.

And all I remember is, friends flock-
    ing round
As I sat with his head 'twixt my
    knees on the ground ;
And no voice but was praising this
    Roland of mine,
As I poured down his throat our last
    measure of wine,
Which (the burgesses voted by com-
    mon consent)
Was no more than his due who
    brought good news from Ghent.

SONG FROM "PARACELSUS."

I.

HEAP cassia, sandal-buds, and stripes
    Of labdanum, and aloe-balls,
Smeared with dull nard an Indian
    wipes
    From out her hair : such balsam
    falls
    Down seaside mountain pedes-
    tals,
From tree-tops where tired winds are
    fain,
Spent with the vast and howling
    main,
To treasure half their island gain.

II.

And strew faint sweetness from some
    old
    Egyptian's fine worm-eaten shroud
Which breaks to dust when once un-
    rolled ;
    Or shredded perfume, like a cloud
    From closet long to quiet vowed,
With mothed and dropping arras
    hung,
Mouldering her lute and books
    among,
As when a queen, long dead, was
    young.

THROUGH THE METIDJA TO ABD-EL-KADR.

[1842.]

I.

As I ride, as I ride,
With a full heart for my guide,
So its tide rocks my side,
As I ride, as I ride,
That, as I were double-eyed,
He, in whom our Tribes confide,
Is descried, ways untried
As I ride, as I ride.

II.

As I ride, as I ride
To our Chief and his Allied,
Who dares chide my heart's pride
As I ride, as I ride?
Or are witnesses denied —
Through the desert waste and wide
Do I glide unespied
As I ride, as I ride?

III.

As I ride, as I ride,
When an inner voice has cried,
The sands slide, nor abide
(As I ride, as I ride)
O'er each visioned homicide
That came vaunting (has he lied?)
To reside — where he died,
As I ride, as I ride.

IV.

As I ride, as I ride,
Ne'er has spur my swift horse plied,
Yet his hide, streaked and pied,
As I ride, as I ride,
Shows where sweat has sprung and
dried,
— Zebra-footed, ostrich-thighed —
How has vied stride with stride
As I ride, as I ride!

V.

As I ride, as I ride,
Could I loose what Fate has tied,
Ere I pride, she should hide
(As I ride, as I ride)
All that's meant me — satisfied
When the Prophet and the Bride
Stop veins I'd have subside
As I ride, as I ride!

INCIDENT OF THE FRENCH CAMP.

I.

You know, we French stormed Rat-
isbon:
A mile or so away
On a little mound, Napoleon
Stood on our storming-day;
With neck out-thrust, you fancy
how,
Legs wide, arms locked behind,
As if to balance the prone brow
Oppressive with its mind.

II.

Just as perhaps he mused, "My plans
That soar, to earth may fall,
Let once my army-leader Lannes
Waver at yonder wall," —
Out 'twixt the battery smokes there
flew
A rider, bound on bound
Full-galloping; nor bridle drew
Until he reached the mound.

III.

Then off there flung in smiling joy,
And held himself erect
By just his horse's mane, a boy:
You hardly could suspect —
(So tight he kept his lips compressed,
Scarce any blood came through)
You looked twice ere you saw his
breast
Was all but shot in two.

IV.

"Well," cried he, "Emperor, by
God's grace
We've got you Ratisbon!
The Marshal's in the market-place,
And you'll be there anon
To see your flag-bird flap his vans
Where I, to heart's desire,
Perched him!" The chief's eye
flashed: his plans
Soared up again like fire.

V.

The chief's eye flashed; but presently
Softened itself, as sheathes
A film the mother-eagle's eye
When her bruised eaglet breathes

"You're wounded!"—"Nay," the
  soldier's pride
Touched to the quick, he said,
"I'm killed, Sire!" And his chief
  beside,
Smiling, the boy fell dead.

THE LOST LEADER.

I.

JUST for a handful of silver he left us,
  Just for a ribbon to stick in his
    coat—
Found the one gift of which fortune
  bereft us,
  Lost all the others, she lets us
    devote;
They, with the gold to give, doled
  him out silver,
  So much was theirs who so little
    allowed:
How all our copper had gone for his
  service!
  Rags—were they purple, his heart
    had been proud!
We that had loved him so, followed
  him, honored him,
  Lived in his mild and magnificent
    eye,
Learned his great language, caught
  his clear accents,
  Made him our pattern to live and
    to die!
Shakspeare was of us, Milton was for
  us,
  Burns, Shelley, were with us,—
    they watch from their graves!
He alone breaks from the van and
  the freemen,
  He alone sinks to the rear and the
    slaves!

II.

We shall march prospering,—not
  through his presence;
  Songs may inspirit us,—not from
    his lyre;
Deeds will be done,—while he boasts
  his quiescence,
  Still bidding crouch whom the rest
    bade aspire;
Blot out his name, then, record one
  lost soul more,
  One task more declined, one more
    footpath untrod,

One more devil's-triumph and sorrow
  for angels,
  One wrong more to man, one more
    insult to God!
Life's night begins: let him never
  come back to us!
  There would be doubt, hesitation,
    and pain,
Forced praise on our part—the glim-
  mer of twilight,
  Never glad confident morning again!
Best fight on well, for we taught him
  —strike gallantly,
  Menace our heart ere we master his
    own;
Then let him receive the new knowl-
  edge and wait us,
  Pardoned in heaven, the first by
    the throne!

IN A GONDOLA.

He sings.

I SEND my heart up to thee, all my
  heart
  In this my singing.
For the stars help me, and the sea
  bears part;
  The very night is clinging
Closer to Venice' streets to leave one
  space
  Above me, whence thy face
May light my joyous heart to thee its
  dwelling-place.

She speaks.

Say after me, and try to say
My very words, as if each word
Came from you of your own accord,
In your own voice, in your own
  way:
"This woman's heart and soul and
  brain
Are mine as much as this gold chain
She bids me wear; which" (say again)
"I choose to make by cherishing
A precious thing, or choose to fling
Over the boat-side, ring by ring."
And yet once more say . . . no word
  more!
Since words are only words. Give
  o'er!

Unless you call me, all the same,
Familiarly by my pet name,
Which if the Three should hear you
　call,
And me reply to, would proclaim
At once our secret to them all.
Ask of me, too, command me, blame —
Do, break down the partition-wall
'Twixt us, the daylight world beholds
Curtained in dusk and splendid folds!
What's left but — all of me to take?
I am the Three's : prevent them, slake
Your thirst! 'Tis said, the Arab sage,
In practising with gems, can loose
Their subtle spirit in his cruce
And leave but ashes : so, sweet image,
Leave them my ashes when thy use
Sucks out my soul, thy heritage!

He sings.

I.

Past we glide, and past, and past!
　What's that poor Agnese doing
Where they make the shutters fast?
　Gray Zanobi's just a-wooing
To his couch the purchased bride :
　Past we glide!

II.

Past we glide, and past, and past!
　Why's the Pucci Palace flaring
Like a beacon to the blast?
　Guests by hundreds, not one caring
If the dear host's neck were wried :
　Past we glide!

She sings.

I.

The moth's kiss, first!
Kiss me as if you made believe
You were not sure, this eve,
How my face, your flower, had pursed
Its petals up ; so, here and there
You brush it, till I grow aware
Who wants me, and wide ope I burst.

II.

The bee's kiss, now!
Kiss me as if you entered gay
My heart at some noonday,
A bud that dares not disallow
The claim, so all is rendered up,
And passively its shattered cup
Over your head to sleep I bow.

He sings.

I.

What are we two?
I am a Jew,
And carry thee, farther than friends
　can pursue,
To a feast of our tribe;
Where they need thee to bribe
The Devil that blasts them unless he
　imbibe
Thy . . . Scatter the vision forever!
　And now,
As of old, I am I, thou art thou!

II.

Say again, what we are?
The sprite of a star,
I lure thee above where the destinies
　bar
My plumes their full play
Till a ruddier ray
Than my pale one announce there is
　withering away
Some . . . Scatter the vision forever!
　And now,
As of old, I am I, thou art thou!

He muses.

Oh! which were best, to roam or
　rest?
The land's lap or the water's breast?
To sleep on yellow millet-sheaves,
Or swim in lucid shallows, just
Eluding water-lily leaves,
An inch from Death's black fingers,
　thrust
To lock you, whom release he must;
Which life were best on summer
　eves?

He speaks, musing.

Lie back; could thought of mine im-
　prove you?
From this shoulder let there spring
A wing; from this, another wing;
Wings, not legs and feet, shall move
　you!
Snow-white must they spring, to
　blend
With your flesh, but I intend
They shall deepen to the end,
Broader, into burning gold,
Till both wings crescent-wise infold

Your perfect self, from 'neath your
  feet
To o'er your head, where, lo, they
  meet
As if a million sword-blades hurled
Defiance from you to the world!

Rescue me thou, the only real!
And scare away this mad ideal
That came, nor motions to depart!
Thanks! Now, stay ever as thou art!

Still he muses.

I.

What if the Three should catch at
  last
Thy serenader? While there's cast
Paul's cloak about my head, and fast
Gian pinions me, Himself has past
His stylet through my back; I reel;
And . . . is it thou I feel?

II.

They trail me, these three godless
  knaves,
Past every church that saints and
  saves,
Nor stop till, where the cold sea
  raves
By Lido's wet accursed graves,
They scoop mine, roll me to its
  brink,
And . . . on thy breast I sink!

She replies, musing.

Dip your arm o'er the boat-side,
  elbow-deep,
As I do: thus: were death so unlike
  sleep,
Caught this way? Death's to fear
  from flame or steel,
Or poison doubtless; but from water
  — feel!
Go find the bottom! Would you stay
  me? There!
Now pluck a great blade of that rib-
  bon-grass
To plait in where the foolish jewel
  was,
I flung away: since you have praised
  my hair,
'Tis proper to be choice in what I
  wear.

He speaks.

Row home? must we row home? Too
  surely
Know I where its front's demurely
Over the Guidecca piled;
Window just with window mating,
Door on door exactly waiting,
All's the set face of a child:
But behind it, where's a trace
Of the staidness and reserve,
And formal lines without a curve,
In the same child's playing-face?
No two windows look one way
O'er the small sea-water thread
Below them. Ah, the autumn day
I, passing, saw you overhead!
First, out a cloud of curtain blew,
Then a sweet cry, and last came
  you —
To catch your lory that must needs
Escape just then, of all times then,
To peck a tall plant's fleecy seeds
And make me happiest of men.
I scarce could breathe to see you
  reach
So far back o'er the balcony,
To catch him ere he climbed too
  high
Above you in the Smyrna peach,
That quick the round smooth cord of
  gold,
This coiled hair on your head, un-
  rolled,
Fell down you like a gorgeous snake
The Roman girls were wont, of old,
When Rome there was, for coolness'
  sake
To let lie curling o'er their bosoms
Dear lory, may his beak retain
Ever its delicate rose stain,
As if the wounded lotus-blossoms
Had marked their thief to know
  again!

Stay longer yet, for others' sake
Than mine! What should your cham-
  ber do?
— With all its rarities that ache
In silence while day lasts, but wake
At night-time and their life renew,
Suspended just to pleasure you
Who brought against their will to-
  gether
These objects, and, while day lasts,
  weave
Around them such a magic tether
That dumb they look: your harp,
  believe,

With all the sensitive tight strings
Which dare not speak, now to itself
Breathes slumberously, as if some
  elf
Went in and out the chords, his wings
Make murmur, wheresoe'er they
  graze,
As an angel may, between the maze
Of midnight palace-pillars, on
And on, to sow God's plagues, have
  gone
Through guilty glorious Babylon.
And while such murmurs flow, the
  nymph
Bends o'er the harp-top from her
  shell
As the dry limpet for the lymph
Come with a tune he knows so well.
And how your statues' hearts must
  swell!
And how your pictures must descend
To see each other, friend with friend!
Oh, could you take them by surprise,
You'd find Schidone's eager Duke
Doing the quaintest courtesies
To that prim saint by Haste-thee-
  Luke!
And, deeper into her rock den,
Bold Castelfranco's Magdalen
You'd find retreated from the ken
Of that robed counsel-keeping Ser —
As if the Tizian thinks of her,
And is not, rather, gravely bent
On seeing for himself what toys
Are these, his progeny invent,
What litter now the board employs
Whereon he signed a document
That got him murdered! Each en-
  joys
Its night so well, you cannot break
The sport up: so, indeed must make
More stay with me, for others' sake.

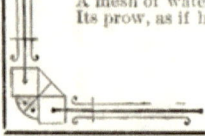

She speaks.

I.

To-morrow, if a harp-string, say,
Is used to tie the jasmine back
That overfloods my room with sweets,
Contrive your Zorzi somehow meets
My Zanze! If the ribbon's black,
The Three are watching: keep away!

II.

Your gondola — let Zorzi wreathe
A mesh of water-weeds about
Its prow, as if he unaware

Had struck some quay or bridge-foot
  stair!
That I may throw a paper out
As you and he go underneath.

There's Zanze's vigilant taper; safe
  are we.
Only one minute more to-night with
  me?
Resume your past self of a month
  ago!
Be you the bashful gallant, I will
  be
The lady with the colder breast than
  snow.
Now bow you, as becomes, nor touch
  my hand
More than I touch yours when I step
  to land,
And say, "All thanks, Siora!" —
                    Heart to heart
And lips to lips! Yet once more, ere
  we part,
Clasp me and make me thine, as mine
  thou art!

He is surprised, and stabbed.

It was ordained to be so, sweet! —
  and best
Comes now, beneath thine eyes, upon
  thy breast.
Still kiss me! Care not for the cow-
  ards! Care
Only to put aside thy beauteous hair
My blood will hurt! The Three, I do
  not scorn,
To death, because they never lived:
  but I
Have lived indeed, and so — (yet one
  more kiss) — can die!

—————

A LOVERS' QUARREL.

I.

OH, what a dawn of day!
How the March sun feels like May!
  All is blue again
  After last night's rain,
And the South dries the hawthorn
  spray.
  Only, my Love's away!
I'd as lief that the blue were gray.

II.

Runnels, which rillets swell,
Must be dancing down the dell,
  With a foaming head
  On the beryl bed
Paven smooth as a hermit's cell:
  Each with a tale to tell,
Could my love but attend as well.

III.

Dearest, three months ago,
When we lived blocked up with
    snow,—
  When the wind would edge
  In and in his wedge,
In, as far as the point could go—
  Not to our ingle, though,
Where we loved each the other so!

IV.

Laughs with so little cause!
We devised games out of straws.
  We would try and trace
  One another's face
In the ash, as an artist draws;
  Free on each other's flaws,
How we chattered like two church
    daws!

V.

What's in the " Times " ?—a scold
At the Emperor deep and cold;
  He has taken a bride
  To his grewsome side,
That's as fair as himself is bold:
  There they sit ermine-stoled,
And she powders her hair with gold.

VI.

Fancy the Pampas' sheen!
Miles and miles of gold and green
  Where the sunflowers blow
  In a solid glow,
And to break now and then the
    screen—
  Black neck and eyeballs keen,
Up a wild horse leaps between!

VII.

Try, will our table turn?
Lay your hands there light, and yearn
  Till the yearning slips
  Through the finger-tips
In a fire which a few discern,
  And a very few feel burn,
And the rest, they may live and
    learn!

VIII.

Then we would up and pace,
For a change, about the place,
  Each with arm o'er neck:
  'T is our quarter-deck,
We are seamen in woeful case.
  Help in the ocean-space!
Or, if no help, we'll embrace.

IX.

See, how she looks now, dressed
In a sledging-cap and vest!
  'T is a huge fur cloak—
  Like a reindeer's roke
Falls the lappet along the breast:
  Sleeves for her arts to rest,
Or to hang, as my Love likes best.

X.

Teach me to flirt a fan
As the Spanish ladies can,
  Or I tint your lip
  With a burnt stick's tip
And you turn into such a man!
  Just the two spots that span
Half the bill of the young male swan.

XI.

Dearest, three months ago
When the mesmerizer Snow
  With his hand's first sweep
  Put the earth to sleep:
'Twas a time when the heart could
    show
  All—how was earth to know,
'Neath the mute hand's to-and-fro?

XII.

Dearest, three months ago
When we loved each other so,
  Lived and loved the same
  Till an evening came
When a shaft from the Devil's bow
  Pierced to our ingle-glow,
And the friends were friend and foe!

XIII.

Not from the heart beneath—
'Twas a bubble born of breath,
  Neither sneer nor vaunt,
  Nor reproach nor taunt.
See a word, how it severeth!
  Oh, power of life and death
In the tongue, as the Preacher saith!

XIV.

Woman, and will you cast
For a word, quite off at last
  Me, your own, your You, —
  Since, as truth is true,
I was You all the happy past —
  Me do you leave aghast
With the memories We amassed?

XV.

Love, if you knew the light
That your soul casts in my sight,
  How I look to you
  For the pure and true,
And the beauteous and the right, —
  Bear with a moment's spite
When a mere mote threats the white!

XVI.

What of a hasty word?
Is the fleshly heart not stirred
  By a worm's pin-prick
  Where its roots are quick?
See the eye, by a fly's-foot blurred —
  Ear, when a straw is heard
Scratch the brain's coat of curd!

XVII.

Foul be the world or fair
More or less, how can I care?
  'Tis the world the same
  For my praise or blame,
And endurance is easy there.
  Wrong in the one thing rare —
Oh, it is hard to bear!

XVIII.

Here's the spring back or close,
When the almond-blossom blows;
  We shall have the word
  In a minor third
There is none but the cuckoo knows:
  Heaps of the guelder-rose!
I must bear with it, I suppose.

XIX.

Could but November come,
Were the noisy birds struck dumb
  At the warning slash
  Of his driver's-lash —
I would laugh like the valiant Thumb
  Facing the castle glum
And the giant's fee-faw-fum!

XX.

Then, were the world well stripped
Of the gear wherein equipped
  We can stand apart,
  Heart dispense with heart
In the sun, with the flowers un-
   nipped, —
  Oh, the world's hangings ripped,
We were both in a bare-walled crypt!

XXI.

Each in the crypt would cry,
" But one freezes here! and why?
  When a heart, as chill,
  At my own would thrill
Back to life, and its fires out-fly?
  Heart, shall we live or die?
The rest . . . settle by and by!"

XXII.

So, she'd efface the score,
And forgive me as before.
  It is twelve o'clock:
  I shall hear her knock
In the worst of a storm's uproar:
  I shall pull her through the door,
I shall have her for evermore!

EARTH'S IMMORTALITIES.

FAME.

SEE, as the prettiest graves will do in
  time,
Our poet's wants the freshness of its
  prime;
Spite of the sexton's browsing horse,
  the sods
Have struggled through its binding
  osier rods;
Headstone and half-sunk footstone
  lean awry,
Wanting the brick-work promised by
  and by;
How the minute gray lichens, plate
  o'er plate,
Have softened down the crisp-cut
  name and date!

LOVE.

So, the year's done with!
  (*Love me forever!*)
All March begun with,
  April's endeavor;

The Last Ride together. — Page 33.

May-wreaths that bound me
  June needs must sever;
Now snows fall round me,
  Quenching June's fever —
    (*Love me forever!*)

THE LAST RIDE TOGETHER.

I.

I said — Then, dearest, since 'tis so,
Since now at length my fate I know,
Since nothing all my love avails,
Since all, my life seemed meant for, fails,
  Since this was written and needs
    must be —
My whole heart rises up to bless
Your name in pride and thankfulness!
Take back the hope you gave, — I claim
Only a memory of the same,
— And this beside, if you will not blame,
  Your leave for one more last ride
    with me.

II.

My mistress bent that brow of hers;
Those deep dark eyes where pride demurs
When pity would be softening through,
Fixed me a breathing-while or two
  With life or death in the balance:
    right!
The blood replenished me again;
My last thought was at least not vain:
I and my mistress, side by side,
Shall be together, breathe and ride,
So, one day more am I deified.
  Who knows but the world may end
    to-night?

III.

Hush! if you saw some western cloud
All billowy-bosomed, over-bowed
By many benedictions — sun's
And moon's and evening-star's at once —
  And so, you, looking and loving
    best,
Conscious grew, your passion drew
Cloud, sunset, moonrise, star-shine too,

Down on you, near and yet more near,
Till flesh must fade for heaven was here! —
Thus leant she and lingered — joy and fear
  Thus lay she a moment on my
    breast.

IV.

Then we began to ride. My soul
Smoothed itself out, a long-cramped scroll
Freshening and fluttering in the wind.
Past hopes already lay behind.
  What need to strive with a life
    awry?
Had I said that, had I done this,
So might I gain, so might I miss.
Might she have loved me? just as well
She might have hated, who can tell!
Where had I been now if the worst befell?
  And here we are riding, she and I.

V.

Fail I alone, in words and deeds?
Why, all men strive and who succeeds?
We rode; it seemed my spirit flew,
Saw other regions, cities new,
  As the world rushed by on either
    side.
I thought, — All labor, yet no less
Bear up beneath their unsuccess.
Look at the end of work, contrast
The petty done, the undone vast,
This present of theirs with the hopeful past!
  I hoped she would love me; here
    we ride.

VI.

What hand and brain went ever paired?
What heart alike conceived and dared?
What act proved all its thought had been?
What will but felt the fleshy screen?
  We ride and I see her bosom heave.
There's many a crown for who can reach.
Ten lines, a statesman's life in each!
The flag stuck on a heap of bones,
A soldier's doing! what atones?
They scratch his name on the Abbey-stones.
  My riding is better, by their leave

VII.

What does it all mean, poet? Well,
Your brains beat into rhythm, you
   tell
What we felt only; you expressed
You hold things beautiful the best,
   And pace them in rhyme so, side
     by side.

'Tis something, nay 'tis much: but
   then,
Have you yourself what's best for
   men?
Are you — poor, sick, old ere your
   time —
Nearer one whit your own sublime
Than we who have never turned a
   rhyme?
   Sing, riding's a joy! For me, I ride.

VIII.

And you, great sculptor — so, you gave
A score of years to Art, her slave,
And that's your Venus, whence we
   turn
To yonder girl that fords the burn!
You acquiesce, and shall I repine?
What, man of music, you grown gray
With notes and nothing else to say,
Is this your sole praise from a friend,
"Greatly his opera's strains intend,
But in music we know how fashions
   end!"
   I gave my youth; but we ride, in
     fine.

IX.

Who knows what's fit for us? Had
   fate
Proposed bliss here should sublimate
My being — had I signed the bond —
Still one must lead some life beyond,
   Have a bliss to die with, dim-de-
     scried.
This foot once planted on the goal,
This glory-garland round my soul,
Could I descry such? Try and test!
I sink back shuddering from the quest.
Earth being so good, would heaven
   seem best?
   Now, heaven and she are beyond
     this ride.

X.

And yet — she has not spoke so long!
What if heaven be that, fair and
   strong
At life's best, with our eyes upturned
Whither life's flower is first dis-
   cerned.

We, fixed so, ever should so abide?
What if we still ride on, we two,
With life forever old yet new,
Changed not in kind but in degree,
The instant made eternity, —
And heaven just prove that I and she
   Ride, ride together, forever ride?

MESMERISM.

I.

ALL I believed is true!
   I am able yet
   All I want, to get
By a method as strange as new,
Dare I trust the same to you?

II.

If at night, when doors are shut,
   And the wood-worm picks,
   And the death-watch ticks,
And the bar has a flag of smut,
And a cat's in the water-butt —

III.

And the socket floats and flares,
   And the house-beams groan,
   And a foot unknown
Is surmised on the garret-stairs,
And the locks slip unawares —

IV.

And the spider, to serve his ends,
   By a sudden thread,
   Arms and legs outspread,
On the table's midst descends,
Comes to find, God knows what
   friends! —

V.

If since eve drew in, I say,
   I have sat and brought
   (So to speak) my thought
To bear on the woman away,
Till I felt my hair turn gray —

VI.

Till I seemed to have and hold,
   In the vacancy
   'Twixt the wall and me
From the hair-plait's chestnut-gold
To the foot in its muslin fold —

VII.

Have and hold, then and there,
 Her, from head to foot,
 Breathing and mute,
Passive and yet aware,
In the grasp of my steady stare —

VIII.

Hold and have, there and then,
 All her body and soul
 That completes my whole,
All that women add to men,
In the clutch of my steady ken —

IX.

Having and holding, till
 I imprint her fast
 On the void at last
As the sun does whom he will
By the calotypist's skill —

X.

Then, — if my heart's strength serve,
 And through all and each
 Of the veils I reach
To her soul and never swerve,
Knitting an iron nerve —

XI.

Command her soul to advance
 And inform the shape
 Which has made escape
And before my countenance
Answers me glance for glance —

XII.

I, still with a gesture fit
 Of my hands that test
 Do my soul's behest,
Pointing the power from it,
While myself do steadfast sit —

XIII.

Steadfast and still the same
 On my object bent,
 While the hands give vent
To my ardor and my aim
And break into very flame —

XIV.

Then I reach, I must believe,
 Not her soul in vain,
 For to me again
It reaches, and past retrieve
Is wound in the toils I weave ;

XV.

And must follow as I require,
 As befits a thrall,
 Bringing flesh and all,
Essence and earth-attire,
To the source of the tractile fire :

XVI.

Till the house called hers, not mine,
 With a growing weight
 Seems to suffocate
If she break not its leaden line
And escape from its close confine.

XVII.

Out of doors into the night !
 On to the maze
 Of the wild wood-ways,
Not turning to left nor right
From the pathway, blind with sight —

XVIII.

Making through rain and wind
 O'er the broken shrubs,
 'Twixt the stems and stubs,
With a still, composed, strong mind,
Not a care for the world behind —

XIX.

Swifter and still more swift,
 As the crowding peace
 Doth to joy increase
In the wide blind eyes uplift
Through the darkness and the drift!

XX.

While I — to the shape, I, too,
 Feel my soul dilate ;
 Nor a whit abate,
And relax not a gesture due,
As I see my belief come true.

XXI.

For, there ! have I drawn or no
 Life to that lip ?
 Do my fingers dip
In a flame which again they throw
On the cheek that breaks aglow ?

XXII.

Ha ! was the hair so first ?
 What, untilleted,
 Made alive, and spread
Through the void with a rich outburst,
Chestnut gold-interspersed ?

XXIII.

Like the doors of a casket-shrine,
  See, on either side,
    Her two arms divide
Till the heart betwixt makes sign,
"Take me, for I am thine!"

XXIV.

"Now—now"—the door is heard!
  Hark, the stairs! and near—
    Nearer—and here—
"Now!" and, at call the third,
She enters without a word.

XXV.

On doth she march and on
  To the fancied shape;
    It is, past escape,
Herself, now: the dream is done,
And the shadow and she are one.

XXVI.

First, I will pray. Do Thou
  That ownest the soul,
    Yet wilt grant control
To another, nor disallow
For a time, restrain me now!

XXVII.

I admonish me while I may,
  Not to squander guilt,
    Since require Thou wilt
At my hand its price one day!
What the price is, who can say?

BY THE FIRESIDE.

I.

How well I know what I mean to
    do
  When the long dark autumn even-
    ings come;
And where, my soul, is thy pleasant
    hue?
  With the music of all thy voices,
    dumb
In life's November too!

II.

I shall be found by the fire, suppose,
  O'er a great wise book, as beseem-
    eth age;
While the shutters flap as the cross-
    wind blows,
  And I turn the page, and I turn the
    page,
Not verse now, only prose!

III.

Till the young ones whisper, finger
    on lip,
  "There he is at it, deep in Greek:
Now then, or never, out we slip
  To cut from the hazels by the creek
A mainmast for our ship!"

IV.

I shall be at it indeed, my friends!
  Greek puts already on either side
Such a branch-work forth as soon ex-
    tends
  To a vista opening far and wide,
And I pass out where it ends.

V.

The outside frame, like your hazel-
    trees—
  But the inside-archway widens fast,
And a rarer sort succeeds to these,
  And we slope to Italy at last
And youth, by green degrees.

VI.

I follow wherever I am led,
  Knowing so well the leader's hand:
O woman-country, wooed not wed,
  Loved all the more by earth's male-
    lands,
Laid to their hearts instead!

VII.

Look at the ruined chapel again
  Half-way up in the Alpine gorge!
Is that a tower, I point you plain,
  Or is it a mill, or an iron forge
Breaks solitude in vain?

VIII.

A turn, and we stand in the heart of
    things;
  The woods are round us, heaped
    and dim:
From slab to slab how it slips and
    springs,
  The thread of water single and slim,
Through the ravage some torrent
    brings!

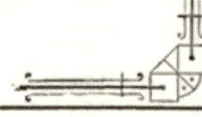

IX.

Does it feed the little lake below?
  That speck of white just on its marge
Is Pella; see, in the evening glow,
  How sharp the silver spear-heads charge
When Alp meets heaven in snow!

X.

On our other side is the straight-up rock;
  And a path is kept 'twixt the gorge and it
By bowlder-stones, where lichens mock
  The marks on a moth, and small ferns fit
Their teeth to the polished block.

XI.

Oh the sense of the yellow mountain flowers,
  And thorny balls, each three in one,
The chestnuts throw on our path in showers!
  For the drop of the woodland fruit's begun,
These early November hours,

XII.

That crimson the creeper's leaf across
  Like a splash of blood, intense, abrupt,
O'er a shield else gold from rim to boss,
  And lay it for show on the fairy-cupped
Elf-needled mat of moss,

XIII.

By the rose-flesh mushrooms, undivulged
  Last evening—nay, in to-day's first dew
Yon sudden coral nipple bulged,
  Where a freaked fawn-colored flaky crew
Of toad-stools peep indulged.

XIV.

And yonder, at foot of the fronting ridge
  That takes the turn to a range beyond,

Is the chapel reached by the one-arched bridge,
  Where the water is stopped in a stagnant pond
Danced over by the midge.

XV.

The chapel and bridge are of stone alike,
  Blackish-gray and mostly wet;
Cut hemp-stalks steep in the narrow dike.
  See here again, how the lichens fret
And the roots of the ivy strike!

XVI.

Poor little place, where its one priest comes
  On a festa-day, if he comes at all,
To the dozen folk from their scattered homes,
  Gathered within that precinct small
By the dozen ways one roams—

XVII.

To drop from the charcoal-burners' huts,
  Or climb from the hemp-dresser's low shed,
Leave the grange where the wood-man stores his nuts,
  Or the wattled cote where the fowlers spread
Their gear on the rock's bare juts,

XVIII.

It has some pretension too, this front,
  With its bit of fresco half-moon-wise
Set over the porch, Art's early wont:
  'Tis John in the Desert, I surmise,
But has borne the weather's brunt—

XIX.

Not from the fault of the builder, though,
  For a pent-house properly projects
Where three carved beams make a certain show,
  Dating—good thought of our architect's—
'Five, six, nine, he lets you know,

XX.

And all day long a bird sings there,
  And a stray sheep drinks at the pond at times;

The place is silent and aware ;
  It has had its scenes, its joys and
      crimes,
But that is its own affair.

XXI.

My perfect wife, my Leonor,
  O heart, my own ! O eyes, mine
      too !
Whom else could I dare look back-
      ward for,
  With whom beside should I dare
      pursue
The path gray heads abhor ?

XXII.

For it leads to a crag's sheer edge with
      them ;
  Youth, flowery all the way, there
      stops —
Not they ; age threatens and they con-
      temn,
  Till they reach the gulf wherein
      youth drops,
One inch from our life's safe hem !

XXIII.

With me, youth led . . . I will speak
      now,
  No longer watch you as you sit
Reading by firelight, that great brow
  And the spirit-small hand propping
      it,
Mutely my heart knows how —

XXIV.

When, if I think but deep enough,
  You are wont to answer, prompt as
      rhyme ;
And you, too, find without rebuff
  Response your soul seeks many a
      time,
Piercing its fine flesh-stuff.

XXV.

My own, confirm me ! If I tread
  This path back, is it not in pride
To think how little I dreamed it led
  To an age so blest that, by its side,
Youth seems the waste instead ?

XXVI.

My own, see where the years con-
      duct !
  At first, 'twas something our two
      souls

Should mix as mists do ; each is
    ' sucked
  In each now : on, the new stream
      rolls,
Whatever rocks obstruct.

XXVII.

Think, when our one soul under-
      stands
  The great Word which makes all
      things new,
When earth breaks up and heaven
      expands,
  How will the change strike me and
      you
In the house not made with hands ?

XXVIII.

Oh ! I must feel your brain prompt
      mine,
  Your heart anticipate my heart,
You must be just before, in fine,
  See and make me see, for your part,
New depths of the divine !

XXIX.

But who could have expected this
  When we two drew together first
Just for the obvious human bliss,
  To satisfy life's daily thirst
With a thing men seldom miss ?

XXX.

Come back with me to the first of
      all,
  Let us lean and love it over again,
Let us now forget and now recall,
  Break the rosary in a pearly rain,
And gather what we let fall !

XXXI.

What did I say ? — that a small bird
      sings
  All day long, save when a brown
      pair
Of hawks from the wood float with
      wide wings
  Strained to a bell : 'gainst noonday
      glare
You count the streaks and rings.

XXXII.

But at afternoon or almost eve
  'Tis better ; then the silence grows
To that degree, you half believe
  It must get rid of what it knows,
Its bosom does so heave.

XXXIII.

Hither we walked then, side by side,
  Arm in arm and cheek to cheek,
And still I questioned or replied,
  While my heart, convulsed to really
    speak,
Lay choking in its pride.

XXXIV.

Silent the crumbling bridge we cross,
  And pity and praise the chapel
    sweet,
And care about the fresco's loss,
  And wish for our souls a like re-
    treat,
And wonder at the moss.

XXXV.

Stoop and kneel on the settle under,
  Look through the window's grated
    square :
Nothing to see ! For fear of plunder,
  The cross is down and the altar
    bare,
As if thieves don't fear thunder.

XXXVI.

We stoop and look in through the
    grate,
  See the little porch and rustic door,
Read duly the dead builder's date ;
  Then cross the bridge that we
    crossed before,
Take the path again — but wait !

XXXVII.

Oh moment one and infinite !
  The water slips o'er stock and
    stone ;
The West is tender, hardly bright :
  How gray at once is the evening
    grown —
One star, its chrysolite !

XXXVIII.

We two stood there with never a
    third,
  But each by each, as each knew
    well :
The sights we saw and the sounds we
    heard,
  The lights and the shades made up
    a spell
Till the trouble grew and stirred.

XXXIX.

Oh, the little more, and how much it
    is !
  And the little less, and what worlds
    away !
How a sound shall quicken content
    to bliss,
  Or a breath suspend the blood's
    best play,
And life be a proof of this !

XL.

Had she willed it, still had stood the
    screen
  So slight, so sure, 'twixt my love
    and her ;
I could fix her face with a guard be-
    tween,
  And find her soul as when friends
    confer,
Friends — lovers that might have
    been.

XLI.

For my heart had a touch of the wood-
    land time,
  Wanting to sleep now over its best.
Shake the whole tree in the summer-
    prime,
  But bring to the last leaf no such
    test !
"Hold the last fast !" runs the
    rhyme.

XLII.

For a chance to make your little
    much,
  To gain a lover and lose a friend,
Venture the tree and a myriad such,
  When nothing you mar but the year
    can mend :
But a last leaf — fear to touch !

XLIII.

Yet should it unfasten itself and fall
  Eddying down till it find your face
At some slight wind — best chance of
    all !
  Be your heart henceforth its dwell-
    ing-place
You trembled to forestall !

XLIV.

Worth how well, those dark gray
    eyes,
  That hair so dark and dear, how
    worth

That a man should strive and agonize,
  And taste a veriest hell on earth
For the hope of such a prize!

XLV.

You might have turned and tried a
  man,
  Set him a space to weary and wear,
And prove which suited more your
  plan,
  His best of hope or his worst de-
    spair,
Yet end as he began.

XLVI.

But you spared me this, like the heart
  you are,
  And filled my empty heart at a
    word.
If two lives join, there is oft a scar,
  They are one and one, with a shad-
    owy third;
One near one is too far.

XLVII.

A moment after, and hands unseen
  Were hanging the night around us
    fast;
But we knew that a bar was broken
  between
  Life and life: we were mixed at last
In spite of the mortal screen.

XLVIII.

The forests had done it; there they
  stood;
  We caught for a moment the pow-
    ers at play:
They had mingled us so, for once and
  good,
  Their work was done — we might
    go or stay,
They relapsed to their ancient mood.

XLIX.

How the world is made for each of us!
  How all we perceive and know in it
Tends to some moment's product
  thus,
  When a soul declares itself — to wit,
By its fruit, the thing it does!

L.

Be hate that fruit, or love that fruit,
  It forwards the general deed of
    man,

And each of the Many helps to recruit
  The life of the race by a general
    plan;
Each living his own, to boot.

LI.

I am named and known by that mo-
  ment's feat;
  There took my station and degree;
So grew my own small life com-
  plete,
  As nature obtained her best of me —
One born to love you, sweet!

LII.

And to watch you sink by the fireside
  now
  Back again, as you mutely sit
Musing by fire-light, that great brow
  And the spirit-small hand propping
    it,
Yonder, my heart knows how!

LIII.

So, earth has gained by one man the
  more,
  And the gain of earth must be
    heaven's gain too;
And the whole is well worth think-
  ing o'er
  When autumn comes: which I
    mean to do
One day, as I said before.

ANY WIFE TO ANY HUS-
BAND.

I.

My love, this is the bitterest, that
  thou —
Who art all truth, and who dost love
  me now
  As thine eyes say, as thy voice
    breaks to say —
Shouldst love so truly, and couldst
  love me still
  A whole long life through, had but
    love its will,
  Would death, that leads me from
    thee, brook delay.

II.

I have but to be by thee, and thy hand
Will never let mine go, nor heart
    withstand
  The beating of my heart to reach
    its place.
When shall I look for thee and feel
    thee gone?
When cry for the old comfort and
    find none?
  Never, I know! Thy soul is in thy
    face.

III.

Oh, I should fade — 'tis willed so!
    Might I save,
Gladly I would, whatever beauty
    gave
  Joy to thy sense, for that was pre-
    cious too.
It is not to be granted. But the soul
Whence the love comes, all ravage
    leaves that whole;
  Vainly the flesh fades; soul makes
    all things new.

IV.

It would not be because my eye grew
    dim
Thou couldst not find the love there,
    thanks to Him
  Who never is dishonored in the
    spark
He gave us from his fire of fires, and
    bade
Remember whence it sprang, nor be
    afraid
  While that burns on, though all the
    rest grow dark.

V.

So, how thou wouldst be perfect,
    white and clean
Outside as inside, soul and soul's de-
    mesne
  Alike, this body given to show it
    by!
Oh, three-parts through the worst of
    life's abyss,
What plaudits from the next world
    after this,
  Couldst thou repeat a stroke and
    gain the sky!

VI.

And is it not the bitterer to think
That, disengage our hands and thou
    wilt sink

Although thy love was love in very
    deed?
I know that nature! Pass a festive
    day,
Thou dost not throw its relic-flower
    away,
  Nor bid its music's loitering echo
    speed.

VII.

Thou let'st the stranger's glove lie
    where it fell;
If old things remain old things all is
    well,
  For thou art grateful as becomes
    man best:
And hadst thou only heard me play
    one tune,
Or viewed me from a window, not so
    soon
  With thee would such things fade
    as with the rest.

VIII.

I seem to see! We meet and part;
    'tis brief;
The book I opened keeps a folded
    leaf,
  The very chair I sat on, breaks the
    rank;
That is a portrait of me on the wall —
Three lines, my face comes at so
    slight a call —
  And for all this, one little hour to
    thank!

IX.

But now, because the hour through
    years was fixed,
Because our inmost beings met and
    mixed,
  Because thou once hast loved me —
    wilt thou dare
Say to thy soul and Who may list be-
    side,
  "Therefore she is immortally my
    bride;
Chance cannot change my love, nor
    time impair.

X.

"So, what if in the dusk of life that's
    left,
I, a tired traveller of my sun bereft,
  Look from my path when, mimick-
    ing the same,
The fire-fly glimpses past me, come
    and gone?

— Where was it till the sunset? where
    anon
  It will be at the sunrise! What's
  to blame?"

XI.

Is it so helpful to thee? Canst thou
  take
The mimic up, nor, for the true thing's
  sake,
  Put gently by such efforts at a beam?
Is the remainder of the way so long,
Thou need'st the little solace, thou
  the strong?
  Watch out thy watch, let weak ones
  doze and dream.

XII.

— Ah, but the fresher faces! "Is it
  true,"
Thou'lt ask, "some eyes are beautiful
  and new?
  Some hair, — how can one choose
  but grasp such wealth?
And if a man would press his lips to
  lips
Fresh as the wilding hedge-rose-cup
  there slips
  The dewdrop out of, must it be by
  stealth?

XIII.

"It cannot change the love still kept
  for her,
More than if such a picture I prefer
  Passing a day with, to a room's bare
  side:
The painted form takes nothing she
  possessed,
Yet, while the Titian's Venus lies at
  rest,
  A man looks. Once more, what is
  there to chide?"

XIV.

So must I see, from where I sit and
  watch,
My own self sell myself, my hand
  attach
  Its warrant to the very thefts from
  me —
Thy singleness of soul that made me
  proud,
Thy purity of heart I loved aloud,
  Thy man's-truth I was bold to bid
  God see!

XV.

Love so, then, if thou wilt! Give all
  thou canst
Away to the new faces — disen-
  tranced,
  (Say it and think it) obdurate no
  more,
Re-issue looks and words from the old
  mint,
Pass them afresh, no matter whose
  the print,
  Image, and superscription once they
  bore!

XVI.

Re-coin thyself, and give it them to
  spend, —
It all comes to the same thing at the
  end,
  Since mine thou wast, mine art,
  and mine shalt be,
Faithful or faithless: sealing up the
  sum
Or lavish of my treasure, thou must
  come
  Back to the heart's place here I
  keep for thee!

XVII.

Only, why should it be with stain at
  all?
Why must I, 'twixt the leaves of
  coronal,
  Put any kiss of pardon on thy
  brow?
Why need the other women know so
  much,
And talk together, "Such the look
  and such
  The smile he used to love with, then
  as now!"

XVIII.

Might I die last and show thee!
  Should I find
Such hardships in the few years left
  behind,
  If free to take and light my lamp,
  and go
Into thy tomb, and shut the door and
  sit,
Seeing thy face on those four sides of
  it
  The better that they are so blank, I
  know!

XIX.

Why, time was what I wanted, to turn
    o'er
Within my mind each look, get more
    and more
  By heart each word, too much to
    learn at first;
And join thee all the fitter for the
    pause
'Neath the low door-way's lintel.
    That were cause
  For lingering, though thou calledst,
    if I durst!

XX.

And yet thou art the nobler of us
    two:
What dare I dream of, that thou canst
    not do,
  Outstripping my ten small steps
    with one stride?
I'll say then, here's a trial and a
    task:
Is it to bear? — if easy, I'll not
    ask:
  Though love fail, I can trust on in
    thy pride.

XXI.

Pride? — when those eyes forestall
    the life behind
The death I have to go through! —
    when I find,
  Now that I want thy help most, all
    of thee!
What did I fear? Thy love shall hold
    me fast
Until the little minute's sleep is
    past
  And I wake saved. — And yet it
    will not be!

IN A YEAR.

I.

NEVER any more,
    While I live,
Need I hope to see his face
    As before.
Once his love grown chill,
    Mine may strive:
Bitterly we re-embrace,
    Single still.

II.

Was it something said,
    Something done,
Vexed him? was it touch of hand,
    Turn of head?
Strange! that very way
    Love begun:
I as little understand
    Love's decay.

III.

When I sewed or drew,
    I recall
How he looked as if I sung,
    — Sweetly too.
If I spoke a word,
    First of all
Up his cheek the color sprung,
    Then he heard.

IV.

Sitting by my side,
    At my feet,
So he breathed but air I breathed,
    Satisfied!
I, too, at love's brim
    Touched the sweet:
I would die if death bequeathed
    Sweet to him.

V.

" Speak, I love thee best!"
    He exclaimed:
" Let thy love my own foretell!"
    I confessed:
" Clasp my heart on thine
    Now unblamed,
Since upon thy soul as well
    Hangeth mine!"

VI.

Was it wrong to own,
    Being truth?
Why should all the giving prove
    His alone?
I had wealth and ease,
    Beauty, youth:
Since my lover gave me love,
    I gave these.

VII.

That was all I meant,
    — To be just,
And the passion I had raised,
    To content.

Since he chose to change
    Gold for dust,
If I gave him what he praised
    Was it strange ?

VIII.

Would he loved me yet,
    On and on,
While I found some way undreamed
    — Paid my debt !
Gave more life and more,
    Till all gone,
He should smile " She never seemed
    Mine before.

IX.

" What, she felt the while,
    Must I think ?
Love's so different with us men ! "
    He should smile :
" Dying for my sake —
    White and pink !
Can't we touch these bubbles then
    But they break ? "

X.

Dear, the pang is brief,
    Do thy part,
Have thy pleasure ! How perplexed
    Grows belief !
Well, this cold clay clod
    Was man's heart :
Crumble it, and what comes next ?
    Is it God ?

SONG FROM "JAMES LEE."

I.

OH, good gigantic smile o' the brown
    old earth,
    This autumn morning ! How he
        sets his bones
To bask i' the sun, and thrusts out
    knees and feet
For the ripple to run over in its mirth :
    Listening the while, where on the
        heap of stones
The white breast of the sea-lark twit-
    ters sweet.

II.

That is the doctrine, simple, ancient,
    true ;
    Such is life's trial, as old earth
        smiles and knows.

If you loved only what were worth
    your love,
Love were clear gain, and wholly well
    for you.
Make the low nature better by your
    throes !
Give earth yourself, go up for gain
    above !

A WOMAN'S LAST WORD.

I.

LET's contend no more, Love,
    Strive nor weep :
All be as before, Love,
    — Only sleep !

II.

What so wild as words are ?
    I and thou
In debate, as birds are,
    Hawk on bough !

III.

See the creature stalking
    While we speak !
Hush and hide the talking,
    Cheek on cheek.

IV.

What so false as truth is,
    False to thee ?
Where the serpent's tooth is,
    Shun the tree —

V.

Where the apple reddens,
    Never pry —
Lest we lose our Edens,
    Eve and I.

VI.

Be a god, and hold me
    With a charm !
Be a man, and fold me
    With thine arm !

VII.

Teach me, only teach, Love !
    As I ought
I will speak thy speech, Love,
    Think thy thought—

Meeting at Night. — Page 45.

WOMEN AND ROSES.

VIII.

Meet, if thou require it,
 Both demands,
Laying flesh and spirit
 In thy hands.

IX.

That shall be to-morrow,
 Not to-night :
I must bury sorrow
 Out of sight :

X.

— Must a little weep, Love,
 (Foolish me !)
And so fall asleep, Love,
 Loved by thee.

MEETING AT NIGHT.

I.

THE gray sea and the long black land;
And the yellow half-moon large and
 low;
And the startled little waves that
 leap
In fiery ringlets from their sleep,
As I gain the cove with pushing prow,
And quench its speed i' the slushy
 sand.

II.

Then a mile of warm sea-scented
 beach ;
Three fields to cross till a farm ap-
 pears :
A tap at the pane, the quick sharp
 scratch
And blue spurt of a lighted match,
And a voice less loud, through joys
 and fears,
Than the two hearts beating each to
 each !

PARTING AT MORNING.

ROUND the cape of a sudden came the
 sea,
And the sun looked over the moun-
 tain's rim :
And straight was a path of gold for
 him,
And the need of a world of men for
 me.

WOMEN AND ROSES.

I.

I DREAM of a red-rose tree.
And which of its roses three
Is the dearest rose to me ?

II.

Round and round, like a dance of
 snow
In a dazzling drift, as its guardians,
 go
Floating the women faded for ages,
Sculptured in stone, on the poet's
 pages.
Then follow women fresh and gay,
Living and loving and loved to-day.
Last, in the rear, flee the multitude
 of maidens,
Beauties yet unborn. And all, to one
 cadence,
They circle their rose on my rose-tree.

III.

Dear rose, thy term is reached,
Thy leaf hangs loose and bleached :
Bees pass it unimpeached.

IV.

Stay, then, stoop, since I cannot
 climb,
You, great shapes of the antique time,
How shall I fix you, fire you, freeze
 you,
Break my heart at your feet to please
 you ?
Oh, to possess and be possessed !
Hearts that beat 'neath each pallid
 breast !
Once but of love, the poesy, the pas-
 sion,
Drink but once and die ! — In vain,
 the same fashion,
They circle their rose on my rose-tree.

V.

Dear rose, thy joy's undimmed ;
Thy cup is ruby-rimmed,
Thy cup's heart nectar-brimmed.

VI.

Deep, as drops from a statue's plinth
The bee sucked in by the hyacinth,
So will I bury me while burning,
Quench like him at a plunge my
 yearning,

Eyes in your eyes, lips on your lips !
Fold me fast where the cincture slips,
Prison all my soul in eternities of
  pleasure,
Girdle me for once ! But no — the
  old measure,
They circle their rose on my rose-tree.

VII.

Dear rose without a thorn,
Thy bud's the babe unborn :
First streak of a new morn.

VIII.

Wings, lend wings for the cold, the
  clear !
What is far conquers what is near.
Roses will bloom nor want behold-
  ers,
Sprung from the dust where our flesh
  moulders.
What shall arrive with the cycle's
  change ?
A novel grace and a beauty strange.
I will make an Eve, be the Artist that
  began her,
Shaped her to his mind ! — Alas ! in
  like manner
They circle their rose on my rose-tree.

MISCONCEPTIONS.

I.

This is a spray the bird clung to,
  Making it blossom with pleasure,
Ere the high tree-top she sprung to,
  Fit for her nest and her treasure.
Oh, what a hope beyond measure
Was the poor spray's, which the fly-
  ing feet hung to, —
So to be singled out, built in, and sung
  to !

II.

That is a heart the queen leant on,
  Thrilled in a minute erratic,
Ere the true bosom she bent on,
  Meet for love's regal dalmatic.
Oh, what a fancy ecstatic
Was the poor heart's, ere the wan-
  derer went on, —
Love to be saved for it, proffered to,
  spent on !

A PRETTY WOMAN.

I.

That fawn-skin-dappled hair of hers,
  And the blue eye
  Dear and dewy,
And that infantine fresh air of hers !

II.

To think men cannot take you, Sweet,
  And infold you,
  Ay, and hold you,
And so keep you what they make
  · you, Sweet !

III.

You like us for a glance, you know —
  For a word's sake
  Or a sword's sake :
All's the same, whate'er the chance,
  you know.

IV.

And in turn we make you ours, we
  say —
  You and youth too,
  Eyes and mouth too,
All the face composed of flowers, we
  say.

V.

All's our own, to make the most of,
  Sweet —
  Sing and say for,
  Watch and pray for,
Keep a secret or go boast of, Sweet !

VI.

But for loving, why, you would not,
  Sweet,
  Though we prayed you,
  Paid you, brayed you
In a mortar — for you could not,
  Sweet !

VII.

So, we leave the sweet face fondly
  there :
  Be its beauty
  Its sole duty !
Let all hope of grace beyond, lie
  there !

VIII.

And while the face lies quiet there,
  Who shall wonder
  That I ponder
A conclusion ? I will try it there.

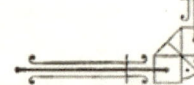

IX.

As, — why must one, for the love fore-
        gone,
    Scout mere liking?
    Thunder-striking
Earth, — the heaven, we looked above
    for, gone!

X.

Why, with beauty, needs there
    money be,
    Love with liking?
    Crush the fly-king
In his gauze, because no honey-bee?

XI.

May not liking be so simple-sweet,
    If love grew there
    'Twould undo there
All that breaks the cheek to dimples
    sweet?

XII.

Is the creature too imperfect, say?
    Would you mend it,
    And so end it?
Since not all addition perfects aye!

XIII.

Or is it of its kind, perhaps,
    Just perfection —
    Whence, rejection
Of a grace not to its mind, perhaps?

XIV.

Shall we burn up, tread that face at
    once
    Into tinder,
    And so hinder
Sparks from kindling all the place at
    once?

XV.

Or else kiss away one's soul on her?
    Your love fancies!
    —A sick man sees
Truer, when his hot eyes roll on her!

XVI.

Thus the craftsman thinks to grace
    the rose, —
    Plucks a mould-flower.
    For his gold flower,
Uses fine things that efface the rose:

XVII.

Rosy rubies make its cup more rose,
    Precious metals
    Ape the petals, —
Last, some old king locks it up, mo-
    rose!

XVIII.

Then how grace a rose? I know a
    way!
    Leave it, rather.
    Must you gather?
Smell, kiss, wear it — at last, throw
    away!

A LIGHT WOMAN.

I.

So far as our story approaches the end,
    Which do you pity the most of us
        three? —
My friend, or the mistress of my
        friend
    With her wanton eyes, or me?

II.

My friend was already too good to lose,
    And seemed in the way of improve-
        ment yet,
When she crossed his path with her
        hunting-noose,
    And over him drew her net.

III.

When I saw him tangled in her toils,
    A shame, said I, if she adds just
        him
To her nine and ninety other spoils,
    The hundredth for a whim!

IV.

And before my friend be wholly hers,
    How easy to prove to him, I said,
An eagle's the game her pride pre-
    fers,
    Though she snaps at a wren instead.

V.

So, I gave her eyes my own eyes to
        take,
    My hand sought hers as in earnest
        need,
And round she turned for my noble
        sake,
    And gave me herself indeed.

VI.

The eagle am I, with my fame in the
   world,
   The wren is he, with his maiden
     face.
— You look away and your lip is
   curled?
Patience, a moment's space!

VII.

For see, my friend goes shaking and
   white;
He eyes me as the basilisk:
I have turned, it appears, his day to
   night,
   Eclipsing his sun's disk.

VIII.

And I did it, he thinks, as a very
   thief:
   "Though I love her — that, he com-
     prehends —
One should master one's passions
   (love, in chief),
   And be loyal to one's friends!"

IX.

And she, — she lies in my hand as
   tame
As a pear late basking over a wall;
Just a touch to try, and off it came;
   'Tis mine, — can I let it fall?

X.

With no mind to eat it, that's the
   worst!
Were it thrown in the road, would
   the case assist?
'Twas quenching a dozen blue-flies'
   thirst
   When I gave its stalk a twist.

XI.

And I, — what I seem to my friend,
   you see;
What I soon shall seem to his love,
   you guess:
What I seem to myself, do you ask of
   me?
   No hero, I confess.

XII.

'Tis an awkward thing to play with
   souls,
   And matter enough to save one's
   own:

Yet think of my friend, and the burn-
   ing coals
   He played with for bits of stone!

XIII.

One likes to show the truth for the
   truth;
   That the woman was light is very
     true:
But suppose she says, — Never mind
   that youth!
   What wrong have I done to you?

XIV.

Well, anyhow, here the story stays,
   So far at least as I understand;
And, Robert Browning, you writer of
   plays,
   Here's a subject made to your hand!

LOVE IN A LIFE.

I.

Room after room,
I hunt the house through
We inhabit together.
Heart, fear nothing, for, heart, thou
   shalt find her —
Next time, herself! — not the trouble
   behind her
Left in the curtain, the couch's per-
   fume!
As she brushed it, the cornice-wreath
   blossomed anew:
Yon looking-glass gleamed at the
   wave of her feather.

II.

Yet the day wears,
And door succeeds door;
I try the fresh fortune —
Range the wide house from the wing
   to the centre.
Still the same chance! she goes out as
   I enter.
Spend my whole day in the quest, —
   who cares?
But 'tis twilight, you see, — with such
   suites to explore,
Such closets to search, such alcoves
   to importune!

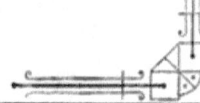

LIFE IN A LOVE.

ESCAPE me?
Never—
Beloved!
While I am I, and you are you,
So long as the world contains us both,
Me the loving and you the loth,
While the one eludes, must the other
    pursue.
My life is a fault at last, I fear:
    It seems too much like a fate, in-
        deed!
    Though I do my best I shall scarce
        succeed.
But what if I fail of my purpose here?
It is but to keep the nerves at strain,
    To dry one's eyes and laugh at a
        fall,
And baffled, get up and begin again,—
    So the chase takes up one's life,
        that's all.
While, look but once from your far-
        thest bound
    At me so deep in the dust and dark,
No sooner the old hope goes to ground
    Than a new one, straight to the self-
        same mark,
I shape me—
Ever
Removed!

THE LABORATORY.

ANCIEN RÉGIME.

I.

Now that I, tying thy glass mask
    tightly,
May gaze through these faint smokes
    curling whitely,
As thou pliest thy trade in this devil's-
    smithy—
Which is the poison to poison her,
    prithee?

II.

He is with her, and they know that I
    know
Where they are, what they do: they
    believe my tears flow
While they laugh, laugh at me, at me
    fled to the drear
Empty church, to pray God in, for
    them!—I am here.

III.

Grind away, moisten and mash up
    thy paste,
Pound at thy powder,—I am not in
    haste!
Better sit thus and observe thy
    strange things,
Than go where men wait me, and
    dance at the King's.

IV.

That in the mortar—you call it a
    gum?
Ah, the brave tree whence such gold
    oozings come!
And yonder soft vial, the exquisite
    blue,
Sure to taste sweetly,—is that poison
    too?

V.

Had I but all of them, thee and thy
    treasures,
What a wild crowd of invisible pleas-
    ures!
To carry pure death in an earring, a
    casket,
A signet, a fan-mount, a filigree bas-
    ket!

VI.

Soon, at the King's, a mere lozenge
    to give,
And Pauline should have just thirty
    minutes to live!
But to light a pastille, and Elise with
    her head
And her breast and her arms and her
    hands, should drop dead!

VII.

Quick—is it finished? The color's
    too grim!
Why not soft like the vial's, enticing
    and dim?
Let it brighten her drink, let her turn
    it and stir,
And try it and taste, ere she fix and
    prefer!

VIII.

What a drop! She's not little, no
    minion like me!
That's why she ensnared him: this
    never will free
The soul from those masculine eyes,
    —say, "No!"
To that pulse's magnificent come and
    go.

IX.

For only last night, as they whispered,
  I brought
My own eyes to bear on her so, that
  I thought
Could I keep them one-half minute
  fixed, she would fall
Shrivelled; she fell not; yet this does
  it all!

X.

Not that I bid you spare her the pain;
Let death be felt and the proof re-
  main :
Brand, burn up, bite into its grace —
He is sure to remember her dying
  face!

XI.

Is it done? Take my mask off! Nay,
  be not morose ;
It kills her, and this prevents seeing
  it close :
The delicate droplet, my whole for-
  tune's fee!
If it hurts her, beside, can it ever hurt
  me ?

XII.

Now, take all my jewels, gorge gold
  to your fill,
You may kiss me, old man, on my
  mouth if you will!
But brush this dust off me, lest horror
  it brings
Ere I know it — next moment I dance
  at the King's!

GOLD HAIR:

A STORY OF PORNIC.

I.

Oh, the beautiful girl, too white,
  Who lived at Pornic down by the
  sea,
Just where the sea and the Loire
  unite !
  And a boasted name in Brittany
She bore, which I will not write.

II.

Too white, for the flower of life is
  red ;
  Her flesh was the soft seraphic
  screen

Of a soul that is meant (her parents
  said)
  To just see earth, and hardly be
  seen,
And blossom in heaven instead.

III.

Yet earth saw one thing, one how
  fair !
  One grace that grew to its full on
  earth :
Smiles might be sparse on her cheek
  so spare,
  And her waist want half a girdle's
  girth,
But she had her great gold hair.

IV.

Hair, such a wonder of flix and floss,
  Freshness and fragrance — floods of
  it, too !
Gold, did I say? Nay, gold's mere
  dross :
  Here, Life smiled, "Think what I
  meant to do !"
And Love sighed, "Fancy my loss !'

V.

So, when she died, it was scarce more
  strange
  Than that, when some delicate
  evening dies,
And you follow its spent sun's pallid
  range,
  There's a shoot of color startles the
  skies
With sudden, violent change, —

VI.

That, while the breath was nearly to
  seek,
  As they put the little cross to her
  lips,
She changed ; a spot came out on her
  cheek,
  A spark from her eye in mid-eclipse,
And she broke forth, " I must speak !

VII.

" Not my hair !" made the girl her
  moan —
  " All the rest is gone or to go ;
But the last, last grace, my all, my
  own,
  Let it stay in the grave, that the
  ghosts may know !
Leave my poor gold hair alone ! "

VIII.

The passion thus vented, dead lay she;
  Her parents sobbed their worst on
    that.
All friends joined in, nor observed
  degree :
  For indeed the hair was to wonder
    at,
As it spread — not flowing free,

IX.

But curled around her brow, like a
  crown,
  And coiled beside her cheeks, like a
    cap,
And calmed about her neck — ay,
  down
  To her breast, pressed flat, without
    a gap
I' the gold, it reached her gown.

X.

All kissed that face, like a silver wedge
  'Mid the yellow wealth, nor dis-
    turbed its hair ;
E'en the priest allowed death's privi-
  lege,
  As he planted the crucifix with care
On her breast, 'twixt edge and edge.

XI.

And thus was she buried, inviolate
  Of body and soul, in the very space
By the altar ; keeping saintly state
  In Pornic church, for her pride of
    race,
Pure life and piteous fate.

XII.

And in after-time would your fresh
  tear fall,
  Though your mouth might twitch
    with a dubious smile,
As they told you of gold both robe
  and pall,
  How she prayed them leave it alone
    a while,
So it never was touched at all.

XIII.

Years flew ; this legend grew at last
  The life of the lady ; all she had
    done,
All been, in the memories fading fast
  Of lover and friend, was summed in
    one
Sentence survivors passed :

XIV.

To wit, she was meant for heaven,
  not earth ;
  Had turned an angel before the
    time :
Yet, since she was mortal, in such
  dearth
  Of frailty, all you could count a
    crime
Was — she knew her gold hair's worth.

XV.

At little pleasant Pornic church,
  It chanced, the pavement wanted
    repair,
Was taken to pieces ; left in the lurch,
  A certain sacred space lay bare,
And the boys began research.

XVI.

'Twas the space where our sires would
  lay a saint,
  A benefactor, — a bishop, suppose,
A baron with armor-adornments
  quaint,
  Dame with chased ring and jewelled
    rose,
Things sanctity saves from taint ;

XVII.

So we come to find them in after-days
  When the corpse is presumed to
    have done with gauds
Of use to the living, in many ways :
  For the boys get pelf, and the town
    applauds,
And the church deserves the praise.

XVIII.

They grubbed with a will ; and at
  length — *O cor*
  Humanum, pectora cœca, and the
    rest ! —
They found — no gaud they were pry-
  ing for,
  No ring, no rose, but — who would
    have guessed ? —
A double Louis-d'or !

XIX.

Here was a case for the priest : he
  heard,
  Marked, inwardly digested, laid

Finger on nose, smiled, " A little bird
 Chirps in my ear:" then, " Bring
  a spade,
Dig deeper ! " — he gave the word.

XX.

And lo, when they came to the coffin-
 lid,
 Or rotten planks which composed it
  once,
Why, there lay the girl's skull wedged
 amid
 A mint of money, it served for the
  nonce
To hold in its hair-heaps hid !

XXI.

Hid there? Why? Could the girl
 be wont
 (She the stainless soul) to treasure
  up
Money, earth's trash and heaven's
 affront?
 Had a spider found out the com-
  munion-cup,
Was a toad in the christening-font ?

XXII.

Truth is truth : too true it was.
 Gold ! She hoarded and hugged it
  first,
Longed for it, leaned o'er it, loved it
  — alas —
 Till the humor grew to a head and
  burst,
And she cried, at the final pass, —

XXIII.

" Talk not of God, my heart is stone !
 Nor lover nor friend — be gold for
  both !
Gold I lack ; and, my all, my own,
 It shall hide in my hair. I scarce
  die loth
If they let my hair alone !"

XXIV.

Louis-d'ors, some six times five,
 And duly double, every piece.
Now, do you see ? With the priest to
 shrive,
 With parents preventing her soul's
  release
By kisses that kept alive, —

XXV.

With heaven's gold gates about to
 ope,
 With friends' praise, gold-like, lin-
  gering still,
An instinct had bidden the girl's hand
 grope
 For gold, the true sort — " Gold in
  heaven, if you will ;
But I keep earth's too, I hope."

XXVI.

Enough ! The priest took the grave's
 grim yield :
 The parents, they eyed that price of
  sin
As if *thirty pieces* lay revealed
 On the place *to bury strangers in*,
The hideous Potter's Field.

XXVII.

But the priest bethought him :
 "'Milk that's spilt'
 — You know the adage ! Watch
  and pray !
Saints tumble to earth with so slight a
 tilt !
 It would build a new altar ; that,
  we may !"
And the altar therewith was built.

XXVIII.

Why I deliver this horrible verse ?
 As the text of a sermon, which now
  I preach.
Evil or good may be better or worse
 In the human heart, but the mix-
  ture of each
Is a marvel and a curse.

XXIX.

The candid incline to surmise of late
 That the Christian faith may be
  false, I find ;
For our Essays-and-Reviews' debate
 Begins to tell on the public mind,
And Colenso's words have weight :

XXX.

I still, to suppose it true, for my part,
 See reasons and reasons ; this, to
  begin :
'Tis the faith that launched point-
 blank her dart
 At the head of a lie — taught Origi-
  nal Sin,
The Corruption of Man's Heart.

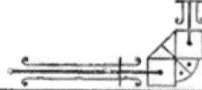

"Ages ago, a lady there,
At the farthest window facing the East." — Page 53.

THE STATUE AND THE BUST.

THERE's a palace in Florence, the
    world knows well,
And a statue watches it from the
    square,
And this story of both do our towns-
    men tell.

Ages ago, a lady there,
At the farthest window facing the East
Asked, " Who rides by with the royal
    air ? "

The bridesmaids' prattle around her
    ceased ;
She leaned forth, one on either hand ;
They saw how the blush of the bride
    increased —

They felt by its beats her heart ex-
    pand —
As one at each ear and both in a
    breath
Whispered, " The Great Duke Fer-
    dinand."

That selfsame instant, underneath,
The Duke rode past in his idle way,
Empty and fine, like a swordless
    sheath.

Gay he rode, with a friend as gay,
Till he threw his head back — " Who
    is she ? "
— " A bride the Riccardi brings home
    to-day."

Hair in heaps lay heavily
Over a pale brow spirit-pure —
Carved like the heart of the coal-
    black tree,

Crisped like a war-steed's encolure —
And vainly sought to dissemble her
    eyes
Of the blackest black our eyes endure.

And lo, a blade for a knight's emprise
Filled the fine empty sheath of a
    man, —
The Duke grew straightway brave
    and wise.

He looked at her, as a lover can
She looked at him, as one who awakes :
The past was a sleep, and her life
    began.

Now, love so ordered for both their
    sakes,
A feast was held, that selfsame night,
In the pile which the mighty shadow
    makes.

(For Via Larga is three-parts light,
But the palace overshadows one,
Because of a crime which may God
    requite !

To Florence and God the wrong was
    done,
Through the first republic's murder
    there
By Cosimo and his cursed son.)

The Duke (with the statue's face in
    the square)
Turned, in the midst of his multi-
    tude,
At the bright approach of the bridal
    pair.

Face to face the lovers stood
A single minute and no more,
While the bridegroom bent as a man
    subdued —

Bowed till his bonnet brushed the
    floor —
For the Duke on the lady a kiss con-
    ferred,
As the courtly custom was of yore.

In a minute can lovers exchange a
    word ?
If a word did pass, which I do not
    think,
Only one out of the thousand heard.

That was the bridegroom. At day's
    brink
He and his bride were alone at last
In a bed-chamber by a taper's blink.

Calmly he said that her lot was cast,
That the door she had passed was
    shut on her
Till the final catafalque repassed.

The world meanwhile, its noise and
    stir,
Through a certain window facing the
    East,
She could watch like a convent's
    chronicler.

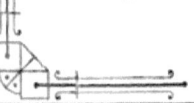

Since passing the door might lead to
  a feast,
And a feast might lead to so much
  beside,
He, of many evils, chose the least.

"Freely I choose too," said the bride—
"Your window and its world suffice,"
Replied the tongue, while the heart
  replied—

"If I spend the night with that devil
  twice,
May his window serve as my loop of
  hell
Whence a damned soul looks on
  paradise!

"I fly to the Duke who loves me well,
Sit by his side and laugh at sorrow
Ere I count another ave-bell.

"'T is only the coat of a page to bor-
  row,
And tie my hair in a horse-boy's trim,
And I save my soul—but not to-mor-
  row"—

(She checked herself and her eye
  grew dim)
"My father tarries to bless my state:
I must keep it one day more for
  him.

"Is one day more so long to wait?
Moreover the Duke rides past, I know;
We shall see each other, sure as fate."

She turned on her side and slept.
  Just so!
So we resolve on a thing, and sleep:
So did the lady, ages ago.

That night the Duke said, "Dear or
  cheap
As the cost of this cup of bliss may
  prove
To body or soul, I will drain it deep."

And on the morrow, bold with love,
He beckoned the bridegroom (close on
  call,
As his duty bade, by the Duke's al-
  cove)

And smiled, "'Twas a very funeral,
Your lady will think, this feast of
  ours,—
A shame to efface, whate'er befall!

"What if we break from the Arno
  bowers,
And try if Petraja, cool and green,
Cure last night's fault with this morn-
  ing's flowers?"

The bridegroom, not a thought to be
  seen
On his steady brow and quiet mouth,
Said, "Too much favor for me so
  mean!

"But, alas! my lady leaves the South;
Each wind that comes from the Apen-
  nine
Is a menace to her tender youth:

"Nor a way exists, the wise opine,
If she quits her palace twice this
  year,
To avert the flower of life's decline."

Quoth the Duke, "A sage and a kind-
  ly fear.
Moreover Petraja is cold this spring:
Be our feast to-night as usual here!"

And then to himself—"Which night
  shall bring
Thy bride to her lover's embraces,
  fool—
Or I am the fool, and thou art the
  king!

"Yet my passion must wait a night,
  nor cool—
For to-night the envoy arrives from
  France
Whose heart I unlock with thyself,
  my tool.

"I need thee still and might miss per-
  chance.
To-day is not wholly lost, beside,
With its hope of my lady's counte-
  nance:

"For I ride—what should I do but
  ride?
And, passing her palace, if I list,
May glance at its window—well be-
  tide!"

So said, so done: nor the lady missed
One ray that broke from the ardent
  brow,
Nor a curl of the lips where the spirit
  kissed.

Be sure that each renewed the vow,
No morrow's sun should arise and set
And leave them then as it left them
   now.

But next day passed, and next day yet,
With still fresh cause to wait one day
   more
Ere each leaped over the parapet.

And still, as love's brief morning wore,
With a gentle start, half smile, half
   sigh,
They found love not as it seemed be-
   fore.

They thought it would work infalli-
   bly,
But not in despite of heaven and
   earth:
The rose would blow when the storm
   passed by.

Meantime they could profit, in win-
   ter's dearth,
By store of fruits that supplant the
   rose:
The world and its ways have a certain
   worth:

And to press a point while these op-
   pose
Were simple policy; better wait:
We lose no friends and we gain no
   foes.

Meantime, worse fates than a lover's
   fate,
Who daily may ride and pass and look
Where his lady watches behind the
   grate!

And she — she watched the square
   like a book
Holding one picture and only one,
Which daily to find she undertook:

When the picture was reached the
   book was done,
And she turned from the picture at
   night to scheme
Of tearing it out for herself next sun.

So weeks grew months, years; gleam
   by gleam
The glory dropped from their youth
   and love,
And both perceived they had dreamed
   a dream;

Which hovered as dreams do, still
   above:
But who can take a dream for a truth?
Oh, hide our eyes from the next re-
   move!

One day as the lady saw her youth
Depart, and the silver thread that
   streaked
Her hair, and, worn by the serpent's
   tooth,

The brow so puckered, the chin so
   peaked, —
And wondered who the woman was,
Hollow-eyed and haggard-cheeked

Fronting her silent in the glass —
" Summon here," she suddenly said,
" Before the rest of my old self pass,

" Him, the Carver, a hand to aid,
Who fashions the clay no love will
   change,
And fixes a beauty never to fade.

" Let Robbia's craft so apt and strange
Arrest the remains of young and fair,
And rivet them while the seasons
   range.

" Make me a face on the window
   there,
Waiting as ever, mute the while,
My love to pass below in the square!

" And let me think that it may beguile
Dreary days which the dead must
   spend
Down in their darkness under the
   aisle,

" To say, ' What matters it at the end?
I did no more while my heart was
   warm
Than does that image, my pale-faced
   friend.'

" Where is the use of the lip's red
   charm,
The heaven of hair, the pride of the
   brow,
And the blood that blues the inside
   arm —

" Unless we turn, as the soul knows
   how,
The earthly gift to an end divine?
A lady of clay is as good, I trow."

But long ere Robbia's cornice, fine
With flowers and fruits which leaves
   inlace,
Was set where now is the empty
   shrine —

(And, leaning out of a bright blue
   space,
As a ghost might lean from a chink of
   sky,
The passionate pale lady's face —

Eying ever, with earnest eye
And quick-turned neck at its breath-
   less stretch,
Some one who ever is passing by —)

The Duke had sighed like the simplest
   wretch
In Florence, "Youth — my dream
   escapes!
Will its record stay!" And he bade
   them fetch

Some subtle moulder of brazen
   shapes —
"Can the soul, the will, die out of a
   man
Ere his body finds the grave that
   gapes?

"John of Douay shall effect my plan,
Set me on horseback here aloft,
Alive, as the crafty sculptor can,

"In the very square I have crossed so
   oft:
That men may admire, when future
   suns
Shall touch the eyes to a purpose soft,

"While the mouth and the brow stay
   brave in bronze —
Admire and say, ' When he was alive
How he would take his pleasure
   once!'

"And it shall go hard but I contrive
To listen the while, and laugh in my
   tomb
At idleness which aspires to strive."

So! While these wait the trump of
   doom,
How do their spirits pass, I wonder,
Nights and days in the narrow room?

Still, I suppose, they sit and ponder
What a gift life was, ages ago,
Six steps out of the chapel yonder.

Only they see not God, I know,
Nor all that chivalry of his,
The soldier-saints who, row on row,

Burn upward each to his point of
   bliss —
Since, the end of life being mani-
   fest,
He had burned his way through the
   world to this.

I hear you reproach, " But delay was
   best,
For their end was a crime." — Oh!
   a crime will do
As well, I reply, to serve for a test,

As a virtue golden through and
   through,
Sufficient to vindicate itself
And prove its worth at a moment's
   view!

Must a game be played for the sake of
   pelf?
Where a button goes, 'twere an epi-
   gram
To offer the stamp of the very Guelph.

The true has no value beyond the
   sham:
As well the counter as coin, I sub-
   mit,
When your table's a hat, and your
   prize, a dram.

Stake your counter as boldly every
   whit,
Venture as warily, use the same
   skill,
Do your best, whether winning or los-
   ing it,

If you choose to play! — is my princi-
   ple.
Let a man contend to the uttermost
For his life's set prize, be it what it
   will!

The counter, our lovers staked, was
   lost
As surely as if it were lawful coin:
And the sin I impute to each frustrate
   ghost

Is, the unlit lamp and the ungirt loin,
Though the end in sight was a vice, I
  say.
You of the virtue (we issue join)
How strive you? *De te, fabula!*

LOVE AMONG THE RUINS.

I.

WHERE the quiet-colored end of even-
  ing smiles,
    Miles and miles,
On the solitary pastures where our
  sheep
    Half-asleep
Tinkle homeward through the twi-
  light, stray or stop
    As they crop—
Was the site once of a city great and
  gay
    (So they say),
Of our country's very capital, its
  prince,
    Ages since,
Held his court in, gathered councils,
  wielding far
    Peace or war.

II.

Now,—the country does not even
  boast a tree,
    As you see,
To distinguish slopes of verdure, cer-
  tain rills
    From the hills
Intersect and give a name to (else
  they run
    Into one),
Where the dome and daring palace
  shot its spires
    Up like fires
O'er the hundred-gated circuit of a
  wall
    Bounding all,
Made of marble, men might march on
  nor be pressed,
    Twelve abreast.

III.

And such plenty and perfection, see,
  of grass
    Never was!
Such a carpet as, this summer-time,
  o'er-spreads
    And embeds

Every vestige of the city, guessed
  alone,
    Stock or stone—
Where a multitude of men breathed
  joy and woe
    Long ago;
Lust of glory pricked their hearts up,
  dread of shame
    Struck them tame;
And that glory and that shame alike,
  the gold
    Bought and sold.

IV.

Now,—the single little turret that
  remains
    On the plains,
By the caper overrooted, by the gourd
  Overscored,
While the patching houseleek's head
  of blossom winks
    Through the chinks—
Marks the basement whence a tower
  in ancient time
    Sprang sublime,
And a burning ring, all round, the
  chariots traced
    As they raced,
And the monarch and his minions
  and his dames
    Viewed the games.

V.

And I know—while thus the quiet-
  colored eve
    Smiles to leave
To their folding, all our many tink-
  ling fleece
    In such peace,
And the slopes and rills in undistin-
  guished gray
    Melt away—
That a girl with eager eyes and yellow
  hair
    Waits me there
In the turret whence the charioteers
  caught soul
    For the goal,
When the king looked, where she
  looks now, breathless, dumb
    Till I come.

VI.

But he looked upon the city, every side,
    Far and wide,
All the mountains topped with tem-
  ples, all the glades
    Colonnades,

All the causeys, bridges, aqueducts,
— and then,
All the men!
When I do come, she will speak not,
she will stand,
Either hand
On my shoulder, give her eyes the
first embrace
Of my face,
Ere we rush, ere we extinguish sight
and speech
Each on each.

VII.

In one year they sent a million fight-
ers forth
South and North,
And they built their gods a brazen
pillar high
As the sky,
Yet reserved a thousand chariots in
full force —
Gold, of course.
O heart! O blood that freezes, blood
that burns!
Earth's returns
For whole centuries of folly, noise and
sin!
Shut them in,
With their triumphs and their glories
and the rest!
Love is best.

TIME'S REVENGES.

I've a Friend, over the sea;
I like him, but he loves me.
It all grew out of the books I write;
They find such favor in his sight
That he slaughters you with savage
looks
Because you don't admire my books.
He does himself though, — and if some
vein
Were to snap to-night in this heavy
brain,
To-morrow month, if I lived to try,
Round should I just turn quietly,
Or out of the bedclothes stretch my
hand
Till I found him, come from his for-
eign land
To be my nurse in this poor place,
And make my broth and wash my
face

And light my fire and, all the while,
Bear with his old good-humored
smile
That I told him " Better have kept
away
Than come and kill me, night and
day,
With, worse than fever throbs and
shoots,
The creaking of his clumsy boots."
I am as sure that this he would do,
As that Saint Paul's is striking two.
And I think I rather . . . woe is me!
— Yes, rather should see him than
not see,
If lifting a hand would seat him there
Before me in the empty chair
To-night, when my head aches indeed,
And I can neither think nor read,
Nor make these purple fingers hold
The pen: this garret's freezing cold!

And I've a Lady — there he wakes
The laughing fiend and prince of
snakes
Within me, at her name, to pray
Fate send some creature in the way
Of my love for her, to be down-torn,
Upthrust and outward-borne,
So I might prove myself that sea
Of passion which I needs must be!
Call my thoughts false and my fancies
quaint,
And my style infirm and its figures
faint,
All the critics say, and more blame
yet,
And not one angry word you get.
But, please you, wonder I would put
My cheek beneath that lady's foot
Rather than trample under mine
The laurels of the Florentine,
And you shall see how the Devil
spends
A fire God gave for other ends!
I tell you, I stride up and down
This garret, crowned with love's best
crown,
And feasted with love's perfect feast,
To think I kill for her, at least,
Body and soul and peace and fame,
Alike youth's end and manhood's
aim,
— So is my spirit, as flesh with sin,
Filled full, eaten out and in
With the face of her, the eyes of her,
The lips, the little chin, the stir
Of shadow round her mouth; and she
— I'll tell you, — calmly would decree

That I should roast at a slow fire,
If that would compass her desire,
And make her one whom they invite
To the famous ball to-morrow night.

There may be heaven ; there must be
   hell ;
Meantime, there is our earth here —
   well !

WARING.

I.

I.

WHAT's become of Waring
Since he gave us all the slip,
Chose land-travel or seafaring,
Boots and chest or staff and scrip,
Rather than pace up and down
Any longer London town ?

II.

Who'd have guessed it from his lip
Or his brow's accustomed bearing.
On the night he thus took ship
Or started landward ? — little caring
For us, it seems, who supped together
(Friends of his too, I remember)
And walked home through the merry
   weather
The snowiest in all December.
I left his arm that night myself
For what's-his-name's, the new prose-
   poet
Who wrote the book there on the
   shelf —
How, forsooth, was I to know it
If Waring meant to glide away
Like a ghost at break of day ?
Never looked he half so gay !

III.

He was prouder than the Devil :
How he must have cursed our revel !
Ay, and many other meetings,
Indoor visits, outdoor greetings,
As up and down he paced this Lon-
   don,
With no work done, but great works
   undone,
Where scarce twenty knew his name.
Why not, then, have earlier spoken,
Written, bustled ? Who's to blame
If your silence kept unbroken ?

"True, but there were sundry jot-
   tings,
Stray-leaves, fragments, blurs and
   blottings,
Certain first steps were achieved
Already which " — (is that your mean-
   ing ?)
" Had well borne out whoe'er believed
In more to come !" But who goes
   gleaning
Hedge-side chance-blades, while full-
   sheaved
Stand cornfields by him ? Pride, o'er-
   weening
Pride alone, puts forth such claims
O'er the day's distinguished names.

IV.

Meantime, how much I loved him,
I find out now I've lost him.
I who cared not if I moved him,
Who could so carelessly accost him,
Henceforth never shall get free
Of his ghostly company,
His eyes that just a little wink
As deep I go into the merit
Of this and that distinguished spirit —
His cheeks' raised color, soon to sink,
As long I dwell on some stupendous
And tremendous (Heaven defend us!)
Monstr'-inform'-ingens-horrend-ous
Demoniaco-seraphic
Penman's latest piece of graphic.
Nay, my very wrist grows warm
With his dragging weight of arm.
E'en so, swimmingly appears,
Through one's after-supper musings,
Some lost lady of old years
With her beauteous vain endeavor
And goodness unrepaid as ever ;
The face, accustomed to refusings,
We, puppies that we were . . . Oh,
   never
Surely, nice of conscience, scrupled
Being aught like false, forsooth, to ?
Telling aught but honest truth to ?
What a sin, had we centupled
Its possessor's grace and sweetness !
No ! she heard in its completeness
Truth, for truth's a weighty matter,
And, truth at issue, we can't flatter !
Well, 'tis done with ; she's exempt
From damning us through such a
   sally ;
And so she glides, as down a valley,
Taking up with her contempt,
Past our reach ; and in, the flowers
Shut her unregarded hours.

V.

Oh, could I have him back once
  more,
This Waring, but one-half day more!
Back, with the quiet face of yore,
So hungry for acknowledgment
Like mine! I'd fool him to his bent.
Feed, should not he, to heart's con-
  tent?
I'd say, "to only have conceived,
Planned your great works, apart from
  progress,
Surpasses little works achieved!"
I'd lie so, I should be believed.
I'd make such havoc of the claims
Of the day's distinguished names
To feast him with, as feasts an ogress
Her feverish sharp-toothed gold-
  crowned child!
Or as one feasts a creature rarely
Captured here, unreconciled
To capture; and completely gives
Its pettish humors license, barely
Requiring that it lives.

VI.

Ichabod, Ichabod,
The glory is departed!
Travels Waring East away?
Who, of knowledge, by hearsay,
Reports a man upstarted
Somewhere as a god,
Hordes grown European-hearted,
Millions of the wild made tame
On a sudden at his fame?
In Vishnu-land what Avatar?
Or who in Moscow, towards the Czar,
With the demurest of footfalls
Over the Kremlin's pavement bright
With serpentine and syenite,
Steps, with five other generals
That simultaneously take snuff,
For each to have pretext enough
And kerchiefwise unfold his sash
Which, softness' self, is yet the stuff
To hold fast where a steel chain snaps,
And leave the grand white neck no
  gash?
Waring in Moscow, to those rough
Cold northern natures borne per-
  haps,
Like the lambwhite maiden dear
From the circle of mute kings
Unable to repress the tear,
Each as his sceptre down he flings,
To Dian's fame at Taurica,
Where now a captive priestess, she
  alway

Mingles her tender grave Hellenic
  speech
With theirs, tuned to the hailstone-
  beaten beach;
As pours some pigeon, from the
  myrrhy lands
Rapt by the whirlblast to fierce Scyth-
  ian strands
Where breed the swallows, her melo-
  dious cry
Amid their barbarous twitter!
In Russia? Never! Spain were
  fitter!
Ay, most likely 'tis in Spain
That we and Waring meet again
Now, while he turns down that cool
  narrow lane
Into the blackness, out of grave Ma-
  drid
All fire and shine, abrupt as when
  there's slid
Its stiff gold blazing pall
From some black coffin-lid.
Or, best of all,
I love to think
The leaving us was just a feint;
Back here to London did he slink,
And now works on without a wink
Of sleep, and we are on the brink
Of something great in fresco-paint:
Some garret's ceiling, walls and floor,
Up and down and o'er and o'er
He splashes, as none splashed before
Since great Caldara Polidore.
Or Music means this land of ours
Some favor yet, to pity won
By Purcell from his Rosy Bowers, —
"Give me my so-long promised son,
Let Waring end what I begun!"
Then down he creeps and out he steals,
Only when the night conceals
His face; in Kent 'tis cherry-time,
Or hops are picking: or at prime
Of March he wanders as, too happy,
Years ago when he was young,
Some mild eve when woods grew
  sappy,
And the early moths had sprung
To life from many a trembling sheath
Woven the warm boughs beneath;
While small birds said to themselves
What should soon be actual song,
And young gnats, by tens and twelves
Made as if they were the throng
That crowd around and carry aloft
The sound they have nursed, so sweet
  and pure,
Out of a myriad noises soft,
Into a tone that can endure

Amid the noise of a July noon
When all God's creatures crave their
    boon,
All at once, and all in tune,
And get it, happy as Waring then,
Having first within his ken
What a man might do with men :
And far too glad, in the even-glow,
To mix with the world he meant to
    take
Into his hand, he told you, so —
And out of it his world to make,
To contract and to expand
As he shut or oped his hand.
O Waring ! what's to really be?
A clear stage and a crowd to see !
Some Garrick, say, out shall not he
The heart of Hamlet's mystery pluck ?
Or, where most unclean beasts are
    rife,
Some Junius — am I right ? — shall
    tuck
His sleeve, and forth with flaying-
    knife !
Some Chatterton shall have the luck
Of calling Rowley into life !
Some one shall somehow run a muck
With this old world, for want of strife
Sound asleep. Contrive, contrive
To rouse us, Waring ! Who's alive ?
Our men scarce seem in earnest now.
Distinguished names ! — but 'tis, some-
    how,
As if they played at being names
Still more distinguished, like the
    games
Of children. Turn our sport to ear-
    nest
With a visage of the sternest !
Bring the real times back, confessed
Still better than our very best !

II.

I.

" When I last saw Waring " . . .
(How all turned to him who spoke !
You saw Waring ? Truth or joke ?
In land-travel or sea-faring ?)

II.

" We were sailing by Triest
Where a day or two we harbored ;
A sunset was in the West,
When, looking over the vessel's side,
One of our company espied
A sudden speck to larboard.

And as a sea-duck flies and swims
At once, so came the light craft up,
With its sole lateen sail that trims
And turns (the water round its rims
Dancing, as round a sinking cup)
And by us like a fish it curled,
And drew itself up close beside,
Its great sail on the instant furled,
And o'er its thwarts a shrill voice
    cried
(A neck as bronzed as a Lascar's)
' Buy wine of us, you English Brig ?
Or fruit, tobacco and cigars ?
A pilot for you to Triest ?
Without one, look you ne'er so big,
They'll never let you up the bay !
We natives should know best.'
I turned, and ' just those fellows'
    way,'
Our captain said, ' The 'long-shore
    thieves
Are laughing at us in their sleeves.'

III.

" In truth, the boy leaned laughing
    back ;
And one half-hidden by his side
Under the furled sail, soon I spied,
With great grass hat and kerchief
    black,
Who looked up with his kingly
    throat,
Said somewhat, while the other
    shook
His hair back from his eyes to look
Their longest at us ; then the boat,
I know not how, turned sharply
    round,
Laying her whole side on the sea
As a leaping fish does ; from the lee
Into the weather, cut somehow
Her sparkling path beneath our bow,
And so went off, as with a bound,
Into the rosy and golden half
O' the sky, to overtake the sun
And reach the shore, like the sea-
    calf
Its singing cave ; yet I caught one
Glance ere away the boat quite
    passed,
And neither time nor toil could mar
Those features : so I saw the last
Of Waring ! " — You ? Oh, never
    star
Was lost here but it rose afar !
Look East, where whole new thou-
    sands are !
In Vishnu-land what Avatar ?

HOME THOUGHTS, FROM ABROAD.

I.

On, to be in England now that April's
there,
And whoever wakes in England sees,
some morning, unaware,
That the lowest boughs and the brush-
wood sheaf
Round the elm-tree bole are in tiny
leaf,
While the chaffinch sings on the
orchard bough
In England — now!
And after April, when May follows
And the white-throat builds, and all
the swallows!
Hark, where my blossomed pear-tree
in the hedge
Leans to the field and scatters on the
clover
Blossoms and dewdrops — at the bent
spray's edge —
That's the wise thrush : he sings each
song twice over
Lest you should think he never could
recapture
The first fine careless rapture!
And though the fields look rough with
hoary dew,
And will be gay when noontide wakes
anew
The buttercups, the little children's
dower
— Far brighter than this gaudy melon-
flower!

THE ITALIAN IN ENGLAND.

That second time they hunted me
From hill to plain, from shore to sea,
And Austria, bounding far and wide
Her blood-hounds through the coun-
tryside
Breathed hot and instant on my
trace, —
I made six days a hiding-place
Of that dry green old aqueduct
Where I and Charles, when boys, have
plucked
The fire-flies from the roof above,
Bright creeping through the moss they
love :

— How long it seems since Charles
was lost!
Six days the soldiers crossed and
crossed
The country in my very sight ;
And when that peril ceased at night,
The sky broke out in red dismay
With signal fires ; well, there I lay
Close covered o'er in my recess,
Up to the neck in ferns and cress,
Thinking on Metternich our friend,
And Charles's miserable end,
And much beside, two days ; the
third,
Hunger o'ercame me when I heard
The peasants from the village go
To work among the maize ; you know,
With us in Lombardy, they bring
Provisions packed on mules, a string,
With little bells that cheer their task,
And casks, and boughs on every cask
To keep the sun's heat from the
wine ;
These I let pass in jingling line,
And, close on them, dear noisy crew,
The peasants from the village, too ;
For at the very rear would troop
Their wives and sisters in a group
To help, I knew ; when these had
passed,
I threw my glove to strike the last,
Taking the chance : she did not start,
Much less cry out, but stooped apart,
One instant rapidly glanced round,
And saw me beckon from the ground :
A wild bush grows and hides my
crypt ;
She picked my glove up while she
stripped
A branch off, then rejoined the rest
With that : my glove lay in her breast:
Then I drew breath ; they disap-
peared :
It was for Italy I feared.

An hour, and she returned alone
Exactly where my glove was thrown.
Meanwhile came many thoughts ; on
me
Rested the hopes of Italy ;
I had devised a certain tale
Which, when 'twas told her, could
not fail
Persuade a peasant of its truth ;
I meant to call a freak of youth
This hiding, and give hopes of pay,
And no temptation to betray.
But when I saw that woman's face,
Its calm simplicity of grace.

Our Italy's own attitude
In which she walked thus far, and
   stood,
Planting each naked foot so firm,
To crush the snake and spare the
   worm —
At first sight of her eyes, I said,
" I am that man upon whose head
They fix the price, because I hate
The Austrians over us : the State
Will give you gold — oh, gold so
   much ! —
If you betray me to their clutch,
And be your death, for aught I know,
If once they find you saved their foe.
Now, you must bring me food and
   drink,
And also paper, pen and ink,
And carry safe what I shall write
To Padua, which you'll reach at night
Before the duomo shuts ; go in,
And wait till Tenebræ begin ;
Walk to the third confessional,
Between the pillar and the wall,
And kneeling whisper, *Whence comes*
   peace ?
Say it a second time, then cease ;
And if the voice inside returns,
From Christ and Freedom ; what con-
   cerns
The cause of Peace ? — for answer, slip
My letter where you placed your lip ;
Then come back happy ; we have done
Our mother service — I, the son,
As you the daughter of our land ! "

   Three mornings more, she took her
    stand
In the same place, with the same
   eyes :
I was no surer of sunrise
Than of her coming : we conferred
Of her own prospects, and I heard
She had a lover — stout and tall,
She said — then let her eyelids fall,
" He could do much " — as if some
   doubt
Entered her heart, — then, passing
   out,
" She could not speak for others, who
Had other thoughts ; herself she
   knew : "
And so she brought me drink and
   food.
After four days, the scouts pursued
Another path ; at last arrived
The help my Paduan friends contrived
To furnish me : she brought the news.
For the first time I could not choose

But kiss her hand, and lay my own
Upon her head — " This faith was
   shown
To Italy, our mother ; she
Uses my hand and blesses thee."
She followed down to the sea-shore ;
I left and never saw her more.

   How very long since I have thought
Concerning — much less wished for —
   aught
Beside the good of Italy,
For which I live and mean to die !
I never was in love ; and since
Charles proved false, what shall now
   convince
My inmost heart I have a friend ?
However, if I pleased to spend
Real wishes on myself — say, three —
I know at least what one should be,
I would grasp Metternich until
I felt his red wet throat distil
In blood through these two hands.
   And next,
— Nor much for that am I perplexed —
Charles, perjured traitor, for his part,
Should die slow of a broken heart
Under his new employers. Last
— Ah ! there, what should I wish ?
   For fast
Do I grow old and out of strength.
If I resolved to seek at length
My father's house again, how scared
They all would look, and unprepared!
My brothers live in Austria's pay
— Disowned me long ago, men say ;
And all my early mates who used
To praise me so — perhaps induced
More than one early step of mine —
Are turning wise : while some opine
" Freedom grows license," some sus-
   pect
" Haste breeds delay," and recollect
They always said, such premature
Beginnings never could endure !
So, with a sullen " All's for best,"
The land seems settling to its rest.
I think then, I should wish to stand
This evening in that dear, lost land,
Over the sea the thousand miles,
And know if yet that woman smiles
With the calm smile ; some little
   farm
She lives in there, no doubt : what
   harm
If I sat on the door-side bench,
And while her spindle made a trench
Fantastically in the dust,
Inquired of all her fortunes — just

Her children's ages and their names,
And what may be the husband's aims
For each of them. I'd talk this out,
And sit there, for an hour about,

Then kiss her hand once more, and lay
Mine on her head, and go my way.

So much for idle wishing — how
It steals the time ! To business now.

THE ENGLISHMAN IN ITALY.

PIANO DI SORRENTO.

Fortù, Fortù, my beloved one, sit here by my side,
On my knees put up both little feet ! I was sure, if I tried,
I could make you laugh spite of Scirocco. Now, open your eyes,
Let me keep you amused, till he vanish in black from the skies,
With telling my memories over, as you tell your beads ;
All the Plain saw me gather, I garland — the flowers or the weeds.

Time for rain ! for your long hot dry autumn had networked with brown
The white skin of each grape on the bunches, marked like a quail's crown,
Those creatures you make such account of, whose heads, — specked with white
Over brown like a great spider's back, as I told you last night, —
Your mother bites off for her supper. Red-ripe as could be,
Pomegranates were chapping and splitting in halves on the tree.
And betwixt the loose walls of great flintstone, or in the thick dust
On the path, or straight out of the rock-side, wherever could thrust
Some burnt sprig of bold hardy rock-flower its yellow face up,
For the prize were great butterflies fighting, some five for one cup.
So, I guessed, ere I got up this morning, what change was in store,
By the quick rustle-down of the quail-nets which woke me before
I could open my shutter, made fast with a bough and a stone,
And look through the twisted dead vine-twigs, sole lattice that's known.
Quick and sharp rang the rings down the net-poles, while, busy beneath,
Your priest and his brother tugged at them, the rain in their teeth.
And out upon all the flat house-roofs, where split figs lay drying,
The girls took the frails under cover : nor use seemed in trying
To get out the boats and go fishing, for, under the cliff,
Fierce the black water frothed o'er the blind rock. No seeing our skiff
Arrive about noon from Amalfi ! — our fisher arrive,
And pitch down his basket before us, all trembling alive,
With pink and gray jellies, your sea-fruit ; you touch the strange lumps,
And mouths gape there, eyes open, all manner of horns and of humps,
Which only the fisher looks grave at, while round him like imps,
Cling screaming the children as naked and brown as his shrimps ;
Himself too as bare to the middle — you see round his neck
The string and its brass coin suspended, that saves him from wreck.
But to-day not a boat reached Salerno : so back, to a man,
Came our friends, with whose help in the vineyards grape-harvest began.
In the vat, half-way up in our house-side, like blood the juice spins,
While your brother all bare-legged is dancing till breathless he grins
Dead-beaten in effort on effort to keep the grapes under,
Since still, when he seems all but master, in pours the fresh plunder
From girls who keep coming and going with basket on shoulder,
And eyes shut against the rain's driving ; your girls that are older, —

For under the hedges of aloe, and where, on its bed
Of the orchard's black mould, the love-apple lies pulpy and red,
All the young ones are kneeling and filling their laps with the snails
Tempted out by this first rainy weather,—your best of regales,
As to-night will be proved to my sorrow, when, supping in state,
We shall feast our grape-gleaners (two dozen, three over one plate)
With lasagne so tempting to swallow in slippery ropes,
And gourds fried in great purple slices, that color of popes.
Meantime, see the grape-bunch they've brought you; the rain-water slips
O'er the heavy blue bloom on each globe which the wasp to your lips
Still follows with fretful persistence. Nay, taste, while awake,
This half of a curd-white smooth cheese-ball that peels, flake by flake,
Like an onion, each smoother and whiter: next, sip this weak wine
From the thin green glass flask, with its stopper, a leaf of the vine;
And end with the prickly pear's red flesh that leaves through its juice
The stony black seeds on your pearl-teeth.

                                Scirocco is loose!
Hark, the quick, whistling pelt of the olives which, thick in one's track,
Tempt the stranger to pick up and bite them, though not yet half black!
How the old twisted olive-trunks shudder, the medlars let fall
Their hard fruit, and the brittle great fig-trees snap off, figs and all.
For here comes the whole of the tempest! no refuge, but creep
Back again to my side and my shoulder, and listen or sleep.

    Oh! how will your country show next week, when all the vine-boughs
Have been stripped of their foliage to pasture the mules and the cows?
Last eve, I rode over the mountains; your brother, my guide,
Soon left me, to feast on the myrtles that offered, each side,
Their fruit-balls, black, glossy, and luscious,—or strip from the sorbs
A treasure, or, rosy and wondrous, those hairy gold orbs!
But my mule picked his sure sober path out, just stopping to neigh
When he recognized down in the valley his mates on their way
With the fagots and barrels of water. And soon we emerged
From the plain where the woods could scarce follow; and still, as we urged
Our way, the woods wondered, and left us. Up, up still we trudged,
Though the wild path grew wilder each instant, and place was e'en grudged
'Mid the rock-chasms and piles of loose stones like the loose broken teeth
Of some monster which climbed there to die, from the ocean beneath—
Place was grudged to the silver-gray fume-weed that clung to the path,
And dark rosemary ever a-dying, that, 'spite the wind's wrath,
So loves the salt rock's face to seaward. and lentisks as stanch
To the stone where they root and bear berries; and . . . what shows a branch
Coral-colored, transparent, with circlets of pale seagreen leaves;
Over all trod my mule with the caution of gleaners o'er sheaves.
Still, foot after foot like a lady, still, round after round,
He climbed to the top of Calvano; and God's own profound
Was above me, and round me the mountains, and under, the sea,
And within me my heart to bear witness what was and shall be.
Oh, heaven and the terrible crystal! no rampart excludes
Your eye from the life to be lived in the blue solitudes.
Oh, those mountains, their infinite movement! still moving with you;
For, ever some new head and breast of them thrusts into view
To observe the intruder; you see it, if quickly you turn
And, before they escape you, surprise them. They grudge you should learn
How the soft plains they look on, lean over and love (they pretend)
—Cower beneath them, the black sea-pine crouches, the wild fruit-trees bend,
E'en the myrtle-leaves curl, shrink and shut: all is silent and grave:
'Tis a sensual and timorous beauty,—how fair! but a slave.

So, I turned to the sea ; and there slumbered, as greenly as ever
Those isles of the siren, your Galli. No ages can sever
The Three, nor enable their sister to join them, — half-way
On the voyage, she looked at Ulysses — no farther to-day !
Though the small one, just launched in the wave, watches breast-high and
        steady
From under the rock her bold sister, swum half-way already.
Forth, shall we sail there together, and see, from the sides,
Quite new rocks show their faces, new haunts where the siren abides ?
Shall we sail round and round them, close over the rocks, though unseen,
That ruffle the gray glassy water to glorious green ?
Then scramble from splinter to splinter, reach land, and explore,
On the largest, the strange square black turret with never a door,
Just a loop to admit the quick lizards ?   Then, stand there and hear
The birds' quiet singing, that tells us what life is, so clear ?
— The secret they sang to Ulysses when, ages ago,
He heard and he knew this life's secret, I hear and I know.

    Ah, see ! The sun breaks o'er Calvano. He strikes the great gloom
And flutters it o'er the mount's summit in airy gold fume.
All is over. Look out, see, the gypsy, our tinker and smith,
Has arrived, set up bellows and forge, and down-squatted forthwith
To his hammering under the wall there ! One eye keeps aloof
The urchins that itch to be putting his Jew's-harp to proof,
While the other, through locks of curled wire, is watching how sleek
Shines the hog, come to share in the windfall. Chew, abbot's own cheek !
All is over. Wake up and come out now, and down let us go,
And see the fine things got in order at church for the show
Of the Sacrament, set forth this evening. To-morrow's the Feast
Of the Rosary's Virgin, by no means of Virgins the least :
As you'll hear in the off-hand discourse which (all nature, no art)
The Dominican brother, these three weeks, was getting by heart.
Not a pillar nor post but is dizened with red and blue papers ;
All the roof waves with ribbons, each altar ablaze with long tapers.
But the great masterpiece is the scaffold rigged glorious to hold
All the fiddlers and fifers and drummers and trumpeters bold
Not afraid of Bellini nor Auber : who, when the priest's hoarse,
Will strike us up something that's brisk for the feast's second course.
And then will the flaxen-wigged Image be carried in pomp
Through the plain, while, in gallant procession, the priests mean to stomp.
All round the glad church lie old bottles with gunpowder stopped,
Which will be, when the Image re-enters, religiously popped.
And at night from the crest of Calvano great bonfires will hang :
On the plain will the trumpets join chorus, and more poppers bang.
At all events, come — to the garden, as far as the wall ;
See me tap with a hoe on the plaster, till out there shall fall
A scorpion with wide angry nippers !

                            — " Such trifles ! " you say ?
Forth, in my England at home, men meet gravely to-day
And debate, if abolishing corn-laws be righteous and wise !
— If t'were proper, Scirocco should vanish in black from the skies !

UP AT A VILLA — DOWN IN THE CITY.

(AS DISTINGUISHED BY AN ITALIAN PERSON OF QUALITY.)

I.

Had I but plenty of money, money enough and to spare,
The house for me, no doubt, were a house in the city-square ;
Ah, such a life, such a life, as one leads at the window there !

II.

Something to see, by Bacchus, something to hear, at least !
There, the whole day long, one's life is a perfect feast ;
While up at a villa one lives, I maintain it, no more than a beast.

III.

Well now, look at our villa ! stuck like the horn of a bull
Just on a mountain edge as bare as the creature's skull,
Save a mere shag of a bush with hardly a leaf to pull !
— I scratch my own, sometimes, to see if the hair's turned wool.

IV.

But the city, oh the city — the square with the houses ! Why ?
They are stone-faced, white as a curd, there's something to take the eye !
Houses in four straight lines, not a single front awry ;
You watch who crosses and gossips, who saunters, who hurries by ;
Green blinds, as a matter of course, to draw when the sun gets high ;
And the shops with fanciful signs which are painted properly.

V.

What of a villa ? Though winter be over in March by rights,
'Tis May perhaps ere the snow shall have withered well off the heights :
You've the brown ploughed land before, where the oxen steam and wheeze,
And the hills over-smoked behind by the faint gray olive-trees.

VI.

Is it better in May, I ask you ? You've summer all at once ;
In a day he leaps complete with a few strong April suns.
'Mid the sharp short emerald wheat, scarce risen three fingers well,
The wild tulip, at end of its tube, blows out its great red bell
Like a thin clear bubble of blood, for the children to pick and sell.

VII.

Is it ever hot in the square ? There's a fountain to spout and splash !
In the shade it sings and springs ; in the shine such foam-bows flash
On the horses with curling fish-tails, that prance and paddle and pash
Round the lady atop in her conch — fifty gazers do not abash,
Though all that she wears is some weeds round her waist in a sort of sash.

VIII.

All the year long at the villa, nothing to see though you linger,
Except yon cypress that points like death's lean lifted forefinger.
Some think fireflies pretty, when they mix i' the corn and mingle,
Or thrid the stinking hemp till the stalks of it seem a-tingle.
Late August or early September, the stunning cicala is shrill,
And the bees keep their tiresome whine round the resinous firs on the hill.
Enough of the seasons, — I spare you the months of the fever and chill.

IX.

Ere you open your eyes in the city, the blessed church-bells begin :
No sooner the bells leave off than the diligence rattles in :
You get the pick of the news, and it costs you never a pin.
By and by there's the travelling doctor gives pills, lets blood, draws teeth
Or the Pulcinello-trumpet breaks up the market beneath.
At the post-office such a scene-picture — the new play, piping hot !
And a notice how, only this morning, three liberal thieves were shot.
Above it, behold the Archbishop's most fatherly of rebukes,
And beneath, with his crown and his lion, some little new law of the Duke's !
Or a sonnet with flowery marge, to the Reverend Don So-and-so
Who is Dante, Boccaccio, Petrarca, St. Jerome, and Cicero,
"And moreover" (the sonnet goes rhyming), "the skirts of Saint Paul has reached,
Having preached us those six Lent-lectures more unctuous than ever he preached."
Noon strikes, — here sweeps the procession ! our Lady borne smiling and smart,
With a pink gauze gown all spangles, and seven swords stuck in her heart !
Bang-whang-whang goes the drum, *tootle-te-tootle* the fife ;
No keeping one's haunches still : it's the greatest pleasure in life.

X.

But bless you, it's dear — it's dear ! fowls, wine, at double the rate.
They have clapped a new tax upon salt, and what oil pays passing the gate
It's a horror to think of. And so, the villa for me, not the city !
Beggars can scarcely be choosers : but still — ah, the pity, the pity !
Look, two and two go the priests, then the monks with cowls and sandals,
And the penitents dressed in white shirts, a-holding the yellow candles ;
One, he carries a flag up straight, and another a cross with handles,
And the Duke's guard brings up the rear, for the better prevention of scandals :
Bang-whang-whang goes the drum, *tootle-te-tootle* the fife.
Oh, a day in the city-square, there is no such pleasure in life !

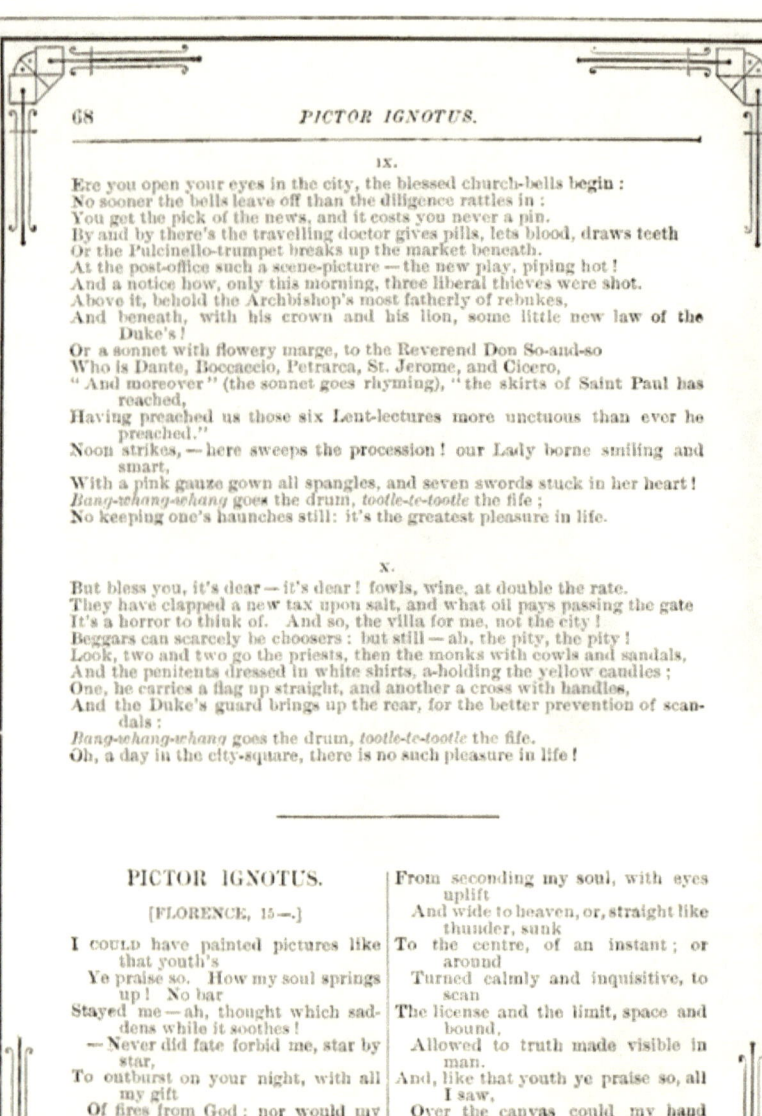

PICTOR IGNOTUS.

[FLORENCE, 15—.]

I could have painted pictures like that youth's
Ye praise so. How my soul springs up ! No bar
Stayed me — ah, thought which saddens while it soothes !
— Never did fate forbid me, star by star,
To outburst on your night, with all my gift
Of fires from God : nor would my flesh have shrunk

From seconding my soul, with eyes uplift
And wide to heaven, or, straight like thunder, sunk
To the centre, of an instant ; or around
Turned calmly and inquisitive, to scan
The license and the limit, space and bound,
Allowed to truth made visible in man.
And, like that youth ye praise so, all I saw,
Over the canvas could my hand have flung,

Each face obedient to its passion's
  law,
  Each passion clear proclaimed with-
    out a tongue :
Whether Hope rose at once in all the
  blood,
  A-tiptoe for the blessing of em-
    brace,
Or Rapture drooped the eyes, as when
  her brood
  Pull down the nesting dove's heart
    to its place ;
Or Confidence lit swift the forehead
  up,
  And locked the mouth fast, like a
    castle braved, —
O human faces ! hath it spilt, my cup ?
  What did ye give me that I have
    not saved ?
Nor will I say I have not dreamed
  (how well !)
  Of going — I, in each new picture,
    — forth,
As, making new hearts beat and
  bosoms swell,
  To Pope or Kaiser, East, West,
    South, or North,
Bound for the calmly satisfied great
  State,
  Or glad aspiring little burgh, it
    went,
Flowers cast upon the car which bore
  the freight,
  Through old streets named afresh
    from the event,
Till it reached home, where learned
  age should greet
  My face, and youth, the star not yet
    distinct
Above his hair, lie learning at my
  feet ! —
  Oh ! thus to live, I and my picture,
    linked
With love about, and praise, till life
  should end,
  And then not go to heaven, but
    linger here,
Here on my earth, earth's every man
  my friend,
  The thought grew frightful, 'twas so
    wildly dear !
But a voice changed it. Glimpses of
  such sights
  Have scared me, like the revels
    through a door
Of some strange house of idols at its
  rites !

This world seemed not the world it
  was, before :
Mixed with my loving trusting ones,
  there trooped
  . . . Who summoned those cold
    faces that begun
To press on me and judge me ?
  Though I stooped
Shrinking, as from the soldiery a
  nun,
They drew me forth, and spite of me
  . . . enough !
These buy and sell our pictures,
  take and give,
Count them for garniture and house-
  hold-stuff,
  And where they live needs must
    our pictures live
And see their faces, listen to their
  prate,
  Partakers of their daily pettiness,
Discussed of, — " This I love, or this I
  hate,
This likes me more, and this affects
  me less ! "
Wherefore I chose my portion. If at
  whiles
My heart sinks, as monotonous I
  paint
These endless cloisters and eternal
  aisles
  With the same series, Virgin, Babe,
    and Saint,
With the same cold calm beautiful
  regard, —
  At least no merchant traffics in my
    heart ;
The sanctuary's gloom at least shall
  ward
  Vain tongues from where my pic-
    tures stand apart :
Only prayer breaks the silence of the
  shrine
  While, blackening in the daily
    candle-smoke,
They moulder on the damp wall's
  travertine,
  'Mid echoes the light footstep never
    woke.
So, die my pictures ! surely, gently
  die !
  O youth ! men praise so, — holds
    their praise its worth ?
Blown harshly, keeps the trump its
  golden cry ?
  Tastes sweet the water with such
    specks of earth ?

FRA LIPPO LIPPI.

I AM poor brother Lippo, by your
    leave
You need not clap your torches to my
    face.
Zooks! what's to blame? you think
    you see a monk!
What, 'tis past midnight, and you go
    the rounds,
And here you catch me at an alley's
    end
Where sportive ladies leave their
    doors ajar?
The Carmine's my cloister: hunt it
    up,
Do, — harry out, if you must show
    your zeal,
Whatever rat, there, haps on his
    wrong hole,
And nip each softling of a wee white
    mouse,
Weke, weke, that's crept to keep him
    company!
Aha! you know your betters? Then,
    you'll take
Your hand away that's fiddling on
    my throat,
And please to know me likewise.
    Who am I?
Why, one, sir, who is lodging with a
    friend
Three streets off — he's a certain . . .
    how d'ye call?
Master — a . . . Cosimo of the Medici,
I' the house that caps the corner.
    Boh! you were best!
Remember and tell me the day you're
    hanged.
How you affected such a gullet's-
    gripe!
But you, sir, it concerns you that your
    knaves
Pick up a manner, nor discredit you:
Zooks! are we pilchards, that they
    sweep the streets
And count fair prize what comes into
    their net?
He's Judas to a tittle, that man is!
Just such a face! Why, sir, you make
    amends.
Lord, I'm not angry! Bid your hang-
    dogs go
Drink out this quarter-florin to the
    health
Of the munificent House that harbors
    me
(And many more beside, lads! more
    beside!)

And all's come square again. I'd like
    his face —
His, elbowing on his comrade in the
    door
With the pike and lantern, — for the
    slave that holds
John Baptist's head a-dangle by the
    hair
With one hand ("Look you, now," as
    who should say)
And his weapon in the other, yet un-
    wiped!
It's not your chance to have a bit of
    chalk,
A wood-coal or the like? or you
    should see!
Yes, I'm the painter, since you style
    me so.
What, brother Lippo's doings, up and
    down,
You know them, and they take you?
    like enough!
I saw the proper twinkle in your
    eye —
'Tell you, I liked your looks at very
    first.
Let's sit and set things straight now,
    hip to haunch.
Here's spring come, and the nights
    one makes up bands
To roam the town and sing out car-
    nival,
And I've been three weeks shut with-
    in my mew,
A-painting for the great man, saints
    and saints
And saints again. I could not paint
    all night —
Ouf! I leaned out of window for fresh
    air.
There came a hurry of feet and little
    feet,
A sweep of lute-strings, laughs, and
    whifs of song, —
Flower o' the broom,
Take away love, and our earth is a tomb!
Flower o' the quince,
I let Lisa go, and what good in life
    since?
Flower o' the thyme — and so on.
    Round they went.
Scarce had they turned the corner
    when a titter
Like the skipping of rabbits by moon-
    light, — three slim shapes,
And a face that looked up . . . zooks,
    sir, flesh and blood
That's all I'm made of! Into shreds
    it went,

Curtain and counterpane and cover-
    let,
All the bed-furniture — a dozen knots,
There was a ladder! Down I let my-
    self,
Hands and feet, scrambling somehow,
    and so dropped,
And after them. I came up with the
    fun
Hard by Saint Lawrence, hail fellow,
    well met, —
Flower o' the rose,
If I've been merry, what matter who
    knows?
And so, as I was stealing back again,
To get to bed and have a bit of sleep
Ere I rise up to-morrow and go work
On Jerome knocking at his poor old
    breast
With his great round stone to subdue
    the flesh,
You snap me of the sudden. Ah, I
    see!
Though your eye twinkles still, you
    shake your head —
Mine's shaved — a monk, you say —
    the sting's in that!
If Master Cosimo announced himself,
Mum's the word naturally; but a
    monk!
Come, what am I a beast for? tell us,
    now!
I was a baby when my mother died
And father died and left me in the
    street.
I starved there, God knows how, a
    year or two
On fig-skins, melon-parings, rinds and
    shucks,
Refuse and rubbish. One fine frosty
    day,
My stomach being empty as your
    hat,
The wind doubled me up and down I
    went.
Old aunt Lapaccia trussed me with
    one hand
(Its fellow was a stinger, as I knew),
And so along the wall, over the
    bridge,
By the straight cut to the convent.
    Six words there,
While I stood munching my first
    bread that month:
"So, boy, you're minded," quoth the
    good fat father
Wiping his own mouth, 'twas refec-
    tion-time, —
"To quit this very miserable world?

Will you renounce" . . . "the month-
    ful of bread?" thought I;
By no means! Brief, they made a
    monk of me;
I did renounce the world, its pride
    and greed,
Palace, farm, villa, shop, and banking-
    house,
Trash, such as these poor devils of
    Medici
Have given their hearts to — all at
    eight years old.
Well, sir, I found in time, you may
    be sure,
'Twas not for nothing — the good
    bellyful,
The warm serge and the rope that
    goes all round,
And day-long blessed idleness beside!
"Let's see what the urchin's fit for"
    — that came next.
Not overmuch their way, I must con-
    fess.
Such a to-do! They tried me with
    their books:
Lord, they'd have taught me Latin in
    pure waste!
Flower o' the clove,
All the Latin I construe is, "Amo" I
    love!
But, mind you, when a boy starves
    in the streets
Eight years together as my fortune
    was,
Watching folk's faces to know who
    will fling
The bit of half-stripped grape-bunch
    he desires,
And who will curse or kick him for
    his pains, —
Which gentleman processional and
    fine,
Holding a candle to the Sacrament,
Will wink and let him lift a plate and
    catch
The droppings of the wax to sell
    again,
Or holla for the Eight and have him
    whipped, —
How say I? — nay, which dog bites,
    which lets drop
His bone from the heap of offal in the
    street, —
Why, soul and sense of him grow
    sharp alike,
He learns the look of things, and none
    the less
For admonition from the hunger-
    pinch.

I had a store of such remarks, be
    sure,
Which, after I found leisure, turned
    to use:
I drew men's faces on my copy-books,
Scrawled them within the antipho-
    nary's marge,
Joined legs and arms to the long
    music-notes,
Found eyes and nose and chin for A's
    and B's,
And made a string of pictures of the
    world
Betwixt the ins and outs of verb and
    noun,
On the wall, the bench, the door.
The monks looked black.
"Nay," quoth the Prior, "turn him
    out, d'ye say?
In no wise. Lose a crow and catch
    a lark.
What if at last we get our man of
    parts,
We Carmelites, like those Camaldo-
    lese
And Preaching Friars, to do our
    church up fine
And put the front on it that ought to
    be!"
And hereupon he bade me daub away.
Thank you! my head being crammed,
    the walls a blank,
Never was such prompt disemburden-
    ing.
First every sort of monk, the black
    and white,
I drew them, fat and lean: then, folks
    at church,
From good old gossips waiting to con-
    fess
Their cribs of barrel-droppings, can-
    dle-ends, —
To the breathless fellow at the altar-
    foot,
Fresh from his murder, safe and sit-
    ting there
With the little children round him in
    a row
Of admiration, half for his beard, and
    half
For that white anger of his victim's
    son
Shaking a fist at him with one fierce
    arm,
Signing himself with the other be-
    cause of Christ
(Whose sad face on the cross sees only
    this
After the passion of a thousand years),

Till some poor girl, her apron o'er her
    head
(Which the intense eyes looked
    through), came at eve
On tiptoe, said a word, dropped in a
    loaf,
Her pair of earrings and a bunch of
    flowers
(The brute took growling), prayed, and
    so was gone.
I painted all, then cried, " 'Tis ask
    and have;
Choose, for more's ready!" — laid the
    ladder flat,
And showed my covered bit of clois-
    ter-wall.
The monks closed in a circle and
    praised loud
Till checked, taught what to see and
    not to see,
Being simple bodies, — "That's the
    very man!
Look at the boy who stoops to pat the
    dog!
That woman's like the Prior's niece
    who comes
To care about his asthma: it's the
    life!"
But there my triumph's straw-fire
    flared and funked;
Their betters took their turn to see
    and say:
The Prior and the learned pulled a face
And stopped all that in no time.
    "How? what's here?
Quite from the mark of painting, bless
    us all!
Faces, arms, legs, and bodies like the
    true
As much as pea and pea! it's devil's
    game!
Your business is not to catch men with
    show,
With homage to the perishable clay,
But lift them over it, ignore it all,
Make them forget there's such a thing
    as flesh.
Your business is to paint the souls of
    men —
Man's soul, and it's a fire, smoke . . .
    no, it's not . . .
It's vapor done up like a new-born
    babe —
(In that shape when you die it leaves
    your mouth),
It's . . . well, what matters talking,
    it's the soul!
Give us no more of body than shows
    soul!

"How? what's here?
Quite from the mark of painting, bless us all!" — Page 72.

Here's Giotto, with his Saint a-prais-
  ing God.
That sets us praising, — why not stop
  with him?
Why put all thoughts of praise out of
  our head
With wonder at lines, colors, and
  what not?
Paint the soul, never mind the legs
  and arms!
Rub all out, try at it a second time!
Oh! that white smallish female with
  the breasts,
She's just my niece . . . Herodias, I
  would say, —
Who went and danced, and got men's
  heads cut off!
Have it all out!" Now, is this sense,
  I ask?
A fine way to paint soul, by painting
  body
So ill, the eye can't stop there, must
  go farther
And can't fare worse! Thus, yellow
  does for white
When what you put for yellow's
  simply black,
And any sort of meaning looks in-
  tense
When all beside itself means and
  looks naught.
Why can't a painter lift each foot in
  turn,
Left foot and right foot, go a double
  step,
Make his flesh liker and his soul more
  like,
Both in their order? Take the pret-
  tiest face,
The Prior's niece . . . patron saint —
  is it so pretty
You can't discover if it means hope,
  fear,
Sorrow or joy? won't beauty go with
  these?
Suppose I've made her eyes all right
  and blue,
Can't I take breath and try to add
  life's flash,
And then add soul and heighten them
  threefold?
Or say there's beauty with no soul
  at all —
(I never saw it — put the case the
  same —)
If you get simple beauty and naught
  else,
You get about the best thing God
  invents:

That's somewhat: and you'll find the
  soul you have missed,
Within yourself, when you return
  him thanks.
"Rub all out!" Well, well, there's
  my life, in short,
And so the thing has gone on ever
  since.
I'm grown a man no doubt, I've
  broken bounds:
You should not take a fellow eight
  years old
And make him swear to never kiss the
  girls.
I'm my own master, paint now as I
  please —
Having a friend, you see, in the
  Corner-house!
Lord, it's fast holding by the rings in
  front —
Those great rings serve more purposes
  than just
To plant a flag in, or tie up a horse!
And yet the old schooling sticks, the
  old grave eyes
Are peeping o'er my shoulder as I
  work,
The heads shake still — "It's art's
  decline, my son!
You're not of the true painters, great
  and old;
Brother Angelico's the man, you'll
  find;
Brother Lorenzo stands his single
  peer:
Fag on at flesh, you'll never make the
  third!"
Flower o' the pine,
You keep your mistr . . . manners, and
  I'll stick to mine!
I'm not the third, then: bless us,
  they must know!
Don't you think they're the likeliest
  to know,
They with their Latin? So, I swallow
  my rage,
Clinch my teeth, suck my lips in
  tight, and paint
To please them — sometimes do, and
  sometimes don't;
For, doing most, there's pretty sure to
  come
A turn, some warm eve finds me at
  my saints —
A laugh, a cry, the business of the
  world —
(Flower o' the peach,
Death for us all, and his own life for
  each!)

And my whole soul revolves, the cup
  runs over,
The world and life's too big to pass for
  a dream,
And I do these wild things in sheer
  despite,
And play the fooleries you catch me
  at
In pure rage! The old mill-horse,
  out at grass
After hard years, throws up his stiff
  heels so,
Although the miller does not preach
  to him
The only good of grass is to make
  chaff.
What would men have? Do they like
  grass or no —
May they or mayn't they? all I want's
  the thing
Settled forever one way. As it is,
You tell too many lies and hurt your-
  self:
You don't like what you only like too
  much,
You do like what, if given you at
  your word,
You find abundantly detestable.
For me, I think I speak as I was
  taught.
I always see the garden, and God
  there
A-making man's wife: and, my lesson
  learned,
The value and significance of flesh,
I can't unlearn ten minutes after-
  wards.
  You understand me: I'm a beast, I
  know.
But see, now — why, I see as cer-
  tainly
As that the morning-star's about to
  shine,
What will hap some day. We've a
  youngster here
Comes to our convent, studies what I
  do,
Slouches and stares and lets no atom
  drop:
His name is Guidi — he'll not mind
  the monks —
They call him Hulking Tom, he lets
  them talk —
He picks my practice up — he'll paint
  apace,
I hope so — though I never live so
  long,
I know what's sure to follow. You
  be judge!

You speak no Latin more than I,
  belike;
However, you're my man, you've
  seen the world
— The beauty and the wonder and
  the power,
The shapes of things, their colors,
  lights, and shades,
Changes, surprises, — and God made
  it all!
— For what? Do you feel thankful,
  ay or no,
For this fair town's face, yonder
  river's line,
The mountain round it and the sky
  above,
Much more the figures of man, woman,
  child,
These are the frame to? What's it
  all about?
To be passed over, despised? or dwelt
  upon,
Wondered at? oh, this last of course!
  — you say.
But why not do as well as say, —
  paint these
Just as they are, careless what comes
  of it?
God's works — paint any one, and
  count it crime
To let a truth slip. Don't object,
  "His works
Are here already; nature is complete:
Suppose you reproduce her — (which
  you can't)
There's no advantage! you must beat
  her, then."
For, don't you mark? we're made so
  that we love
First when we see them painted,
  things we have passed
Perhaps a hundred times nor cared to
  see;
And so they are better, painted —
  better to us,
Which is the same thing. Art was
  given for that;
God uses us to help each other so,
Lending our minds out. Have you
  noticed, now
Your cullion's hanging face? A bit
  of chalk,
And trust me but you should, though!
  How much more
If I drew higher things with the same
  truth!
That were to take the Prior's pulpit-
  place,
Interpret God to all of you! Oh, oh,

It makes me mad to see what men
shall do
And we in our graves! This world's
no blot for us
Nor blank; it means intensely, and
means good:
To find its meaning is my meat and
drink.
"Ay, but you don't so instigate to
prayer!"
Strikes in the Prior: "when your
meaning's plain
It does not say to folks — remember
matins,
Or, mind you fast next Friday!"
Why, for this
What need of art at all? A skull
and bones,
Two bits of stick nailed cross-wise,
or, what's best,
A bell to chime the hour with, does
as well.
I painted a Saint Lawrence six months
since
At Prato, splashed the fresco in fine
style:
"How looks my painting, now the
scaffold's down?"
I ask a brother: "Hugely," he re-
turns —
"Already not one phiz of your three
slaves
Who turn the Deacon off his toasted
side,
But's scratched and prodded to our
heart's content,
The pious people have so eased their
own
With coming to say prayers there in
a rage:
We get on fast to see the bricks be-
neath.
Expect another job this time next
year,
For pity and religion grow i' the
crowd —
Your painting serves its purpose!"
Hang the fools!

— That is — you'll not mistake an
idle word
Spoke in a huff by a poor monk, Got
wot
Tasting the air this spicy night which
turns
The unaccustomed head like Chianti
wine!
Oh, the church knows! don't misre-
port me, now

It's natural a poor monk out of bounds
Should have his apt word to excuse
himself:
And hearken how I plot to make
amends.
I have bethought me: I shall paint a
piece
. . . There's for you! Give me six
months, then go, see
Something in Sant' Ambrogio's!
Bless the nuns!
They want a cast o' my office. I shall
paint
God in the midst, Madonna and her
babe,
Ringed by a bowery, flowery angel-
brood,
Lilies and vestments and white faces,
sweet
As puff on puff of grated orris-root
When ladies crowd to church at mid-
summer.
And then i' the front, of course a saint
or two —
Saint John, because he saves the
Florentines,
Saint Ambrose, who puts down in
black and white
The convent's friends and gives them
a long day,
And Job, I must have him there past
mistake,
The man of Uz (and Us without
the z,
Painters who need his patience). Well, all these
Secured at their devotion, up shall
come
Out of a corner when you least ex-
pect,
As one by a dark stair into a great
light,
Music and talking, who but Lippo!
I! —
Mazed, motionless, and moon-struck
— I'm the man!
Back I shrink — what is this I see
and hear?
I, caught up with my monk's things
by mistake,
My old serge gown and rope that goes
all round,
I, in this presence, this pure company!
Where's a hole, where's a corner for
escape?
Then steps a sweet angelic slip of a
thing
Forward, puts out a soft palm — "No
so fast!"

— Addresses the celestial presence,
  " nay —
He made you and devised you, after
  all,
Though he's none of you! Could
  Saint John there, draw —
His camel-hair make up a painting-
  brush?
We come to brother Lippo for all that,
Iste perfecit opus!'' So, all smile —
I shuffle sideways with my blushing
  face
Under the cover of a hundred wings
Thrown like a spread of kirtles when
  you're gay
And play hot cockles, all the doors
  being shut
Till, wholly unexpected, in there pops
The hot-head husband! Thus I scut-
  tle off
To some safe bench behind, not let-
  ting go
The palm of her, the little lily thing
That spoke the good word for me in
  the nick,
Like the Prior's niece . . . Saint
  Lucy, I would say.
And so all's saved for me, and for the
  church
A pretty picture gained. Go, six
  months hence!
Your hand, sir, and good-by: no
  lights, no lights!
The street's hushed, and I know my
  own way back,
Don't fear me! There's the gray
  beginning. Zooks!

ANDREA DEL SARTO.

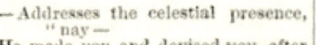

[CALLED "THE FAULTLESS PAINT-
ER.")

BUT do not let us quarrel any more,
No, my Lucrezia! bear with me for
  once:
Sit down and all shall happen as you
  wish.
You turn your face, but does it bring
  your heart?
I'll work then for your friend's friend,
  never fear,
Treat his own subject after his own
  way,

Fix his own time, accept too his own
  price,
And shut the money into this small
  hand
When next it takes mine. Will it?
  tenderly?
Oh, I'll content him, — but to-morrow,
  Love!
I often am much wearier than you
  think,
This evening more than usual: and it
  seems
As if — forgive now — should you let
  me sit
Here by the window, with your hand
  in mine,
And look a half-hour forth on Fiesole,
Both of one mind, as married people
  use,
Quietly, quietly the evening through,
I might get up to-morrow to my work
Cheerful and fresh as ever. Let us
  try.
To-morrow, how you shall be glad for
  this!
Your soft hand is a woman of itself,
And mine, the man's bared breast
  she curls inside.
Don't count the time lost, neither;
  you must serve
For each of the five pictures we re-
  quire:
It saves a model. So! keep looking
  so —
My serpentining beauty, rounds on
  rounds!
— How could you ever prick those
  perfect ears,
Even to put the pearl there! oh, so
  sweet —
My face, my moon, my everybody's
  moon,
Which everybody looks on and calls
  his,
And, I suppose, is looked on by in
  turn,
While she looks — no one's: very
  dear, no less.
You smile? why, there's my picture
  ready made,
There's what we painters call our
  harmony!
A common grayness silvers every
  thing, —
All in a twilight, you and I alike
— You, at the point of your first pride
  in me
(That's gone, you know) — but I, at
  every point;

My youth, my hope, my art, being all
  toned down
To yonder sober pleasant Fiesole.
There's the bell clinking from the
  chapel-top;
That length of convent-wall across
  the way
Holds the trees safer, huddled more
  inside;
The last monk leaves the garden;
  days decrease,
And autumn grows, autumn in every
  thing.
Eh? the whole seems to fall into a
  shape,
As if I saw alike my work and self
And all that I was born to be and
  do,
A twilight-piece. Love, we are in
  God's hand.
How strange now, looks the life he
  makes us lead;
So free we seem, so fettered fast we
  are!
I feel he laid the fetter: let it lie!
This chamber, for example — turn
  your head —
All that's behind us! You don't un-
  derstand
Nor care to understand about my art,
But you can hear at least when peo-
  ple speak:
And that cartoon, the second from the
  door
— It is the thing, Love! so such things
  should be:
Behold Madonna! — I am bold to say.
I can do with my pencil what I know,
What I see, what at bottom of my
  heart
I wish for, if I ever wish so deep —
Do easily, too — when I say, perfectly,
I do not boast, perhaps: yourself are
  judge,
Who listened to the Legate's talk last
  week;
And just as much they used to say in
  France.
At any rate 'tis easy, all of it!
No sketches first, no studies, that's
  long past:
I do what many dream of, all their
  lives,
— Dream? strive to do, and agonize
  to do,
And fail in doing. I could count
  twenty such
On twice your fingers, and not leave
  this town,

Who strive — you don't know how
  the others strive
To paint a little thing like that you
  smeared
Carelessly passing with your robes
  afloat, —
Yet do much less, so much less, Some-
  one says,
(I know his name, no matter) — so
  much less!
Well, less is more, Lucrezia: I am
  judged.
There burns a truer light of God in
  them,
In their vexed beating stuffed and
  stopped-up brain,
Heart, or whate'er else, than goes on
  to prompt
This low-pulsed forthright craftsman's
  hand of mine.
Their works drop groundward, but
  themselves, I know,
Reach many a time a heaven that's
  shut to me,
Enter and take their place there sure
  enough,
Though they come back and cannot
  tell the world.
My works are nearer heaven, but I
  sit here.
The sudden blood of these men! at a
  word —
Praise them, it boils, or blame them,
  it boils too.
I, painting from myself and to myself,
Know what I do, am unmoved by
  men's blame
Or their praise either. Somebody
  remarks
Morello's outline there is wrongly
  traced,
His hue mistaken; what of that? or
  else,
Rightly traced and well ordered;
  what of that?
Speak as they please, what does the
  mountain care?
Ah, but a man's reach should exceed
  his grasp,
Or what's a heaven for? All is silver-
  gray,
Placid and perfect with my art: the
  worse!
I know both what I want and what
  might gain,
And yet how profitless to know, to
  sigh
"Had I been two, another and my-
  self,

Our head would have o'erlooked the
   world!" No doubt.
Yonder's a work now, of that famous
   youth
The Urbinate who died five years ago.
('Tis copied, George Vasari sent it
   me.)
Well, I can fancy how he did it all,
Pouring his soul, with kings and
   popes to see,
Reaching, that heaven might so re-
   plenish him,
Above and through his art — for it
   gives way;
That arm is wrongly put — and there
   again —
A fault to pardon in the drawing's
   lines,
Its body, so to speak: its soul is right,
He means right — that, a child may
   understand.
Still, what an arm! and I could alter
   it:
But all the play, the insight and the
   stretch —
Out of me, out of me! And where-
   fore out?
Had you enjoined them on me, given
   me soul,
We might have risen to Rafael, I and
   you.
Nay, Love, you did give all I asked,
   I think —
More than I merit, yes, by many
   times.
But had you — oh, with the same per-
   fect brow,
And perfect eyes, and more than per-
   fect mouth,
And the low voice my soul hears, as
   a bird
The fowler's pipe, and follows to the
   snare —
Had you, with these the same, but
   brought a mind!
Some women do so. Had the mouth
   there urged
"God and the glory! never care for
   gain.
The present by the future, what is
   that?
Live for fame, side by side with Ag-
   nolo!
Rafael is waiting: up to God, all
   three!"
I might have done it for you. So it
   seems:
Perhaps not. All is as God over-
   . rules.

Beside, incentives come from the soul's
   self;
The rest avail not. Why do I need
   you?
What wife had Rafael, or has Agnolo?
In this world, who can do a thing,
   will not;
And who would do it, cannot, I per-
   ceive:
Yet the will's somewhat — somewhat,
   too, the power —
And thus we half-men struggle. At
   the end,
God, I conclude, compensates, pun-
   ishes.
'Tis safer for me, if the award be
   strict,
That I am something underrated here,
Poor this long while, despised, to
   speak the truth.
I dared not, do you know, leave home
   all day,
For fear of chancing on the Paris
   lords.
The best is when they pass and look
   aside;
But they speak sometimes: I must
   bear it all.
Well may they speak! That Francis,
   that first time,
And that long festal year at Fontaine-
   bleau!
I surely then could sometimes leave
   the ground,
Put on the glory, Rafael's daily wear,
In that humane great monarch's gold-
   en look, —
One finger in his beard or twisted
   curl
Over his mouth's good mark that
   made the smile,
One arm about my shoulder, round
   my neck,
The jingle of his gold chain in my
   ear,
I painting proudly with his breath on
   me,
All his court round him, seeing with
   his eyes,
Such frank French eyes, and such a
   fire of souls
Profuse, my hand kept plying by
   those hearts, —
And, best of all, this, this, this face
   beyond,
This in the background, waiting on
   my work,
To crown the issue with a last re-
   ward!

A good time, was it not, my kingly
  days?
And had you not grown restless . . .
  but I knew —
'Tis done and past; 'twas right, my
  instinct said :
Too live the life grew, golden and not
  gray :
And I'm the weak-eyed bat no sun
  should tempt
Out of the grange whose four walls
  make his world.
How could it end in any other way ?
You called me, and I came home to
  your heart.
The triumph was, to have ended
  there; then, if
I reached it ere the triumph, what is
  lost ?
Let my hands frame your face in
  your hair's gold,
You beautiful Lucrezia that are mine !
"Rafael did this, Andrea painted
  that ;
The Roman's is the better when you
  pray,
But still the other's Virgin was his
  wife" —
Men will excuse me. I am glad to
  judge
Both pictures in your presence ;
  clearer grows
My better fortune. I resolve to think.
For, do you know, Lucrezia, as God
  lives,
Said one day Agnolo his very self,
To Rafael . . . I have known it all
  these years . . .
(When the young man was flaming
  out his thoughts
Upon a palace-wall for Rome to see,
Too lifted up in heart because of
  it)
"Friend, there's a certain sorry little
  scrub
Goes up and down our Florence,
  none cares how,
Who, were he set to plan and exe-
  cute
As you are, pricked on by your
  popes and kings,
Would bring the sweat into that
  brow of yours !"
To Rafael's ! — And indeed the arm
  is wrong,
I hardly dare . . . yet, only you to
  see,
Give the chalk here — quick, thus the
  line should go !

Ay, but the soul ! he's Rafael ! rub it
  out !
Still, all I care for, if he spoke the
  truth.
(What he? why, who but Michel
  Agnolo ?
Do you forget already words like
  those ?)
If really there was such a chance, so
  lost, —
Is, whether you're — not grateful —
  but more pleased.
Well, let me think so. And you smile
  indeed !
This hour has been an hour ! An-
  other smile ?
If you would sit thus by me every
  night
I should work better, do you compre-
  hend ?
I mean that I should earn more, give
  you more.
See, it is settled dusk now ; there's a
  star ;
Morello's gone, the watch-lights show
  the wall,
The cue-owls speak the name we
  call them by.
Come from the window, love, — come
  in, at last,
Inside the melancholy little house
We built to be so gay with. God is
  just.
King Francis may forgive me : oft at
  nights
When I look up from painting, eyes
  tired out,
The walls become illumined, brick
  from brick
Distinct, instead of mortar, fierce
  bright gold,
That gold of his I did cement them
  with !
Let us but love each other. Must
  you go ?
That cousin here again ? he waits
  outside ?
Must see you — you, and not with
  me ? Those loans ?
More gaming debts to pay ? you smiled
  for that ?
Well, let smiles buy me ! have you
  more to spend ?
While hand and eye and something
  of a heart
Are left me, work's my ware, and
  what's it worth ?
I'll pay my fancy. Only let me
  sit

The gray remainder of the evening out,
Idle, you call it, and muse perfectly
How I could paint, were I but back in France,
One picture, just one more — the Virgin's face,
Not your's this time ! I want you at my side
To hear them — that is, Michel Agnolo —
Judge all I do and tell you of its worth.
Will you ? To-morrow satisfy your friend.
I take the subjects for his corridor,
Finish the portrait out of hand — there, there,
And throw him in another thing or two
If he demurs : the whole should prove enough
To pay for this same cousin's freak. Beside,
What's better and what's all I care about,
Get you the thirteen scudi for the ruff !
Love, does that please you ? Ah, but what does he.
The cousin ! what does he to please you more ?

I am grown peaceful as old age to-night
I regret little, I would change still less
Since there my past life lies, why alter it ?
The very wrong to Francis ! — it is true
I took his coin, was tempted and complied,
And built this house and sinned, and all is said.
My father and my mother died of want.
Well, had I riches of my own ? you see
How one gets rich ! Let each one bear his lot.
They were born poor, lived poor, and poor they died :
And I have labored somewhat in my time
And not been paid profusely. Some good son
Paint my two hundred pictures — let him try !

No doubt, there's something strikes a balance. Yes,
You loved me quite enough, it seems to-night.
This must suffice me here. What would one have ?
In heaven, perhaps, new chances, one more chance —
Four great walls in the New Jerusalem,
Meted on each side by the angel's reed,
For Leonard, Rafael, Agnolo, and me
To cover — the three first without a wife,
While I have mine ! So — still they overcome
Because there's still Lucrezia, — as I choose.

Again the cousin's whistle ! Go, my love.

THE BISHOP ORDERS HIS TOMB AT SAINT PRAXED'S CHURCH

ROME, 15—.

VANITY, saith the preacher, vanity !
Draw round my bed : is Anselm keeping back ?
Nephews — sons mine . . . ah God, I know not ! Well —
She, men would have to be your mother once,
Old Gandolf envied me, so fair she was !
What's done is done, and she is dead beside,
Dead long ago, and I am Bishop since,
And as she died so must we die ourselves,
And thence ye may perceive the world's a dream.
Life, how and what is it ? As here I lie
In this state-chamber, dying by degrees,
Hours and long hours in the dead night, I ask
" Do I live, am I dead ? " Peace, peace seems all.

Saint Praxed's ever was the church
  for peace ;
And so, about this tomb of mine. I
  fought
With tooth and nail to save my niche,
  ye know :
-- Old Gandolf cozened me, despite
  my care ;
Shrewd was that snatch from out the
  corner South
He graced his carrion with, God curse
  the same !
Yet still my niche is not so cramped
  but thence
One sees the pulpit on the epistle-
  side,
And somewhat of the choir, those
  silent seats,
And up into the aëry dome where live
The angels, and a sunbeam's sure to
  lurk ;
And I shall fill my slab of basalt
  there,
And 'neath my tabernacle take my
  rest,
With those nine columns round me,
  two and two,
The odd one at my feet where Anselm
  stands ;
Peach-blossom marble all, the rare,
  the ripe
As fresh-poured red wine of a mighty
  pulse,
-- Old Gandolf with his paltry onion-
  stone,
Put me where I may look at him !
  True peach,
Rosy and flawless : how I earned the
  prize !
Draw close : that conflagration of my
  church
-- What then ? So much was saved
  if aught were missed !
My sons, ye would not be my death ?
  Go dig
The white-grape vineyard where the
  oil-press stood,
Drop water gently till the surface
  sink,
And if ye find . . . Ah God, I know
  not, I ! . . . .
Bedded in store of rotten fig-leaves
  soft,
And corded up in a tight olive-frail,
Some lump, ah God, of *lapis lazuli*,
Big as a Jew's head cut off at the
  nape,
Blue as a vein o'er the Madonna's
  breast . . .

Sons, all have I bequeathed you,
  villas, all,
That brave Frascati villa with its
  bath,
So, let the blue lump poise between
  my knees,
Like God the Father's globe on both
  his hands
Ye worship in the Jesu Church so
  gay,
For Gandolf shall not choose but see
  and burst !
Swift as a weaver's shuttle fleet our
  years :
Man goeth to the grave, and where is
  he ?
Did I say, basalt for my slab, sons ?
  Black --
'Twas ever antique-black I meant !
  How else
Shall ye contrast my frieze to come
  beneath ?
The bass-relief in bronze ye promised
  me,
Those Pans and Nymphs ye wot of,
  and perchance
Some tripod, thyrsus, with a vase or
  so,
The Saviour at his sermon on the
  mount,
Saint Praxed in a glory, and one
  Pan
Ready to twitch the Nymph's last
  garment off,
And Moses with the tables . . . but I
  know
Ye mark me not ! What do they
  whisper thee,
Child of my bowels, Anselm ? Ah,
  ye hope
To revel down my villas while I gasp
Bricked o'er with beggar's mouldy
  travertine
Which Gandolf from his tomb-top
  chuckles at !
Nay, boys, ye love me -- all of jasper,
  then !
'Tis jasper ye stand pledged to, lest
  I grieve
My bath must needs be left behind
  alas !
One block, pure green as a pistachio-
  nut,
There's plenty jasper somewhere in
  the world --
And have I not Saint Praxed's ear to
  pray
Horses for ye, and brown Greek
  manuscripts,

And mistresses with great smooth
    marbly limbs?
— That's if ye carve my epitaph aright,
Choice Latin, picked phrase, Tully's
    every word,
No gaudy ware like Gandolf's second
    line —
Tully, my masters? Ulpian serves
    his need!
And then how I shall lie through cen-
    turies,
And hear the blessed mutter of the
    mass,
And see God made and eaten all day
    long,
And feel the steady candle-flame, and
    taste
Good strong thick stupefying incense-
    smoke!
For as I lie here, hours of the dead
    night,
Dying in state and by such slow de-
    grees,
I fold my arms as if they clasped a
    crook,
And stretch my feet forth straight as
    stone can point,
And let the bedclothes, for a mort-
    cloth, drop
Into great laps and folds of sculptor's
    work:
And as yon tapers dwindle, and
    strange thoughts
Grow, with a certain humming in my
    ears,
About the life before I lived this life,
And this life too, popes, cardinals,
    and priests,
Saint Praxed at his sermon on the
    mount,
Your tall pale mother with her talk-
    ing eyes,
And new-found agate urns as fresh
    as day,
And marble's language, Latin pure,
    discreet,
— Aha, ELUCESCEBAT quoth our
    friend?

No Tully, said I, Ulpian at the best!
Evil and brief hath been my pilgrim-
    age.
All *lapis*, all, sons! Else I give the
    Pope
My villas! Will ye ever eat my
    heart?
Ever your eyes were as a lizard's
    quick,
They glitter like your mother's for
    my soul,
Or ye would heighten my impover-
    ished frieze,
Piece out its starved design, and fill
    my vase
With grapes, and add a vizor and a
    Term,
And to the tripod ye would tie a lynx
That in his struggle throws the thyr-
    sus down,
To comfort me on my entablature
Whereon I am to lie till I must ask
"Do I live? am I dead?" There,
    leave me, there!
For ye have stabbed me with ingrati-
    tude
To death: ye wish it — God, ye wish
    it! Stone —
Gritstone, a-crumble! Clammy
    squares which sweat
As if the corpse they keep were ooz-
    ing through —
And no more *lapis* to delight the
    world!
Well go! I bless ye. Fewer tapers
    there,
But in a row: and, going, turn your
    backs
— Ay, like departing altar-minis-
    trants,
And leave me in my church, the
    church for peace,
That I may watch at leisure if he
    leers —
Old Gandolf at me, from his onion-
    stone,
As still he envied me, so fair she
    was!

A TOCCATA OF GALUPPI'S.

I.

O GALUPPI, Baldassaro, this is very sad to find!
I can hardly misconceive you; it would prove me deaf and blind:
But, although I take your meaning, 'tis with such a heavy mind!

II.

Here you come with your old music, and here's all the good it brings.
What, they lived once thus at Venice where the merchants were the kings,
Where Saint Mark's is, where the Doges used to wed the sea with rings?

III.

Ay, because the sea's the street there; and 'tis arched by . . . . what you call!
. . . . Shylock's bridge with houses on it, where they kept the carnival.
I was never out of England — it's as if I saw it all.

IV.

Did young people take their pleasure when the sea was warm in May?
Balls and masks begun at midnight, burning ever to mid-day,
When they made up fresh adventures for the morrow, do you say?

V.

Was a lady such a lady, cheeks so round and lips so red, —
On her neck the small face buoyant, like a bell-flower on its bed,
O'er the breast's superb abundance where a man might base his head?

VI.

Well, and it was graceful of them: they'd break talk off and afford
— She, to bite her mask's black velvet, he, to finger on his sword,
While you sat and played Toccatas, stately at the clavichord?

VII.

What? Those lesser thirds so plaintive, sixths diminished, sigh on sigh,
Told them something? Those suspensions, those solutions — "Must we
    die?"
Those commiserating sevenths — "Life might last! we can but try!"

VIII.

"Were you happy?" — "Yes." — "And are you still as happy?" — "Yes.
    And you?"
— "Then, more kisses!" — "Did I stop them, when a million seemed so
    few?"
Hark, the dominant's persistence till it must be answered to!

IX.

So, an octave struck the answer. Oh, they praised you, I dare say!
"Brave Galuppi! that was music! good alike at grave and gay!
I can always leave off talking when I hear a master play!"

X.

Then they left you for their pleasure: till in due time, one by one,
Some with lives that came to nothing, some with deeds as well undone,
Death stepped tacitly, and took them where they never see the sun.

XI.

But when I sit down to reason, think to take my stand nor swerve,
While I triumph o'er a secret wrung from nature's close reserve,
In you come with your cold music till I creep through every nerve.

XII.

Yes, you, like a ghostly cricket, creaking where a house was burned:
"Dust and ashes, dead and done with, Venice spent what Venice earned.
The soul, doubtless, is immortal — where a soul can be discerned.

XIII.

" Yours for instance: you know physics, something of geology,
Mathematics are your pastime; souls shall rise in their degree;
Butterflies may dread extinction, — you'll not die, it cannot be !

XIV.

" As for Venice and her people, merely born to bloom and drop,
Here on earth they bore their fruitage, mirth and folly were the crop:
What of soul was left, I wonder, when the kissing had to stop ?

XV.

" Dust and ashes !" So you creak it, and I want the heart to scold.
Dear dead women, with such hair, too — what's become of all the gold
Used to hang and brush their bosoms ? I feel chilly and grown old.

HOW IT STRIKES A CON-TEMPORARY.

I only knew one poet in my life :
And this, or something like it, was
 his way.

You saw go up and down Vallado-
 lid,
A man of mark, to know next time
 you saw,
His very serviceable suit of black
Was courtly once and conscientious
 still,
And many might have worn it, though
 none did :
The cloak, that somewhat shone and
 showed the threads,
Had purpose, and the ruff, signifi-
 cance.
He walked, and tapped the pavement
 with his cane,
Scenting the world, looking it full in
 face :
An old dog, bald and blindish, at his
 heels.
They turned up, now, the alley by
 the church,
That leads no whither; now, they
 breathed themselves
On the main promenade just at the
 wrong time.
You'd come upon his scrutinizing hat,
Making a peaked shade blacker than
 itself
Against the single window spared
 some house
Intact yet with its mouldered Moor-
 ish work, —

Or else surprise the ferrel of his stick
Trying the mortar's temper 'tween
 the chinks
Of some new shop a-building, French
 and fine.
He stood and watched the cobbler at
 his trade,
The man who slices lemons into drink,
The coffee-roaster's brazier, and the
 boys
That volunteer to help him turn its
 winch.
He glanced o'er books on stalls with
 half an eye,
And fly-leaf ballads on the vendor's
 string,
And broad-edge bold-print posters by
 the wall.
He took such cognizance of men and
 things,
If any beat a horse, you felt he saw;
If any cursed a woman, he took note;
Yet stared at nobody, — you stared at
 him,
And found, less to your pleasure than
 surprise,
He seemed to know you and expect
 as much.
So, next time that a neighbor's
 tongue was loosed,
It marked the shameful and notorious
 fact
We had among us, not so much a
 spy,
As a recording chief-inquisitor,
The town's true master if the town
 but knew !
We merely kept a governor for form,
While this man walked about and
 took account

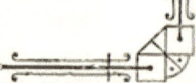

How it strikes a Contemporary. — Page 84.

Of all thought, said and acted, then
    went home,
And wrote it fully to our Lord the
    King
Who has an itch to know things, he
    knows why,
And reads them in his bedroom of a
    night.
Oh, you might smile! there wanted
    not a touch,
A tang of . . . well, it was not wholly
    ease,
As back into your mind the man's
    look came.
Stricken in years a little, such a brow
His eyes had to live under! — clear
    as flint
On either side o' the formidable nose
Curved, cut and colored like an eagle's
    claw.
Had he to do with A.'s surprising
    fate?
When altogether old B. disappeared,
And young C. got his mistress, — was't
    our friend,
His letter to the King, that did it
    all?
What paid the bloodless man for so
    much pains?
Our Lord the King has favorites mani-
    fold,
And shifts his ministry some once a
    month;
Our city gets new governors at
    whiles, —
But never word or sign, that I could
    hear,
Notified, to this man about the streets,
The King's approval of those letters
    conned
The last thing duly at the dead of
    night.
Did the man love his office? Frowned
    our Lord,
Exhorting when none heard — " Be-
    seech me not!
Too far above my people, — beneath
    me!
I set the watch, — how should the
    people know?
Forget them, keep me all the more in
    mind!"
Was some such understanding 'twixt
    the two?

    I found no truth in one report at
    least —
That if you tracked him to his home,
    down lanes

Beyond the Jewry, and as clean to
    pace,
You found he ate his supper in a
    room
Blazing with lights, four Titians on
    the wall,
And twenty naked girls to change his
    plate!
Poor man, he lived another kind of
    life
In that new stuccoed third house by
    the bridge,
Fresh-painted, rather smart than
    otherwise!
The whole street might o'erlook him
    as he sat,
Leg crossing leg, one foot on the dog's
    back,
Playing a decent cribbage with his
    maid
(Jacynth, you're sure her name was)
    o'er the cheese,
And fruit, three red halves of starved
    winter-pears,
Or treat of radishes in April. Nine,
Ten, struck the church clock, straight
    to bed went he.

    My father! like the man of sense he
    was,
Would point him out to me a dozen
    times
" St — St," he'd whisper, " the Corre-
    gidor!"
I had been used to think that person-
    age
Was one with lacquered breeches,
    lustrous belt,
And feathers like a forest in his hat,
Who blew a trumpet and proclaimed
    the news,
Announced the bull-fights, gave each
    church its turn,
And memorized the miracle in vogue!
He had a great observance from us
    boys;
We were in error; that was not the
    man.

    I'd like now, yet had haply been
    afraid,
To have just looked, when this man
    came to die,
And seen who lined the clean gay
    garret sides,
And stood about the neat low truckle-
    bed,
With the heavenly manner of reliev-
    ing guard

Here had been, mark, the general-in-
chief,
Through a whole campaign of the
world's life and death,
Doing the King's work all the dim
day long,
In his old coat and up to knees in
mud,
Smoked like a herring, dining on a
crust, —
And, now the day was won, relieved
at once !
No further show or need of that old
coat,
You are sure, for one thing ! Bless
us, all the while
How sprucely we are dressed out,
you and I !
A second, and the angels alter that,
Well, I could never write a verse, —
could you ?
Let's to the Prado and make the most
of time.

PROTUS.

AMONG these latter busts we count
by scores,
Half-emperors and quarter-emperors,
Each with his bay-leaf fillet, loose-
thonged vest,
Loric and low-browed Gorgon on the
breast, —
One loves a baby face, with violets
there,
Violets instead of laurel in the hair,
As those were all the little locks could
bear.

Now read here. "Protus ends a pe-
riod
Of empery beginning with a god ;
Born in the porphyry chamber at
Byzant,
Queens by his cradle, proud and min-
istrant :
And if he quickened breath there,
t'would like fire
Pantingly through the dim vast realm
transpire.
A fame that he was missing, spread
afar :
The world, from its four corners, rose
in war,

Till he was borne out on a balcony
To pacify the world when it should
see.
The captains ranged before him, one,
his hand
Made baby points at, gained the chief
command.
And day by day more beautiful he
grew
In shape, all said, in feature and in hue,
While young Greek sculptors gaz-
ing on the child
Became, with old Greek sculpture
reconciled.
Already sages labored to condense
In easy tomes a life's experience :
And artists took grave counsel to
impart
In one breath and one hand-sweep,
all their art,
And make his graces prompt as blos-
soming
Of plentifully watered palms in spring:
Since well beseems it, whoso mounts
the throne,
For beauty, knowledge, strength,
should stand alone,
And mortals love the letters of his
name.''

— Stop ! Have you turned two pages ?
Still the same.
New reign, same date. The scribe
goes on to say
How that same year, on such a month
and day,
"John the Pannonian, groundedly
believed
A blacksmith's bastard, whose hard
hand reprieved
The Empire from its fate the year
before, —
Came, had a mind to take the crown,
and wore
The same for six years (during which
the Huns
Kept off their fingers from us), till
his sons
Put something in his liquor'' — and
so forth.
Then a new reign. Stay — "Take at
its just worth''
(Subjoins an annotator) "What I give
As hearsay. Some think, John let
Protus live
And slip away. 'Tis said, he reached
man's age
At some blind northern court ; made
first a page,

Then tutor to the children ; last, of
use
About the hunting stables. I deduce
He wrote the little tract 'On worm-
ing dogs,'
Whereof the name in sundry cata-
logues
Is extant yet. A Protus of the race
Is rumored to have died a monk in
Thrace, —
And, if the same, he reached senili-
ty."

Here's John the smith's rough-ham-
mered head. Great eye,
Gross jaw and griped lips do what
granite can
To give you the crown-grasper.
What a man !

MASTER HUGUES OF SAXE-GOTHA.

I.

Hist, but a word, fair and soft !
  Forth and be judged, Master
    Hugues !
Answer the question I've put you so
  oft :
  What do you mean by your moun-
    tainous fugues ?
See, we're alone in the loft, —

II.

I, the poor organist here,
  Hugues, the composer of note,
Dead though, and done with, this
  many a year :
  Let's have a colloquy, something to
    quote,
Make the world prick up its ear !

III.

See, the church empties apace ;
  Fast they extinguish the lights.
Hallo there, sacristan ! Five min-
  utes' grace !
  Here's a crank pedal wants set-
    ting to rights,
Balks one of holding the base.

IV.

See, our huge house of the sounds,
  Hushing its hundreds at once,
Bids the last loiterer back to his
  bounds !
  — Oh, you may challenge them !
    not a response
Get the church-saints on their rounds!

V.

(Saints go their rounds, who shall
  doubt ?
  — March, with the moon to admire,
Up nave, down chancel, turn tran-
  sept about,
  Supervise all betwixt pavement and
    spire,
Put rats and mice to the rout —

VI.

Aloys and Jurien and Just —
  Order things back to their place,
Have a sharp eye lest the candlesticks
  rust,
  Rub the church-plate, darn the sac-
    rament-lace,
Clear the desk-velvet of dust.)

VII.

Here's your book, younger folks
  shelve !
  Played I not off-hand and run-
    ningly,
Just now, your masterpiece, hard
  number twelve ?
  Here's what should strike, could
    one handle it cunningly :
Help the axe, give it a helve !

VIII.

Page after page as I played,
  Every bar's rest, where one wipes
Sweat from one's brow, I looked up
  and surveyed,
  O'er my three claviers, yon forest
    of pipes
Whence you still peeped in the shade.

IX.

Sure you were wishful to speak,
  You, with brow ruled like a score,
Yes, and eyes buried in pits on each
  cheek,
  Like two great breves, as they
    wrote them of yore,
Each side that bar, your straight beak!

X.

Sure you said—"Good, the mere
    notes!
    Still, could'st thou take my intent,
Know what procured me our Com-
    pany's votes—
    A master were lauded and sciolists
      shent,
Parted the sheep from the goats!"

XI.

Well then, speak up, never flinch!
    Quick, ere my candle's a snuff
—Burnt, do you see? to its uttermost
    inch—
    I believe in you, but that's not
      enough:
Give my conviction a clinch!

XII.

First you deliver your phrase
    — Nothing propound, that I see,
Fit in itself for much blame or much
    praise—
    Answered no less, where no answer
      needs be:
Off start the Two on their ways.

XIII.

Straight must a Third interpose,
    Volunteer needlessly help;
In strikes a Fourth, a Fifth thrusts in
    his nose,
    So the cry's open, the kennel's
    a-yelp,
Argument's hot to the close.

XIV.

One dissertates, he is candid;
    Two must discept,—has distin-
    guished;
Three helps the couple, if ever yet
    man did;
    Four protests; Five makes a dart at
    the thing wished:
Back to One, goes the case bandied.

XV.

One says his say with a difference:
    More of expounding, explaining!
All now is wrangle, abuse, and vocif-
    erance;
    Now there's a truce, all's subdued,
    self-restraining:
Five, though, stands out all the stiffer
    hence.

XVI.

One is incisive, corrosive;
    Two retorts, nettled, curt, crepi-
    tant;
Three makes rejoinder, expansive,
    explosive;
    Four overbears them all, strident
    and strepitant:
Five . . . O Danaides, O Sieve!

XVII.

Now, they ply axes and crowbars;
    Now, they prick pins at a tissue
Fine as a skein of the casuist Escobar's
    Worked on the bone of a lie. To
    what issue?
Where is our gain at the Two-bars?

XVIII.

Est fuga, volvitur rota.
    On we drift: where looms the dim
    port?
One, Two, Three, Four, Five, contrib
    ute their quota;
    Something is gained, if one caught
    but the import:
Show it us, Hugues of Saxe-Gotha!

XIX.

What with affirming, denying,
    Holding, risposting, subjoining,
All's like . . . it's like . . . for an in-
    stance I'm trying . . .
    There! See our roof, its gilt mould
    ing and groining
Under those spider-webs lying!

XX.

So your fugue broadens and thickens,
    Greatens and deepens and length
    ens,
Till we exclaim — "But where's
    music, the dickens?
    Blot ye the gold, while your spider-
    web strengthens
— Blacked to the stoutest of tickens?"

XXI.

I for man's effort am zealous:
    Prove me such censure unfounded!
Seems it surprising a lover grows
    jealous—
    Hopes 'twas for something, his or-
    gan-pipes sounded,
Tiring three boys at the bellows?

XXII.

Is it your moral of Life ?
Such a web, simple and subtle,
Weave we on earth here in impotent
 strife,
Backward and forward each throw-
 ing his shuttle,
Death ending all with a knife ?

XXIII.

Over our heads truth and nature --
Still our life's zigzags and dodges,
Ins and outs, weaving a new legisla-
 ture--
God's gold just shining its last
 where that lodges,
Palled beneath man's usurpature.

XXIV.

So we o'ershroud stars and roses,
Cherub and trophy and garland ;
Nothings grow something which
 quietly closes
Heaven's earnest eye ; not a glimpse
 of the far land
Gets through our comments and
 glozes.

XXV.

Ah, but traditions, inventions
 (Say we and make up a visage),
So many men with such various in-
 tentions,
 Down the past ages, must know
 more than this age !
Leave we the web its dimensions !

XXVI.

Who thinks Hugues wrote for the
 deaf,
 Proved a mere mountain in labor ?

Better submit ; try again ; what's the
 clef ?
 'Faith, 'tis no trifle for pipe and for
 tabor --
Four flats, the minor in F.

XXVII.

Friend, your fugue taxes the finger :
 Learning it once, who would lose
 it ?
Yet all the while a misgiving will
 linger,
 Truth's golden o'er us although we
 refuse it --
Nature, through cobwebs we string
 her.

XXVIII.

Hugues ! I advise *meâ pœnâ*
 (Counterpoint glares like a Gorgon)
Bid One, Two, Three, Four, Five,
 clear the arena !
 Say the word, straight I unstop the
 full-organ,
Blare out the *mode Palestrina.*

XXIX.

While in the roof, if I'm right there,
 . . . Lo you, the wick in the socket !
Hallo, you sacristan, show us a light
 there !
 Down it dips, gone like a rocket.
What, you want, do you, to come una-
 wares,
 Sweeping the church up for first
 morning-prayers,
And find a poor devil has ended his
 cares
At the foot of your rotten-runged rat-
 riddled stairs ?
 Do I carry the moon in my pocket ?

ABT VOGLER.

(AFTER HE HAS BEEN EXTEMPORIZING UPON THE MUSICAL INSTRU-
MENT OF HIS INVENTION.)

1.

Would that the structure brave, the manifold music I build,
 Bidding my organ obey, calling its keys to their work,
Claiming each slave of the sound, at a touch, as when Solomon willed
 Armies of angels that soar, legions of demons that lurk,

Man, brute, reptile, fly, — alien of end and of aim,
  Adverse, each from the other heaven-high, hell-deep removed, —
Should rush into sight at once as he named the ineffable Name,
  And pile him a palace straight, to pleasure the princess he loved !

II.

Would it might tarry like his, the beautiful building of mine,
  This which my keys in a crowd pressed and importuned to raise !
Ah, one and all, how they helped, would dispart now and now combine,
  Zealous to hasten the work, heighten their master his praise !
And one would bury his brow with a blind plunge down to hell,
  Burrow a while and build, broad on the roots of things,
Then up again swim into sight, having based me my palace well,
  Founded it, fearless of flame, flat on the nether springs.

III.

And another would mount and march, like the excellent minion he was,
  Ay, another and yet another, one crowd but with many a crest,
Raising my rampired walls of gold as transparent as glass,
  Eager to do and die, yield each his place to the rest ;
For higher still and higher (as a runner tips with fire,
  When a great illumination surprises a festal night —
Outlining round and round Rome's dome from space to spire)
  Up, the pinnacled glory reached, and the pride of my soul was in sight.

IV.

In sight ? Not half ! for it seemed, it was certain, to match man's birth,
  Nature in turn conceived, obeying an impulse as I ;
And the emulous heaven yearned down, made effort to reach the earth,
  As the earth had done her best, in my passion, to scale the sky :
Novel splendors burst forth, grew familiar and dwelt with mine,
  Not a point nor peak but found, but fixed its wandering star ;
Meteor-moons, balls of blaze : and they did not pale nor pine,
  For earth had attained to heaven, there was no more near nor far.

V.

Nay more ; for there wanted not who walked in the glare and glow,
  Presences plain in the place ; or, fresh from the Protoplast,
Furnished for ages to come, when a kindlier wind should blow,
  Lured now to begin and live, in a house to their liking at last ;
Or else the wonderful Dead who have passed through the body and gone,
  But were back once more to breathe in an old world worth their new :
What never had been, was now ; what was, as it shall be anon ;
  And what is, — shall I say, matched both ? for I was made perfect too.

VI.

All through my keys that gave their sounds to a wish of my soul,
  All through my soul that praised as its wish flowed visibly forth,
All through music and me ! For think, had I painted the whole,
  Why, there it had stood, to see, nor the process so wonder-worth.
Had I written the same, made verse — still, effect proceeds from cause,
  Ye know why the forms are fair, ye hear how the tale is told ;
It is all triumphant art, but art in obedience to laws,
  Painter and poet are proud, in the artist-list enrolled : —

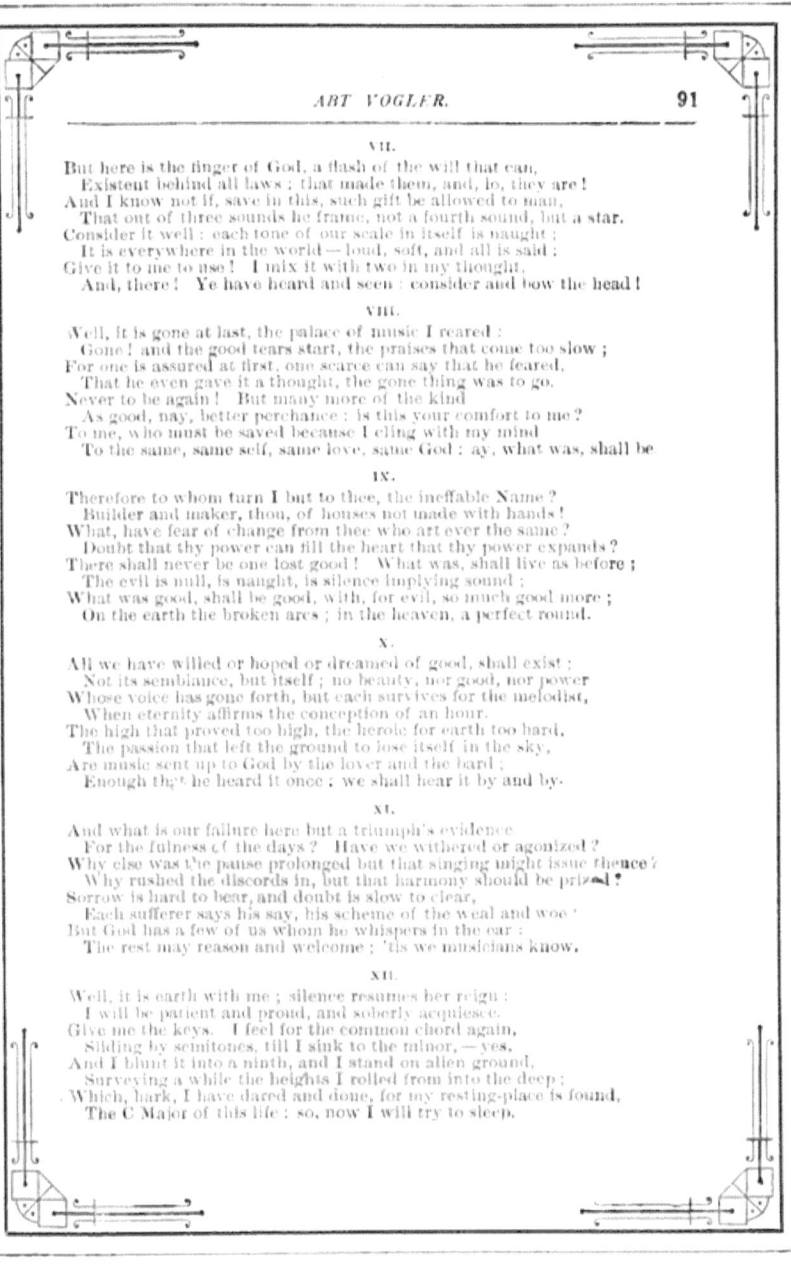

VII.

But here is the finger of God, a flash of the will that can,
  Existent behind all laws ; that made them, and, lo, they are !
And I know not if, save in this, such gift be allowed to man,
  That out of three sounds he frame, not a fourth sound, but a star.
Consider it well : each tone of our scale in itself is naught ;
  It is everywhere in the world — loud, soft, and all is said ;
Give it to me to use ! I mix it with two in my thought,
  And, there ! Ye have heard and seen : consider and bow the head !

VIII.

Well, it is gone at last, the palace of music I reared :
  Gone ! and the good tears start, the praises that come too slow ;
For one is assured at first, one scarce can say that he feared,
  That he even gave it a thought, the gone thing was to go.
Never to be again ! But many more of the kind
  As good, nay, better perchance : is this your comfort to me ?
To me, who must be saved because I cling with my mind
  To the same, same self, same love, same God : ay, what was, shall be

IX.

Therefore to whom turn I but to thee, the ineffable Name ?
  Builder and maker, thou, of houses not made with hands !
What, have fear of change from thee who art ever the same ?
  Doubt that thy power can fill the heart that thy power expands ?
There shall never be one lost good ! What was, shall live as before ;
  The evil is null, is naught, is silence implying sound ;
What was good, shall be good, with, for evil, so much good more ;
  On the earth the broken arcs ; in the heaven, a perfect round.

X.

All we have willed or hoped or dreamed of good, shall exist ;
  Not its semblance, but itself ; no beauty, nor good, nor power
Whose voice has gone forth, but each survives for the melodist,
  When eternity affirms the conception of an hour.
The high that proved too high, the heroic for earth too hard,
  The passion that left the ground to lose itself in the sky,
Are music sent up to God by the lover and the bard ;
  Enough that he heard it once ; we shall hear it by and by.

XI.

And what is our failure here but a triumph's evidence
  For the fulness of the days ? Have we withered or agonized ?
Why else was the pause prolonged but that singing might issue thence ?
  Why rushed the discords in, but that harmony should be prized ?
Sorrow is hard to bear, and doubt is slow to clear,
  Each sufferer says his say, his scheme of the weal and woe '
But God has a few of us whom he whispers in the ear :
  The rest may reason and welcome ; 'tis we musicians know.

XII.

Well, it is earth with me ; silence resumes her reign :
  I will be patient and proud, and soberly acquiesce.
Give me the keys. I feel for the common chord again,
  Sliding by semitones, till I sink to the minor, — yes,
And I blunt it into a ninth, and I stand on alien ground,
  Surveying a while the heights I rolled from into the deep ;
Which, hark, I have dared and done, for my resting-place is found,
  The C Major of this life : so, now I will try to sleep.

TWO IN THE CAMPAGNA.

I.

I wonder do you feel to-day
  As I have felt since, hand in hand,
We sat down on the grass, to stray
  In spirit better through the land,
This morn of Rome and May?

II.

For me, I touched a thought, I know,
  Has tantalized me many times
(Like turns of thread the spiders
    throw
  Mocking across our path), for
    rhymes
To catch at and let go.

III.

Help me to hold it! First it left
  The yellowing fennel, run to seed
There, branching from the brick-
    work's cleft,
  Some old tomb's ruin: yonder weed
Took up the floating weft,

IV.

Where one small orange cup amassed
  Five beetles, — blind and green they
    grope
Among the honey-meal : and last,
  Everywhere on the grassy slope,
I traced it. Hold it fast!

V.

The champaign with its endless fleece
  Of feathery grasses everywhere!
Silence and passion, joy and peace,
  An everlasting wash of air —
Rome's ghost since her decease.

VI.

Such life here, through such lengths
    of hours,
  Such miracles performed in play,
Such primal naked forms of flowers,
  Such letting nature have her way
While heaven looks from its towers!

VII.

How say you? Let us, O my dove,
  Let us be unashamed of soul,
As earth lies bare to heaven above!
  How is it under our control
To love or not to love?

VIII.

I would that you were all to me,
  You that are just so much, no more.
Nor yours nor mine, nor slave nor
    free!
  Where does the fault lie? What
    the core
O' the wound, since wound must be?

IX.

I would I could adopt your will,
  See with your eyes, and set my
    heart
Beating by yours, and drink my fill
  At your soul's springs, — your part,
    my part
In life, for good and ill.

X.

No. I yearn upward, touch you
    close,
  Then stand away. I kiss your
    cheek,
Catch your soul's warmth, — I pluck
    the rose
  And love it more than tongue can
    speak —
Then the good minute goes.

XI.

Already how am I so far
  Out of that minute? Must I go
Still like the thistle-ball, no bar,
  Onward, whenever light winds
    blow,
Fixed by no friendly star?

XII.

Just when I seemed about to learn!
  Where is the thread now? Off
    again!
The old trick! Only I discern —
  Infinite passion, and the pain
Of finite hearts that yearn.

"DE GUSTIBUS—"

I.

Your ghost will walk, you lover of
    trees
  (If our loves remain),
  In an English lane,
By a cornfield-side a-flutter with pop-
    pies.

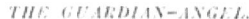

Hark, those two in the hazel cop-
 pice —
A boy and a girl, if the good fates
 please,
 Making love, say, —
 The happier they!
Draw yourself up from the light of
 the moon,
And let them pass, as they will too
 soon,
 With the beanflower's boon,
 And the blackbird's tune,
 And May, and June!

II.

What I love best in all the world
Is a castle, precipice-encurled,
In a gash of the wind-grieved Apen-
 nine.
Or look for me, old fellow of mine,
(If I get my head from out the mouth
O' the grave, and loose my spirit's
 bands,
And come again to the land of lands),
In a seaside house to the farther
 South,
Where the baked cicala dies of
 drouth,
And one sharp tree — 'tis a cypress —
 stands,
By the many hundred years red-
 rusted,
Rough, iron-spiked, ripe fruit-o'er-
 crusted,
My sentinel to guard the sands
To the water's edge. For, what ex-
 pands
Before the house, but the great
 opaque
Blue breadth of sea without a break?
While, in the house, forever crumbles
Some fragment of the frescoed walls,
From blisters where a scorpion
 sprawls.
A girl bare-footed brings, and tumbles
Down on the pavement, green-flesh
 melons,
And says there's news to-day, — the
 king
Was shot at, touched in the liver-
 wing,
Goes with his Bourbon arm in a sling:
— She hopes they have not caught the
 felons.
Italy, my Italy!
Queen Mary's saying serves for me —
 (When fortune's malice
 Lost her, Calais)

Open my heart and you will see
Graved inside of it, "Italy."
Such lovers old are I and she:
So it always was, so shall ever be!

THE GUARDIAN-ANGEL.

A PICTURE AT FANO.

I.

DEAR and great Angel, wouldst thou
 only leave
 That child, when thou hast done
 with him, for me!
Let me sit all the day here, that when
 eve
 Shall find performed thy special
 ministry,
And time come for departure, thou,
 suspending
Thy flight, may'st see another child
 for tending,
Another still to quiet and retrieve.

II.

Then I shall feel thee step one step,
 no more,
 From where thou standest now, to
 where I gaze,
— And suddenly my head is covered
 o'er
 With those wings, white above the
 child who prays
Now on that tomb — and I shall feel
 thee guarding
Me, out of all the world; for me, dis-
 carding
 Yon heaven thy home, that waits
 and opes its door.

III.

I would not look up thither past thy
 head
 Because the door opes, like that
 child, I know,
For I should have thy gracious face
 instead,
 Thou bird of God! And wilt thou
 bend me low
Like him, and lay, like his, my hands
 together,
And lift them up to pray, and gently
 tether
 Me, as thy lamb there, with thy
 garment's spread?

IV.

If this was ever granted, I would
    rest
    My head beneath thine, while thy
      healing hands
Close-covered both my eyes beside
    thy breast,
    Pressing the brain which too much
      thought expands,
Back to its proper size again, and
    smoothing
Distortion down till every nerve had
    soothing,
    And all lay quiet, happy, and sup-
      pressed.

V.

How soon all worldly wrong would
    be repaired !
    I think how I should view the
      earth and skies
And sea, when once again my brow
    was bared
    After thy healing, with such differ-
      ent eyes.
O world, as God has made it ! All is
    beauty :
And knowing this is love, and love is
    duty.
    What further may be sought for or
      declared ?

VI.

Guercino drew this angel I saw
    teach
    (Alfred, dear friend !) — that little
      child to pray,
Holding the little hands up, each to
    each
    Pressed gently, — with his own
      head turned away
Over the earth where so much lay be-
    fore him
Of work to do, though heaven was
    opening o'er him,
    And he was left at Fano by the
      beach.

VII.

We were at Fano, and three times we
    went
    To sit and see him in his chapel
      there,
And drink his beauty to our soul's
    content
    — My angel with me too : and since
      I care

For dear Guercino's fame (to which in
    power
And glory comes this picture for a
    dower,
    Fraught with a pathos so magnifi-
      cent)

VIII.

And since he did not work thus ear-
    nestly
    At all times, and has else endured
      some wrong —
I took one thought his picture struck
    from me,
    And spread it out, translating it to
      song.
My love is here. Where are you, dear
    old friend ?
How rolls the Wairoa at your world's
    far end ?
    This is Ancona, yonder is the sea.

EVELYN HOPE.

I.

BEAUTIFUL Evelyn Hope is dead !
    Sit and watch by her side an hour.
That is her book-shelf, this her bed ;
    She plucked that piece of geranium-
      flower,
Beginning to die too, in the glass ;
    Little has yet been changed, I
      think :
The shutters are shut, no light may
    pass
    Save two long rays through the
      hinge's chink.

II.

Sixteen years old when she died !
    Perhaps she had scarcely heard my
      name ;
It was not her time to love ; beside,
    Her life had many a hope and aim,
Duties enough and little cares,
    And now was quiet, now astir,
Till God's hand beckoned unawares, —
    And the sweet white brow is all of
      her.

III.

Is it too late then, Evelyn Hope ?
    What, your soul was pure and true,
The good stars met in your horoscope,
    Made you of spirit, fire, and dew —

And just because I was thrice as old,
  And our paths in the world diverged
    so wide,
Each was naught to each, must I be
    told ?
  We were fellow mortals, naught
    beside ?

IV.

No, indeed ! for God above
  Is great to grant, as mighty to make,
And creates the love to reward the
    love :
  I claim you still, for my own love's
    sake !
Delayed it may be for more lives yet,
  Through worlds I shall traverse,
    not a few ;
Much is to learn, much to forget
  Ere the time be come for taking
    you.

V.

But the time will come, — at last it
    will,
  When, Evelyn Hope, what meant
    (I shall say)
In the lower earth, in the years long
    still,
  That body and soul so pure and gay ?
Why your hair was amber, I shall
    divine,
  And your mouth of your own gera-
    nium's red —
And what you would do with me, in
    fine,
  In the new life come in the old one's
    stead.

VI.

I have lived (I shall say) so much
    since then,
  Given up myself so many times,
Gained me the gains of various men,
  Ransacked the ages, spoiled the
    climes ;
Yet one thing, one, in my soul's full
    scope,
  Either I missed or itself missed me:
And I want and find you, Evelyn Hope !
  What is the issue ? let us see !

VII.

I loved you, Evelyn, all the while !
  My heart seemed full as it could
    hold ;
There was place and to spare for the
    frank young smile,
  And the red young mouth, and the
    hair's young gold.

So hush, — I will give you this leaf to
    keep :
  See, I shut it inside the sweet cold
    hand !
There, that is our secret : go to sleep !
  You will wake, and remember, and
    understand.

MEMORABILIA.

I.

Ah ! did you once see Shelley plain,
  And did he stop and speak to you,
And did you speak to him again ?
  How strange it seems, and new !

II.

But you were living before that,
  And also you are living after ;
And the memory I started at —
  My starting moves your laughter !

III.

I crossed a moor, with a name of its
    own
  And a certain use in the world, no
    doubt,
Yet a hand's-breadth of it shines alone
  'Mid the blank miles round about :

IV.

For there I picked up on the heather
  And there I put inside my breast
A moulted feather, an eagle-feather !
  Well, I forget the rest.

APPARENT FAILURE.

"We shall soon lose a celebrated building."
  Paris Newspaper.

I.

No, for I'll save it ! Seven years
    since,
  I passed through Paris, stopped a
    day
To see the baptism of your Prince ;
  Saw, made my bow, and went my
    way :

Walking the heat and headache off,
  I took the Seine-side, you surmise,
Thought of the Congress, Gortscha-
    koff,
  Cavour's appeal and Buol's replies,
So sauntered till — what met my
    eyes?

II.

Only the Doric little Morgue!
  The dead-house where you show
    your drowned :
Petrarch's Vaucluse makes proud the
    Sorgue,
  Your Morgue has made the Seine
    renowned.
One pays one's debt in such a case ;
  I plucked up heart and entered, —
    stalked,
Keeping a tolerable face
  Compared with some whose cheeks
    were chalked :
Let them! No Briton's to be
    balked !

III.

First came the silent gazers ; next,
  A screen of glass, we're thankful
    for ;
Last, the sight's self, the sermon's
    text,
  The three men who did most abhor
Their life in Paris yesterday,
  So killed themselves ; and now,
    enthroned
Each on his copper couch, they lay
  Fronting me, waiting to be owned.
I thought, and think, their sin's
    atoned.

IV.

Poor men, God made, and all for
    that !
  The reverence struck me ; o'er each
    head
Religiously was hung its hat,
  Each coat dripped by the owner's
    bed,
Sacred from touch : each had his
    berth,
  His bounds, his proper place of
    rest,
Who last night tenanted on earth
  Some arch, where twelve such slept
    abreast, —
Unless the plain asphalte seemed
    best.

V.

How did it happen, my poor boy?
  You wanted to be Buonaparte
And have the Tuileries for toy,
  And could not, so it broke you?
    heart?
You, old one by his side, I judge,
  Were, red as blood, a socialist,
A leveller! Does the Empire grudge
  You've gained what no Republic
    missed ?
Be quiet, and unclinch your fist !

VI.

And this — why, he was red in vain,
  Or black, — poor fellow that is blue !
What fancy was it, turned your brain ?
  Oh, women were the prize for you !
Money gets women, cards and dice
  Get money, and ill-luck gets just
The copper couch and one clear nice
  Cool squirt of water o'er your bust,
The right thing to extinguish lust !

VII.

It's wiser being good than bad ;
  It's safer being meek than fierce :
It's fitter being sane than mad.
  My own hope is, a sun will pierce
The thickest cloud earth ever
    stretched ;
That, after Last, returns the First,
Though a wide compass round be
    fetched ;
  That what began best, can't end
    worst,
Nor what God blessed once, prove
    accurst.

PROSPICE.

Fear death? — to feel the fog in my
    throat,
  The mist in my face,
When the snows begin, and the blasts
    denote
  I am nearing the place,
The power of the night, the press of
    the storm,
  The post of the foe ;
Where he stands, the Arch Fear in a
    visible form,
  Yet the strong man must go :

For the journey is done and the sum-
      mit attained,
   And the barriers fall,
Though a battle's to fight ere the
      guerdon be gained,
   The reward of it all.
I was ever a fighter, so — one fight
      more,
   The best and the last !
I would hate that death bandaged
      my eyes, and forbore,
   And bade me creep past.
No ! let me taste the whole of it, fare
      like my peers
   The heroes of old,
Bear the brunt, in a minute pay glad
      life's arrears
   Of pain, darkness, and cold.
For sudden the worst turns the best
      to the brave,
   The black minute's at end,
And the elements' rage, the fiend-
      voices that rave,
   Shall dwindle, shall blend,
Shall change, shall become first a
      peace out of pain,
   Then a light, then thy breast,
O thou soul of my soul ! I shall clasp
      thee again,
   And with God be the rest !

"CHILDE ROLAND TO THE DARK TOWER CAME."

(See Edgar's song in " LEAR.")

I.

My first thought was, he lied in every
      word,
   That hoary cripple, with malicious
      eye
   Askance to watch the working of
      his lie
On mine, and mouth scarce able to
      afford
Suppression of the glee, that pursed
      and scored
   Its edge, at one more victim gained
      thereby.

II.

What else should he be set for, with
      his staff ?
   What, save to waylay with his lies,
      insnare

All travellers who might find him
      posted there,
And ask the road ? I guessed what
      skull-like laugh
Would break, what crutch gin write
      my epitaph
   For pastime in the dusty thorough-
      fare,

III.

If at his counsel I should turn aside
   Into that ominous tract which, all
      agree,
   Hides the Dark Tower. Yet acqui-
      escingly
I did turn as he pointed: neither pride
Nor hope rekindling at the end de-
      scried,
   So much as gladness that some end
      might be.

IV.

For, what with my whole world-wide
      wandering,
   What with my search drawn out
      through years, my hope
   Dwindled into a ghost not fit to cope
With that obstreperous joy success
      would bring. —
I hardly tried now to rebuke the
      spring
   My heart made, finding failure in
      its scope.

V.

As when a sick man very near to
      death
   Seems dead indeed, and feels begin
      and end
   The tears, and takes the farewell of
      each friend,
And hears one bid the other go, draw
      breath,
Freelier outside ("since all is o'er,"
      he saith,
   "And the blow fallen no grieving
      can amend ") ;

VI.

While some discuss if near the other
      graves
   Be room enough for this, and when
      a day
   Suits best for carrying the corpse
      away,
With care about the banners, scarves,
      and staves :

And still the man hears all, and only craves
He may not shame such tender love and stay.

VII.

Thus, I had so long suffered in this quest,
Heard failure prophesied so oft, been writ
So many times among "The Band" — to wit,
The knights who to the Dark Tower's search addressed
Their steps — that just to fail as they, seemed best,
And all the doubt was now — should I be fit?

VIII.

So, quiet as despair, I turned from him,
That hateful cripple, out of his highway
Into the path he pointed. All the day
Had been a dreary one at best, and dim
Was settling to its close, yet shot one grim
Red leer to see the plain catch its estray.

IX.

For mark! no sooner was I fairly found
Pledged to the plain, after a pace or two,
Than, pausing to throw backward a last view
O'er the safe road, 'twas gone; gray plain all round :
Nothing but plain to the horizon's bound.
I might go on : naught else remained to do.

X.

So, on I went. I think I never saw
Such starved ignoble nature; nothing throve :
For flowers — as well expect a cedar grove !
But cockle, spurge, according to their law
Might propagate their kind, with none to awe,
You'd think; a burr had been a treasure trove.

XI.

No ! penury, inertness, and grimace,
In some strange sort, were the land's portion. "See
Or shut your eyes," said Nature peevishly,
"It nothing skills : I cannot help my case :
'Tis the Last Judgment's fire must cure this place,
Calcine its clods and set my prisoners free."

XII.

If there pushed any ragged thistle-stalk
Above its mates, the head was chopped ; the bents
Were jealous else. What made those holes and rents
In the dock's harsh swarth leaves, bruised as to balk
All hope of greenness ? 'tis a brute must walk
Pashing their life out, with a brute's intents.

XIII.

As for the grass, it grew as scant as hair
In leprosy : thin dry blades pricked the mud
Which underneath looked kneaded up with blood.
One stiff blind horse, his every bone a-stare,
Stood stupefied, however he came there :
Thrust out past service from the Devil's stud !

XIV.

Alive ? he might be dead for aught I know,
With that red gaunt and colloped neck a-strain,
And shut eyes underneath the rusty mane ;
Seldom went such grotesqueness with such woe ;
I never saw a brute I hated so ;
He must be wicked to deserve such pain.

XV.

I shut my eyes and turned them on my heart.
As a man calls for wine before he fights,

"Childe Roland to the Dark Tower came " — Page 99, Stanza xxi.

I asked one draught of earlier, hap-
  pier sights,
Ere fitly I could hope to play my part
Think first, fight afterwards — the
  soldier's art :
  One taste of the old time sets all to
  rights.

XVI.

Not it ! I fancied Cuthbert's redden-
  ing face
Beneath its garniture of curly gold,
Dear fellow, till I almost felt him
  fold
An arm in mine to fix me to the place,
That way he used. Alas, one night's
  disgrace !
  Out went my heart's new fire and
  left it cold.

XVII.

Giles then, the soul of honor — there
  he stands
Frank as ten years ago when
  knighted first.
What honest man should dare (he
  said) he durst.
Good — but the scene shifts — faugh !
  what hangman hands
Pin to his breast a parchment ? His
  own hands
  Read it. Poor traitor, spit upon
  and curst !

XVIII.

Better this present than a past like
  that ;
  Back therefore to my darkening
  path again !
  No sound, no sight as far as eye
  could strain.
Will the night send a howlet or a bat ?
I asked : when something on the dis-
  mal flat
  Came to arrest my thoughts and
  change their train.

XIX.

A sudden little river crossed my path
As unexpected as a serpent comes.
No sluggish tide congenial to the
  glooms ;
This, as it frothed by, might have
  been a bath
For the fiend's glowing hoof — to see
  the wrath
  Of its black eddy bespate with
  flakes and spumes.

XX.

So petty yet so spiteful ! All along,
  Low scrubby alders kneeled down
  over it ;
  Drenched willows flung them head-
  long in a fit
Of mute despair, a suicidal throng :
The river which had done them all
  the wrong,
  Whate'er that was, rolled by, de-
  terred no whit.

XXI.

Which, while I forded, — good saints,
  how I feared
  To set my foot upon a dead man's
  cheek,
  Each step, or feel the spear I thrust
  to seek
For hollows, tangled in his hair or
  beard !
—It may have been a water-rat I
  speared,
  But, ugh ! it sounded like a baby's
  shriek.

XXII.

Glad was I when I reached the other
  bank.
  Now for a better country. Vain
  presage !
  Who were the stragglers, what war
  did they wage
Whose savage trample thus could
  pad the dank
Soil to a plash ? Toads in a poisoned
  tank,
  Or wild cats in a red-hot iron cage —

XXIII.

The fight must so have seemed in that
  fell cirque.
  What penned them there, with all
  the plain to choose ?
  No footprint leading to that horrid
  mews,
None out of it. Mad brewage set to
  work
Their brains, no doubt, like galley-
  slaves the Turk
  Pits for his pastime, Christians
  against Jews.

XXIV.

And more than that — a furlong on —
  why, there !
  What bad use was that engine for,
  that wheel,

Or brake, not wheel — that harrow
    fit to reel
Men's bodies out like silk? with all
    the air
Of Tophet's tool, on earth left una-
    ware,
    Or brought to sharpen its rusty
    teeth of steel.

XXV.

Then came a bit of stubbed ground,
    once a wood,
    Next a marsh, it would seem, and
    now mere earth
Desperate and done with; (so a fool
    finds mirth,
Makes a thing and then mars it, till
    his mood
Changes and off he goes!) within a
    rood —
    Bog, clay, and rubble, sand and
    stark black dearth.

XXVI.

Now blotches rankling, colored gay
    and grim,
    Now patches where some leanness
    of the soil's
Broke into moss or substances like
    boils ;
Then came some palsied oak, a cleft
    in him
Like a distorted mouth that splits its
    rim
    Gaping at death, and dies while it
    recoils.

XXVII.

And just as far as ever from the
    end :
    Naught in the distance but the even-
    ing, naught
To point my footstep farther ! At
    the thought,
A great black bird, Apollyon's bosom
    friend,
Sailed past, nor beat his wide wing
    dragon-penned
    That brushed my cap — perchance
    the guide I sought.

XXVIII.

For, looking up, aware I somehow
    grew,
    'Spite of the dusk, the plain had
    given place

All round to mountains — with such
    name to grace
Mere ugly heights and heaps now
    stolen in view.
How thus they had surprised me, —
    solve it, you !
    How to get from them was no
    clearer case.

XXIX.

Yet half I seemed to recognize some
    trick
    Of mischief happened to me, God
    knows when —
In a bad dream perhaps. Here
    ended, then,
Progress this way. When, in the
    very nick
Of giving up, one time more, came a
    click
    As when a trap shuts — you're in-
    side the den

XXX.

Burningly it came on me all at once,
    This was the place ! those two hills
    on the right,
    Crouched like two bulls locked
    horn in horn in fight :
While to the left, a tall scalped moun-
    tain . . . Dunce,
Dotard, a-dozing at the very nonce,
    After a life spent training for the
    sight !

XXXI.

What in the midst lay but the Tower
    itself ?
    The round squat turret, blind as
    the fool's heart,
    Built of brown stone, without a
    counterpart
In the whole world. The tempest's
    mocking elf
Points to the shipman thus the unseen
    shelf
    He strikes on, only when the tim-
    bers start.

XXXII.

Not see ? because of night perhaps ? —
    why, day
    Came back again for that ! before it
    left,
    The dying sunset kindled through
    a cleft :
The hills, like giants at a hunting,
    lay,

Chin upon hand, to see the game at
bay, —
"Now stab and end the creature —
to the heft!"

XXXIII.

Not hear? when noise was every-
where! it tolled
Increasing like a bell. Names in
my ears
Of all the lost adventurers my
peers, —
How such a one was strong, and such
was bold,
And such was fortunate, yet each of
old
Lost, lost! one moment knelled the
woe of years.

XXXIV.

There they stood, ranged along the
hill-sides, met
To view the last of me, a living
frame
For one more picture! in a sheet of
flame
I saw them and I knew them all,
And yet
Dauntless the slug-horn to my lips I
set,
And blew "*Childe Roland to the
Dark Tower came.*"

A GRAMMARIAN'S
FUNERAL.

SHORTLY AFTER THE REVIVAL
OF LEARNING IN EUROPE.

LET us begin and carry up this corpse,
Singing together.
Leave we the common crofts, the
vulgar thorpes,
Each in its tether
Sleeping safe in the bosom of the
plain,
Cared-for till cock-crow:
Look out if yonder be not day again
Rimming the rock-row!
That's the appropriate country; there,
man's thought,
Rarer, intenser,
Self-gathered for an outbreak, as it
ought,
Chafes in the censer.

Leave we the unlettered plain its herd
and crop;
Seek we sepulture
On a tall mountain, citied to the top,
Crowded with culture!
All the peaks soar, but one the rest
excels;
Clouds overcome it;
No, yonder sparkle is the citadel's
Circling its summit.
Thither our path lies; wind we up the
heights!
Wait ye the warning?
Our low life was the level's and the
night's;
He's for the morning.
Step to a tune, square chests, erect
each head,
'Ware the beholders!
This is our master, famous, calm, and
dead,
Borne on our shoulders.

Sleep, crop and herd! sleep, darkling
thorpe and croft
Safe from the weather!
He, whom we convoy to his grave
aloft,
Singing together.
He was a man born with thy face and
throat,
Lyric Apollo!
Long he lived nameless: how should
spring take note
Winter would follow?
Till lo, the little touch, and youth
was gone!
Cramped and diminished,
Moaned he, "New measures, other
feet anon!
My dance is finished?"
No, that's the world's way; (keep the
mountain side,
Make for the city!)
He knew the signal, and stepped on
with pride
Over men's pity;
Left play for work, and grappled with
the world
Bent on escaping:
"What's in the scroll," quoth he,
"thou keepest furled?
Show me their shaping,
Theirs who most studied man, the
bard and sage, —
Give!" — So, he gowned him,
Straight got by heart that book to its
last page:
Learned, we found him.

Yea, but we found him bald too, eyes like lead,
Accents uncertain :
"Time to taste life," another would have said,
"Up with the curtain !"
This man said rather, "Actual life comes next ?
Patience a moment !
Grant I have mastered learning's crabbed text,
Still there's the comment.
Let me know all ! Prate not of most or least,
Painful or easy !
Even to the crumbs I'd fain eat up the feast,
Ay, nor feel queasy."
Oh, such a life as he resolved to live,
When he had learned it,
When he had gathered all books had to give !
Sooner, he spurned it.
Image the whole, then execute the parts —
Fancy the fabric
Quite, ere you build, ere steel strike fire from quartz,
Ere mortar dab brick !

(Here's the town-gate reached ; there's the market-place
Gaping before us.)
Yea, this in him was the peculiar grace
(Hearten our chorus !)
That before living he'd learn how to live —
No end to learning :
Earn the means first — God surely will contrive
Use for our earning.
Others mistrust and say, "But time escapes !
Live now or never !"
He said, "What's time ? Leave Now for dogs and apes !
Man has Forever."
Back to his book then : deeper drooped his head :
Calculus racked him :
Leaden before, his eyes grew dross of lead :
Tussis attacked him.
"Now, master, take a little rest !" — not he !
(Caution redoubled !
Step two abreast, the way winds narrowly !)
Not a whit troubled,

Back to his studies, fresher than at first,
Fierce as a dragon
He (soul-hydroptic with a sacred thirst)
Sucked at the flagon.
Oh, if we draw a circle premature,
Heedless of far gain,
Greedy for quick returns of profit, sure
Bad is our bargain !
Was it not great ? did not he throw on God
(He loves the burthen)—
God's task to make the heavenly period
Perfect the earthen ?
Did not he magnify the mind, show clear
Just what it all meant ?
He would not discount life, as fools do here,
Paid by instalment.
He ventured neck or nothing — heaven's success
Found, or earth's failure :
"Wilt thou trust death or not ?" He answered, "Yes !
Hence with life's pale lure !"
That low man seeks a little thing to do,
Sees it and does it :
This high man, with a great thing to pursue,
Dies ere he knows it.
That low man goes on adding one to one,
His hundred's soon hit :
This high man, aiming at a million,
Misses an unit.
That, has the world here — should he need the next,
Let the world mind him !
This, throws himself on God, and un perplexed
Seeking shall find him.
So, with the throttling hands of death at strife,
Ground he at grammar ;
Still, through the rattle, parts of speech were rife :
While he could stammer
He settled *Hoti's* business — let it be !—
Properly based *Oun* —
Gave us the doctrine of the enclitic *De*,
Dead from the waist down.

Well, here's the platform, here's the
   proper place :
      Hail to your purlieus,
All ye highfliers of the feathered race,
      Swallows and curlews !
Here's the top-peak ; the multitude
   below
      Live, for they can, there ;
This man decided not to Live but
   Know —
      Bury this man there ?
Here — here's his place, where mete-
   ors shoot, clouds form,
      Lightnings are loosened,
Stars come and go ! Let joy break
   with the storm,
      Peace let the dew send !
Lofty designs must close in like ef-
   fects ;
      Loftily lying.
Leave him — still loftier than the
   world suspects,
      Living and dying.

CLEON.

" As certain also of your own poets have
said " —

CLEON the poet (from the sprinkled
   isles,
Lily on lily, that o'erlace the sea,
And laugh their pride when the light
      wave lisps " Greece "), —
To Protus in his Tyranny : much
   health !

   They give thy letter to me, even
   now :
I read and seem as if I heard thee
   speak.
The master of thy galley still unlades
Gift after gift ; they block my court
   at last
And pile themselves along its portico
Royal with sunset, like a thought of
   thee ;
And one white she-slave, from the
   group dispersed
Of black and white slaves (like the
   checker-work
Pavement, at once my nation's work
   and gift,
Now covered with this settle-down of
   doves)

One lyric woman, in her crocus vest
Woven of sea-wools, with her two
      white hands
Commends to me the strainer and the
   cup
Thy lip hath bettered ere it blesses
   mine.

   Well counselled, king, in thy mu-
   nificence !
For so shall men remark, in such an
   act
Of love for him whose song gives life
      its joy,
Thy recognition of the use of life ;
Nor call thy spirit barely adequate
To help on life in straight ways, broad
   enough
For vulgar souls, by ruling and the
   rest.
Thou, in the daily building of thy
   tower, —
Whether in fierce and sudden spasms
   of toil,
Or through dim lulls of unapparent
   growth,
Or when the general work, 'mid good
   acclaim,
Climbed with the eye to cheer the
   architect, —
Didst ne'er engage in work for mere
   work's sake ;
Hadst ever in thy heart the luring
   hope
Of some eventual rest a-top of it,
Whence, all the tumult of the build-
   ing hushed,
Thou first of men mightst look out to
   the East :
The vulgar saw thy tower, thou saw-
   est the sun.
For this, I promise on thy festival
To pour libation, looking o'er the sea,
Making this slave narrate thy for-
   tunes, speak
Thy great words, and describe thy
   royal face —
Wishing thee wholly where Zeus lives
   the most,
Within the eventual element of calm.

   Thy letter's first requirement meets
   me here.
It is as thou hast heard : in one short
   life
I, Cleon, have effected all those things
Thou wonderingly dost enumerate.
That epos on thy hundred plates of
   gold

Is mine, and also mine the little chant
So sure to rise from every fishing-
  bark
When, lights at prow, the seamen
  haul their net.
The image of the sun-god on the
  phare,
Men turn from the sun's self to see, is
  mine ;
The Pœcile, o'er-storied its whole
  length,
As thou didst hear, with painting, is
  mine too.
I know the true proportions of a man
And woman also, not observed before;
And I have written three books on
  the soul,
Proving absurd all written hitherto,
And putting us to ignorance again.
For music, — why, I have combined
  the moods,
Inventing one. In brief, all arts are
  mine ;
Thus much the people know and rec-
  ognize,
Throughout our seventeen islands.
  Marvel not !
We of these latter days, with greater
  mind
Than our forerunners, since more
  composite,
Look not so great, beside their simple
  way,
To a judge who only sees one way at
  once,
One mind-point and no other at a
  time, —
Compares the small part of a man of
  us
With some whole man of the heroic
  age,
Great in his way — not ours, nor
  meant for ours.
And ours is greater, had we skill to
  know :
For, what we call this life of men on
  earth,
This sequence of the soul's achieve-
  ments here,
Being, as I find much reason to con-
  ceive,
Intended to be viewed eventually
As a great whole, not analyzed to
  parts,
But each part having reference to
  all, —
How shall a certain part, pronounced
  complete,
Endure effacement by another part ?

Was the thing done ? — then, what's
  to do again ?
See, in the checkered pavement oppo-
  site,
Suppose the artist made a perfect
  rhomb,
And next a lozenge, then a trape-
  zoid —
He did not overlay them, superim-
  pose
The new upon the old and blot it out,
But laid them on a level in his work,
Making at last a picture ; there it
  lies.
So first the perfect separate forms
  were made,
The portions of mankind ; and after,
  so,
Occurred the combination of the
  same.
For where had been a progress, other-
  wise ?
Mankind, made up of all the single
  men, —
In such a synthesis the labor ends.
Now mark me ! those divine men of
  old time
Have reached, thou sayest well, each
  at one point
The outside verge that rounds our
  faculty ;
And where they reached, who can do
  more than reach ?
It takes but little water just to touch
At some one point the inside of a
  sphere,
And, as we turn the sphere, touch all
  the rest
In due succession : but the finer air
Which not so palpably nor obviously,
Though no less universally, can touch
The whole circumference of that
  emptied sphere,
Fills it more fully than the water
  did ;
Holds thrice the weight of water in
  itself
Resolved into a subtler element.
And yet the vulgar call the sphere
  first full
Up to the visible height — and after,
  void ;
Not knowing air's more hidden prop-
  erties.
And thus our soul, misknown, cries
  out to Zeus
To vindicate his purpose in our life :
Why stay we on the earth unless to
  grow ?

Long since, I imaged, wrote the fic-
tion out,
That he or other god descended here
And, once for all, showed simultane-
ously
What, in its nature, never can be
shown
Piecemeal or in succession ; showed,
I say,
The worth both absolute and relative
Of all his children from the birth of
time,
His instruments for all appointed
work.
I now go on to image, - might we
hear
The judgment which should give the
due to each,
Show where the labor lay and where
the ease,
And prove Zeus' self, the latent
everywhere !
This is a dream : — but no dream, let
us hope,
That years and days, the summers
and the springs,
Follow each other with unwaning
powers.
The grapes which dye thy wine, are
richer far
Through culture, than the wild wealth
of the rock ;
The suave plum than the savage-
tasted drupe ;
The pastured honey-bee drops choicer
sweet ;
The flowers turn double, and the
leaves turn flowers ;
That young and tender crescent
moon, thy slave,
Sleeping upon her robe as if on
clouds,
Refines upon the women of my youth
What, and the soul alone deteriorates ?
I have not chanted verse like Homer,
no —
Nor swept string like Terpander, no —
nor carved
And painted men like Phidias and
his friend :
I am not great as they are, point by
point.
But I have entered into sympathy
With these four, running these into
one soul,
Who, separate, ignored each others'
arts.
Say, is it nothing that I know them
all ?

The wild-flower was the larger ; I
have dashed
Rose-blood upon its petals, pricked
its cup's
Honey with wine, and driven its seed
to fruit,
And show a better flower if not so
large .
I stand myself. Refer this to the
gods
Whose gift alone it is ! which shall I
dare
(All pride apart) upon the absurd
pretext
That such a gift by chance lay in my
hand,
Discourse of lightly or depreciate ?
It might have fallen to another's
hand : what then ?
I pass too surely ; let at least truth
stay !

And next, of what thou followest
on to ask.
This being with me, as I declare, O
king !
My works in all these varicolored
kinds,
So done by me, accepted so by men —
Thou askest, if (my soul thus in men's
hearts)
I must not be accounted to attain
The very crown and proper end of
life ?
Inquiring thence how, now life closeth
up,
I face death with success in my right
hand .
Whether I fear death less than dost
thyself
The fortunate of men ?   "For"
(writest thou),
"Thou leavest much behind, while I
leave naught.
Thy life stays in the poems men shall
sing,
The pictures men shall study ; while
my life,
Complete and whole now in its power
and joy,
Dies altogether with my brain and
arm,
Is lost indeed ; since, what survives
myself ?
The brazen statue to o'erlook my
grave,
Set on the promontory which I named,
And that — some supple courtier of
my heir

Shall use its robed and sceptred arm, perhaps
To fix the rope to, which best drags it down.
I go then : triumph thou, who dost not go ! "

Nay, thou art worthy of hearing my whole mind.
Is this apparent, when thou turn'st to muse
Upon the scheme of earth and man in chief,
That admiration grows as knowledge grows ?
That imperfection means perfection hid,
Reserved in part, to grace the after-time ?
If, in the morning of philosophy,
Ere aught had been recorded, nay perceived,
Thou, with the light now in thee, couldst have looked
On all earth's tenantry, from worm to bird,
Ere man, her last, appeared upon the stage —
Thou wouldst have seen them perfect, and deduced
The perfectness of others yet unseen.
Conceding which, — had Zeus then questioned thee
" Shall I go on a step, improve on this,
Do more for visible creatures than is done ? "
Thou wouldst have answered, " Ay, by making each
Grow conscious in himself — by that alone.
All's perfect else : the shell sucks fast the rock,
The fish strikes through the sea, the snake both swims
And slides, forth range the beasts, the birds take flight,
Till life's mechanics can no farther go —
And all this joy in natural life, is put,
Like fire from off thy finger into each,
So exquisitely perfect is the same.
But 'tis pure fire, and they mere matter are :
It has them, not they it ; and so I choose
For man, thy last premeditated work
(If I might add a glory to the scheme)

That a third thing should stand apart from both,
A quality arise within his soul,
Which, intro-active, made to supervise
And feel the force it has, may view itself,
And so be happy." Man might live at first
The animal life : but is there nothing more ?
In due time, let him critically learn
How he lives ; and, the more he gets to know
Of his own life's adaptabilities,
The more joy-giving will his life become.
Thus man, who hath this quality, is best.

But thou, king, hadst more reasonably said :
" Let progress end at once, — man make no step
Beyond the natural man, the better beast,
Using his senses, not the sense of sense ! "
In man there's failure, only since he left
The lower and inconscious forms of life.
We called it an advance, the rendering plain
Man's spirit might grow conscious of man's life,
And, by new lore so added to the old,
Take each step higher over the brute's head.
This grew the only life, the pleasure-house,
Watch-tower and treasure-fortress of the soul,
Which whole surrounding flats of natural life
Seemed only fit to yield subsistence to ;
A tower that crowns a country. But alas,
The soul now climbs it just to perish there !
For thence we have discovered ('tis no dream —
We know this, which we had not else perceived)
That there's a world of capability
For joy, spread round about us, meant for us.

Inviting us ; and still the soul craves all,
And still the flesh replies, " Take no jot more
Than ere thou clombst the tower to look abroad !
Nay, so much less as that fatigue has brought
Deduction to it." We struggle, fain to enlarge
Our bounded physical recipiency,
Increase our power, supply fresh oil to life,
Repair the waste of age and sickness ; no,
It skills not ! life's inadequate to joy,
As the soul sees joy, tempting life to take.
They praise a fountain in my garden here
Wherein a Naiad sends the water-bow
Thin from her tube : she smiles to see it rise.
What if I told her, it is just a thread
From that great river which the hills shut up,
And mock her with my leave to take the same ?
The artificer has given her one small tube
Past power to widen or exchange — what boots
To know she might spout oceans if she could ?
She cannot lift beyond her first thin thread :
And so a man can use but a man's joy
While he sees God's. Is it for Zeus to boast.
" See, man, how happy I live, and despair —
That I may be still happier — for thy use ! "
If this were so, we could not thank our lord,
As hearts beat on to doing : 'tis not so —
Malice it is not. Is it carelessness ?
Still, no. If care — where is the sign ? I ask,
And get no answer, and agree in sum,
O king ! with thy profound discouragement,
Who seest the wider but to sigh the more.
Most progress is most failure : thou sayest well.

The last point now. Thou dost except a case —
Holding joy not impossible to one
With artist-gifts — to such a man as I
Who leave behind me living works indeed ;
For, such a poem, such a painting lives.
What ? dost thou verily trip upon a word,
Confound the accurate view of what joy is
(Caught somewhat clearer by my eyes than thine)
With feeling joy ? confound the knowing how
And showing how to live (my faculty)
With actually living ? — Otherwise
Where is the artist's vantage o'er the king ?
Because in my great epos I display
How divers men young, strong, fair, wise, can act —
Is this as though I acted ? if I paint,
Carve the young Phœbus, am I therefore young ?
Methinks I'm older that I bowed myself
The many years of pain that taught me art !
Indeed, to know is something, and to prove
How all this beauty might be enjoyed, is more :
But, knowing naught, to enjoy is something too.
You rower, with the moulded muscles there,
Lowering the sail, is nearer it than I.
I can write love-odes : thy fair slave's an ode.
I get to sing of love, when grown too gray
For being beloved ; she turns to that young man,
The muscles all a-ripple on his back.
I know the joy of kingship : well, thou art king !
" But," sayest thou — (and I marvel, I repeat,
To find thee tripping on a mere word) " what
Thou writest, paintest, stays ; that does not die.
Sappho survives, because we sing her songs,
And Æschylus, because we read his plays ! "

Why, if they live still, let them come
   and take
Thy slave in my despite, drink from
   thy cup,
Speak in my place. Thou diest while
   I survive?
Say rather that my fate is deadlier
   still,
In this, that every day my sense of
   joy
Grows more acute, my soul (intensi-
   fied
By power and insight) more enlarged,
   more keen;
While every day my hair falls more
   and more,
My hand shakes, and the heavy years
   increase —
The horror quickening still from year
   to year,
The consummation coming past es-
   cape,
When I shall know most, and yet
   least enjoy —
When all my works wherein I prove
   my worth,
Being present still to mock me in
   men's mouths,
Alive still, in the phrase of such as
   thou,
I, I the feeling, thinking, acting
   man,
The man who loved his life so over-
   much,
Shall sleep in my urn. It is so hor-
   rible,
I dare at times imagine to my need
Some future state revealed to us by
   Zeus,
Unlimited in capability
For joy, as this is in desire for joy,
—To seek which, the joy-hunger
   forces us :
That, stung by straitness of our life,
   made strait
On purpose to make prized the life at
   large —
Freed by the throbbing impulse we
   call death,
We burst there, as the worm into the
   fly,
Who, while a worm still, wants his
   wings. But no !
Zeus has not yet revealed it ; and alas,
He must have done so, were it possi-
   ble !

   Live long and happy, and in that
     thought die,

Glad for what was ! Farewell. And
   for the rest,
I cannot tell thy messenger aright
Where to deliver what he bears of
   thine
To one called Paulus ; we have heard
   his fame
Indeed, if Christus be not one with
   him —
I know not, nor am I troubled much to
   know.
Thou canst not think a mere barbarian
   Jew
As Paulus proves to be, one circum-
   cised,
Hath access to a secret shut from us ?
Thou wrongest our philosophy, O
   king,
In stooping to inquire of such an
   one,
As if his answer could impose at all !
He writeth, doth he ? well, and he
   may write.
Oh, the Jew findeth scholars ! certain
   slaves
Who touched on this same isle,
   preached him and Christ ;
And (as I gathered from a by-stander)
Their doctrine could be held by no
   sane man.

INSTANS TYRANNUS.

I.

Of the million or two, more or less,
I rule and possess,
One man, for some cause undefined,
Was least to my mind.

II.

I struck him, he grovelled of course —
For, what was his force ?
I pinned him to earth with my weight
And persistence of hate ;
And he lay, would not moan, would
   not curse,
As his lot might be worse.

III.

" Were the object less mean, would
   he stand
At the swing of my hand !
For obscurity helps him, and blots
The hole where he squats."

So, I set my five wits on the stretch
To inveigle the wretch.
All in vain! Gold and jewels I
    threw,
Still he couched there perdue;
I tempted his blood and his flesh,
Hid in roses my mesh,
Choicest cates and the flagon's best
    spilth:
Still he kept to his filth.

IV.

Had he kith now or kin, were access
To his heart, did I press:
Just a son or a mother to seize!
No such booty as these.
Were it simply a friend to pursue
'Mid my million or two,
Who could pay me, in person or pelf,
What he owes me himself!
No: I could not but smile through
    my chafe:
For the fellow lay safe
As his mates do, the midge and the
    nit,
— Through minuteness, to wit.

V.

Then a humor more great took its
    place
At the thought of his face:
The droop, the low cares of the
    mouth,
The trouble uncouth
'Twixt the brows, all that air one is
    fain
To put out of its pain.
And, "no!" I admonished myself,
"Is one mocked by an elf,
Is one baffled by toad or by rat?
The gravamen's in that!
How the lion, who crouches to suit
His back to my foot,
Would admire that I stand in debate!
But the small turns the great
If it vexes you, — that is the thing!
Toad or rat vex the king?
Though I waste half my realm to
    unearth
Toad or rat, 'tis well worth!"

VI.

So, I soberly laid my last plan
To extinguish the man.
Round his creep-hole, with never a
    break,
Ran my fires for his sake;

Over-head, did my thunder combine
With my under-ground mine:
Till I looked from my labor content
To enjoy the event

VII.

When sudden . . . how think ye, the
    end?
Did I say "without friend"?
Say rather, from marge to blue marge
The whole sky grew his targe
With the sun's self for visible boss,
While an Arm ran across,
Which the earth heaved beneath like
    a breast,
Where the wretch was safe prest!
Do you see? Just my vengeance
    complete,
The man sprang to his feet,
Stood erect, caught at God's skirts,
    and prayed!
— So, I was afraid!

AN EPISTLE

CONTAINING THE STRANGE MEDI-
CAL EXPERIENCE OF KARSHISH,
THE ARAB PHYSICIAN.

KARSHISH, the picker-up of learning's
    crumbs,
The not-incurious in God's handi-
    work
(This man's-flesh he hath admirably
    made,
Blown like a bubble, kneaded like a
    paste,
To coop up and keep down on earth
    a space
That puff of vapor from his mouth,
    man's soul)
— To Abib, all-sagacious in our art,
Breeder in me of what poor skill I
    boast,
Like me inquisitive how pricks and
    cracks
Befall the flesh through too much
    stress and strain,
Whereby the wily vapor fain would
    slip
Back and rejoin its source before the
    term, —
And aptest in contrivance (under
    God)

To baffle it by deftly stopping such : —
The vagrant Scholar to his Sage at
    home
Sends greeting (health and knowl-
    edge, fame with peace)
Three samples of true snake-stone —
    rarer still,
One of the other sort, the melon-
    shaped
(But fitter, pounded fine, for charms
    than drugs),
And writeth now the twenty-second
    time.

My journeyings were brought to
    Jericho :
Thus I resume. Who, studious in
    our art,
Shall count a little labor unrepaid ?
I have shed sweat enough, left flesh
    and bone
On many a flinty furlong of this land.
Also, the country-side is all on fire
With rumors of a marching hither-
    ward.
Some say Vespasian cometh, some,
    his son.
A black lynx snarled and pricked a
    tufted ear ;
Lust of my blood inflamed his yellow
    balls :
I cried and threw my staff, and he
    was gone.
Twice have the robbers stripped and
    beaten me,
And once a town declared me for a
    spy ;
But at the end, I reach Jerusalem,
Since this poor covert where I pass
    the night,
This Bethany, lies scarce the distance
    thence
A man with plague-sores at the third
    degree
Runs till he drops down dead. Thou
    laughest here !
'Sooth, it elates me, thus reposed and
    safe,
To void the stuffing of my travel-
    scrip,
And share with thee whatever Jewry
    yields.
A viscid choler is observable
In tertians, I was nearly bold to
    say ;
And falling-sickness hath a happier
    cure
Than our school wots of : there's a
    spider here

Weaves no web, watches on the ledge
    of tombs,
Sprinkled with mottles on an ash-
    gray back ;
Take five and drop them . . . but
    who knows his mind,
The Syrian runagate I trust this to?
His service payeth me a sublimate
Blown up his nose to help the ailing
    eye.
Best wait : I reach Jerusalem at morn,
There set in order my experiences,
Gather what most deserves, and give
    thee all —
Or I might add, Judæa's gum-traga-
    canth
Scales off in purer flakes, shines
    clearer-grained,
Cracks 'twixt the pestle and the por-
    phyry,
In fine exceeds our produce. Scalp-
    disease
Confounds me, crossing so with lep-
    rosy :
Thou hadst admired one sort I gained
    at Zoar —
But zeal outruns discretion. Here I
    end.

Yet stay ! my Syrian blinketh grate-
    fully,
Protesteth his devotion is my price —
Suppose I write what harms not,
    though he steal ?
I half resolve to tell thee, yet I blush,
What set me off a-writing first of
    all.
An itch I had, a sting to write, a
    tang !
For, be it this town's barrenness, —
    or else
The Man had something in the look
    of him, —
His case has struck me far more than
    'tis worth.
So, pardon if — (lest presently I lose,
In the great press of novelty at hand,
The care and pains this somehow
    stole from me)
I bid thee take the thing while fresh
    in mind,
Almost in sight — for, wilt thou have
    the truth ?
The very man is gone from me but
    now,
Whose ailment is the subject of dis-
    course.
Thus then, and let thy better wit
    help all !

"A black lynx snarled and pricked a tufted ear." — Page 110.

'Tis but a case of mania: sub-
  induced
By epilepsy, at the turning-point
Of trance prolonged unduly some
  three days
When, by the exhibition of some drug
Or spell, exorcization, stroke of art
Unknown to me and which 'twere
  well to know,
The evil thing, out-breaking, all at
  once,
Left the man whole and sound of body
  indeed, —
But, flinging (so to speak) life's gates
  too wide,
Making a clear house of it too sud-
  denly,
The first conceit that entered might
  inscribe
Whatever it was minded on the wall
So plainly at that vantage, as it were
(First come, first served), that nothing
  subsequent
Attaineth to erase those fancy-scrawls
The just-returned and new-established
  soul
Hath gotten now so thoroughly by
  heart
That henceforth she will read or these
  or none.
And first — the man's own firm con-
  viction rests
That he was dead (in fact they buried
  him)
— That he was dead and then restored
  to life
By a Nazarene physician of his tribe:
— 'Sayeth, the same bade " Rise," and
  he did rise.
" Such cases are diurnal," thou wilt
  cry.
Not so this figment! — not, that such
  a fume,
Instead of giving way to time and
  health,
Should eat itself into the life of life,
As saffron tingeth flesh, blood, bones,
  and all!
For see, how he takes up the after-
  life.
The man — it is one Lazarus a Jew,
Sanguine, proportioned, fifty years of
  age,
The body's habit wholly laudable,
As much, indeed, beyond the common
  health
As he were made and put aside to
  show.
Think, could we penetrate by any drug

And bathe the wearied soul and wor-
  ried flesh,
And bring it clear and fair, by three
  days' sleep!
Whence has the man the balm that
  brightens all ?
This grown man eyes the world now
  like a child.
Some elders of his tribe, I should pre-
  mise,
Led in their friend, obedient as a
  sheep,
To bear my inquisition. While they
  spoke,
Now sharply, now with sorrow, — told
  the case, —
He listened not except I spoke to
  him,
But folded his two hands and let
  them talk,
Watching the flies that buzzed: and
  yet no fool.
And that's a sample how his years
  must go.
Look if a beggar, in fixed middle-life,
Should find a treasure, — can he use
  the same
With straitened habitude and tastes
  starved small,
And take at once to his impoverished
  brain
The sudden element that changes
  things,
That sets the undreamed-of rapture
  at his hand,
And puts the cheap old joy in the
  scorned dust?
Is he not such an one as moves to
  mirth —
Warily parsimonious, when no need,
Wasteful as drunkenness at undue
  times?
All prudent counsel as to what befits
The golden mean, is lost on such an
  one :
The man's fantastic will is the man's
  law.
So here — we call the treasure knowl-
  edge, say,
Increased beyond the fleshly facul-
  ty —
Heaven opened to a soul while yet on
  earth,
Earth forced on a soul's use while
  seeing heaven :
The man is witless of the size, the
  sum,
The value in proportion of all things,
Or whether it be little or be much.

Discourse to him of prodigious arma-
 ments
Assembled to besiege his city now,
And of the passing of a mule with
 gourds —
'Tis one! Then take it on the other
 side,
Speak of some trifling fact, — he will
 gaze rapt
With stupor at its very littleness
(Far as I see), as if in that indeed
He caught prodigious import, whole
 results ;
And so will turn to us the by-standers
In ever the same stupor (note this
 point),
That we, too, see not with his opened
 eyes.
Wonder and doubt come wrongly into
 play,
Preposterously, at cross purposes.
Should his child sicken unto death, —
 why, look
For scarce abatement of his cheerful-
 ness,
Or pretermission of the daily craft !
While a word, gesture, glance from
 that same child
At play or in the school or laid
 asleep,
Will startle him to an agony of fear,
Exasperation, just as like. Demand
The reason why — "'tis but a word,"
 object —
"A gesture " — he regards thee as our
 lord
Who lived there in the pyramid alone,
Looked at us (dost thou mind ?) when,
 being young,
We both would unadvisedly recite
Some charm's beginning, from that
 book of his,
Able to bid the sun throb wide and
 burst
All into stars, as suns grown old are
 wont.
Thou and the child have each a veil
 alike
Thrown o'er your heads, from under
 which ye both
Stretch your blind hands and trifle
 with a match
Over a mine of Greek fire, did ye
 know !
He holds on firmly to some thread of
 life —
(It is the life to lead perforcedly)
Which runs across some vast, distract-
 ing orb

Of glory on either side that meagre
 thread,
Which, conscious of, he must not enter
 yet —
The spiritual life around the earthly
 life :
The law of that is known to him as
 this,
His heart and brain move there, his
 feet stay here.
So is the man perplext with impulses
Sudden to start off crosswise, not
 straight on,
Proclaiming what is right and wrong
 across,
And not along, this black thread
 through the blaze —
"It should be" balked by " here it
 cannot be."
And oft the man's soul springs into
 his face
As if he saw again and heard again
His sage that bade him " Rise," and
 he did rise,
Something, a word, a tick o' the blood
 within
Admonishes : then back he sinks at
 once
To ashes, who was very fire before,
In sedulous recurrence to his trade
Whereby he earneth him the daily
 bread ;
And studiously the humbler for that
 pride,
Professedly the faultier that he knows
God's secret, while he holds the thread
 of life.
Indeed the especial marking of the
 man
Is prone submission to the heavenly
 will —
Seeing it, what it is, and why it is.
'Sayeth, he will wait patient to the
 last
For that same death which must re-
 store his being
To equilibrium, body loosening soul
Divorced even now by premature full
 growth ;
He will live, nay, it pleaseth him to
 live
So long as God please, and just how
 God please.
He even seeketh not to please God
 more
(Which meaneth, otherwise) than as
 God please.
Hence, I perceive not he affects to
 preach

The doctrine of his sect whate'er it be,
Make proselytes as madmen thirst to do:
How can he give his neighbor the real ground,
His own conviction? Ardent as he is —
Call his great truth a lie, why, still the old
"Be it as God please" re-assureth him.
I probed the sore as thy disciple should;
"How, beast," said I, "this stolid carelessness
Sufficeth thee, when Rome is on her march
To stamp out like a little spark thy town,
Thy tribe, thy crazy tale and thee at once?"
He merely looked with his large eyes on me.
The man is apathetic, you deduce?
Contrariwise, he loves both old and young,
Able and weak, affects the very brutes
And birds — how say I? flowers of the field —
As a wise workman recognizes tools
In a master's workshop, loving what they make,
Thus is the man as harmless as a lamb:
Only impatient, let him do his best,
At ignorance and carelessness and sin —
An indignation which is promptly curbed:
As when in certain travel I have feigned
To be an ignoramus in our art
According to some preconceived design,
And happened to hear the land's practitioners
Steeped in conceit sublimed by ignorance,
Prattle fantastically on disease,
Its cause and cure — and I must hold my peace!

Thou wilt object — Why have I not ere this
Sought out the sage himself, the Nazarene
Who wrought this cure, inquiring at the source.

Conferring with the frankness that befits?
Alas! it grieveth me, the learned leech
Perished in a tumult many years ago,
Accused, — our learning's fate, — of wizardry,
Rebellion, to the setting up a rule
And creed prodigious as described to me.
His death, which happened when the earthquake fell
(Prefiguring, as soon appeared, the loss
To occult learning in our lord the sage
Who lived there in the pyramid alone),
Was wrought by the mad people — that's their wont!
On vain recourse, as I conjecture it,
To his tried virtue, for miraculous help —
How could he stop the earthquake? That's their way!
The other imputations must be lies:
But take one, though I loath to give it thee,
In mere respect for any good man's fame.
And after all, our patient Lazarus
Is stark mad; should we count on what he says?
Perhaps not: though in writing to a leech
'Tis well to keep back nothing of a case.)
This man so cured regards the curer, then,
As — God forgive me! who but God himself,
Creator and sustainer of the world,
That came and dwelt in flesh on it a while!
— 'Sayeth that such an one was born and lived,
Taught, healed the sick, broke bread at his own house,
Then died, with Lazarus by, for aught I know,
And yet was . . . what I said nor choose repeat,
And must have so avouched himself, in fact,
In hearing of this very Lazarus
Who saith — but why all this of what he saith?
Why write of trivial matters, things of price

Calling at every moment for remark?
I noticed on the margin of a pool
Blue-flowering borage, the Aleppo
   sort,
Aboundeth, very nitrous. It is
   strange!

Thy pardon for this long and tedious
   case,
Which, now that I review it, needs
   must seem
Unduly dwelt on, prolixly set forth!
Nor I myself discern in what is
   writ
Good cause for the peculiar interest
And awe indeed this man has touched
   me with.
Perhaps the journey's end, the weari-
   ness
Had wrought upon me first. I met
   him thus:
I crossed a ridge of short sharp broken
   hills
Like an old lion's cheek teeth. Out
   there came
A moon made like a face with certain
   spots
Multiform, manifold, and menacing:
Then a wind rose behind me. So we
   met
In this old sleepy town at unaware,
The man and I. I send thee what is
   writ.
Regard it as a chance, a matter risked
To this ambiguous Syrian: he may
   lose,
Or steal, or give it thee with equal
   good.
Jerusalem's repose shall make
   amends
For time this letter wastes, thy time
   and mine;
Till when, once more thy pardon and
   farewell!

The very God! think, Abib; dost
   thou think?
So, the All-Great, were the All-Loving
   too—
So, through the thunder comes a hu-
   man voice
Saying, "O heart I made, a heart beats
   here!
Face, my hands fashioned, see it in
   myself!
Thou hast no power nor may'st con-
   ceive of mine:
But love I gave thee, with myself to
   love,

And thou must love me who have
   died for thee!"
The madman saith He said so: it is
   strange.

CALIBAN UPON SETEBOS;

OR, NATURAL THEOLOGY IN THE ISLAND.

"*Thou thoughtest that I was altogether such a one as thyself.*"

['WILL sprawl], now that the heat of
   day is best,
Flat on his belly in the pit's much
   mire,
With elbows wide, fists clinched to
   prop his chin.
And, while he kicks both feet in the
   cool slush,
And feels about his spine small eft-
   things course,
Run in and out each arm, and make
   him laugh:
And while above his head a pompion-
   plant,
Coating the cave-top as a brow its
   eye,
Creeps down to touch and tickle hair
   and beard,
And now a flower drops with a bee
   inside,
And now a fruit to snap at, catch and
   crunch,—
He looks out o'er yon sea which sun-
   beams cross
And recross till they weave a spider-
   web
(Meshes of fire, some great fish breaks
   at times),
And talks to his own self, howe'er he
   please,
Touching that other, whom his dam
   called God.
Because to talk about Him, vexes
   —ha,
Could He but know! and time to vex
   is now,
When talk is safer than in winter-
   time.
Moreover Prosper and Miranda sleep
In confidence he drudges at their
   task:

And it is good to cheat the pair, and
   gibe,
Letting the rank tongue blossom into
   speech.]

Setebos, Setebos, and Setebos!
'Thinketh, He dwelleth i' the cold o'
   the moon.

'Thinketh He made it, with the sun to
   match,
But not the stars; the stars came
   otherwise;
Only made clouds, winds, meteors,
   such as that:
Also this isle, what lives and grows
   thereon,
And snaky sea which rounds and
   ends the same.

'Thinketh, it came of being ill at
   ease:
He hated that He cannot change His
   cold,
Nor cure its ache. 'Hath spied an icy
   fish
That longed to 'scape the rock-stream
   where she lived,
And thaw herself within the luke-
   warm brine
O' the lazy sea, her stream thrusts far
   amid,
A crystal spike 'twixt two warm
   walls of wave;
Only, she ever sickened, found re-
   pulse
At the other kind of water, not her
   life
(Green-dense and dim-delicious, bred
   o' the sun),
Flounced back from bliss she was not
   born to breathe,
And in her old bounds buried her
   despair,
Hating and loving warmth alike; so
   He.

'Thinketh, He made thereat the sun,
   this isle,
Trees and the fowls here, beast and
   creeping thing.
Yon otter, sleek-wet, black, lithe as a
   leech;
Yon auk, one fire-eye in a ball of
   foam,
That floats and feeds; a certain bad-
   ger brown,
He hath watched hunt with that
   slant white-wedge eye

By moonlight; and the pie with the
   long tongue
That pricks deep into oakwarts for a
   worm,
And says a plain word when she finds
   her prize,
But will not eat the ants; the ants
   themselves
That build a wall of seeds and settled
   stalks
About their hole — He made all these
   and more,
Made all we see, and us, in spite:
   how else?
He could not, Himself, make a second
   self
To be His mate; as well have made
   Himself:
He would not make what He mislikes
   or slights,
An eyesore to Him, or not worth His
   pains;
But did, in envy, listlessness, or sport,
Make what Himself would fain, in a
   manner, be —
Weaker in most points, stronger in a
   few,
Worthy, and yet mere playthings all
   the while,
Things He admires and mocks too, —
   that is it.
Because, so brave, so better though
   they be,
It nothing skills if He begin to plague.
Look now, I melt a gourd-fruit into
   mash,
Add honeycomb and pods, I have
   perceived,
Which bite the finches when they
   bill and kiss, —
Then, when froth rises bladdery,
   drink up all,
Quick, quick, till maggots scamper
   through my brain;
Last, throw me on my back i' the
   seeded thyme,
And wanton, wishing I were born a
   bird.
Put case, unable to be what I wish,
I yet could make a live bird out of
   clay:
Would not I take clay, pinch my
   Caliban
Able to fly? — for, there, see, he hath
   wings,
And great comb like the hoopoe's to
   admire,
And there, a sting to do his foes of-
   fence,

There, and I will that he begin to
      live,
Fly to yon rock-top, nip me off the
      horns
Of grigs high up that make the
      merry din
Saucy through their veined wings,
      and mind me not.
In which feat, if his leg snapped,
      brittle clay,
And he lay stupid-like, — why, I
      should laugh ;
And if he, spying me, should fall to
      weep,
Beseech me to be good, repair his
      wrong,
Bid his poor leg smart less or grow
      again, —
Well, as the chance were, this might
      take or else
Not take my fancy : I might hear his
      cry,
And give the manikin three legs for
      one,
Or pluck the other off, leave him like
      an egg,
And lessoned he was mine and merely
      clay.
Were this no pleasure, lying in the
      thyme,
Drinking the mash, with brain be-
      come alive,
Making and marring clay at will ?
      So He.

'Thinketh, such shows nor right nor
      wrong in Him,
Nor kind, nor cruel : He is strong and
      Lord.
'Am strong myself compared to yon-
      der crabs
That march now from the mountain
      to the sea ;
'Let twenty pass, and stone the
      twenty-first,
Loving not, hating not, just choosing
      so.
'Say, the first straggler that boasts
      purple spots
Shall join the file, one pincer twisted
      off ;
'Say, This bruised fellow shall receive
      a worm,
And two worms he whose nippers
      end in red
As it likes me each time, I do : so He.

Well then, 'supposeth He is good i'
      the main,

Placable if His mind and ways were
      guessed,
But rougher than His handiwork, be
      sure !
Oh, He hath made things worthier
      than Himself,
And envieth that, so helped, such
      things do more
Than He who made them ! What
      consoles but this ?
That they, unless through Him, do
      naught at all,
And must submit : what other use in
      things ?
'Hath cut a pipe of pithless elder-
      joint
That, blown through, gives exact the
      scream o' the jay
When from her wing you twitch the
      feathers blue :
Sound this, and little birds that hate
      the jay
Flock within stone's throw, glad their
      foe is hurt :
Put case such pipe could prattle and
      boast forsooth
" I catch the birds, I am the crafty
      thing,
I make the cry my maker cannot
      make
With his great round mouth ; he must
      blow through mine ! "
Would not I smash it with my foot ?
      So He.

But wherefore rough, why cold and
      ill at ease ?
Aha, that is a question ! Ask, for
      that,
What knows, — the something over
      Setebos
That made Him, or He, may be, found
      and fought,
Worsted, drove off and did to noth-
      ing, perchance.
There may be something quiet o'er
      His head,
Out of His reach, that feels nor joy
      nor grief,
Since both derive from weakness in
      some way.
I joy because the quails come ; would
      not joy
Could I bring quails here when I have
      a mind :
This Quiet, all it hath a mind to,
      doth.
'Esteemeth stars the outposts of its
      couch,

But never spends much thought nor
  care that way.
It may look up, work up, — the worse
  for those
It works on! 'Careth but for Sete-
  bos
The many-handed as a cuttle-fish,
Who, making Himself feared through
  what He does,
Looks up, first, and perceives he can-
  not soar
To what is quiet and hath happy life;
Next looks down here, and out of
  very spite
Makes this a bauble-world to ape yon
  real,
These good things to match those, as
  his do grapes.
'Tis solace making baubles, ay, and
  sport.
Himself peeped late, eyed Prosper at
  his books
Careless and lofty, lord now of the
  isle:
Vexed, 'stitched a book of broad
  leaves, arrow-shaped,
Wrote thereon, he knows what, pro-
  digious words;
Has peeled a wand and called it by a
  name;
Weareth at whiles for an enchanter's
  robe
The eyed skin of a supple ocelot;
And hath an ounce sleeker than
  youngling mole,
A four-legged serpent he makes cower
  and couch,
Now snarl, now hold its breath and
  mind his eye,
And saith she is Miranda and my
  wife;
'Keeps for his Ariel a tall pouch-bill
  crane
He bids go wade for fish and straight
  disgorge;
Also a sea-beast, lumpish, which he
  snared,
Blinded the eyes of, and brought
  somewhat tame,
And split its toe-webs, and now pens
  the drudge
In a hole o' the rock, and calls him
  Caliban;
A bitter heart that bides its time and
  bites.
'Plays thus at being Prosper in a
  way,
Taketh his mirth with make-believes:
  so He.

His dam held that the Quiet made all
  things
Which Setebos vexed only: 'holds
  not so.
Who made them weak, meant weak-
  ness He might vex.
Had He meant other, while His hand
  was in,
Why not make horny eyes no thorn
  could prick,
Or plate my scalp with bone against
  the snow,
Or overscale my flesh 'neath joint and
  joint,
Like an orc's armor? Ay, — so spoil
  His sport!
He is the One now: only He doth all.

'Saith, He may like, perchance, what
  profits Him.
Ay, himself loves what does him
  good; but why?
'Gets good no otherwise. This blinded
  beast
Loves whoso places flesh-meat on his
  nose,
But, had he eyes, would want no
  help, would hate
Or love, just as it liked him: He hath
  eyes.
Also it pleaseth Setebos to work,
Use all His hands, and exercise much
  craft,
By no means for the love of what is
  worked.
'Tasteth, himself, no finer good i' the
  world
When all goes right, in this safe sum-
  mer-time,
And he wants little, hungers, aches
  not much,
Than trying what to do with wit and
  strength.
'Falls to make something: 'piled yon
  pile of turfs,
And squared and stuck there squares
  of soft white chalk,
And, with a fish-tooth, scratched a
  moon on each,
And set up endwise certain spikes of
  tree,
And crowned the whole with a sloth's
  skull a-top,
Found dead i' the woods, too hard
  for one to kill.
No use at all i' the work, for work's
  sole sake;
'Shall some day knock it down again:
  so He.

'Saith He is terrible : watch His feats
  in proof !
One hurricane will spoil six good
  months' hope.
He hath a spite against me, that I
  know,
Just as He favors Prosper, who knows
  why ?
So it is, all the same, as well I find.
'Wove wattles half the winter, fenced
  them firm
With stone and stake to stop she-
  tortoises
Crawling to lay their eggs here : well,
  one wave,
Feeling the foot of Him upon its
  neck,
Gaped as a snake does, lolled out its
  large tongue,
And licked the whole labor flat : so
  much for spite.
'Saw a ball flame down late (yonder
  it lies)
Where, half an hour before, I slept
  i' the shade :
Often they scatter sparkles : there is
  force !
'Dug up a newt He may have envied
  once
And turned to stone, shut up inside a
  stone
Please Him and hinder this ?— What
  Prosper does ?
Aha, if he would tell me how ! Not
  He !
There is the sport : discover how or
  die !
All need not die, for of the things o'
  the isle
Some flee afar, some dive, some run
  up trees ;
Those at His mercy, — why, they
  please Him most
When . . . when . . . well, never try
  the same way twice !
'Repeat what act has pleased, He may
  grow wroth.
You must not know His ways, and
  play Him off,
Sure of the issue. 'Doth the like him-
  self :
'Spareth a squirrel that it nothing
  fears
But steals the nut from underneath
  my thumb,
And when I threat, bites stoutly in
  defence :
'Spareth an urchin that contrariwise,
Curls up into a ball, pretending death

For fright at my approach : the two
  ways please.
But what would move my choler more
  than this,
That either creature counted on its
  life
To-morrow and next day and all days
  to come,
Saying forsooth in the inmost of its
  heart,
"Because he did so yesterday with me,
And otherwise with such another
  brute,
So must he do henceforth and al-
  ways."— Ay ?
'Would teach the reasoning couple
  what "must" means :
'Doth as he likes, or wherefore Lord ?
  So He.

'Conceiveth all things will continue
  thus,
And we shall have to live in fear of
  Him
So long as He lives, keeps His
  strength : no change,
If He have done His best, make no
  new world
To please Him more, so leave off
  watching this, —
If He surprise not even the Quiet's
  self
Some strange day, — or, suppose,
  grow into it
As grubs grow butterflies : else, here
  are we,
And there is He, and nowhere help at
  all.

'Believeth with the life, the pain shall
  stop.
His dam held different, that after
  death
He both plagued enemies and feasted
  friends :
Idly ! He doth His worst in this our
  life,
Giving just respite lest we die through
  pain,
Saving last pain for worst, — with
  which, an end.
Meanwhile, the best way to escape
  His ire
Is, not to seem too happy. 'Sees
  himself,
Yonder two flies, with purple films
  and pink,
Bask on the pompion-bell above : kills
  both.

'Sees two black painful beetles roll
 their ball
On head and tail as if to save their
 lives:
Moves them the stick away they
 strive to clear.

Even so, 'would have Him miscon-
 ceive, suppose
This Caliban strives hard and ails no
 less,
And always, above all else, envies
 Him;
Wherefore he mainly dances on dark
 nights,
Moans in the sun, gets under holes to
 laugh,
And never speaks his mind save
 housed as now:
Outside, 'groans, curses. If He caught
 me here,
O'erheard this speech, and asked,
 " What chucklest at?"
'Would, to appease Him, cut a finger
 off,
Or of my three kid yearlings burn
 the best,
Or let the toothsome apples rot on tree,
Or push my tame beast for the ore to
 taste:
While myself lit a fire, and made a
 song
And sung it, " What I hate, be conse-
 crate
To celebrate Thee and Thy state, no mate
For Thee; what see for envy in poor
 me?"

Hoping the while, since evils some-
 times mend,
Warts rub away and sores are cured
 with slime,
That some strange day, will either
 the Quiet catch
And conquer Setebos, or likelier
 He
Decrepit may doze, doze, as good as
 die.

———————

[What, what? A curtain o'er the
 world at once!
Crickets stop hissing; not a bird —
 or, yes,
There scuds His raven that hath told
 Him all!
It was fool's play, this prattling!
 Ha! The wind
Shoulders the pillared dust, death's
 house o' the move,
And fast invading fires begin! White
 blaze —
A tree's head snaps — and there,
 there, there, there, there,
His thunder follows! Fool to gibe
 at Him!
Lo! 'Lieth flat and loveth Setebos!
'Maketh his teeth meet through his
 upper lip,
Will let those quails fly, will not eat
 this month
One little mess of whelks, so he may
 'scape!]

———————

SAUL.

I.

Said Abner, " At last thou art come!
Kiss my cheek, wish me well!"
 Ere I tell, ere thou speak,
 Then I wished it, and did kiss his
 cheek.
And he, " Since the King, O my friend! for thy countenance sent,
Neither drunken nor eaten have we; nor until from his tent
Thou return with the joyful assurance the King liveth yet,
Shall our lip with the honey be bright, with the water be wet.
For out of the black mid-tent's silence, a space of three days,
Not a sound hath escaped to thy servants, of prayer nor of praise,
To betoken that Saul and the Spirit have ended their strife,
And that, faint in his triumph, the monarch sinks back upon life.

II.

"Yet now my heart leaps, O beloved ! God's child with his dew
On thy gracious gold hair, and those lilies still living and blue
Just broken to twine round thy harp-strings, as if no wild heat
Were now raging to torture the desert ! "

III.

Then I, as was meet,
Knelt down to the God of my fathers, and rose on my feet,
And ran o'er the sand burnt to powder. The tent was unlooped ;
I pulled up the spear that obstructed, and under I stooped ;
Hands and knees on the slippery grass-patch, all withered and gone,
That extends to the second enclosure, I groped my way on
Till I felt where the foldskirts fly open. Then once more I prayed,
And opened the foldskirts and entered, and was not afraid
But spoke, "Here is David, thy servant !" And no voice replied.
At the first I saw naught but the blackness ; but soon I descried
A something more black than the blackness — the vast, the upright
Main prop which sustains the pavilion : and slow into sight
Grew a figure against it, gigantic and blackest of all.
Then a sunbeam, that burst through the tent-roof, showed Saul.

IV.

He stood as erect as that tent-prop, both arms stretched out wide
On the great cross-support in the centre, that goes to each side ;
He relaxed not a muscle, but hung there as, caught in his pangs
And waiting his change, the king serpent all heavily hangs,
Far away from his kind, in the pine, till deliverance come
With the spring-time, — so agonized Saul, drear and stark, blind and dumb.

V.

Then I tuned my harp, — took off the lilies we twine round its chords
Lest they snap 'neath the stress of the noontide — those sunbeams like
swords !
And I first played the tune all our sheep know, as, one after one,
So docile they come to the pen-door till folding be done.
They are white, and untorn by the bushes, for lo, they have fed
Where the long grasses stifle the water within the stream's bed ;
And now one after one seeks its lodging, as star follows star
Into eve and the blue far above us, — so blue and so far !

VI.

--Then the tune, for which quails on the cornland will each leave his mate
To fly after the player ; then, what makes the crickets elate
Till for boldness they fight one another : and then, what has weight
To set the quick jerboa a-musing outside his sand house —
There are none such as he for a wonder, half bird and half mouse !
God made all the creatures and gave them our love and our fear,
To give sign, we and they are his children, one family here.

VII.

Then I played the help-tune of our reapers, their wine-song, when hand
Grasps at hand, eye lights eye in good friendship, and great hearts expand
And grow one in the sense of this world's life. — And then, the last song
When the dead man is praised on his journey — "Bear, bear him along
With his few faults shut up like dead flowerets ! Are balm seeds not here
To console us ? The land has none left such as he on the bier.

Oh, would we might keep thee, my brother!" — And then, the glad chant
Of the marriage, — first go the young maidens, next, she whom we vaunt
As the beauty, the pride of our dwelling — And then, the great march
Wherein man runs to man to assist him and buttress an arch
Naught can break; who shall harm them, our friends? — Then, the chorus
    intoned
As the Levites go up to the altar in glory enthroned.
But I stopped here: for here in the darkness Saul groaned.

VIII.

And I paused, held my breath in such silence, and listened apart;
And the tent shook, for mighty Saul shuddered: and sparkles 'gan dart
From the jewels that woke in his turban at once with a start
All its lordly male-sapphires, and rubies courageous at heart.
So the head: but the body still moved not, still hung there erect.
And I bent once again to my playing, pursued it unchecked,
As I sang, —

IX.

    "Oh, our manhood's prime vigor! No spirit feels waste,
Not a muscle is stopped in its playing nor sinew unbraced.
Oh, the wild joys of living! the leaping from rock up to rock,
The strong rending of boughs from the fir-tree, the cool silver shock
Of the plunge in a pool's living water, the hunt of the bear,
And the sultriness showing the lion is couched in his lair.
And the meal, the rich dates yellowed over with gold dust divine,
And the locust-flesh steeped in the pitcher, the full draught of wine,
And the sleep in the dried river-channel where bulrushes tell
That the water was wont to go warbling so softly and well.
How good is man's life, the mere living! how fit to employ
All the heart and the soul and the senses forever in joy!
Hast thou loved the white locks of thy father, whose sword thou didst guard
When he trusted thee forth with the armies, for glorious reward?
Didst thou see the thin hands of thy mother, held up as men sang
The low song of the nearly departed, and hear her faint tongue
Joining in while it could to the witness, 'Let one more attest,
I have lived, seen God's hand through a lifetime, and all was for best!'
Then they sung through their tears in strong triumph, not much, but the
    rest.
And thy brothers, the help and the contest, the working whence grew
Such result as, from seething grape-bundles, the spirit strained true;
And the friends of thy boyhood — that boyhood of wonder and hope,
Present promise and wealth of the future beyond the eye's scope, —
Till lo, thou art grown to a monarch; a people is thine;
And all gifts, which the world offers singly, on one head combine!
On one head, all the beauty and strength, love and rage (like the throe
That, a-work in the rock, helps its labor and lets the gold go)
High ambition and deeds which surpass it, fame crowning them, — all
Brought to blaze on the head of one creature — King Saul!'"

X.

And lo, with that leap of my spirit, — heart, hand, harp, and voice,
Each lifting Saul's name out of sorrow, each bidding rejoice
Saul's fame in the light it was made for — as when, dare I say,
The Lord's army, in rapture of service, strains through its array,
And upsoareth the cherubim-chariot — "Saul!" cried I, and stopped,
And waited the thing that should follow. Then Saul, who hung propped
By the tent's cross-support in the centre, was struck by his name.
Have ye seen when Spring's arrowy summons goes right to the aim,

And some mountain, the last to withstand her, that held (he alone,
While the vale laughed in freedom and flowers) on a broad bust of stone
A year's snow bound about for a breastplate,— leaves grasp of the sheet?
Fold on fold all at once it crowds thunderously down to his feet,
And there fronts you, stark, black, but alive yet, your mountain of old,
With his rents, the successive bequeathings of ages untold—
Yea, each harm got in fighting your battles, each furrow and scar
Of his head thrust 'twixt you and the tempest—all hail, there they are!
— Now again to be softened with verdure, again hold the nest
Of the dove, tempt the goat and its young to the green on his crest
For their food in the ardors of summer.   One long shudder thrilled
All the tent till the very air tingled, then sank and was stilled
At the King's self left standing before me, released and aware.
What was gone, what remained?   All to traverse 'twixt hope and despair,
Death was past, life not come: so he waited.   A while his right hand
Held the brow, helped the eyes, left too vacant, forthwith to remand
To their place what new objects should enter: 'twas Saul as before.
I looked up and dared gaze at those eyes, nor was hurt any more
Than by slow pallid sunsets in autumn, ye watch from the shore,
At their sad level gaze o'er the ocean—a sun's slow decline
Over hills which, resolved in stern silence, o'erlap and intwine
Base with base to knit strength more intensely: so, arm folded arm
O'er the chest whose slow heavings subsided.

XI.

                                       What spell or what charm
(For, a while there was trouble within me), what next should I urge
To sustain him where song had restored him?—   Song filled to the verge
His cup with the wine of this life, pressing all that it yields
Of mere fruitage, the strength and the beauty: beyond, on what fields,
Glean a vintage more potent and perfect to brighten the eye
And bring blood to the lip, and commend them the cup they put by?
He saith, " It is good; " still he drinks not: he lets me praise life,
Gives assent, yet would die for his own part.

XII.

                                       Then fancies grew rife
Which had come long ago on the pasture, when round me the sheep
Fed in silence — above, the one eagle wheeled slow as in sleep;
And I lay in my hollow and mused on the world that might lie
'Neath his ken, though I saw but the strip 'twixt the hill and the sky.
And I laughed — " Since my days are ordained to be passed with my flocks,
Let me people at least, with my fancies, the plains and the rocks,
Dream the life I am never to mix with, and image the show
Of mankind as they live in those fashions I hardly shall know!
Schemes of life, its best rules and right uses, the courage that gains,
And the prudence that keeps what men strive for."   And now these old
      trains
Of vague thought came again; I grew surer; so, once more the string
Of my harp made response to my spirit, as thus—

XIII.

                                       " Yea, my King,"
I began — " thou dost well in rejecting mere comforts that spring
From the mere mortal life held in common by man and by brute:
In our flesh grows the branch of this life, in our soul it bears fruit.
Thou hast marked the slow rise of the tree,—how its stem trembled first
Till it passed the kid's lip, the stag's antler; then safely outburst

The fan-branches all round ; and thou mindest when these too, in turn
Broke a-bloom and the palm-tree seemed perfect ; yet more was to learn,
E'en the good that comes in with the palm-fruit. Our dates shall we slight,
When their juice brings a cure for all sorrow ? or care for the plight
Of the palm's self whose slow growth produced them ? Not so ! stem and
    branch
Shall decay, nor be known in their place, while the palm-wine shall stanch
Every wound of man's spirit in winter. I pour thee such wine.
Leave the flesh to the fate it was fit for ! the spirit be thine !
By the spirit, when age shall o'ercome thee, thou still shalt enjoy
More indeed, than at first when, inconscious, the life of a boy.
Crush that life, and behold its wine running ! Each deed thou hast done
Dies, revives, goes to work in the world ; until e'en as the sun
Looking down on the earth, though clouds spoil him, though tempests efface,
Can find nothing his own deed produced not, must every where trace
The results of his past summer-prime, — so, each ray of thy will,
Every flash of thy passion and prowess, long over, shall thrill
Thy whole people, the countless, with ardor, till they too give forth
A like cheer to their sons : who in turn, till the South and the North
With the radiance thy deed was the germ of, Carouse in the past !
But the license of age has its limit ; thou diest at last,
As the lion when age dims his eyeball, the rose at her height,
So with man — so his power and his beauty forever take flight
No ! Again a long draught of my soul-wine ! Look forth o'er the years !
Thou hast done now with eyes for the actual ; begin with the seer's !
Is Saul dead ? In the depth of the vale make his tomb — bid arise
A gray mountain of marble heaped four-square, till, built to the skies,
Let it mark where the great First King slumbers : whose fame would ye
    know ?
Up above see the rock's naked face, where the record shall go
In great characters cut by the scribe, — Such was Saul, so he did ;
With the sages directing the work, by the populace chid, —
For not half, they'll affirm, is comprised there ! Which fault to amend,
In the grove with his kind grows the cedar, whereon they shall spend
(See, in tablets 'tis level before them) their praise, and record
With the gold of the graver, Saul's story, — the statesman's great word
Side by side with the poet's sweet comment. The river's a-wave
With smooth paper-reeds grazing each other when prophet-winds rave :
So the pen gives unborn generations their due and their part
In thy being ! Then, first of the mighty, thank God that thou art !"

XIV.

And behold while I sang . . . but O Thou who didst grant me, that day,
And, before it, not seldom hast granted thy help to essay,
Carry on and complete an adventure, — my shield and my sword
In that act where my soul was thy servant, thy word was my word, —
Still be with me, who then at the summit of human endeavor
And scaling the highest, man's thought could, gazed hopeless as ever
On the new stretch of heaven above me — till, mighty to save,
Just one lift of thy hand cleared that distance — God's throne from man's
    grave !
Let me tell out my tale to its ending — my voice to my heart
Which can scarce dare believe in what marvels last night I took part,
As this morning I gather the fragments, alone with my sheep !
And still fear lest the terrible glory evanish like sleep,
For I wake in the gray dewy covert, while Hebron upheaves
The dawn struggling with night on his shoulder, and Kidron retrieves
Slow the damage of yesterday's sunshine.

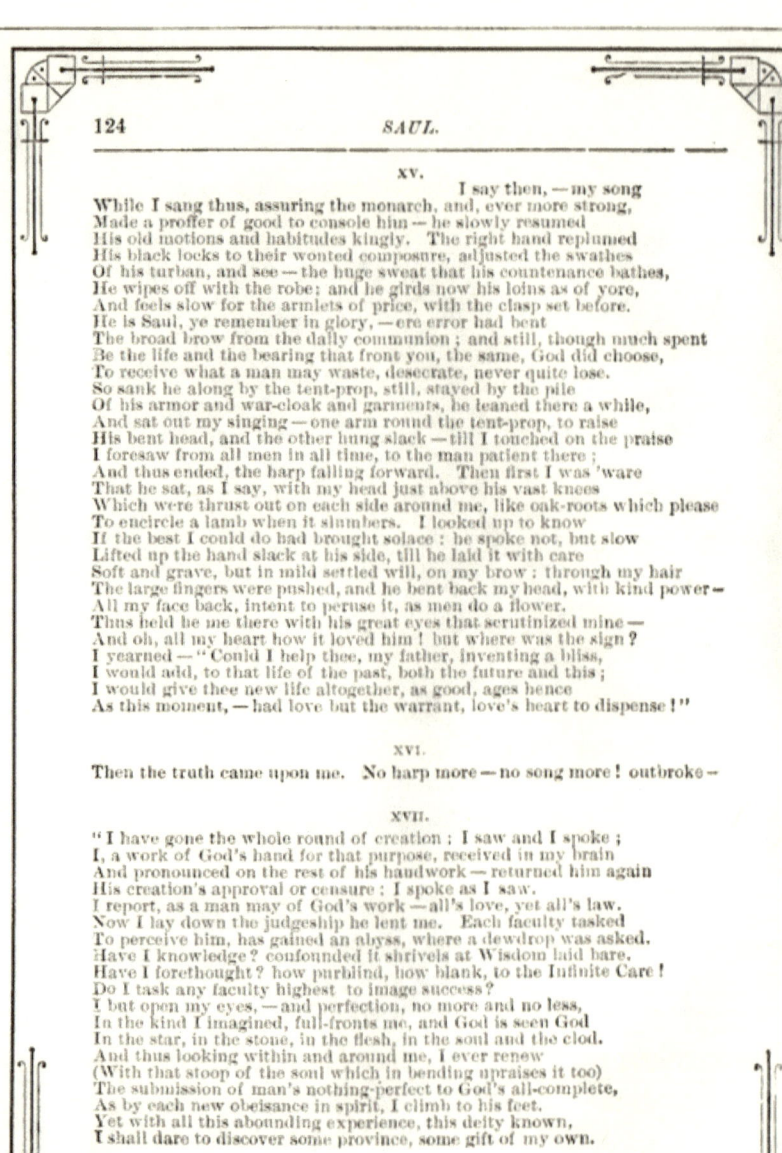

xv.

        I say then, — my song
While I sang thus, assuring the monarch, and, ever more strong,
Made a proffer of good to console him — he slowly resumed
His old motions and habitudes kingly. The right hand replumed
His black locks to their wonted composure, adjusted the swathes
Of his turban, and see — the huge sweat that his countenance bathes,
He wipes off with the robe; and he girds now his loins as of yore,
And feels slow for the armlets of price, with the clasp set before.
He is Saul, ye remember in glory, — ere error had bent
The broad brow from the daily communion ; and still, though much spent
Be the life and the bearing that front you, the same, God did choose,
To receive what a man may waste, desecrate, never quite lose.
So sank he along by the tent-prop, still, stayed by the pile
Of his armor and war-cloak and garments, he leaned there a while,
And sat out my singing — one arm round the tent-prop, to raise
His bent head, and the other hung slack — till I touched on the praise
I foresaw from all men in all time, to the man patient there ;
And thus ended, the harp falling forward. Then first I was 'ware
That he sat, as I say, with my head just above his vast knees
Which were thrust out on each side around me, like oak-roots which please
To encircle a lamb when it slumbers. I looked up to know
If the best I could do had brought solace : he spoke not, but slow
Lifted up the hand slack at his side, till he laid it with care
Soft and grave, but in mild settled will, on my brow : through my hair
The large fingers were pushed, and he bent back my head, with kind power —
All my face back, intent to peruse it, as men do a flower.
Thus held he me there with his great eyes that scrutinized mine —
And oh, all my heart how it loved him ! but where was the sign ?
I yearned — "Could I help thee, my father, inventing a bliss,
I would add, to that life of the past, both the future and this ;
I would give thee new life altogether, as good, ages hence
As this moment, — had love but the warrant, love's heart to dispense !"

xvi.

Then the truth came upon me. No harp more — no song more ! outbroke —

xvii.

"I have gone the whole round of creation ; I saw and I spoke ;
I, a work of God's hand for that purpose, received in my brain
And pronounced on the rest of his handwork — returned him again
His creation's approval or censure : I spoke as I saw.
I report, as a man may of God's work — all's love, yet all's law.
Now I lay down the judgeship he lent me. Each faculty tasked
To perceive him, has gained an abyss, where a dewdrop was asked.
Have I knowledge ? confounded it shrivels at Wisdom laid bare.
Have I forethought ? how purblind, how blank, to the Infinite Care !
Do I task any faculty highest to image success ?
I but open my eyes, — and perfection, no more and no less,
In the kind I imagined, full-fronts me, and God is seen God
In the star, in the stone, in the flesh, in the soul and the clod.
And thus looking within and around me, I ever renew
(With that stoop of the soul which in bending upraises it too)
The submission of man's nothing-perfect to God's all-complete,
As by each new obeisance in spirit, I climb to his feet.
Yet with all this abounding experience, this deity known,
I shall dare to discover some province, some gift of my own.

There's a faculty pleasant to exercise, hard to hoodwink,
I am fain to keep still in abeyance (I laugh as I think),
Lest, insisting to claim and parade in it, wot ye, I worst
E'en the Giver in one gift.— Behold, I could love if I durst!
But I sink the pretension as fearing a man may o'ertake
God's own speed in the one way of love: I abstain for love's sake.
—What, my soul? see thus far and no farther? when doors great and small,
Nine and ninety flew ope at our touch, should the hundredth appal?
In the least things have faith, yet distrust in the greatest of all?
Do I find love so full in my nature, God's ultimate gift,
That I doubt his own love can compete with it? Here the parts shift?
Here, the creature surpass the creator,—the end, what began?
Would I fain in my impotent yearning do all for this man,
And dare doubt he alone shall not help him, who yet alone can?
Would it ever have entered my mind, the bare will, much less power,
To bestow on this Saul what I sang of, the marvellous dower
Of the life he was gifted and filled with? to make such a soul,
Such a body, and then such an earth for insphering the whole?
And doth it not enter my mind (as my warm tears attest)
These good things being given, to go on, and give one more, the best?
Ay, to save and redeem and restore him, maintain at the height
This perfection,—succeed, with life's dayspring, death's minute of night?
Interpose at the difficult minute, snatch Saul, the mistake,
Saul, the failure, the ruin he seems now,—and bid him awake
From the dream, the probation, the prelude, to find himself set
Clear and safe in new light and new life,—a new harmony yet
To be run and continued, and ended—who knows?—or endure!
The man taught enough by life's dream, of the rest to make sure;
By the pain-throb, triumphantly winning intensified bliss,
And the next world's reward and repose, by the struggles in this.

XVIII.

"I believe it! 'Tis thou, God, that givest, 'tis I who receive:
In the first is the last, in thy will is my power to believe.
All's one gift: thou canst grant it moreover, as prompt to my prayer,
As I breathe out this breath, as I open these arms to the air.
From thy will, stream the worlds, life and nature, thy dread Sabaoth:
I will?—the mere atoms despise me! Why am I not loth
To look that, even that in the face too? Why is it I dare
Think but lightly of such impuissance? What stops my despair?
This;—'tis not what man Does which exalts him, but what man Would do!
See the King—I would help him, but cannot, the wishes fall through.
Could I wrestle to raise him from sorrow, grow poor to enrich,
To fill up his life, starve my own out, I would—knowing which,
I know that my service is perfect. Oh, speak through me now!
Would I suffer for him that I love? So wouldst thou—so wilt thou!
So shall crown thee the topmost, ineffablest, uttermost crown—
And thy love fill infinitude wholly, nor leave up nor down
One spot for the creature to stand in! It is by no breath,
Turn of eye, wave of hand, that salvation joins issue with death!
As thy love is discovered almighty, almighty be proved
Thy power, that exists with and for it, of being beloved!
He who did most, shall bear most; the strongest shall stand the most weak.
'Tis the weakness in strength, that I cry for! my flesh, that I seek
In the Godhead! I seek and I find it. O Saul, it shall be
A Face like my face that receives thee; a Man like to me,
Thou shalt love and be loved by, forever: a Hand like this hand
Shall throw open the gates of new life to thee! See the Christ stand!"

XIX.

I know not too well how I found my way home in the night.
There were witnesses, cohorts about me, to left and to right,
Angels, powers, the unuttered, unseen, the alive, the aware :
I repressed, I got through them as hardly, as strugglingly there,
As a runner beset by the populace famished for news—
Life or death. The whole earth was awakened, hell loosed with her crews ;
And the stars of night beat with emotion, and tingled and shot
Out in fire the strong pain of pent knowledge : but I fainted not,
For the Hand still impelled me at once and supported, suppressed
All the tumult, and quenched it with quiet, and holy behest,
Till the rapture was shut in itself, and the earth sank to rest.
Anon at the dawn, all that trouble had withered from earth —
Not so much, but I saw it die out in the day's tender birth ;
In the gathered intensity brought to the gray of the hills ;
In the shuddering forests' held breath ; in the sudden wind-thrills ;
In the startled wild beasts that bore oft, each with eye sidling still
Though averted with wonder and dread ; in the birds stiff and chill
That rose heavily as I approached them, made stupid with awe :
E'en the serpent that slid away silent — he felt the new law.
The same stared in the white humid faces upturned by the flowers ;
The same worked in the heart of the cedar and moved the vine-bowers :
And the little brooks witnessing murmured, persistent and low,
With their obstinate, all but hushed voices — " E'en so, it is so ! "

RABBI BEN EZRA.

I.

Grow old along with me !
The best is yet to be,
The last of life, for which the first
    was made :
Our times are in His hand
Who saith, " A whole I planned,
Youth shows but half ; trust God :
    see all, nor be afraid ! "

II.

Not that, amassing flowers,
Youth sighed, " Which rose make
    ours,
Which lily leave and then as best
    recall ! "
Not that, admiring stars,
It yearned, " Nor Jove, nor Mars ;
Mine be some figured flame which
    blends, transcends them all ! "

III.

Not for such hopes and fears
Annulling youth's brief years,
Do I remonstrate : folly wide the
    mark !

Rather I prize the doubt
Low kinds exist without,
Finished and finite clods, untroubled
    by a spark.

IV.

Poor vaunt of life indeed,
Were man but formed to feed
On joy, to solely seek and find and
    feast.
Such feasting ended, then
As sure an end to men ;
Irks care the crop-full bird ? Frets
    doubt the maw-crammed beast ?

V.

Rejoice we are allied
To That which doth provide
And not partake, effect and not
    receive !
A spark disturbs our clod :
Nearer we hold of God
Who gives, than of His tribes that
    take, I must believe.

VI.

Then, welcome each rebuff
That turns earth's smoothness rough,
Each sting that bids nor sit nor stand
    but go !

Be our joys three-parts pain!
Strive, and hold cheap the strain;
Learn, nor account the pang; dare,
    never grudge the throe!

VII.

For thence,—a paradox
Which comforts while it mocks,—
Shall life succeed in that it seems to
    fail:
What I aspired to be,
And was not, comforts me:
A brute I might have been, but would
    not sink i' the scale.

VIII.

What is he but a brute
Whose flesh hath soul to suit,
Whose spirit works lest arms and legs
    want play?
To man, propose this test—
Thy body at its best,
How far can that project thy soul on
    its lone way?

IX.

Yet gifts should prove their use:
I own the Past profuse
Of power each side, perfection every
    turn:
Eyes, ears took in their dole,
Brain treasured up the whole;
Should not the heart beat once "How
    good to live and learn"?

X.

Not once beat "Praise be thine!
I see the whole design,
I, who saw power, see now love per-
    fect too.
Perfect I call Thy plan:
Thanks that I was a man!
Maker, remake, complete,—I trust
    what Thou shalt do!"

XI.

For pleasant is this flesh;
Our soul, in its rose-mesh
Pulled ever to the earth, still yearns
    for rest:
Would we some prize might hold
To match those manifold
Possessions of the brute,—gain most,
    as we did best!"

XII.

Let us not always say
"Spite of this flesh to-day
I strove, made head, gained ground
    upon the whole!"
As the bird wings and sings,
Let us cry "All good things
Are ours, nor soul helps flesh more,
    now, than flesh helps soul!"

XIII.

Therefore I summon age
To grant youth's heritage,
Life's struggle having so far reached
    its term:
Thence shall I pass, approved
A man, for aye removed
From the developed brute; a God
    though in the germ.

XIV.

And I shall thereupon
Take rest, ere I be gone
Once more on my adventure brave
    and new:
Fearless and unperplexed,
When I wage battle next,
What weapons to select, what armor
    to indue.

XV.

Youth ended, I shall try
My gain or loss thereby;
Leave the fire ashes, what survives
    is gold:
And I shall weigh the same,
Give life its praise or blame:
Young, all lay in dispute; I shall
    know, being old.

XVI.

For, note when evening shuts,
A certain moment cuts
The deed off, calls the glory from the
    gray:
A whisper from the west
Shoots—"Add this to the rest,
Take it and try its worth: here dies
    another day."

XVII.

So, still within this life,
Though lifted o'er its strife,
Let me discern, compare, pronounce
    at last,

"This rage was right i' the main,
That acquiescence vain:
The Future I may face now I have
　　proved the Past."

XVIII.

For more is not reserved
To man, with soul just nerved
To act to-morrow what he learns to-
　　day:
Here, work enough to watch
The Master work, and catch
Hints of the proper craft, tricks of
　　the tool's true play.

XIX.

As it was better, youth
Should strive, through acts uncouth,
Toward making, than repose on aught
　　found made:
So, better, age, exempt
From strife, should know, than tempt
Further. Thou waitedst age · wait
　　death, nor be afraid!

XX.

Enough now, if the Right
And Good and Infinite
Be named here, as thou callest thy
　　hand thine own,
With knowledge absolute,
Subject to no dispute
From fools that crowded youth, nor
　　let thee feel alone.

XXI.

Be there, for once and all,
Severed great minds from small,
Announced to each his station in the
　　Past!
Was I, the world arraigned,
Were they, my soul disdained,
Right? Let age speak the truth and
　　give us peace at last!

XXII.

Now, who shall arbitrate?
Ten men love what I hate,
Shun what I follow, slight what I re-
　　ceive:
Ten, who in ears and eyes
Match me: we all surmise,
They, this thing, and I, that: whom
　　shall my soul believe?

XXIII.

Not on the vulgar mass
Called "work," must sentence pass,
Things done, that took the eye and
　　had the price;
O'er which, from level stand,
The low world laid its hand,
Found straightway to its mind, could
　　value in a trice:

XXIV.

But all, the world's coarse thumb
And finger failed to plumb,
So passed in making up the main ac-
　　count:
All instincts immature,
All purposes unsure,
That weighed not as his work, yet
　　swelled the man's amount:

XXV.

Thoughts hardly to be packed
Into a narrow act,
Fancies that broke through language
　　and escaped:
All I could never be,
All, men ignored in me,
This, I was worth to God, whose
　　wheel the pitcher shaped.

XXVI.

Ay, note that Potter's wheel,
That metaphor! and feel
Why time spins fast, why passive lies
　　our clay, —
Thou, to whom fools propound,
When the wine makes its round,
"Since life fleets, all is change; the
　　Past gone, seize to-day!"

XXVII.

Fool! All that is, at all,
Lasts ever, past recall;
Earth changes, but thy soul and God
　　stand sure:
What entered into thee,
That was, is, and shall be:
Time's wheel runs back or stops:
　　Potter and clay endure.

XXVIII.

He fixed thee mid this dance
Of plastic circumstance,
This Present, thou, forsooth, wouldst
　　fain arrest:

Machinery just meant
To give thy soul its bent,
Try thee, and turn thee forth suffi-
    ciently impressed.

XXIX.

What though the earlier grooves
Which ran the laughing loves
Around thy base, no longer pause and
    press?
What though, about thy rim,
Skull-things in order grim
Grow out, in graver mood, obey the
    sterner stress?

XXX.

Look not thou down but up!
To uses of a cup,
The festal board, lamp's flash, and
    trumpet's peal,
The new wine's foaming flow,
The Master's lips aglow!
Thou, heaven's consummate cup, what
    needst thou with earth's wheel?

XXXI.

But I need, now as then,
Thee, God, who mouldest men!
And since, not even while the whirl
    was worst,
Did I, — to the wheel of life
With shapes and colors rife,
Bound dizzily, — mistake my end, to
    slake Thy thirst:

XXXII.

So, take and use Thy work,
Amend what flaws may lurk,
What strain o' the stuff, what warp-
    ings past the aim!
My times be in Thy hand!
Perfect the cup as planned!
Let age approve of youth, and death
    complete the same!

EPILOGUE.

FIRST SPEAKER, *as David.*

I.

On the first of the Feast of Feasts,
    The Dedication Day,
When the Levites joined the priests
    At the altar in robed array,
Gave signal to sound and say, —

II.

When the thousands, rear and van,
    Swarming with one accord,
Became as a single man
    (Look, gesture, thought, and word),
In praising and thanking the Lord, —

III.

When the singers lift up their voice,
    And the trumpets made endeavor,
Sounding, "In God rejoice!"
    Saying, "In Him rejoice
Whose mercy endureth forever!"

IV.

Then the Temple filled with a cloud,
    Even the House of the Lord;
Porch bent and pillar bowed:
    For the presence of the Lord,
In the glory of His cloud,
    Had filled the House of the Lord.

SECOND SPEAKER, *as Renan.*

Gone now! All gone across the dark
    so far,
Sharpening fast, shuddering ever,
    shutting still,
Dwindling into the distance, dies
    that star
Which came, stood, opened once!
    We gazed our fill
With upturned faces on as real a Face
That, stooping from grave music
    and mild fire,
Took in our homage, made a visible
    place
Through many a depth of glory,
    gyre on gyre,
For the dim human tribute. Was
    this true?
Could man indeed avail, mere praise
    of his,
To help by rapture God's own rap-
    ture too,
Thrill with a heart's red tinge that
    pure pale bliss?
Why did it end? Who failed to beat
    the breast,
And shriek, and throw the arms
    protesting wide,
When a first shadow showed the star
    addressed
Itself to motion, and on either side
The rims contracted as the rays
    retired;
The music, like a fountain's sicken-
    ing pulse,

Subsided on itself : a while transpired
　　Some vestige of a Face no pangs
　　　　convulse,
No prayers retard ; then even this
　　　　was gone,
　　Lost in the night at last.　We, lone
　　　　and left
Silent through centuries, ever and
　　　anon
　　Venture to probe again the vault
　　　　bereft
Of all now save the lesser lights, a mist
　　Of multitudinous points, yet suns,
　　　men say —
And this leaps ruby, this lurks ame-
　　　thyst,
　　But where may hide what came
　　　　and loved our clay ?
How shall the sage detect in yon ex-
　　　panse
　　The star which chose to stoop and
　　　　stay for us?
Unroll the records !　Hailed ye such
　　　advance
　　Indeed, and did your hope evanish
　　　　thus ?
Watchers of twilight, is the worst
　　　averred ?
　　We shall not look up, know our-
　　　　selves are seen.
Speak, and be sure that we again are
　　　heard,
　　Acting or suffering, have the disk's
　　　　serene
Reflect our life, absorb an earthly
　　　flame,
　　Nor doubt that, were mankind inert
　　　　and numb,
Its core had never crimsoned all the
　　　same,
　　Nor, missing ours, its music fallen
　　　　dumb?
Oh, dread succession to a dizzy post,
　　Sad sway of sceptre whose mere
　　　　touch appals,
Ghastly dethronement, cursed by
　　　those the most
　　On whose repugnant brow the
　　　　crown next falls !

THIRD SPEAKER.

I.

Witless alike of will and way divine,
How heaven's high with earth's low
　　should intertwine !
Friends, I have seen through your
　　eyes : now use mine !

II.

Take the least man of all mankind,
　　as I :
Look at his head and heart, find how
　　and why
He differs from his fellows utterly :

III.

Then, like me, watch when nature by
　　degrees
Grows alive round him, as in Arctic
　　seas
(They said of old) the instinctive
　　water flees

IV.

Toward some elected point of central
　　rock,
As though, for its sake only, roamed
　　the flock
Of waves about the waste : a while
　　they mock

V.

With radiance caught for the occa-
　　sion, — hues
Of blackest hell now, now such reds
　　and blues
As only heaven could fitly interfuse, —

VI.

The mimic monarch of the whirlpool,
　　king
O' the current for a minute : then they
　　wring
Up by the roots and oversweep the
　　thing,

VII.

And hasten off, to play again else-
　　where
The same part, choose another peak
　　as bare,
They find and flatter, feast and fin-
　　ish there.

VIII.

When you see what I tell you, — na-
　　ture dance
About each man of us, retire, ad-
　　vance,
As though the pageant's end were to
　　enhance

IX.

His worth, and — once the life, his
  product, gained —
Roll away elsewhere, keep the strife
  sustained,
And show thus real, a thing the North
  but feigned, —

X.

When you acknowledge that one
  world could do
All the diverse work, old yet ever
  new,
Divide us, each from other, me from
  you, —

XI.

Why! where's the need of Temple,
  when the walls
O' the world are that? What use of
  swells and falls
From Levites' choir, priests' cries,
  and trumpet-calls?

XII.

That one Face, far from vanish, rather
  grows,
Or decomposes but to recompose,
Become my universe that feels and
  knows!

A WALL.

I.

On the old wall here! How I could
  pass
  Life in a long midsummer day,
My feet confined to a plot of grass,
  My eyes from a wall not once away!

II.

And lush and lithe do the creepers
  clothe
  Yon wall I watch, with a wealth of
  green:
Its bald red bricks draped, nothing
  loth,
  In lappets of tangle they laugh be-
  tween.

III.

Now, what is it makes pulsate the
  robe?
  Why tremble the sprays? What
  life o'erbrims

The body, — the house, no eye can
  probe, —
  Divined as, beneath a robe, the
  limbs?

IV.

And there again! But my heart may
  guess
  Who tripped behind; and she sang
  perhaps:
So, the old wall throbbed, and its
  life's excess
  Died out and away in the leafy
  wraps.

V.

Wall upon wall are between us: life
  And song should away from heart
  to heart!
I — prison-bird, with a ruddy strife
  At breast, and a lip whence storm-
  notes start —

VI.

Hold on, hope hard in the subtle thing
  That's spirit: though cloistered fast,
  soar free!
Account as wood, brick, stone, this
  ring
  Of the rueful neighbors, and — forth
  to thee!

APPARITIONS.

I

Such a starved bank of moss
  Till, that May-morn,
Blue ran the flash across:
  Violets were born!

II

Sky — what a scowl of cloud
  Till, near and far,
Ray on ray split the shroud:
  Splendid, a star!

III

World — how it walled about
  Life with disgrace
Till God's own smile came out:
  That was thy face!

NATURAL MAGIC.

I.

ALL I can say is — I saw it!
The room was as bare as your hand.
I locked in the swarth little lady, —
  I swear,
From the head to the foot of her —
  well, quite as bare!
"No Nautch shall cheat me," said I,
  "taking my stand
At this bolt which I draw!" And
  this bolt — I withdraw it,
And there laughs the lady, not bare,
  but embowered
With — who knows what verdure,
  o'erfruited, o'erflowered?
Impossible! Only — I saw it!

II.

All I can sing is — I feel it!
This life was as blank as that room;
I let you pass in here. Precaution,
  indeed?
Walls, ceiling, and floor, — not a
  chance for a weed!
Wide opens the entrance: where's
  cold now, where's gloom?
No May to sow seed here, no June to
  reveal it,
Behold you enshrined in these blooms
  of your bringing,
These fruits of your bearing — nay,
  birds of your winging!
A fairy-tale! Only — I feel it!

MAGICAL NATURE.

I.

FLOWER — I never fancied, jewel —
  I profess you!
  Bright I see and soft I feel the out-
    side of a flower.
Save but glow inside and — jewel, I
  should guess you,
  Dim to sight and rough to touch:
    the glory is the dower.

II.

You, forsooth, a flower? Nay, my
  love, a jewel —
  Jewel at no mercy of a moment in
    your prime!

Time may fray the flower-face: kind
  be time or cruel,
  Jewel, from each facet, flash your
    laugh at time!

GARDEN FANCIES.

I. THE FLOWER'S NAME.

I.

HERE's the garden she walked across,
  Arm in my arm, such a short while
    since;
Hark, now I push its wicket, the
    moss
  Hinders the hinges and makes them
    wince!
She must have reached this shrub ere
  she turned,
  As back with that murmur the
    wicket swung;
For she laid the poor snail, my chance
  foot spurned,
  To feed and forget it the leaves
    among.

II.

Down this side of the gravel-walk
  She went while her robe's edge
    brushed the box:
And here she paused in her gracious
    talk
  To point me a moth on the milk-
    white phlox.
Roses, ranged in valiant row,
  I will never think that she passed
    you by!
She loves you noble roses, I know;
  But yonder, see, where the rock-
    plants lie!

III.

This flower she stopped at, finger on
  lip,
  Stooped over, in doubt, as settling
    its claim;
Till she gave me, with pride to make
  no slip,
  Its soft meandering Spanish name.
What a name! Was it love, or praise?
  Speech half-asleep, or song half-
    awake?
I must learn Spanish, one of these
  days,
  Only for that slow sweet name's
    sake.

" Lay on the grass and forgot the oaf
Over a jolly chapter of Rabelais." — Page 133.

IV.

Roses, — if I live and do well,
  I may bring her, one of these days,
To fix you fast with as fine a spell,
  Fit you each with his Spanish
    phrase.
But do not detain me now ; for she
  lingers
  There, like sunshine over the ground,
And ever I see her soft white fingers
  Searching after the bud she found.

V.

Flower, you Spaniard, look that you
  grow not,
  Stay as you are and be loved for-
    ever !
Bud, if I kiss you 'tis that you blow
  not,
  Mind, the shut pink mouth opens
    never !
For while it pouts, her fingers wres-
  tle,
  Twinkling the audacious leaves be-
    tween,
Till round they turn and down they
  nestle ;
  Is not the dear mark still to be
    seen ?

VI.

Where I find her not, beauties vanish ;
  Whither I follow her, beauties flee :
Is there no method to tell her in
  Spanish
  June's twice June since she breathed
    it with me ?
Come, bud, show me the least of her
  traces,
  Treasure my lady's lightest footfall !
— Ah, you may flout and turn up your
  faces —
  Roses, you are not so fair after all !

II.

SIBRANDUS SCHAFNABURGENSIS.

I.

PLAGUE take all your pedants, say I !
  He who wrote what I hold in my
  hand,
Centuries back was so good as to die,
  Leaving this rubbish to cumber the
    land :
This, that was a book in its time,
  Printed on paper and bound in
    leather,

Last month in the white of a matin-
  prime
  Just when the birds sang all to-
    gether.

II.

Into the garden I brought it to read,
  And under the arbute and laurus-
    tine
Read it, so help me grace in my need,
  From title-page to closing line.
Chapter on chapter did I count,
  As a curious traveller counts Stone-
    henge ;
Added up the mortal amount,
  And then proceeded to my revenge.

III.

Yonder's a plum-tree with a crevice
  An owl would build in, were he but
    sage ;
For a lap of moss, like a fine pont-
  levis
  In a castle of the middle age,
Joins to a lip of gum, pure amber ;
  When he'd be private, there might
    he spend
Hours alone in his lady's chamber :
  Into this crevice I dropped our
    friend.

IV.

Splash, went he, as under he ducked,
  — At the bottom, I knew, rain-drip-
  pings stagnate ;
Next, a handful of blossoms I plucked
  To bury him with, my bookshelf's
    magnate ;
Then I went indoors, brought out a
  loaf,
  Half a cheese, and a bottle of Cha-
  blis ;
Lay on the grass and forgot the oaf
  Over a jolly chapter of Rabelais.

V.

Now, this morning, betwixt the moss
  And gum that locked our friend in
    limbo,
A spider had spun his web across,
  And sat in the midst with arms
    akimbo :
So, I took pity, for learning's sake,
  And, *de profundis, accentibus lætis,*
Cantate ! quoth I, as I got a rake ;
  And up I fished his delectable trea-
    tise.

VI.

Here you have it, dry in the sun,
  With all the binding all of a blister,
And great blue spots where the ink
    has run,
  And reddish streaks that wink and
    glister
O'er the page so beautifully yellow :
  Oh, well have the droppings played
    their tricks !
Did he guess how toadstools grow,
  this fellow ?
Here's one stuck in his chapter six !

VII.

How did he like it when the live
  creatures
  Tickled and toused and browsed
    him all over,
And worm, slug, eft, with serious
  features,
  Came in, each one, for his right of
    trover ?
— When the water-beetle with great
    blind deaf face
  Made of her eggs the stately de-
    posit,
And the newt borrowed just so much
    of the preface
  As tiled in the top of his black
    wife's closet ?

VIII.

All that life and fun and romping,
  All that frisking and twisting and
    coupling,
While slowly our poor friend's leaves
    were swamping,
  And clasps were cracking, and cov-
    ers suppling !
As if you had carried sour John
  Knox
  To the playhouse at Paris, Vienna,
    or Munich,
Fastened him into a front-row box,
  And danced off the ballet with
    trousers and tunic.

IX.

Come, old martyr ! What, torment
  enough is it ?
  Back to my room shall you take
    your sweet self.
Good-by, mother-beetle ; husband-
  eft, *sufficit !*
  See the snug niche I have made on
    my shelf !

A.'s book shall prop you up, B.'s shall
  cover you,
  Here's C. to be grave with, or D. to
    be gay,
And with E. on each side, and F. right
    over you,
  Dry-rot at ease till the Judgment-
    day !

IN THREE DAYS.

I.

So, I shall see her in three days
And just one night, but nights are
  short,
Then two long hours, and that is
  morn.
See how I come, unchanged, unworn !
Feel, where my life broke off from
  thine,
How fresh the splinters keep and
  fine, —
Only a touch, and we combine !

II.

Too long, this time of year, the days !
But nights, at least the nights are
  short.
As night shows where her one moon
  is,
A hand's-breadth of pure light and
  bliss,
So life's night gives my lady birth
And my eyes hold her ! What is
  worth
The rest of heaven, the rest of earth ?

III.

O loaded curls ! release your store
Of warmth and scent, as once before
The tingling hair did, lights and darks
Outbreaking into fairy sparks,
When under curl and curl I pried
After the warmth and scent inside,
Through lights and darks how mani-
  fold —
The dark inspired, the light con-
  trolled,
As early Art embrowns the gold !

IV.

What great fear, should one say,
  " Three days,
That change the world, might change
  as well

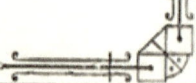

Your fortune ; and if joy delays,
Be happy that no worse befell !"
What small fear, if another says,
" Three days and one shortnight be-
    side
May throw no shadow on your ways ;
But years must teem with change
    untried,
With chance not easily defied,
With an end somewhere undescried."
No fear ! — or, if a fear be born
This minute, fear dies out in scorn.
Fear ? I shall see her in three days
And one night, now the nights are
    short,
Then just two hours, and that is
    morn !

THE LOST MISTRESS.

I.

ALL's over, then ; does truth sound
    bitter
As one at first believes ?
Hark, 'tis the sparrows' good-night
    twitter
About your cottage eaves !

II.

And the leaf-buds on the vine are
    woolly,
I noticed that to-day ;
One day more bursts them open fully :
You know the red turns gray.

III.

To-morrow we meet the same then,
    dearest ?
May I take your hand in mine ?
Mere friends are we,— well, friends
    the merest
Keep much that I resign.

IV.

Each glance of the eye so bright and
    black,
Though I keep with heart's en-
    deavor,—
Your voice, when you wish the snow-
    drops back,
Though it stay in my soul forever,—

V.

Yet I will but say what mere friends
    say,
Or only a thought stronger ;
I will hold your hand but as long as
    all may,
Or so very little longer !

ONE WAY OF LOVE.

I.

ALL June I bound the rose in sheaves
Now, rose by rose, I strip the leaves
And strew them where Pauline may
    pass.
She will not turn aside ? Alas !
Let them lie. Suppose they die ?
The chance was they might take her
    eye.

II.

How many a month I strove to suit
These stubborn fingers to the lute !
To-day I venture all I know.
She will not hear my music ? So !
Break the string ; fold music's wing :
Suppose Pauline had bade me sing !

III.

My whole life long I learned to love.
This hour my utmost art I prove
And speak my passion — heaven or
    hell ?
She will not give me heaven ? 'Tis
    well !
Lose who may — I still can say,
Those who win heaven, blest are
    they !

RUDEL TO THE LADY OF TRIPOLI

I

I KNOW a Mount, the gracious Sun
    perceives
First, when he visits, last, too, when
    he leaves
The world ; and, vainly favored, it
    repays
The day-long glory of his steadfast
    gaze

By no change of its large calm front
     of snow.
And, underneath the Mount, a Flower
     I know,
He cannot have perceived, that
     changes ever
At his approach; and, in the lost
     endeavor
To live his life, has parted, one by
     one,
With all a flower's true graces, for the
     grace
Of being but a foolish mimic sun,
With ray-like florets round a disk-
     like face.
Men nobly call by many a name the
     Mount
As over many a land of theirs its
     large
Calm front of snow like a triumphal
     targe
Is reared, and still with old names,
     fresh names vie,
Each to its proper praise and own ac-
     count:
Men call the Flower, the Sunflower,
     sportively.

II.

O Angel of the East! one, one gold
     look
Across the waters to this twilight
     nook,
—The far sad waters, Angel, to this
     nook!

III.

Dear Pilgrim, art thou for the East
     indeed?
Go!—saying ever as thou dost pro-
     ceed,
That I, French Rudel, choose for my
     device
A sunflower outspread like a sacri-
     fice
Before its idol. See! These inex-
     pert
And hurried fingers could not fail to
     hurt
The woven picture; 'tis a woman's
     skill
Indeed; but nothing baffled me, so, ill
Or well, the work is finished. Say,
     men feed
On songs I sing, and therefore bask
     the bees
On my flower's breast as on a plat-
     form broad:

But, as the flower's concern is not
     for these
But solely for the sun, so men ap-
     plaud
In vain this Rudel, he not looking
     here
But to the East—the East! Go, say
     this, Pilgrim dear!

NUMPHOLEPTOS.

STILL you stand, still you listen, still
     you smile!
Still melts your moonbeam through
     me, white a while,
Softening, sweetening, till sweet and
     soft
Increase so round this heart of mine,
     that oft
I could believe your moonbeam-smile
     has past
The pallid limit and, transformed at
     last,
Lies, sunlight and salvation—warms
     the soul
It sweetens, softens! Would you
     pass that goal,
Gain love's birth at the limit's hap-
     pier verge,
And, where an iridescence lurks, but
     urge
The hesitating pallor on to prime
Of dawn!—true blood-streaked, sun-
     warmth, action-time,
By heart-pulse ripened to a ruddy glow
Of gold above my clay—I scarce
     should know
From gold's self, thus suffused! For
     gold means love.
What means the sad slow silver smile
     above
My clay but pity, pardon?—at the
     best,
But acquiescence that I take my rest,
Contented to be clay, while in your
     heaven
The sun reserves love for the Spirit-
     Seven
Companioning God's throne they lamp
     before,
—Leaves earth a mute waste only
     wandered o'er
By that pale soft sweet disempas-
     sioned moon
Which smiles me slow forgiveness!
     Such, the boon

I beg? Nay, dear, submit to this —
    just this
Supreme endeavor! As my lips now
    kiss
Your feet, my arms convulse your
    shrouding robe,
My eyes, acquainted with the dust,
    dare probe
Your eyes above for — what, if born,
    would blind
Mine with redundant bliss, as flash
    may find
The inert nerve, sting awake the pal-
    sied limb,
Bid with life's ecstasy sense over-
    brim
And suck back death in the resurging
    joy —
So grant me — love, whole, sole, with-
    out alloy!

Vainly! The promise withers! I
    employ
Lips, arms, eyes, pray the prayer
    which finds the word,
Make the appeal which must be felt,
    not heard,
And none the more is changed your
    calm regard:
Rather, its sweet and soft grow harsh
    and hard —
Forbearance, then repulsion, then dis-
    dain.
Avert the rest! I rise, see! — make,
    again
Once more, the old departure for
    some track
Untried yet through a world which
    brings me back
Ever thus fruitlessly to find your
    feet,
To fix your eyes, to pray the soft and
    sweet
Which smile there — take from his
    new pilgrimage
Your outcast, once your inmate, and
    assuage
With love — not placid pardon now —
    his thirst
For a mere drop from out the ocean
    erst
He drank at! Well, the quest shall
    be renewed.
Fear nothing! Though I linger, un-
    imbued
With any drop, my lips thus close. I
    go!
So did I leave you, I have found you
    so,

And doubtlessly, if fated to return,
So shall my pleading persevere and
    earn
Pardon — not love — in that same
    smile, I learn,
And lose the meaning of, to learn
    once more,
Vainly!

            What fairy track do I ex-
    plore?
What magic hall return to, like the
    gem
Centuply-angled o'er a diadem?
You dwell there, hearted; from your
    midmost home
Rays forth — through that fantastic
    world I roam
Ever — from centre to circumference,
Shaft upon colored shaft: this crim-
    sons thence,
That purples out its precinct through
    the waste.
Surely I had your sanction when I
    faced,
Fared forth upon that untried yellow
    ray
Whence I retrack my steps? They
    end to-day
Where they began, before your feet,
    beneath
Your eyes, your smile: the blade is
    shut in sheath,
Fire quenched in flint; irradiation,
    late
Triumphant through the distance,
    finds its fate,
Merged in your blank pure soul, alike
    the source
And tomb of that prismatic glow:
    divorce
Absolute, all-conclusive! Forth I
    fared,
Treading the lambent flamelet: little
    cared
If now its flickering took the topaz
    tint,
If now my dull-caked path gave sul-
    phury hint
Of subterranean rage — no stay nor
    stint
To yellow, since you sanctioned that
    I bathe,
Burnish me, soul and body, swim and
    swathe
In yellow license. Here I reek suf-
    fused
With crocus, saffron, orange, as I
    used

With scarlet, purple, every dye o' the
   bow
Born of the storm-cloud. As before,
   you show
Scarce recognition, no approval, some
Mistrust, more wonder at a man be-
   come
Monstrous in garb, nay — flesh dis-
   guised as well,
Through his adventure. Whatsoe'er
   befell,
I followed, wheresoe'er it wound, that
   vein
You authorized should leave your
   whiteness, stain
Earth's sombre stretch beyond your
   midmost place
Of vantage, — trode that tinct where-
   of the trace
On garb and flesh repel you! Yes, I
   plead
Your own permission — your com-
   mand, indeed,
That who would worthily retain the
   love
Must share the knowledge shrined
   those eyes above,
Go boldly on adventure, break
   through bounds
O' the quintessential whiteness that
   surrounds
Your feet, obtain experience of each
   tinge
That bickers forth to broaden out,
   impinge
Plainer his foot its pathway all dis-
   tinct
From every other. Ah, the wonder,
   linked
With fear, as exploration manifests
What agency it was first tipped the
   crests
Of unnamed wild-flower, soon pro-
   truding grew
Portentous mid the sands, as when
   his hue
Betrays him and the burrowing snake
   gleams through ;
Till, last . . . but why parade more
   shame and pain?
Are not the proofs upon me? Here
   again
I pass into your presence, I receive
Your smile of pity, pardon, and I
   leave . . .
No, not this last of times I leave you,
   mute,
Submitted to my penance, so my
   foot

May yet again adventure, tread, from
   source
To issue, one more ray of rays which
   course
Each other, at your bidding, from the
   sphere
Silver and sweet, their birthplace,
   down that drear
Dark of the world, — you promise
   shall return
Your pilgrim jewelled as with drops
   o' the urn
The rainbow paints from, and no
   smatch at all
Of ghastliness at edge of some cloud-
   pall
Heaven cowers before, as earth awaits
   the fall
O' the bolt and flash of doom. Who
   trusts your word
Tries the adventure : and returns —
   absurd
As frightful — in that sulphur-steeped
   disguise
Mocking the priestly cloth-of-gold,
   sole prize
The arch-heretic was wont to bear
   away
Until he reached the burning. No, I
   say :
No fresh adventure ! No more seek-
   ing love
At end of toil, and finding, calm
   above
My passion, the old statuesque re-
   gard,
The sad petrific smile !

            O you — less hard
And hateful than mistaken and ob-
   tuse
Unreason of a she-intelligence !
You very woman with the pert pre-
   tence
To match the male achievement !
   Like enough !
Ay, you were easy victors, did the
   rough
Straightway efface itself to smooth,
   the gruff
Grind down and grow a whisper, —
   did man's truth
Subdue, for sake of chivalry and
   ruth,
Its rapier edge to suit the bulrush-
   spear
Womanly falsehood fights with! O
   that ear

All fact pricks rudely, that thrice-
  superfine
Feminity of sense, with right divine
To waive all process, take result
  stain-free
From out the very muck wherein . . .
      Ah me !
The true slave's querulous outbreak !
  All the rest
Be resignation ! Forth at your behest
I fare. Who knows but this — the
  crimson-quest —
May deepen to a sunrise, not decay
To that cold sad sweet smile ? — which
  I obey.

APPEARANCES.

I.

AND so you found that poor room
  dull,
  Dark, hardly to your taste, my
    Dear ?
Its features seemed unbeautiful :
  But this I know — 'twas there, not
    here,
You plighted troth to me, the word
Which — ask that poor room how it
  heard !

II.

And this rich room obtains your praise
Unqualified, — so bright, so fair,
So all whereat perfection stays ?
  Ay, but remember — here, not there,
The other word was spoken ! Ask
This rich room how you dropped the
  mask !

THE WORST OF IT.

I.

WOULD it were I had been false, not
  you !
  I that am nothing, not you that are
    all :
I, never the worse for a touch or two
  On my speckled hide ; not you, the
    pride
Of the day, my swan, that a first
  fleck's fall
  On her wonder of white must un-
    swan, undo !

II.

I had dipped in life's struggle and,
  out again,
  Bore specks of it here, there, easy
    to see,
When I found my swan and the cure
  was plain ;
  The dull turned bright as I caught
    your white
On my bosom ; you saved me — saved
  in vain
  If you ruined yourself, and all
    through me !

III.

Yes, all through the speckled beast
  I am,
  Who taught you to stoop ; you gave
    me yourself,
And bound your soul by the vows
  which damn :
  Since on better thought you break,
    as you ought,
Vows — words, no angel set down,
  some elf
  Mistook, — for an oath, an epigram !

IV.

Yes, might I judge you, here were my
  heart,
  And a hundred its like, to treat as
    you pleased !
I choose to be yours, for my proper
  part,
  Yours, leave me or take, or mar or
    make ;
If I acquiesce, why should you be
  teased
  With the conscience-prick and the
    memory-smart ?

V.

But what will God say ? O my
  Sweet,
  Think, and be sorry you did this
    thing !
Though earth were unworthy to feel
  your feet,
  There's a heaven above may de-
    serve your love :
Should you forfeit heaven for a snapt
  gold ring
  And a promise broke, were it just
    or meet ?

VI.

And I to have tempted you! I, who tried
  Your soul, no doubt, till it sank!
    Unwise,
I loved and was lowly, loved and aspired,
  Loved, grieving or glad, till I made you mad,
And you meant to have hated and despised —
  Whereas, you deceived me nor inquired!

VII.

She, ruined? How? No heaven for her?
  Crowns to give, and none for the brow
That looked like marble and smelt like myrrh?
  Shall the robe be worn, and the palm-branch borne,
And she go graceless, she graced now
  Beyond all saints, as themselves aver?

VIII.

Hardly! That must be understood!
  The earth is your place of penance, then ;
And what will it prove? I desire your good,
  But, plot as I may, I can find no way
How a blow should fall, such as falls on men,
  Nor prove too much for your womanhood.

IX.

It will come, I suspect, at the end of life,
  When you walk alone, and review the past ;
And I, who so long shall have done with strife,
  And journeyed my stage and earned my wage
And retired as was right, — I am called at last
  When the Devil stabs you, to lend the knife.

X.

He stabs for the minute of trivial wrong,
  Nor the other hours are able to save,

The happy, that lasted my whole life long :
  For a promise broke, not for first words spoke,
The true, the only, that turn my grave
  To a blaze of joy and a crash of song.

XI.

Witness beforehand! Off I trip
  On a safe path gay through the flowers you flung :
My very name made great by your lip,
  And my heart aglow with the good I know
Of a perfect year when we both were young,
  And I tasted the angels' fellowship.

XII.

And witness, moreover . . . Ah, but wait !
  I spy the loop whence an arrow shoots !
It may be for yourself, when you meditate,
  That you grieve — for slain ruth, murdered truth :
"Though falsehood escape in the end, what boots ?
  How truth would have triumphed !"
  — you sigh too late.

XIII.

Ay, who would have triumphed like you, I say !
  Well, it is lost now ; well, you must bear,
Abide and grow fit for a better day,
  You should hardly grudge, could I be your judge !
But hush! For you, can be no despair :
  There's amends ; 'tis a secret ; hope and pray !

XIV.

For I was true at least — oh, true enough !
  And, Dear, truth is not as good as it seems !
Commend me to conscience! Idle stuff !
  Much help is in mine, as I mope and pine,
And skulk through day, and scowl in my dreams
  At my swan's obtaining the crow's rebuff.

XV.

Men tell me of truth now — "False!"
  I cry :
  Of beauty — "A mask, friend! Look
    beneath!"
We take our own method, the Devil
  and I,
  With pleasant and fair and wise
    and rare :
And the best we wish to what lives,
  is — death ;
  Which even in wishing, perhaps we
    lie!

XVI.

Far better commit a fault and have
  done —
  As you, Dear! — forever : and
    choose the pure,
And look where the healing waters
  run,
  And strive and strain to be good
    again,
And a place in the other world in-
  sure,
  All glass and gold, with God for its
    sun.

XVII.

Misery! What shall I say or do?
  I cannot advise, or, at least, per-
    suade :
Most like, you are glad you deceived
  me — rue
  No whit of the wrong : you endured
    too long,
Have done no evil and want no aid,
  Will live the old life out and chance
    the new.

XVIII.

And your sentence is written all the
  same,
  And I can do nothing, — pray, per-
    haps :
But somehow the world pursues its
  game, —
  If I pray, if I curse, — for better or
    worse :
And my faith is torn to a thousand
  scraps,
  And my heart feels ice while my
    words breathe flame.

XIX.

Dear, I look from my hiding-place.
  Are you still so fair? Have you
    still the eyes?

Be happy! Add but the other grace,
  Be good! Why want what the
    angels vaunt?
I knew you once : but in Paradise,
  If we meet, I will pass nor turn
    my face.

TOO LATE.

I.

HERE was I with my arm and heart
  And brain, all yours for a word, a
    want
Put into a look — just a look, your
  part, —
  While mine, to repay it . . . vainest
    vaunt,
Were the woman, that's dead, alive
  to hear,
  Had her lover, that's lost, love's
    proof to show!
But I cannot show it ; you cannot
  speak
  From the churchyard neither, miles
    removed,
Though I feel by a pulse within my
  cheek,
  Which stabs and stops, that the
    woman I loved
Needs help in her grave and finds
  none near,
  Wants warmth from the heart which
    sends it — so!

II.

Did I speak once angrily, all the drear
  days
  You lived, you woman I loved so
    well,
Who married the other? Blame or
  praise,
  Where was the use then? Time
    would tell,
And the end declare what man for you,
  What woman for me was the choice
    of God.
But, Edith dead! no doubting more!
  I used to sit and look at my life
As it rippled and ran till, right before,
  A great stone stopped it : oh, the
    strife
Of waves at the stone some devil
  threw
  In my life's mid-current, thwarting
    God!

III.

But either I thought, "They may churn and chide
  A while,— my waves which came for their joy
And found this horrible stone full-tide:
  Yet I see just a thread escape, deploy
Through the evening-country, silent and safe,
  And it suffers no more till it finds the sea."
Or else I would think, "Perhaps some night
  When new things happen, a meteor-ball
May slip through the sky in a line of light,
  And earth breathe hard, and land-marks fall,
And my waves no longer champ nor chafe,
  Since a stone will have rolled from its place: let be!"

IV.

But, dead! All's done with: wait who may,
  Watch and wear and wonder who will.
Oh, my whole life that ends to-day!
  Oh, my soul's sentence, sounding still,
"The woman is dead, that was none of his;
  And the man, that was none of hers, may go!"
There's only the past left: worry that!
  Wreak, like a bull, on the empty coat,
Rage, its late wearer is laughing at!
  Tear the collar to rags, having missed his throat;
Strike stupidly on—"This, this, and this,
  Where I would that a bosom received the blow!"

V.

I ought to have done more: once my speech
  And once your answer, and there, the end,
And Edith was henceforth out of reach!
  Why, men do more to deserve a friend,
Be rid of a foe, get rich, grow wise,
  Nor, folding their arms, stare fate in the face.
Why, better even have burst like a thief
  And borne you away to a rock for us two,
In a moment's horror, bright, bloody, and brief,
  Then changed to myself again—"I slew
Myself in that moment; a ruffian lies
  Somewhere: your slave, see, born in his place!"

VI.

What did the other do? You be judge!
  Look at us, Edith! Here are we both!
Give him his six whole years: I grudge
  None of the life with you, nay, I loathe
Myself that I grudged his start in advance
  Of me who could overtake and pass.
But, as if he loved you! No, not he,
  Nor any one else in the world, 'tis plain:
Who ever heard that another, free
  As I, young, prosperous, sound, and sane,
Poured life out, proffered it—"Half a glance
  Of those eyes of yours and I drop the glass!"

VII.

Handsome, were you? 'Tis more than they held,
  More than they said; I was 'ware and watched:
I was the 'scapegrace, this rat belled
  The cat, this fool got his whiskers scratched:
The others? No head that was turned, no heart
  Broken, my lady, assure yourself!
Each soon made his mind up; so and so
  Married a dancer, such and such
Stole his friend's wife, stagnated slow,
  Or maundered, unable to do as much.

And muttered of peace where he had
  no part:
  While, hid in the closet, laid on the
    shelf, —

VIII.

On the whole, you were let alone, I
  think!
  So, you looked to the other, who
    acquiesced;
My rival, the proud man, — prize
  your pink
  Of poets! A poet he was! I've
    guessed:
He rhymed you his rubbish nobody
  read,
  Loved you and doved you — did not
    I laugh!
There was a prize! But we both
  were tried.
  O heart of mine, marked broad
    with her mark,
Tekel, found wanting, set aside,
  Scorned! See, I bleed these tears
    in the dark
Till comfort come and the last be
  bled:
  He? He is tagging your epitaph.

IX.

If it would only come over again!
  — Time to be patient with me, and
    probe
This heart till you punctured the
  proper vein,
  Just to learn what blood is: twitch
    the robe
From that blank lay-figure your fancy
  draped,
  Prick the leathern heart till the —
    verses spirt!
And late it was easy; late, you
  walked
  Where a friend might meet you;
    Edith's name
Arose to one's lip if one laughed or
  talked;
  If I heard good news, you heard the
    same;
When I woke, I knew that your breath
  escaped;
  I could bide my time, keep alive,
    alert.

X.

And alive I shall keep and long, you
  will see!
  I knew a man, was kicked like a
    dog

From gutter to cesspool; what cared
  he
  So long as he picked from the filth
    his prog?
He saw youth, beauty, and genius die,
  And jollily lived to his hundredth
    year.
But I will live otherwise; none of
  such life!
  At once I begin as I mean to end.
Go on with the world, get gold in its
  strife,
  Give your spouse the slip, and be-
    tray your friend!
There are two who decline, a woman
  and I,
  And enjoy our death in the dark-
    ness here.

XI.

I liked that way you had with your
  curls
  Wound to a ball in a net behind:
Your cheek was chaste as a Quaker-
  girl's,
  And your mouth — there was never,
    to my mind,
Such a funny mouth, for it would not
  shut;
  And the dented chin too — what a
    chin!
There were certain ways when you
  spoke, some words
  That you know you never could pro-
    nounce:
You were thin, however; like a bird's
  Your hand seemed — some would
    say, the pounce
Of a scaly-footed hawk — all but!
  The world was right when it called
    you thin.

XII.

But I turn my back on the world: I
  take
  Your hand, and kneel, and lay to
    my lips.
Bid me live, Edith! Let me slake
  Thirst at your presence! Fear no
    slips!
'Tis your slave shall pay, while his
  soul endures,
  Full due, love's whole debt, *sum-
    mum jus.*
My queen shall have high observance,
  planned
  Courtship made perfect, no least
    line

Crossed without warrant. There you
stand,
  Warm too, and white too : would
this wine
Had washed all over that body of
yours,
  Ere I drank it, and you down with
it, thus !

BIFURCATION.

WE were two lovers ; let me lie by
her,
My tomb beside her tomb. On hers
inscribe —
" I loved him ; but my reason bade
prefer
Duty to love, reject the tempter's
bribe
Of rose and lily when each path di-
verged,
And either I must pace to life's far
end
As love should lead me, or, as duty
urged,
Plod the worn causeway arm in arm
with friend.
So, truth turned falsehood : ' How I
loathe a flower,
How prize the pavement !' still ca-
ressed his ear —
The deafish friend's — through life's
day, hour by hour.
As he laughed (coughing) ' Ay, it
would appear !'
But deep within my heart of hearts
there hid
Ever the confidence, amends for all,
That heaven repairs what wrong
earth's journey did,
When love from life-long exile comes
at call.
Duty and love, one broadway, were
the best —
Who doubts ? But one or other was
to choose.
I chose the darkling half, and wait
the rest
In that new world where light and
darkness fuse."

Inscribe on mine — " I loved her :
love's track lay
O'er sand and pebble, as all travellers
know.

Duty led through a smiling country,
gay
With greensward where the rose and
lily blow.
'Our roads are diverse : farewell,
love !' said she :
' 'Tis duty I abide by : homely sward
And not the rock-rough picturesque
for me !
Above, where both roads join, I wait
reward.
Be you as constant to the path where-
on
I leave you planted !' But man needs
must move,
Keep moving — whither, when the
star is gone
Whereby he steps secure nor strays
from love ?
No stone but I was tripped by, stum-
bling-block
But brought me to confusion. Where
I fell,
There I lay flat, if moss disguised the
rock ;
Thence, if flint pierced, I rose and
cried, ' All's well !
Duty be mine to tread in that high
sphere
Where love from duty ne'er disparts,
I trust,
And two halves make that whole,
whereof — since here
One must suffice a man — why, this
one must ! ' "

Inscribe each tomb thus : then, some
sage acquaint
The simple — which holds sinner,
which holds saint !

A LIKENESS.

SOME people hang portraits up
In a room where they dine or sup :
And the wife clinks tea-things under,
And her cousin, he stirs his cup,
Asks, " Who was the lady, I won-
der ?" —
" 'Tis a daub John bought at a sale,"
Quoth the wife, — looks black as
thunder.
" What a shade beneath her nose !
Snuff-taking, I suppose," —
Adds the cousin, while John's corns
ail.

A Likeness. — Page 144.

Or else, there's no wife in the case,
But the portrait's queen of the place,
Alone mid the other spoils
Of youth, — masks, gloves, and foils,
And pipe-sticks, rose, cherry-tree,
    jasmine,
And the long whip, the tandem-
    lasher,
And the cast from a fist ("not, alas!
    mine,
But my master's, the Tipton Slasher")
And the cards where pistol-balls mark
    ace,
And a satin shoe used for a cigar-
    case,
And the chamois-horns ("shot in the
    Chablais ")
And prints — Earey drumming on
    Cruiser,
And Sayers, our champion, the
    bruiser,
And the little edition of Rabelais ;
Where a friend, with both hands in
    his pockets
May saunter up close to examine it,
And remark a good deal of Jane
    Lamb in it,
" But the eyes are half out of their
    sockets ;
That hair's not so bad, where the
    gloss is,
But they've made the girl's nose a
    proboscis
Jane Lamb, that we danced with at
    Vichy !
What, is not she Jane? Then, who
    is she ? "

All that I own is a print,
An etching, a mezzotint ;
'Tis a study, a fancy, a fiction,
Yet a fact (take my conviction),
Because it has more than a hint
Of a certain face, I never
Saw elsewhere touch or trace of
In women I've seen the face of ;
Just an etching, and, so far, clever.

I keep my prints an imbroglio,
Fifty in one portfolio.
When somebody tries my claret,
We turn round chairs to the fire,
Chirp over days in a garret,
Chuckle o'er increase of salary,
Taste the good fruits of our leisure,
Talk about pencil and lyre,
And the National Portrait Gallery :
Then I exhibit my treasure.

After we've turned over twenty,
And the debt of wonder my crony
    owes
Is paid to my Marc Antonios,
He stops me — " *Festina lente !* "
What's that sweet thing there, the
    etching ? "
How my waistcoat strings want
    stretching,
How my cheeks grow red as toma-
    toes,
How my heart leaps ! But hearts
    after leaps, ache.

" By the by, you must take, for a
    keepsake,
That other, you praised, of Volpato's."
The fool ! would he try a flight far-
    ther and say —
He never saw, never before to-day,
What was able to take his breath
    away,
A face to lose youth for, to occupy
    age
With the dream of, meet death with, —
    why, I'll not engage
But that, half in a rapture and half in
    a rage,
I should toss him the thing's self —
    " 'Tis only a duplicate,
A thing of no value ! Take it, I
    supplicate ! "

MAY AND DEATH.

I.

I wish that when you died last May,
    Charles, there had died along with
        you
Three parts of spring's delightful
    things ;
    Ay, and, for me, the fourth part too.

II.

A foolish thought, and worse, perhaps!
    There must be many a pair of
        friends
Who, arm in arm, deserve the warm
    Moon-births and the long evening-
        ends.

III.

So, for their sake, be May still May !
    Let their new time, as mine of old,
Do all it did for me : I bid
    Sweet sights and sounds throng
        manifold.

IV.

Only, one little sight, one plant,
 Woods have in May, that starts up
  green
Save a sole streak which, so to speak,
 Is spring's blood, spilt its leaves be-
  tween, —

V.

That, they might spare; a certain
  wood
 Might miss the plant; their loss
  were small :
But I, — whene'er the leaf grows
  there,
 Its drop comes from my heart,
  that's all.

A FORGIVENESS.

I AM indeed the personage you know.
As for my wife, — what happened
  long ago —
You have a right to question me, as I
Am bound to answer.

    ("Son, a fit reply !"
The monk half spoke, half ground
  through his clinched teeth,
At the confession-grate I knelt
  beneath.)

Thus then all happened, Father !
  Power and place
I had as still I have. I ran life's
  race,
With the whole world to see, as only
  strains
His strength some athlete whose pro-
  digious gains
Of good appal him : happy to ex-
  cess, —
Work freely done should balance
  happiness
Fully enjoyed ; and, since beneath
  my roof
Housed she who made home heaven,
  in heaven's behoof
I went forth every day, and all day
  long
Worked for the world. Look, how
  the laborer's song
Cheers him ! Thus sang my soul,
  at each sharp throe
Of laboring flesh and blood — "She
  loves me so !"

One day, perhaps such song so knit
  the nerve
That work grew play and vanished.
  "I deserve
Haply my heaven an hour before the
  time !"
I laughed, as silverly the clockhouse-
  chime
Surprised me passing through the pos-
  tern gate
— Not the main entry where the
  menials wait
And wonder why the world's affairs
  allow
The master sudden leisure. That
  was how
I took the private garden-way for
  once.

Forth from the alcove, I saw start,
  ensconce
Himself behind the porphyry vase, a
  man.

My fancies in the natural order ran :
"A spy, — perhaps a foe in ambus-
  cade, —
A thief, — more like, a sweetheart of
  some maid
Who pitched on the alcove for tryst
  perhaps."

"Stand there !" I bid.

    Whereat my man but wraps
His face the closelier with uplifted
  arm
Whereon the cloak lies, strikes in
  blind alarm
This and that pedestal as, — stretch
  and stoop, —
Now in, now out of sight, he thrids
  the group
Of statues, marble god and goddess
  ranged
Each side the pathway, till the gate's
  exchanged
For safety : one step thence, the
  street, you know !

Thus far I followed with my gaze
  Then, slow,
Near on admiringly, I breathed again,
And — back to that last fancy of the
  train —
"A danger risked for hope of just a
  word
With — which of all my nest may be
  the bird

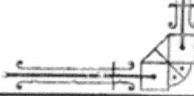

This poacher coverts for her plumage,
  pray?
Carmen? Juana? Carmen seems too
  gay
For such adventure, while Juana's
  grave
— Would scorn the folly. I applaud
  the knave!
He had the eye, could single from
  my brood
His proper fledgeling!"

      As I turned, there stood
In face of me, my wife stone-still
  stone-white.
Whether one bound had brought her,
  — at first sight!
Of what she judged the encounter,
  sure to be
Next moment, of the venturous man
  and me, —
Brought her to clutch and keep me
  from my prey:
Whether impelled because her death
  no day
Could come so absolutely opportune
As now at joy's height, like a year in
  June
Stayed at the fall of its first ripened
  rose;
Or whether hungry for my hate —
  who knows? —
Eager to end an irksome lie, and taste
Our tingling true relation, hate em-
  braced
By hate one naked moment: — any-
  how
There stone-still stone-white stood
  my wife, but now
The woman who made heaven within
  my house.
Ay, she who faced me was my very
  spouse
As well as love — you are to recollect!

"Stay!" she said. "Keep at least
  one soul unspecked
With crime, that's spotless hitherto
  — your own!
Kill me who court the blessing, who
  alone
Was, am, and shall be guilty, first to
  last!
The man lay helpless in the toils I
  cast
About him, helpless as the statue
  there
Against that strangling bell-flower's
  bondage: tear

Away and tread to dust the para-
  site,
But do the passive marble no despite!
I love him as I hate you. Kill me!
  Strike
At one blow both infinitudes alike
Out of existence — hate and love!
  Whence love?
That's safe inside my heart, nor will
  remove
For any searching of your steel, I
  think,
Whence hate? The secret lay on lip,
  at brink
Of speech, in one fierce tremble to
  escape,
At every form wherein your love took
  shape,
At each new provocation of your kiss.
Kill me!"

    We went in.

      Next day after this
I felt as if the speech might come,
  spoke —
Easily, after all.

      "The lifted cloak
Was screen sufficient: I concern my-
  self
Hardly with laying hands on who for
  pelf —
Whate'er the ignoble kind — may
  prowl and brave
Cuffing and kicking proper to a knave
Detected by my household's vigilance.
Enough of such! As for my love-ro-
  mance —
I, like our good Hidalgo, rub my
  eyes
And wake and wonder how the film
  could rise
Which changed for me a barber's
  basin straight
Into — Mambrino's helm? I hesitate
Nowise to say — God's sacramental
  cup!
Why should I blame the brass which,
  burnished up,
Will blaze, to all but me, as good as
  gold?
To me — a warning I was overbold
In judging metals. The Hidalgo
  waked
Only to die, if I remember, — staked
His life upon the basin's worth, and
  lost:
While I confess torpidity at most

In here and there a limb ; but, lame
   and halt,
Still should I work on, still repair my
   fault
Ere I took rest in death, — no fear at
   all !
Now, work — no word before the cur-
   tain fall ! "

   The " curtain " ? That of death on
     life, I meant ;
My " word " permissible in death's
   event,
Would be — truth, soul to soul ; for,
   otherwise,
Day by day, three years long, there
   had to rise
And, night by night, to fall upon our
   stage —
Ours, doomed to public play by heri-
   tage —
Another curtain, when the world,
   perforce
Our critical assembly, in due course
Came and went, witnessing, gave
   praise or blame
To art-mimetic. It had spoiled the
   game
If, suffered to set foot behind our
   scene,
   he world had witnessed how stage-
   king and queen,
Gallant and lady, but a minute since
Enarming each the other, would
   evince
No sign of recognition as they took
His way and her way to whatever nook
Waited them in the darkness either
   side
Of that bright stage where lately
   groom and bride
Had fired the audience to a frenzy-fit
Of sympathetic rapture — every whit
Earned as the curtain fell on her and
   me,
— Actors. Three whole years, noth-
   ing was to see
But calm and concord : where a
   speech was due
There came the speech ; when smiles
   were wanted too
Smiles were as ready. In a place like
   mine,
Where foreign and domestic cares
   combine,
There's audience every day and all
   day long ;
But finally the last of the whole
   throng

Who linger lets one see his back. For
   her —
Why, liberty and liking ; I aver,
Liking and liberty ! For me — I
   breathed,
Let my face rest from every wrinkle
   wreathed
Smile-like about the mouth, unlearned
   my task
Of personation till next day bade
   mask.
And quietly betook me from that
   world
To the real world, not pageant : there
   unfurled
In work, its wings, my soul, the fretted
   power.
Three years I worked, each minute of
   each hour
Not claimed by acting : — work I may
   dispense
With talk about, since work in evi-
   dence,
Perhaps in history ; who knows or
   cares ?

After three years, this way, all una-
   wares,
Out acting ended. She and I, at close
Of a loud night-feast, led, between two
   rows
Of bending male and female loyalty,
Our lord the king down staircase,
   while, held high
At arm's length did the twisted tapers'
   flare
Herald his passage from our palace
   where
Such visiting left glory evermore.
Again the ascent in public, till at door
As we two stood by the saloon — now
   blank
And disencumbered of its guests —
   there sank
A whisper in my ear, so low and yet
So unmistakable !
         " I half forget
The chamber you repair to, and I want
Occasion for one short word — if you
   grant
That grace — within a certain room
   you called
Our ' *Study*,' for you wrote there while
   I scrawled
Some paper full of faces for my sport.
That room I can remember. Just one
   short
Word with you there, for the remem-
   brance' sake ' "

"Follow me thither!" I replied.

          We break
The gloom a little, as with guiding lamp
I lead the way, leave warmth and cheer, by damp,
Blind, disused, serpentining ways afar
From where the habitable chambers are,—
Ascend, descend stairs tunnelled through the stone,—
Always in silence,—till I reach the lone
Chamber sepulchred for my very own
Out of the palace-quarry. When a boy,
Here was my fortress, stronghold from annoy,
Proof-positive of ownership; in youth
I garnered up my gleanings here—uncouth
But precious relics of vain hopes, vain fears;
Finally, this became in after-years
My closet of intrenchment to withstand
Invasion of the foe on every hand—
The multifarious herd in bower and hall,
State-room,—rooms whatsoe'er the style, which call
On masters to be mindful that, before
Men, they must look like men and something more.
Here,—when our lord the king's bestowment ceased
To deck me on the day that, golden-fleeced,
I touched ambition's height,—'twas here, released
From glory (always symbolled by a chain!)
No sooner was I privileged to gain
My secret domicile than glad I flung
That last toy on the table—gazed where hung
On hook my father's gift, the arquebuss—
And asked myself "Shall I envisage thus
The new prize and the old prize, when I reach
Another year's experience?—own that each
Equalled advantage—sportsman's—statesman's tool?
That brought me down an eagle, this—a fool!"

Into which room on entry, I set down
The lamp, and turning saw whose rustled gown
Had told me my wife followed, pace for pace.
Each of us looked the other in the face.
She spoke. "Since I could die now" . . .

          (To explain
Why that first struck me, know—not once again
Since the adventure at the porphyry's edge
Three years before, which sundered like a wedge
Her soul from mine,—though daily, smile to smile,
We stood before the public,—all the while
Not once had I distinguished, in that face
I paid observance to, the faintest trace
Of feature more than requisite for eyes
To do their duty by and recognize:
So did I force mine to obey my will
And pry no farther. There exists such skill,—
Those know who need it. What physician shrinks
From needful contact with a corpse? He drinks
No plague so long as thirst for knowledge,—not
An idler impulse,—prompts inquiry. What,
And will you disbelieve in power to bid
Our spirit back to bounds, as though we child
A child from scrutiny that's just and right
In manhood? Sense, not soul, accomplished sight,
Reported daily she it was—not how
Nor why a change had come to cheek and brow.)

"Since I could die now of the truth concealed,
Yet dare not, must not die,—so seems revealed
The Virgin's mind to me,—for death means peace,
Wherein no lawful part have I, whose lease

Of life and punishment the truth
  avowed
May haply lengthen,—let me push
  the shroud
Away, that steals to muffle ere is just
My penance-fire in snow! I dare—I
  must
Live, by avowal of the truth—this
  truth—
I loved you! Thanks for the fresh
  serpent's tooth
That, by a prompt new pang more
  exquisite
Than all preceding torture, proves
  me right!
I loved you yet I lost you! May I
  go
Burn to the ashes, now my shame you
  know?"

I think there never was such—how
  express?—
Horror coquetting with voluptnous-
  ness,
As in those arms of Eastern work-
  manship—
Yataghan, kandjar, things that rend
  and rip,
Gash rough, slash smooth, help hate
  so many ways,
Yet ever keep a beauty that betrays
Love still at work with the artificer
Throughout his quaint devising. Why
  prefer,
Except for love's sake, that a blade
  should writhe
And bicker like a flame?—now play
  the scythe
As if some broad neck tempted,—
  now contract
And needle off into a fineness lacked
For just that puncture which the heart
  demands?
Then, such adornment! Wherefore
  need our hands
Enclose not ivory alone, nor gold
Roughened for use, but jewels? Nay,
  behold!
Fancy my favorite—which I seem to
  grasp
While I describe the luxury. No asp
Is diapered more delicate round
  throat
Than this below the handle! These
  denote
—These mazy lines meandering, to
  end
Only in flesh they open—what in-
  tend

They else but water-purlings—pale
  contrast
With the life-crimson where they
  blend at last?
And mark the handle's dim pellucid
  green,
Carved, the hard jadestone, as you
  pinch a bean,
Into a sort of parrot-bird! He pecks
A grape-bunch; his two eyes are
  ruby-specks
Pure from the mine: seen this way,
  —glassy blank,
But turn 'them,—lo the inmost fire,
  that shrank
From sparkling, sends a red dart right
  to aim!
Why did I choose such toys? Per-
  haps the game
Of peaceful men is warlike, just as
  men
War-wearied get amusement from that
  pen
And paper we grow sick of—statesfolk
  tired
Of merely (when such measures are
  required)
Dealing out doom to people by three
  words,
A signature and seal: we play with
  swords
Suggestive of quick process. That is
  how
I came to like the toys described you
  now,
Store of which glittered on the walls
  and strewed
The table, even, while my wife pur-
  sued
Her purpose to its ending. "Now you
  know
This shame, my three years' torture,
  let me go,—'
Burn to the very ashes! You—I
  lost,
Yet you—I loved!"

            The thing I pity most
In men is—action prompted by sur-
  prise
Of anger; men? nay, bulls—whose
  onset lies
At instance of the firework and the
  goad!
Once the foe prostrate,—trampling
  once bestowed,—
Prompt follows placability, regret,
Atonement. Trust me, blood-warmth
  never yet

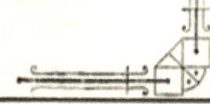

Betokened strong will! As no leap
    of pulse
Pricked me, that first time, so did
    none convulse
My veins at this occasion for resolve.
Had that devolved which did not then
    devolve
Upon me, I had done—what now to
    do
Was quietly apparent.

                    "Tell me who
The man was, crouching by the por-
    phyry vase!"

"No, never! All was folly in his
    case,
All guilt in mine. I tempted, he com-
    plied."

"And yet you loved me?"

            "Loved you. Doubtless—yed
In folly and in guilt, I thought you
    gave
Your heart and soul away from me to
    slave
At statecraft. Since my sight in you
    seemed lost,
I stung myself to teach you, to your
    cost,
What you rejected could be prized
    beyond
Life, heaven, by the first fool I threw
    a fond
Look on, a fatal word to."

                "And you still
Love me? Do I conjecture well, or
    ill?"

"Conjecture—well, or ill! I had
    three years
To spend in learning you."

            "We both are peers
In knowledge, therefore: since three
    years are spent
Ere thus much of yourself I learn—
    who went
Back to the house, that day, and
    brought my mind
To bear upon your action: uncom-
    bined
Motive from motive, till the dross,
    deprived
Of every purer particle, survived
At last in native simple hideousness,
Utter contemptibility, nor less

Nor more. Contemptibility—exempt
How could I, from its proper due—
    contempt?
I have too much despised you to di-
    vert
My life from its set course by help or
    hurt
Of your all-despicable life—perturb
The calm I work in, by—men's
    mouths to curb,
Which at such news were clamorous
    enough—
Men's eyes to shut before my broid-
    ered stuff
With the huge hole there, my em-
    blazoned wall
Blank where a scutcheon hung,—by,
    worse than all,
Each day's procession, my paraded life
Robbed and impoverished through the
    wanting wife
—Now that my life (which means—
    my work) was grown
Riches indeed! Once, just this worth
    alone
Seemed work to have, that profit
    gained thereby
Of good and praise would—how re-
    wardingly!—
Fall at your feet,—a crown I hoped
    to cast
Before your love, my love should
    crown at last.
No love remaining to cast crown
    before,
My love stopped work now: but con-
    tempt the more
Impelled me task as ever head and
    hand,
Because the very fiends weave ropes
    of sand
Rather than taste pure hell in idle-
    ness.
Therefore I kept my memory down
    by stress
Of daily work I had no mind to stay
For the world's wonder at the wife
    away.
Oh, it was easy all of it, believe,
For I despised you! But your words
    retrieve
Importantly the past. No hate as-
    sumed
The mask of love at any time! There
    gloomed
A moment when love took hate's
    semblance, urged
By causes you declare; but love's
    self purged

Away a fancied wrong I did both loves
— Yours and my own : by no hate's
  help, it proves,
Purgation was attempted. Then, you
  rise
High by how many a grade! I did
  despise —
I do but hate you. Let hate's pun-
  ishment
Replace contempt's! First step to
  which ascent —
Write down your own words I re-
  utter you!
I loved my husband and I hated —
  who
He was, I took up as my first chance,
  mere
Mud-ball to fling and make love foul
  with!' Here
Lies paper!"

    " Would my blood for ink suffice!"

  " It may: this minion from a land of
    spice,
Silk, feather — every bird of jewelled
  breast —
This poniard's beauty, ne'er so
  lightly prest
Above your heart there." . . .

        " Thus? "

        " It flows, I see.
Dip there the point and write!"

        "Dictate to me!
Nay, I remember."

      And she wrote the words.
I read them. Then — " Since love, in
  you, affords
License for hate, in me, to quench (I
  say)
Contempt — why, hate itself has
  passed away
In vengeance — foreign to contempt.
  Depart
Peacefully to that death which East-
  ern art
Imbued this weapon with, if tales be
  true!
Love will succeed to hate. I pardon
  you —
Dead in our chamber!"

      True as truth the tale.
She died ere morning; then, I saw
  how pale

Her cheek was ere it wore day's paint-
  disguise.
And what a hollow darkened 'neath
  her eyes,
Now that I used my own. She sleeps
  as erst
Beloved, in this your church: ay,
  yours!

          Immersed
In thought so deeply, Father? Sad,
  perhaps?
For whose sake, hers or mine or his
  who wraps
— Still plain I seem to see! — about
  his head
The idle cloak, — about his heart (in-
  stead
Of cuirass) some fond hope he may
  elude
My vengeance in the cloister's soli-
  tude?
Hardly, I think! As little helped
  his brow
The cloak then, Father — as your
  grate helps now!

CENCIAJA.

Ogni cencio vuol entrare in bucato. — Ital-
ian Proverb.

MAY I print, Shelley, how it came to
  pass
That when your Beatrice seemed —
  by lapse
Of many a long month since her sen-
  tence fell —
Assured of pardon for the parricide,
By intercession of stanch friends, or,
  say,
By certain pricks of conscience in the
  Pope,
Conniver at Francesco Cenci's guilt,—
Suddenly all things changed, and
  Clement grew
" Stern," as you state, " nor to be
  moved nor bent,
But said these three words coldly, ' *She*
  must die;'
Subjoining ' *Pardon ? Paolo Santa*
  Croce
Murdered his mother also yestereve,
And he is fled: she shall not flee, at
  least!' "

— So, to the letter, sentence was ful-
   filled?
Shelley, may I condense verbosity
That lies before me, into some few
   words
Of English, and illustrate your superb
Achievement by a rescued anecdote,
No great things, only new and true
   beside?
As if some mere familiar of a house
Should venture to accost the group
   at gaze
Before its Titian, famed the wide
   world through,
And supplement such pictured mas-
   terpiece
By whisper "Searching in the ar-
   chives here,
I found the reason of the Lady's fate,
And how by accident it came to pass
She wears the halo and displays the
   palm:
Who, haply, else had never suffered
   — no,
Nor graced our gallery, by conse-
   quence."
Who loved the work would like the
   little news:
Who lauds your poem lends an ear to
   me
Relating how the penalty was paid
By one Marchese dell' Oriolo, called
Onofrio Santa Croce otherwise,
For his complicity in matricide
With Paolo his own brother, — he
   whose crime
And flight induced "those three words
   — She must die."
Thus I unroll you then the manu-
   script.

   "God's justice" — (of the multi-
   plicity
Of such communications extant still,
Recording, each, injustice done by
   God
In person of his Vicar-upon-earth,
Scarce one but leads off to the self-
   same tune) —
"God's justice, tardy though it prove
   perchance,
Rests never on the track until it reach
Delinquency. In proof I cite the
   case
Of Paolo Santa Croce."

            Many times
The youngster, — having been impor-
   tunate

That Marchesine Costanza, who re-
   mained
His widowed mother, should supplant
   the heir
Her elder son, and substitute himself
In sole possession of her faculty, —
And meeting just as often with re-
   buff, —
Blinded by so exorbitant a lust
Of gold, the youngster straightway
   tasked his wits,
Casting about to kill the lady — thus

He first, to cover his iniquity,
Writes to Onofrio Santa Croce, then
Authoritative lord, acquainting him
Their mother was contamination —
   wrought
Like hell-fire in the beauty of their
   House
By dissoluteness and abandonment
Of soul and body to impure delight.
Moreover, since she suffered from
   disease,
Those symptoms which her death
   made manifest
Hydroptic, he affirmed were fruits of
   sin
About to bring confusion and dis-
   grace
Upon the ancient lineage and high
   fame
O' the family, when published. Duty-
   bound,
He asked his brother — what a son
   should do?

Which when Marchese dell' Oriolo
   heard
By letter, being absent at his land
Oriolo, he made answer, this, no more:
"It must behoove a son, — things
   haply so, —
To act as honor prompts a cavalier
And son, perform his duty to all
   three,
Mother and brothers" — here advice
   broke off.

By which advice informed and for-
   tified
As he professed himself — as bound
   by birth
To hear God's voice in primogeni-
   ture —
Paolo, who kept his mother company
In her domain Subiaco, straightway
   dared
His whole enormity of enterprise

And, falling on her, stabbed the lady
   dead ;
Whose death demonstrated her inno-
   cence,
And happened, — by the way, — since
   Jesus Christ
Died to save man, just sixteen hun-
   dred years.
Costanza was of aspect beautiful
Exceedingly, and seemed, although
   in age
Sixty about, to far surpass her peers
The coëtaneous dames, in youth and
   grace.

Done the misdeed, its author takes
   to flight,
Foiling thereby the justice of the
   world :
Not God's however, — God, be sure,
   knows well
The way to clutch a culprit. Witness
   here !
The present sinner, when he least ex-
   pects,
Snug-cornered somewhere i' the Basi-
   licate,
Stumbles upon his death by vio-
   lence.
A man of blood assaults the man of
   blood
And slays him somehow. This was
   afterward :
Enough, he promptly met with his
   deserts,
And, ending thus, permits we end
   with him,
And push forthwith to this impor-
   tant point —
His matricide fell out, of all .he
   days,
Precisely when the law-procedure
   closed
Respecting Count Francesco Cenci's
   death
Chargeable on his daughter, sons, and
   wife.
" Thus patricide was matched with
   matricide,"
A poet not inelegantly rhymed :
Nay, fratricide — those Princes Mas-
   sini ! —
Which so disturbed the spirit of the
   Pope
That all the likelihood Rome enter-
   tained
Of   Beatrice's   pardon   vanished
   straight,
And she endured the piteous death.

Now see
The sequel — what effect command-
   ment had
For strict inquiry into this last case,
When Cardinal Aldobrandini (great
His efficacy — nephew to the Pope !)
Was bidden crush — ay, though his
   very hand
Got soiled i' the act — crime spawning
   everywhere !
Because, when all endeavor had been
   used
To catch the aforesaid Paolo, all in
   vain —
" Make perquisition," quoth our Emi-
   nence,
" Throughout his now deserted domi-
   cile !
Ransack the palace, roof, and floor, to
   find
If haply any scrap of writing, hid
In nook or corner, may convict — who
   knows ? —
Brother Onofrio of intelligence
With brother Paolo, as in brother-
   hood
Is but too likely : crime spawns every-
   where ! "

And, every cranny searched accord-
   ingly,
There comes to light — O lynx-eyed
   Cardinal ! —
Onofrio's unconsidered writing-scrap,
The letter in reply to Paolo's prayer,
The word of counsel that — things
   proving so,
Paolo should act the proper knightly
   part,
And do as was incumbent on a son,
A brother — and a man of birth, be
   sure !

Whereat immediately the officers
Proceeded to arrest Onofrio — found
At foot-ball, child's play, unaware of
   harm,
Safe with his friends, the Orsini, at
   their seat
Monte Giordano ; as he left the house
He came upon the watch in wait for
   him
Set by the Barigel, — was caught and
   caged.

News of which capture being, that
   same hour,
Conveyed to Rome, forthwith our
   Eminence

Commands Taverna, Governor and
  Judge,
To have the process in especial care,
Be, first to last, not only president
In person, but inquisitor as well,
Nor trust the by-work to a substitute;
Bids him not, squeamish, keep the
  bench, but scrub
The floor of Justice, so to speak,—go
  try
His best in prison with the criminal;
Promising, as reward for by-work
  done
Fairly on all-fours, that, success ob-
  tained
And crime avowed, or such conniv-
  ency
With crime as should procure a de-
  cent death—
Himself will humbly beg—which
  means, procure—
The Hat and Purple from his relative
The Pope, and so repay a diligence
Which, meritorious in the Cenci-case,
Mounts plainly here to Purple and
  the Hat.

  Whereupon did my lord the Gov-
    ernor
So masterfully exercise the task
Enjoined him, that he, day by day,
  and week
By week, and month by month, from
  first to last
Deserved the prize: now, punctual at
  his place,
Played Judge, and now, assiduous at
  his post,
Inquisitor—pressed cushion and
  scoured plank,
Early and late, Noon's fervor and
  night's chill,
Naught moved whom 'morn would,
  purpling, make amends!
So that observers laughed as, many a
  day,
He left home, in July when day is
  flame,
Posted to Tordinona-prison, plunged
Into the vault where daylong night is
  ice,
There passed his eight hours on a
  stretch, content,
Examining Onofrio: all the stress
Of all examination steadily
Converging into one pin-point,—he
  pushed
Tentative now of head and now of
  heart.

As when the nut-hatch taps and tries
  the nut
This side and that side till the kernel
  sounds,—
So did he press the sole and single
  point
—What was the very meaning of the
  phrase
"Do what beseems an honored cava-
  lier!"

  Which one persistent question-tor-
    ture,—plied
Day by day, week by week, and month
  by month,
Morn, noon, and night,—fatigued
  away a mind
Grown imbecile by darkness, solitude,
And one vivacious memory gnawing
  there
As when a corpse is coffined with a
  snake:
—Fatigued Onofrio into what might
  seem
Admission that perchance his judg-
  ment groped
So blindly, feeling for an issue—aught
With semblance of an issue from the
  toils
Cast of a sudden round feet late so
  free,—
He possibly might have envisaged,
  scarce
Recoiled from—even were the issue
  death
—Even her death whose life was death
  and worse!
Always provided that the charge of
  crime,
Each jot and tittle of the charge were
  true,
In such a sense, belike, he might ad-
  vise
His brother to expurgate crime with
  . . . well,
With blood, if blood must follow on
  "the course
Taken as might beseem a cavalier."

  Whereupon process ended, and re-
    port
Was made without a minute of delay
To Clement, who, because of those two
  crimes
O' the Massimi and Cenci flagrant late,
Must needs impatiently desire result.

Result obtained, he bade the Gov-
  ernor

Summon the Congregation and de-
spatch.
Summons made, sentence passed ac-
cordingly
—Death by beheading. When his
death-decree
Was intimated to Onofrio, all
Man could do — that did he to save
himself.
'Twas much, the having gained for his
defence
The Advocate o' the Poor, with natural
help
Of many noble friendly persons fain
To disengage a man of family,
So young too, from his grim entangle-
ment.
But Cardinal Aldobrandini ruled
There must be no diversion of the law.
Justice is justice, and the magistrate
Bears not the sword in vain. Who
sins must die.

So, the Marchese had his head cut
off
In Place Saint Angelo beside the
Bridge,
With Rome to see, a concourse infi-
nite ;
Where magnanimity demonstrating
Adequate to his birth and breed, —
poor boy ! —
He made the people the accustomed
speech,
Exhorted them to true faith, honest
works,
And special good behavior as regards
A parent of no matter what the sex,
Bidding each son take warning from
himself.
Truly, it was considered in the boy
Stark staring lunacy, no less, to snap
So plain a bait, be hooked and hauled
ashore
By such an angler as the Cardinal !
Why make confession of his privity
To Paolo's enterprise ? Mere seal-
ing lips —
Or, better, saying, " When I coun-
selled him
' *To do as might beseem a cavalier,*'
What could I mean but, ' *Hide our
parent's shame*
*As Christian ought, by aid of Holy
Church !*
Bury it in a convent — ay, beneath
*Enough dotation to prevent its ghost
From troubling earth !* '" Mere saying
thus, — 'tis plain,

Not only were his life the recompense,
But he had manifestly proved him-
self
True Christian, and in lieu of pun-
ishment
Been praised of all men ! — So the
populace.

Anyhow, when the Pope made
promise good
(That of Aldobrandini, near and dear)
And gave Taverna, who had toiled
so much,
A cardinal's equipment, some such
word
As this from mouth to ear went
saucily ;
" Taverna's cap is dyed in what he
drew
From Santa Croce's veins !" So
joked the world.

I add : Onofrio left one child behind,
A daughter named Valeria, dowered
with grace
Abundantly of soul and body, doomed
To life the shorter for her father's
fate.
By death of her, the Marquisate re-
turned
To that Orsini House from whence it
came :
Oriolo having passed as donative
To Santa Croce from their ancestors.

And no word more ? By all means !
Would you know
The authoritative answer, when folks
urged
" What made Aldobrandini, hound-
like stanch,
Hunt out of life a harmless simple-
ton ? "
The answer was — " Hatred implaca-
ble,
By reason they were rivals in their
love."
The Cardinal's desire was to a dame
Whose favor was Onofrio's. Pricked
with pride,
The simpleton must ostentatiously
Display a ring, the Cardinal's love-
gift.
Given to Onofrio as the lady's gage ;
Which ring on finger, as he put forth
hand
To draw a tapestry, the Cardinal
Saw and knew, gift and owner, old
and young ;

Whereon a fury entered him — the
  fire
He quenched with what could quench
  fire only — blood.
Nay, more : "there want not who
  affirm to boot,
The unwise boy, a certain festal eve,
Feigned ignorance of who the wight
  might be
That pressed too closely on him with
  a crowd.
He struck the Cardinal a blow : and
  then,
To put a face upon the incident,
Dared next day, smug as ever, go pay
  court
I' the Cardinal's ante-chamber. Mark
  and mend.
Ye youth, by this example how may
  greed
Vainglorious operate in worldly
  souls !"

  So ends the chronicler, beginning
  with
"God's justice, tardy though it prove
  perchance,
Rests never till it reach delinquency."
Ay, or how otherwise had come to
  pass
That Victor rules, this present year,
  in Rome ?

PORPHYRIA'S LOVER.

I.

THE rain set early in to-night,
  The sullen wind was soon awake,
It tore the elm-tops down for spite,
  And did its worst to vex the lake,
I listened with heart fit to break.

II.

When glided in Porphyria ; straight
  She shut the cold out and the storm,
And kneeled, and made the cheerless
  grate
  Blaze up, and all the cottage warm ;
Which done, she rose, and from her
  form

III.

Withdrew the dripping cloak and
  shawl,
  And laid her soiled gloves by, un-
  tied

Her hat and let the damp hair fall,
  And, last, she sat down by my side
And called me. When no voice re-
  plied,

IV.

She put my arm about her waist,
  And made her smooth white shoul-
  der bare,
And all her yellow hair displaced,
  And, stooping, made my cheek lie
  there,
And spread, o'er all, her yellow
  hair, —

V.

Murmuring how she loved me — she
  Too weak, for all her heart's en-
  deavor,
To set its struggling passion free
  From pride, and vainer ties dis-
  sever,
And give herself to me forever.

VI.

But passion sometimes would pre-
  vail,
  Nor could to-night's gay feast re-
  strain
A sudden thought of one so pale
  For love of her, and all in vain :
So, she was come through wind and
  rain.

VII.

Be sure I looked up at her eyes
  Happy and proud : at last I knew
Porphyria worshipped me ; surprise
  Made my heart swell, and still it
  grew
While I debated what to do.

VIII.

That moment she was mine, mine
  fair,
  Perfectly pure and good : I found
A thing to do, and all her hair
  In one long yellow string I wound
Three times her little throat around,

IX.

And strangled her. No pain felt she ;
  I am quite sure she felt no pain.
As a shut bud that holds a bee,
  I warily oped her lids : again
Laughed the blue eyes without a
  stain.

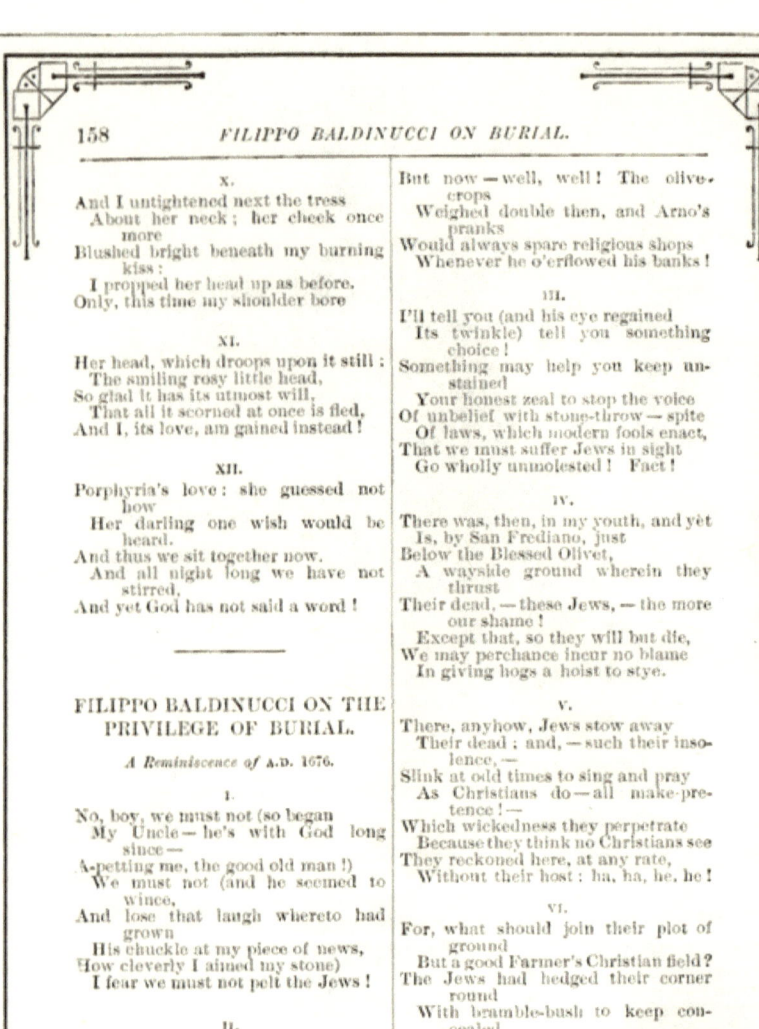

X.

And I untightened next the tress
  About her neck ; her cheek once
    more
Blushed bright beneath my burning
    kiss :
  I propped her head up as before,
Only, this time my shoulder bore

XI.

Her head, which droops upon it still :
  The smiling rosy little head,
So glad it has its utmost will,
  That all it scorned at once is fled,
And I, its love, am gained instead !

XII.

Porphyria's love : she guessed not
    how
  Her darling one wish would be
    heard.
And thus we sit together now,
  And all night long we have not
    stirred,
And yet God has not said a word !

FILIPPO BALDINUCCI ON THE PRIVILEGE OF BURIAL.

A Reminiscence of A.D. 1676.

I.

No, boy, we must not (so began
  My Uncle — he's with God long
    since —
A-petting me, the good old man !)
  We must not (and he seemed to
    wince,
And lose that laugh whereto had
    grown
  His chuckle at my piece of news,
How cleverly I aimed my stone)
  I fear we must not pelt the Jews !

II.

When I was young indeed, — ah, faith
  Was young and strong in Florence
    too !
We Christians never dreamed of
    scathe
  Because we cursed or kicked the
    crew.

But now — well, well ! The olive-
    crops
  Weighed double then, and Arno's
    pranks
Would always spare religious shops
  Whenever he o'erflowed his banks !

III.

I'll tell you (and his eye regained
  Its twinkle) tell you something
    choice !
Something may help you keep un-
    stained
  Your honest zeal to stop the voice
Of unbelief with stone-throw — spite
  Of laws, which modern fools enact,
That we must suffer Jews in sight
  Go wholly unmolested ! Fact !

IV.

There was, then, in my youth, and yet
  Is, by San Frediano, just
Below the Blessed Olivet,
  A wayside ground wherein they
    thrust
Their dead, — these Jews, — the more
    our shame !
  Except that, so they will but die,
We may perchance incur no blame
  In giving hogs a hoist to stye.

V.

There, anyhow, Jews stow away
  Their dead ; and, — such their inso-
    lence, —
Slink at odd times to sing and pray
  As Christians do — all make-pre-
    tence ! —
Which wickedness they perpetrate
  Because they think no Christians see
They reckoned here, at any rate,
  Without their host : ha, ha, he, he !

VI.

For, what should join their plot of
    ground
  But a good Farmer's Christian field ?
The Jews had hedged their corner
    round
  With bramble-bush to keep con-
    cealed
Their doings : for the public road
  Ran betwixt this their ground and
    that
The Farmer's, where he ploughed and
    sowed,
  Grew corn for barn and grapes for
    vat.

VII.

So, properly to guard his store
  And gall the unbelievers too,
He builds a shrine and, what is more,
  Procures a painter whom I knew,
One Buti (he's with God) to paint
  A holy picture there — no less
Than Virgin Mary free from taint
  Borne to the sky by angels : yes !

VIII.

Which shrine he fixed, — who says
    him nay ? —
  A-facing with its picture-side
Not, as you'd think, the public way,
  But just where sought these hounds
      to hide
Their carrion from that very truth
  Of Mary's triumph : not a hound
Could act his mummeries uncouth
  But Mary shamed the pack all
      round !

IX.

Now, if it was amusing, judge !
  — To see the company arrive,
Each Jew intent to end his trudge
  And take his pleasure (though alive)
With all his Jewish kith and kin
  Below ground, have his venom out,
Sharpen his wits for next day's sin,
  Curse Christians, and so home, no
      doubt !

X.

Whereas, each phiz upturned beholds
  Mary, I warrant, soaring brave !
And in a trice, beneath the folds
  Of filthy garb which gowns each
      knave,
Down drops it — there to hide grimace,
  Contortion of the mouth and nose
At finding Mary in the place
  They'd keep for Pilate, I suppose !

XI.

At last, they will not brook — not
    they ! —
  Longer such outrage on their tribe :
So, in some hole and corner, lay
  Their heads together — how to bribe
The meritorious Farmer's self
  To straight undo his work, restore
Their chance to meet, and muse on
    { elf —
  Pretending sorrow, as before !

XII.

Forthwith, a posse, if you please,
  Of Rabbi This and Rabbi That
Almost go down upon their knees
  To get him lay the picture flat.
The spokesman, eighty years of age,
  Gray as a badger, with a goat's
— Not only beard but bleat, 'gins wage
  War with our Mary. Thus he
      dotes : —

XIII.

" Friends, grant a grace ! How He-
      brews toil
  Through life in Florence — why re-
      late
To those who lay the burden, spoil
  Our paths of peace ? We bear our
      fate.
But when with life the long toil ends,
  Why must you — the expression
      craves
Pardon, but truth compels me,
      friends ! —
  Why must you plague us in our
      graves ?

XIV.

" Thoughtlessly plague, I would be-
      lieve !
  For how can you — the lords of ease
By nurture, birthright — e'en conceive
  Our luxury to lie with trees
And turf, — the cricket and the bird
  Left for our last companionship :
No harsh deed, no unkindly word,
  No frowning brow nor scornful lip !

XV.

" Death's luxury, we now rehearse
  While, living, through your streets
      we fare
And take your hatred : nothing worse
  Have we, once dead and safe, to
      bear !
So we refresh our souls, fulfil
  Our works, our daily tasks ; and
      thus
Gather you grain — earth's harvest —
      still
  The wheat for you, the straw for us.

XVI.

" ' What floating in a face, what harm,
  In just a lady borne from bier
By boys' heads, wings for leg and
      arm ? '
  You question. Friends, the harm
      is here —

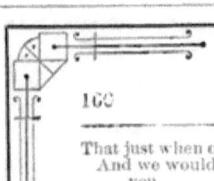

That just when our last sigh is heaved,
  And we would fain thank God and you
For labor done and peace achieved,
  Back comes the Past in full review!

XVII.

" At sight of just that simple flag,
  Starts the foe-feeling serpent-like
From slumber. Leave it lulled, nor drag —
  Though fangless — forth, what needs must strike
When stricken sore, though stroke be vain
  Against the mailed oppressor! Give
Play to our fancy that we gain
  Life's rights when once we cease to live!

XVIII.

" Thus much to courtesy, to kind,
  To conscience! Now to Florence folk!
There's core beneath this apple-rind,
  Beneath this white of egg there's yolk!
Beneath this prayer to courtesy,
  Kind, conscience — there's a sum to pouch!
How many ducats down will buy
  Our shame's removal, sirs? Avouch!

XIX.

" Removal, not destruction, sirs!
  Just turn your picture! Let it front
The public path! Or memory errs,
  Or that same public path is wont
To witness many a chance befall
  Of lust, theft, bloodshed — sins enough,
Wherein our Hebrew part is small.
  Convert yourselves!" — he cut up rough.

XX.

Look you, how soon a service paid
  Religion yields the servant fruit!
A prompt reply our Farmer made
  So following : " Sirs, to grant your suit
Involves much danger! How? Transpose
  Our Lady? Stop the chastisement,
All for your good, herself bestows?
  What wonder if I grudge consent?

XXI.

— " Yet grant it : since, what cash I take
  Is so much saved from wicked use.
We know you! And, for Mary's sake,
  A hundred ducats shall induce
Concession to your prayer. One day
  Suffices : Master Buti's brush
Turns Mary round the other way,
  And deluges your side with slush.

XXII.

" Down with the ducats therefore !" Dump,
  Dump, dump it falls, each counted piece,
Hard gold. Then out of door they stump,
  These dogs, each brisk as with new lease
Of life, I warrant, — glad he'll die
  Henceforward just as he may choose,
Be buried and in clover lie!
  Well said Esaias — " stiff-necked Jews !"

XXIII.

Off posts without a minute's loss
  Our Farmer, once the cash in poke,
And summons Buti — ere its gloss
  Have time to fade from off the joke —
To chop and change his work, undo
  The done side, make the side, now blank.
Recipient of our Lady — who,
  Displaced thus, had these dogs to thank!

XXIV.

Now, you're no boy I need instruct
  In technicalities of Art!
My nephew's childhood sure has sucked
  Along with mother's-milk some part
Of painter's-practice — learned, at least,
  How expeditiously is plied
A work in fresco — never ceased
  When once begun — a day, each side.

XXV.

So, Buti — he's with God — begins :
  First covers up the shrine all round
With hoarding ; then, as like as twins,
  Paints, t'other side the burial-ground.

New Mary, every point the same ;
  Next, sluices over, as agreed,
The old ; and last — but, spoil the
    game
  By telling you ? Not I, indeed !

XXVI.

Well, ere the week was half at end,
  Out came the object of this zeal,
This fine alacrity to spend
  Hard money for mere dead men's
    weal !
How think you ? That old spokes-
    man Jew
  Was High Priest, and he had a
    wife
As old, and she was dying too,
  And wished to end in peace her
    life !

XXVII.

And he must humor dying whims,
  And soothe her with the idle hope
They'd say their prayers and sing
    their hymns
  As if her husband were the Pope !
And she did die — believing just
  This privilege was purchased !
    Dead
In comfort through her foolish trust !
  "Stiff-necked ones," well Esaias
    said !

XXVIII.

So, Sabbath morning, out of gate
  And on to way, what sees our arch
Good Farmer ? Why, they hoist their
    freight —
  The corpse — on shoulder, and so,
    march !
" Now for it, Buti !" In the nick
  Of time 'tis pully-hauly, hence
With hoarding ! O'er the wayside
    quick
  There's Mary plain in evidence !

XXIX.

And here's the convoy halting : right !
  Oh, they are bent on howling psalms
And growling prayers, when oppo-
    site !
  And yet they glance, for all their
    qualms,
Approve that promptitude of his,
  The Farmer's — duly at his post
To take due thanks from every phiz,
  Sour smirk — nay, surly smile
    almost !

XXX.

Then earthward drops each brow
    again ;
  The solemn task's resumed ; they
    reach
Their holy field — the unholy train :
  Enter its precinct, all and each,
Wrapt somehow in their godless rites ;
  Till, rites at end, up-waking, lo
They lift their faces ! What delights
  The mourners as they turn to go ?

XXXI.

Ha, ha, he, he ! On just the side
  They drew their purse-strings to
    make quit
Of Mary, — Christ the Crucified
  Fronted them now — these biters
    bit !
Never was such a hiss and snort,
  Such screwing nose and shooting
    lip !
Their purchase — honey in report —
  Proved gall and verjuice at first sip !

XXXII.

Out they break, on they bustle, where,
  A-top of wall, the Farmer waits
With Buti : never fun so rare !
  The Farmer has the best ; he rates
The rascal, as the old High Priest
  Takes on himself to sermonize —
Nay, sneer " We Jews supposed, at
    least,
  Theft was a crime in Christian
    eyes !"

XXXIII.

"Theft ?" cries the Farmer, " Eat
    your words !
  Show me what constitutes a breach
Of faith in aught was said or heard !
  I promised you in plainest speech
I'd take the thing you count disgrace
  And put it here — and here 'tis put !
Did you suppose I'd leave the place
  Blank therefore, just your rage to
    glut ?

XXXIV.

" I guess you dared not stipulate
  For such a damned impertinence !
So, quick, my graybeard, out of gate
  And in at Ghetto ! Haste you
    hence !

As long as I have house and land,
  To spite you irreligious chaps
Here shall the Crucifixion stand —
  Unless you down with cash, per-
    haps!"

XXXV.

So snickered he and Buti both.
  The Jews said nothing, interchanged
A glance or two, renewed their oath
  To keep ears stopped and hearts
    estranged
From grace, for all our Church can do.
  Then off they scuttle : sullen jog
Homewards, against our Church to
    brew
  Fresh mischief in their synagogue.

XXXVI.

But next day — see what happened,
    boy !
  See why I bid you have a care
How you pelt Jews ! The knaves em-
    ploy
  Such methods of revenge, forbear
No outrage on our faith, when free
  To wreak their malice ! Here they
    took
So base a method — plague o' me
  If I record it in my Book !

XXXVII.

For, next day, while the Farmer sat
  Laughing with Buti, in his shop,
At their successful joke, — rat-tat, —
  Door opens, and they're like to drop
Down to the floor as in there stalks
  A six-feet-high herculean-built
Young he-Jew with a beard that balks
  Description. "Help, ere blood be
    spilt !"

XXXVIII.

— Screamed Buti : for he recognized
  Whom but the son, no less no more,
Of that High Priest his work surprised
  So pleasantly the day before !
Son of the mother, then, whereof
  The bier he lent a shoulder to,
And made the moans about, dared
    scoff
  At sober, Christian grief — the Jew !

XXXIX.

"Sirs, I salute you ! Never rise !
  No apprehension !" (Buti, white
And trembling like a tub of size,
  Had tried to smuggle out of sight

The picture's self — the thing in oils,
  You know, from which a fresco's
    dashed
Which courage speeds while caution
    spoils)
  "Stay and be praised, sir, una-
    bashed !

XL.

"Praised, — ay, and paid too : for I
    come
  To buy that very work of yours,
My poor abode, which boasts — well,
    some
  Few specimens of Art, secures
Haply, a masterpiece indeed
  If I should find my humble means
Suffice the outlay. So, proceed !
  Propose — ere prudence inter-
    venes !"

XLI.

On Buti, cowering like a child,
  These words descended from aloft,
In tone so ominously mild,
  With smile terrifically soft
To that degree — could Buti dare
  (Poor fellow) use his brains, think
    twice ?
He asked, thus taken unaware,
  No more than just the proper price !

XLII.

"Done !" cries the monster. "I dis-
    burse
  Forthwith your moderate demand.
Count on my custom — if no worse
  Your future work be, understand,
Than this I carry off ! No aid !
  My arm, sir, lacks nor bone nor
    thews :
The burden's easy, and we're made,
  Easy or hard, to bear — we Jews !"

XLIII.

Crossing himself at such escape,
  Buti by turns the money eyes
And, timidly, the stalwart shape
  Now moving doorwards ; but, more
    wise,
The Farmer, — who, though dumb,
    this while
  Had watched advantage, — straight
    conceived
A reason for that tone and smile
  So mild and soft ! The Jew — be-
    lieved !

XLIV.

Mary in triumph borne to deck
  A Hebrew household! Pictured
    where
No one was used to bend the neck
  In praise or bow the knee in prayer!
Borne to that domicile by whom?
  The son of the High Priest!
    Through what?
An insult done his mother's tomb!
  Saul changed to Paul—the case
    came pat!

XLV.

"Stay, dog-Jew . . . gentle sir, that
  is!
  Resolve me! Can it be, she
    crowned—
Mary, by miracle— Oh bliss!—
  My present to your burial-ground?
Certain, a ray of light has burst
  Your veil of darkness! Had you
    else,
Only for Mary's sake, unpursed
  So much hard money? Tell—oh,
    tell's!"

XLVI.

Round—like a serpent that we took
  For worm and trod on—turns his
    bulk
About the Jew. First dreadful look
  Sends Buti in a trice to skulk
Out of sight somewhere, safe—alack!
  But our good Farmer faith made
    bold:
And firm (with Florence at his back)
  He stood, while gruff the gutturals
    rolled—

XLVII.

"Ay, sir, a miracle was worked,
  By quite another power, I trow,
Than ever yet in canvas lurked,
  Or you would scarcely face me now!
A certain impulse did suggest
  A certain grasp with this right-
    hand,
Which probably had put to rest
  Our quarrel,—thus your throat once
    spanned!

XLVIII.

"But I remembered me, subdued
  That impulse, and you face me still!
And soon a philosophic mood
  Succeeding (hear it, if you will!)

Has altogether changed my views
  Concerning Art. Blind prejudice!
Well may you Christians tax us Jews
  With scrupulosity too nice!

XLIX.

"For, don't I see,—let's issue
  join!—
  Whenever I'm allowed pollute
(I—and my little bag of coin)
  Some Christian palace of repute,—
Don't I see stuck up everywhere
  Abundant proof that cultured taste
Has Beauty for its only care,
  And upon Truth no thought to
    waste?

L.

"'Jew, since it must be, take in
  pledge
  Of payment'—so a Cardinal
Has sighed to me as if a wedge
  Entered his heart—'this best of all
My treasures!' Leda, Ganymede,
  Or Antiope: swan, eagle, ape
(Or what's the beast of what's the
    breed),
  And Jupiter in every shape!

LI.

"Whereat if I presume to ask
  'But, Eminence, though Titian's
    whisk
Of brush have well performed its task,
  How comes it these false godships
    frisk
In presence of—what yonder frame
  Pretends to image? Surely, odd
It seems, you let confront The Name
  Each beast the heathen called his
    god!'

LII.

"Benignant smiles me pity straight
  The Cardinal. 'Tis Truth, we
    prize!
Art's the sole question in debate!
  These subjects are so many lies.
We treat them with a proper scorn
  When we turn lies—called gods for-
    sooth—
To lies' fit use, now Christ is born.
  Drawing and coloring are Truth.

LIII.

"'Think you I honor lies so much
  As scruple to parade the charms
Of Leda—Titian, every touch—
  Because the thing within her arms

Means Jupiter who had the praise
  And prayer of a benighted world?
Benighted I too, if, in days
  Of light, I kept the canvas furled!'

LIV.

"So ending, with some easy gibe.
  What power has logic! I, at once,
Acknowledged error in our tribe,
  So squeamish that, when friends
    ensconce
A pretty picture in its niche
  To do us honor, deck our graves,
We fret and fume and have an itch
  To strangle folk — ungrateful
    knaves!

LV.

"No, sir! Be sure that — what's its
    style,
  Your picture? — shall possess un-
    grudged
A place among my rank and file
  Of Ledas and what not — be judged
Just as a picture! — and (because
  I fear me much I scarce have bought
A Titian) Master Buti's flaws
  Found there, will have the laugh
    flaws ought!"

LVI.

So, with a scowl, it darkens door —
  This bulk — no longer! Buti makes
Prompt glad re-entry; there's a score
  Of oaths, as the good Farmer wakes
From what must needs have been a
    trance,
  Or he had struck (he swears) to
    ground
The bold bad mouth that dared ad-
    vance
  Such doctrine the reverse of sound!

LVII.

Was magic here? Most like! For,
    since,
  Somehow our city's faith grows still
More and more lukewarm, and our
    Prince
  Or loses heart or wants the will
To check increase of cold. 'Tis
    "Live
  And let live! Languidly repress
The Dissident! In short, — contrive
  Christians must bear with Jews: no
    less!"

LVIII.

The end seems, any Israelite
  Wants any picture, — pishes, poohs,
Purchases, hangs it full in sight
  In any chamber he may choose!
In Christ's crown, one more thorn we
    rue!
  In Mary's bosom, one more sword!
No, boy, you must not pelt a Jew!
  O Lord, how long? How long, O
    Lord?

SOLILOQUY OF THE SPAN-
ISH CLOISTER.

I.

GR-R-R — there go, my heart's abhor-
    rence!
  Water your damned flower-pots,
    do!
If hate killed men, Brother Lawrence,
  God's blood, would not mine kill
    you!
What? your myrtle-bush wants trim-
    ming?
  Oh, that rose has prior claims —
Needs its leaden vase filled brim-
    ming?
  Hell dry you up with its flames!

II.

At the meal we sit together:
  Salve tibi! I must hear
Wise talk of the kind of weather,
  Sort of season, time of year:
*Not a plenteous cork-crop: scarcely
  Dare we hope oak-galls, I doubt:*
What's the Latin name for "parsley"?
  What's the Greek name for Swine's
    Snout?

III.

Whew! We'll have our platter bur-
    nished,
  Laid with care on our own shelf!
With a fire-new spoon we're fur-
    nished,
  And a goblet for ourself,
Rinsed like something sacrificial
  Ere 'tis fit to touch our chaps —
Marked with L. for our initial!
  (He-he! There his lily snaps!)

Soliloquy of the Spanish Cloister. — Page 164.

IV.

Saint, forsooth! While brown Dolores
 Squats outside the Convent bank
With Sanchicha, telling stories,
 Steeping tresses in the tank,
Blue-black, lustrous, thick like horsehairs,
 — Can't I see his dead eye glow,
Bright as 'twere a Barbary corsair's?
 (That is, if he'd let it show!)

V.

When he finishes refection,
 Knife and fork he never lays
Cross-wise, to my recollection,
 As do I, in Jesu's praise.
I the Trinity illustrate,
 Drinking watered orange-pulp —
In three sips the Arian frustrate;
 While he drains his at one gulp.

VI.

Oh, those melons? If he's able
 We're to have a feast! so nice!
One goes to the Abbot's table,
 All of us get each a slice.
How go on your flowers? None double?
 Not one fruit-sort can you spy?
Strange! — And I, too, at such trouble
 Keep them close-nipped on the sly!

VII.

There's a great text in Galatians,
 Once you trip on it, entails
Twenty-nine distinct damnations,
 One sure, if another fails:
If I trip him just a-dying,
 Sure of heaven as sure can be,
Spin him round and send him flying
 Off to hell, a Manichee?

VIII.

Or, my scrofulous French novel
 On gray paper with blunt type!
Simply glance at it, you grovel
 Hand and foot in Belial's gripe:
If I double down its pages
 At the woful sixteenth print,
When he gathers his greengages,
 Ope a sieve and slip it in 't?

IX.

Or, there's Satan! — one might venture
 Pledge one's soul to him, yet leave

Such a flaw in the indenture
 As he'd miss till, past retrieve,
Blasted lay that rose-acacia
 We're so proud of! *Hy, Zy, Hine . . .*
'St, there's Vespers! *Plena gratiâ*
 Ave, Virgo! Gr-r-r — you swine!

THE HERETIC'S TRAGEDY.

A MIDDLE-AGE INTERLUDE.

ROSA MUNDI; SEU, FULCITE ME FLORIBUS. A CONCEIT OF MASTER GYSBRECHT, CANON-REGULAR OF SAINT JODOCUS-BY-THE-BAR, YPRES CITY. CANTUQUE, *Virgilius.* AND HATH OFTEN BEEN SUNG AT HOCK-TIDE AND FESTIVALS. GAVISUS ERAM, *Jessides.*

(It would seem to be a glimpse from the burning of Jacques du Bourg-Molay, at Paris, A.D. 1314; as distorted by the refraction from Flemish brain to brain, during the course of a couple of centuries.)

I.

PREADMONISHETH THE ABBOT DEODAET.

THE Lord, we look to once for all,
 Is the Lord we should look at, all at once:
He knows not to vary, saith Saint Paul,
 Nor the shadow of turning, for the nonce.
See him no other than as he is!
 Give both the infinitudes their due —
Infinite mercy, but, I wis,
 As infinite a justice too.
   [*Organ: plagal-cadence.*
 As infinite a justice too.

II.

ONE SINGETH.

John, Master of the Temple of God,
 Falling to sin the Unknown Sin,
What he bought of Emperor Aldabrod,
 He sold it to Sultan Saladin:
Till, caught by Pope Clement, a-buzzing there,
 Hornet-prince of the mad wasps' hive,

And clipt of his wings in Paris square,
  They bring him now to be burned
  alive.
  [*And wanteth there grace of lute
    or clavicithern, ye shall say to
    confirm him who singeth—*
We bring John now to be burned
  alive.

III.

In the midst is a goodly gallows built;
  'Twixt fork and fork, a stake is
  stuck;
But first they set divers tumbrils
  a-tilt,
  Make a trench all round with the
  city muck;
Inside they pile log upon log, good
  store;
  Fagots not few, blocks great and
  small,
Reach a man's mid-thigh, no less, no
  more,—
  For they mean he should roast in
  the sight of all.

CHORUS.

We mean he should roast in the
  sight of all.

IV.

Good sappy bavins that kindle forth-
  with;
  Billets that blaze substantial and
  slow;
Pine-stump split deftly, dry as pith;
  Larch-heart that chars to a chalk-
  white glow:
Then up they hoist me John in a chafe,
  Sling him fast like a hog to scorch,
Spit in his face, then leap back safe,
  Sing "Laudes," and bid clap-to the
  torch.

CHORUS.

Laus Deo—who bids clap-to the
  torch.

V.

John of the Temple, whose fame so
  bragged,
  Is burning alive in Paris square!
How can he curse, if his mouth is
  gagged?
  Or wriggle his neck, with a collar
  there?
Or heave his chest, while a band goes
  round?
  Or threat with his fist, since his
  arms are spliced?

Or kick with his feet, now his legs are
  bound?
  —Thinks John, I will call upon
  Jesus Christ.
  [*Here one crosseth himself.*

VI.

Jesus Christ—John had bought and
  sold,
  Jesus Christ—John had eaten and
  drunk;
To him, the Flesh meant silver and
  gold.
(*Salvâ reverentiâ.*)
Now it was, "Saviour, bountiful lamb,
  I have roasted thee Turks, though
  men roast me!
See thy servant, the plight wherein I
  am!
  Art thou a saviour? Save thou
  me!"

CHORUS.

'Tis John the mocker cries, "Save
  thou me!"

VII.

Who maketh God's menace an idle
  word?
  —Saith, it no more means what it
  proclaims,
Than a damsel's threat to her wanton
  bird?—
  For she too prattles of ugly names.
—Saith, he knoweth but one thing,—
  what he knows?
  That God is good and the rest is
  breath;
Why else is the same styled Sharon's
  rose?
  Once a rose, ever a rose, he saith.

CHORUS.

Oh, John shall yet find a rose, he
  saith.

VIII.

Alack, there be roses and roses, John!
  Some honeyed of taste like your
  leman's tongue;
Some, bitter; for why? (roast gayly
  on!)
  Their tree struck root in devil's
  dung.
When Paul once reasoned of righteous-
  ness
  And of temperance and of judgment
  to come,

Good Felix trembled, he could no less :
  John, snickering, crooked his
    wicked thumb.

CHORUS.

What cometh to John of the wicked
  thumb ?

IX.

Ha, ha ! John plucketh now at his
   rose
To rid himself of a sorrow at heart !
Lo, — petal on petal, fierce rays un-
   close ;
Anther on anther, sharp spikes out-
   start ;
And with blood for dew, the bosom
   boils ;
And a gust of sulphur is all its smell ;
And lo, he is horribly in the toils
  Of a coal-black giant flower of hell !

CHORUS.

What maketh heaven, That maketh
  hell.

X.

So, as John called now, through the
   fire amain,
On the Name, he had cursed with,
   all his life —
To the Person, he bought and sold
   again —
  For the Face, with his daily buffets
   rife —
Feature by feature It took its place ;
  And his voice, like a mad dog's
   choking bark,
At the steady whole of the Judge's
   face —
  Died. Forth John's soul flared into
   the dark.

SUBJOINETH THE ABBOT DEODAET.

God help all poor souls lost in the
  dark !

HOLY-CROSS DAY.

ON WHICH THE JEWS WERE FORCED
TO ATTEND AN ANNUAL CHRIS-
TIAN SERMON IN ROME.

[" Now was come about Holy-Cross Day,
and now must my lord preach his first ser-
mon to the Jews : as it was of old cared for
in the merciful bowels of the Church, that,
so to speak, a crumb, at least, from her con-
spicuous table here in Rome, should be,
though but once yearly, cast to the famish-
ing dogs, under-trampled and bespitten-upon
beneath the feet of the guests. And a mov-
ing sight in truth, this, of so many of the
besotted blind restif and ready to perish He-
brews! now maternally brought — nay (for
He saith, 'Compel them to come in'), haled,
as it were, by the head and hair, and against
their obstinate hearts, to partake of the
heavenly grace. What awakening, what
striving with tears, what working of a yeasty
conscience! Nor was my lord wanting to
himself on so apt an occasion ; witness the
abundance of conversions which did inconti-
nently reward him ; though not to my lord
be altogether the glory." — *Diary by the
Bishop's Secretary,* 1600.]

What the Jews really said, on thus being
driven to church, was rather to this effect : —

I.

Fee, faw, fum ! bubble and squeak !
Blessedest Thursday's the fat of the
   week.
Rumble and tumble, sleek and rough,
Stinking and savory, smug and gruff,
Take the church-road, for the bell's
   due chime
Gives us the summons — 'tis sermon-
   time !

II.

Boh, here's Barnabas ! Job, that's
   you ?
Up stumps Solomon — bustling too ?
Shame, man ! greedy beyond your
   years
To handsel the bishop's shaving-
   shears ?
Fair play's a jewel ! Leave friends
   in the lurch ?
Stand on a line ere you start for the
   church !

III

Higgledy piggledy, packed we lie,
Rats in a hamper, swine in a sty,
Wasps in a bottle, frogs in a sieve,
Worms in a carcass, fleas in a sleeve.
Hist ! square shoulders, settle your
   thumbs
And buzz for the bishop — here he
   comes.

IV.

Bow, wow, wow — a bone for the
   dog !
I liken his Grace to an acorned hog.

What, a boy at his side, with the
    bloom of a lass,
To help and handle my lord's hour-
    glass!
Didst ever behold so lithe a chine?
His cheek hath laps like a fresh-
    singed swine.

V.

Aaron's asleep — shove hip to haunch,
Or somebody deal him a dig in the
    paunch!
Look at the purse with the tassel and
    knob,
And the gown with the angel and
    thingumbob!
What's he at, quotha? reading his
    text!
Now you've his curtsey — and what
    comes next?

VI.

See to our converts — you doomed
    black dozen —
No stealing away — nor cog nor
    cozen!
You five, that were thieves, deserve
    it fairly;
You seven, that were beggars, will
    live less sparely;
You took your turn and dipped in the
    hat,
Got fortune — and fortune gets you;
    mind that!

VII.

Give your first groan — compunction's
    at work;
And soft! from a Jew you mount to
    a Turk.
Lo, Micah, — the selfsame beard on
    chin
He was four times already converted
    in!
Here's a knife, clip quick — it's a sign
    of grace —
Or he ruins us all with his hanging-
    face.

VIII.

Whom now is the bishop a-leering at?
I know a point where his text falls
    pat.
I'll tell him to-morrow, a word just
    now
Went to my heart and made me vow
To meddle no more with the worst of
    trades:
Let somebody else play his serenades!

IX.

Groan all together now, whee — hee
    — hee!
It's a-work, it's a-work, ah, woe is
    me!
It began, when a herd of us, picked
    and placed,
Were spurred through the Corso,
    stripped to the waist;
Jew brutes, with sweat and blood
    well spent
To usher in worthily Christian Lent.

X.

It grew, when the hangman entered
    our bounds,
Yelled, pricked us out to his church
    like hounds:
It got to a pitch, when the hand in-
    deed
Which gutted my purse, would throt-
    tle my creed:
And it overflows, when, to even the
    odd,
Men I helped to their sins, help me to
    their God.

XI.

But now, while the scapegoats leave
    our flock,
And the rest sit silent and count the
    clock,
Since forced to muse the appointed
    time
On these precious facts and truths
    sublime, —
Let us fitly employ it, under our
    breath,
In saying Ben Ezra's Song of Death.

XII.

For Rabbi Ben Ezra, the night he
    died,
Called sons and sons' sons to his side,
And spoke, "This world has been
    harsh and strange;
Something is wrong: there needeth a
    change.
But what, or where? at the last or
    first?
In one point only we sinned, at worst.

XIII.

"The Lord will have mercy on Jacob
    yet,
And again in his border see Israel
    set.

When Judah beholds Jerusalem,
The stranger-seed shall be joined to
    them :
To Jacob's House shall the Gentiles
    cleave,
So the Prophet saith and his sons be-
    lieve.

XIV.

"Ay, the children of the chosen race
Shall carry and bring them to their
    place ;
In the land of the Lord shall lead the
    same,
Bondsmen and handmaids. Who
    shall blame,
When the slaves enslave, the op-
    pressed ones o'er
The oppressor triumph for evermore !

XV.

"God spoke, and gave us the word to
    keep :
Bade never fold the hands nor sleep
'Mid a faithless world, — at watch and
    ward,
Till Christ at the end relieve our
    guard
By his servant Moses the watch was
    set ;
Though near upon cock-crow, we keep
    it yet.

XVI.

"Thou ! if thou wast he, who at mid-
    watch came,
By the starlight, naming a dubious
    name !
And if, too heavy with sleep — too
    rash
With fear — O thou, if that martyr-
    gash
Fell on thee coming to take thine own,
And we gave the Cross, when we
    owed the Throne —

XVII.

"Thou art the Judge. We are
    bruised thus.
But, the Judgment over, join sides
    with us !
Thine too is the cause ! and not more
    thine
Than ours, is the work of those dogs
    and swine,
Whose life laughs through and spits
    at their creed.
Who maintain thee in word, and defy
    thee in deed !

XVIII.

"We withstood Christ then ? Be
    mindful how
At least we withstand Barabbas now !
Was our outrage sore ? But the worst
    we spared,
To have called these — Christians, had
    we dared !
Let defiance to them pay mistrust of
    thee,
And Rome make amends for Calvary !

XIX.

"By the torture, prolonged from age
    to age,
By the infamy, Israel's heritage,
By the Ghetto's plague, by the garb's
    disgrace,
By the badge of shame, by the felon's
    place,
By the branding-tool, the bloody
    whip,
And the summons to Christian fellow-
    ship, —

XX.

"We boast our proof that at least the
    Jew
Would wrest Christ's name from the
    Devil's crew.
Thy face took never so deep a shade
But we fought them in it, God our
    aid !
A trophy to bear, as we march, thy
    band
South, East, and on to the Pleasant
    Land !"
    [*The late Pope abolished this bad
    business of the sermon.* — R. B.]

AMPHIBIAN.

I.

The fancy I had to-day,
    Fancy which turned a fear !
I swam far out in the bay,
    Since waves laughed warm and
    clear.

II.

I lay and looked at the sun,
    The noon-sun looked at me :
Between us two, no one
    Live creature, that I could see.

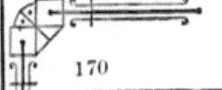

III.

Yes ! There came floating by
  Me, who lay floating too,
Such a strange butterfly !
  Creature as dear as new :

IV.

Because the membraned wings
  So wonderful, so wide,
So sun-suffused, were things
  Like soul and naught beside.

V.

A handbreadth over head !
  All of the sea my own,
It owned the sky instead ;
  Both of us were alone.

VI.

I never shall join its flight,
  For naught buoys flesh in air.
If it touch the sea — good-night !
  Death sure and swift waits there.

VII.

Can the insect feel the better
  For watching the uncouth play
Of limbs that slip the fetter,
  Pretend as they were not clay ?

VIII.

Undoubtedly I rejoice
  That the air comports so well
With a creature which had the choice
  Of the land once. Who can tell ?

IX.

What if a certain soul
  Which early slipped its sheath,
And has for its home the whole
  Of heaven, thus look beneath,

X.

Thus watch one who, in the world,
  Both lives and likes life's way,
Nor wishes the wings unfurled
  That sleep in the worm, they say ?

XI.

But sometimes when the weather
  Is blue, and warm waves tempt
To free one's self of tether,
  And try a life exempt

XII.

From worldly noise and dust,
  In the sphere which overbrims
With passion and thought, — why, just
  Unable to fly, one swims !

XIII.

By passion and thought upborne,
  One smiles to one's self — "They fare
Scarce better, they need not scorn
  Our sea, who live in the air !"

XIV.

Emancipate through passion
  And thought, with sea for sky,
We substitute, in a fashion,
  For heaven — poetry :

XV.

Which sea, to all intent,
  Gives flesh such noon-disport
As a finer element
  Affords the spirit-sort.

XVI.

Whatever they are, we seem :
  Imagine the thing they know ;
All deeds they do, we dream ;
  Can heaven be else but so ?

XVII.

And meantime, yonder streak
  Meets the horizon's verge ;
That is the land, to seek
  If we tire or dread the surge ;

XVIII.

Land the solid and safe —
  To welcome again (confess !)
When, high and dry, we chafe
  The body, and don the dress.

XIX.

Does she look, pity, wonder
  At one who mimics flight,
Swims — heaven above, sea under,
  Yet always earth in sight ?

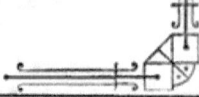

ST. MARTIN'S SUMMER.

I.

No protesting, dearest!
  Hardly kisses even!
    Don't we both know how it ends?
How the greenest leaf turns searest?
Bluest outbreak — blankest heaven?
    Lovers — friends?

II.

You would build a mansion,
  I would weave a bower
    — Want the heart for enterprise.
Walls admit of no expansion:
Trellis-work may haply flower
    Twice the size.

III.

What makes glad Life's Winter?
  New buds, old blooms after.
    Sad the sighing "How suspect
Beams would ere mid-autumn splin-
    ter,
  Rooftree scarce support a rafter,
    Walls lie wrecked?"

IV.

You are young, my princess!
  I am hardly older:
    Yet — I steal a glance behind!
Dare I tell you what convinces
Timid me that you, if bolder,
    Bold — are blind?

V.

Where we plan our dwelling
  Glooms a graveyard surely!
    Headstone, footstone moss may
      drape, —
Name, date, violets hide from spell-
    ing, —
  But, though corpses rot obscurely,
    Ghosts escape.

VI.

Ghosts! O breathing Beauty,
  Give my frank word pardon!
    What if I — somehow, some-
      where —
Pledged my soul to endless duty
Many a time and oft? Be hard on
    Love — laid there?

VII.

Nay, blame grief that's fickle,
  Time that proves a traitor,
    Chance, change, all that purpose
      warps, —
Death who spares to thrust the sickle,
  Which laid Love low, through flow-
    ers which later
    Shroud the corpse!

VIII.

And you, my winsome lady,
  Whisper me with like frankness!
    Lies nothing buried long ago?
Are you — which shimmer mid what's
      shady
  Where moss and violet run to rank-
    ness —
    Tombs, or no?

IX.

Who taxes you with murder?
  My hands are clean — or nearly!
    Love being mortal needs must
      pass.
Repentance? Nothing were absurder.
  Enough: we felt Love's loss se-
    verely;
    Though now — alas!

X.

Love's corpse lies quiet therefore,
  Only Love's ghost plays truant,
    And warns us have in wholesome
      awe
Durable mansionry; that's wherefore
  I weave but trellis-work, pursuant
    — Life, to law.

XI.

The solid, not the fragile,
  Tempts rain and hail and thunder.
    If bower stand firm at autumn's
      close,
Beyond my hope, — why, boughs were
      agile;
  If bower fall flat, we scarce need
      wonder
    Wreathing — rose!

XII.

So, truce to the protesting,
  So, muffled be the kisses!
    For, would we but avow the truth,
Sober is genuine joy. No jesting!
  Ask else Penelope, Ulysses —
    Old in youth!

XIII.

For why should ghosts feel angered?
  Let all their interference
    Be faint march-music in the air!
"Up! Join the rear of us the van-
    guard!
  Up, lovers, dead to all appearance,
    Laggard pair!"

XIV.

The while you clasp me closer,
  The while I press you deeper,
    As safe we chuckle,—under
    breath,
Yet all the slyer, the jocoser,—
  "So, life can boast its day, like leap-
    year,
    Stolen from death!"

XV.

Ah me — the sudden terror!
  Hence quick — avaunt, avoid me,
    You cheat, the ghostly flesh-dis-
    guised!
Nay, all the ghosts in one! Strangè
    error!
So, 'twas Death's self that clipped
    and coyed me,
    Loved — and lied!

XVI.

Ay, dead loves are the potent!
  Like any cloud they used you,
    Mere semblance you, but sub-
    stance they!
Build we no mansion, weave we no
    tent!
    Mere flesh — their spirit interfused
    you!
    Hence, I say!

XVII.

All theirs, none yours the glamour!
  Theirs each low word that won
    me,
    Soft look that found me Love's,
    and left
What else but you — the tears and
    clamor
That's all your very own! Undone
    me —
    Ghost-bereft!

JAMES LEE'S WIFE.

I.

JAMES LEE'S WIFE SPEAKS AT THE WINDOW.

I.

Ah, Love, but a day,
  And the world has changed!
The sun's away,
  And the bird estranged;
The wind has dropped,
  And the sky's deranged:
Summer has stopped.

II.

Look in my eyes!
  Wilt thou change too?
Should I fear surprise?
  Shall I find aught new
In the old and dear,
  In the good and true,
With the changing year?

III.

Thou art a man,
  But I am thy love.
For the lake, its swan;
  For the dell, its dove;
And for thee — (oh, haste!)
  Me to bend above,
Me, to hold embraced.

II.

BY THE FIRESIDE.

I.

Is all our fire of shipwreck wood,
  Oak and pine?
Oh, for the ills half-understood,
  The dim dead woe
  Long ago
Befallen this bitter coast of France!
Well, poor sailors took their chance;
  I take mine.

II.

A ruddy shaft our fire must shoot
  O'er the sea;
Do sailors eye the casement — mute
  Drenched and stark,
  From their bark —

And envy, gnash their teeth for hate
O' the warm safe house and happy
    freight
  — Thee and me?

III.

God help you, sailors, at your need!
    Spare the curse!
For some ships, safe in port indeed,
    Rot and rust,
    Run to dust,
All through worms i' the wood, which
    crept,
Gnawed our hearts out while we
    slept,
    That is worse.

IV.

Who lived here before us two?
    Old-world pairs.
Did a woman ever — would I knew! —
    Watch the man
    With whom began
Love's voyage full-sail, — (now, gnash
    your teeth!)
When planks start, open hell beneath
    Unawares?

III

IN THE DOORWAY.

I.

THE swallow has set her six young on
    the rail,
  And looks seaward:
The water's in stripes like a snake,
    olive-pale
  To the leeward, —
On the weather-side, black, spotted
    white with the wind.
"Good fortune departs, and disaster's
    behind," —
Hark, the wind with its wants and its
    infinite wail!

II.

Our fig-tree, that leaned for the salt-
    ness, has furled
  Her five fingers,
Each leaf like a hand opened wide to
    the world
  Where there lingers

No glint of the gold, Summer sent for
    her sake
How the vines writhe in rows, each
    impaled on its stake!
My heart shrivels up and my spirit
    shrinks curled.

III

Yet here are we two; we have love,
    house enough,
  With the field there;
This house of four rooms, that field
    red and rough,
  Though it yield there,
For the rabbit that robs, scarce a
    blade or a bent;
If a magpie alight now, it seems an
    event;
And they both will be gone at Novem-
    ber's rebuff.

IV

But why must cold spread? but
    wherefore bring change
  To the spirit,
God meant should mate his with an
    infinite range,
  And inherit
His power to put life in the darkness
    and cold?
O, live and love worthily, bear and
    be bold!
Whom Summer made friends of, let
    Winter estrange!

IV.

ALONG THE BEACH.

I.

I WILL be quiet and talk with you,
  And reason why you are wrong.
You wanted my love — is that much
    true?
And so I did love, so I do:
  What has come of it all along?

II.

I took you — how could I otherwise?
  For a world to me, and more;
For all, love greatens and glorifies
Till God's a-glow, to the loving
    eyes,
  In what was mere earth before.

III.

Yes, earth — yes, mere ignoble earth!
  Now do I misstate, mistake?
Do I wrong your weakness and call
  it worth?
Expect all harvest, dread no dearth,
  Seal my sense up for your sake?

IV.

O Love, Love, no, Love! not so, in-
  deed
You were just weak earth, I knew:
With much in you waste, with many
  a weed,
And plenty of passions run to seed,
  But a little good grain too.

V.

And such as you were, I took you for
  mine:
  Did not you find me yours,
To watch the olive and wait the
  vine,
And wonder when rivers of oil and
  wine
  Would flow, as the Book assures?

VI.

Well, and if none of these good things
  came,
  What did the failure prove?
The man was my whole world, all
  the same,
With his flowers to praise or his
  weeds to blame,
  And, either or both, to love.

VII.

Yet this turns now to a fault — there!
  there!
  That I do love, watch too long,
And wait too well, and weary and
  wear;
And 'tis all an old story, and my de-
  spair
  Fit subject for some new song:

VIII.

"How the light, light love, he has
  wings to fly
  At suspicion of a bond:
My wisdom has bidden your pleasure
  good-by,

Which will turn up next in a laughing
  eye,
  And why should you look be-
  yond?"

V.

ON THE CLIFF.

I.

I LEANED on the turf,
I looked at a rock
Left dry by the surf;
For the turf, to call it grass were to
  mock:
Dead to the roots, so deep was done
The work of the summer sun.

II.

And the rock lay flat
As an anvil's face:
No iron like that!
Baked dry; of a weed, of a shell, no
  trace:
Sunshine outside, but ice at the core,
Death's altar by the lone shore.

III.

On the turf, sprang gay
With his films of blue,
No cricket, I'll say,
But a warhorse, barded and chan-
  froned too,
The gift of a quixote-mage to his
  knight,
Real fairy, with wings all right.

IV.

On the rock, they scorch
Like a drop of fire
From a brandished torch,
Fall two red fans of a butterfly;
No turf, no rock, — in their ugly stead,
See, wonderful blue and red!

V.

Is it not so
With the minds of men?
The level and low,
The burnt and bare, in themselves;
  but then
With such a blue and red grace, not
  theirs,
Love settling unawares!

VI.

READING A BOOK, UNDER THE CLIFF.

I.

"Still ailing, Wind? Wilt be ap-
    peased or no?
Which needs the other's office, thou
    or I?
Dost want to be disburthened of a
    woe,
    And can, in truth, my voice untie
Its links, and let it go?

II.

"Art thou a dumb, wronged thing
    that would be righted,
Intrusting thus thy cause to me?
    Forbear!
No tongue can mend such pleadings;
    faith, requited
With falsehood, — love, at last aware
Of scorn, — hopes, early blighted, —

III.

"We have them; but I know not any
    tone
    So fit as thine to falter forth a sor-
    row:
Dost think men would go mad with-
    out a moan,
    If they knew any way to borrow
A pathos like thy own?

IV.

"Which sigh wouldst mock, of all the
    sighs? The one
    So long escaping from lips starved
    and blue,
That lasts while on her pallet-bed the
    nun
    Stretches her length; her foot
    comes through
The straw she shivers on;

V.

"You had not thought she was so
    tall: and spent,
    Her shrunk lids open, her lean fin-
    gers shut
Close, close, their sharp and livid nails
    indent
    The clammy palm; then all is
    mute:
That way, the spirit went.

VI.

"Or wouldst thou rather that I un-
    derstand
    Thy will to help me? — like the dog
    I found
Once, pacing sad this solitary strand,
    Who would not take my food, poor
    hound,
But whined, and licked my hand."

VII.

All this, and more, comes from some
    young man's pride
    Of power to see, — in failure and
    mistake,
Relinquishment, disgrace, on every
    side, —
    Merely examples for his sake,
Helps to his path untried:

VIII.

Instances he must — simply recog-
    nize?
    Oh, more than so! — must, with a
    learner's zeal,
Make doubly prominent, twice em-
    phasize,
    By added touches that reveal
The god in babe's disguise.

IX.

Oh, he knows what defeat means,
    and the rest!
    Himself the undefeated that shall
    be:
Failure, disgrace, he flings them you
    to test, —
    His triumph, in eternity
Too plainly manifest!

X.

Whence, judge if he learn forthwith
    what the wind
    Means in its moaning — by the
    happy prompt
Instinctive way of youth, I mean:
    for kind
    Calm years, exacting their accompt
Of pain, mature the mind:

XI.

And some midsummer morning, at
    the lull
    Just about daybreak, as he looks
    across
A sparkling foreign country, wonder-
    ful

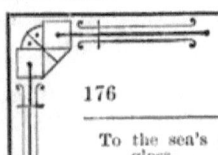

To the sea's edge for gloom and
    gloss,
Next minute must annul, —

XII.

Then, when the wind begins among
    the vines,
    So low, so low, what shall it say
      but this?
" Here is the change beginning, here
    the lines
    Circumscribe beauty, set to bliss
The limit time assigns."

XIII.

Nothing can be as it has been be-
    fore ;
    Better, so call it, only not the same.
To draw one beauty into our hearts'
    core,
    And keep it changeless ! such our
      claim ;
So answered, — Never more !

XIV.

Simple ? Why this is the old woe o'
    the world ;
    Tune, to whose rise and fall we
      live and die.
Rise with it, then ! Rejoice that man
    is hurled
    From change to change unceas-
      ingly,
His soul's wings never furled !

XV.

That's a new question ; still replies
    the fact,
    Nothing endures : the wind moans,
      saying so ;
We moan in acquiescence : there's
    life's pact,
    Perhaps probation — do *I* know ?
God does : endure his act !

XVI.

Only, for man, how bitter not to
    grave
    On his soul's hands' palms one fair
      good wise thing
Just as he grasped it ! For himself,
    death's wave ;
    While time first washes — ah, the
      sting ! —
O'er all he'd sink to save.

VII.

AMONG THE ROCKS.

I.

Oh, good gigantic smile o' the brown
    old earth,
    This autumn morning ! How he
      sets his bones
To bask i' the sun, and thrusts out
    knees and feet
For the ripple to run over in its
    mirth ;
    Listening the while, where on the
      heap of stones
The white breast of the sea-lark twit-
    ters sweet.

II.

That is the doctrine, simple, ancient,
    true ;
    Such is life's trial, as old earth
      smiles and knows.
If you loved only what were worth
    your love,
    Love were clear gain, and wholly
      well for you :
Make the low nature better by your
    throes !
Give earth yourself, go up for gain
    above !

VIII.

BESIDE THE DRAWING-BOARD.

I.

" As like as a Hand to another
    Hand ! "
    Whoever said that foolish thing,
Could not have studied to understand
    The counsels of God in fashioning,
Out of the infinite love of his heart,
This Hand, whose beauty I praise,
    apart
From the world of wonder left to
    praise,
If I tried to learn the other ways
Of love, in its skill, or love, in its
    power.
    " As like as a Hand to another
    Hand : "
    Who said that, never took his stand,
Found and followed, like me, an hour,

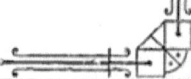

" If haply I might reproduce
One motive of the mechanism." — Page 177.

The beauty in this, — how free, how
  fine
To fear, almost, — of the limit-line !
As I looked at this, and learned and
    drew,
  Drew and learned, and looked
    again,
While fast the happy minutes flew,
  Its beauty mounted into my brain,
  And a fancy seized me : I was fain
To efface my work, begin anew,
Kiss what before I only drew ;
Ay, laying the red chalk 'twixt my
    lips,
  With soul to help if the mere lips
    failed,
  I kissed all right where the draw-
    ing ailed,
Kissed fast the grace that somehow
    slips
Still from one's soulless finger-tips.

II.

'Tis a clay cast, the perfect thing,
  From Hand live once, dead long
    ago :
Princess-like it wears the ring
  To fancy's eye, by which we know
That here at length a master found
  His match, a proud lone soul its
    mate,
As soaring genius sank to ground
And pencil could not emulate
The beauty in this, — how free, how
  fine
To fear almost ! — of the limit-line.
Long ago the god, like me
The worm, learned, each in our de-
    gree :
Looked and loved, learned and drew,
  Drew and learned and loved again,
While fast the happy minutes flew,
  Till beauty mounted into his brain
And on the finger which outvied
  His art he placed the ring that's
    there,
Still by fancy's eye descried,
  In token of a marriage rare :
For him on earth, his art's despair,
For him in heaven, his soul's fit
    bride.

III.

Little girl with the poor coarse hand !
  I turned from her to a cold clay cast —
I have my lesson, understand
  The worth of flesh and blood at
    last !

Nothing but beauty in a Hand ?
  Because he could not change the
    hue,
  Mend the lines and make them true
To this which met his soul's de-
    mand, —
  Would Da Vinci turn from you ?
I hear him laugh my woes to scorn —
" The fool forsooth is all forlorn
Because the beauty, she thinks best,
Lived long ago or was never born, —
Because no beauty bears the test
In this rough peasant Hand ! Con-
    fessed
' Art is null and study void ! '
So sayest thou ? So said not I,
Who threw the faulty pencil by,
And years instead of hours employed,
Learning the veritable use
Of flesh and bone and nerve beneath
Lines and hue of the outer sheath,
If haply I might reproduce
One motive of the mechanism,
Flesh and bone and nerve that make
The poorest coarsest human hand
An object worthy to be scanned
A whole life long for their sole sake.
Shall earth and the cramped moment-
    space
Yield the heavenly crowning grace ?
Now the parts and then the whole !
Who art thou, with stinted soul
And stinted body, thus to cry
' I love, — shall that be life's strait
    dole ?
I must live beloved or die ! '
This peasant hand that spins the wool
And bakes the bread, why lives it on,
Poor and coarse with beauty gone, —
What use survives the beauty ?
    Fool ! "

Go, little girl with the poor coarse
    hand !
I have my lesson, shall understand.

IX

ON DECK

I.

THERE is nothing to remember in me,
  Nothing I ever said with a grace,
Nothing I did that you care to see,
  Nothing I was that deserves a place
In your mind, now I leave you, set
    you free.

II.

Conceded! In turn, concede to me,
  Such things have been as a mutual
    flame.
Your soul's locked fast; out, love for
    a key,
  You might let it loose, till I grew
    the same
In your eyes, as in mine you stand:
    strange plea!

III.

For then, then, what would it matter
  to me
  That I was the harsh, ill-favored
    one?
We both should be like as pea and
  pea;
  It was ever so since the world be-
    gun;
So, let me proceed with my reverie.

IV.

How strange it were if you had all
  me,
  As I have all you in my heart and
    brain,
You, whose least word brought gloom
  or glee,
  Who never lifted the hand in vain
Will hold mine yet, from over the sea!

V.

Strange, if a face, when you thought
  of me,
  Rose like your own face present
    now,
With eyes as dear in their due de-
  gree,
  Much such a mouth, and as bright a
    brow,
Till you saw yourself, while you cried
  " 'Tis She!"

VI.

Well, you may, you must, set down to
  me
  Love that was life, life that was
    love;
A tenure of breath at your lips' de-
  cree,
  A passion to stand as your thoughts
    approve,
  A rapture to fall where your foot
    might be.

VII.

But did one touch of such love for me
  Come in a word or a look of yours,
Whose words and looks will, circling,
  flee
  Round me and round while life en-
    dures, —
Could I fancy "As I feel, thus feels
  He;"

VIII.

Why, fade you might to a thing like
  me,
  And your hair grow these coarse
    hanks of hair,
Your skin, this bark of a gnarled
  tree, —
  You might turn myself! — should
    I know or care,
When I should be dead of joy, James
  Lee?

RESPECTABILITY.

I.

DEAR, had the world in its caprice
  Deigned to proclaim "I know you
    both,
  Have recognized your plighted
    troth,
Am sponsor for you: live in
    peace!" —
How many precious months and years
  Of youth had passed, that speed so
    fast,
  Before we found it out at last,
The world, and what it fears?

II.

How much of priceless life were spent
  With men that every virtue decks,
  And women models of their sex,
Society's true ornament, —
  Ere we dared wander, nights like
    this,
  Through wind and rain, and watch
    the Seine,
  And feel the Boulevart break again
To warmth and light and bliss?

III.

I know! the world proscribes not
  love;
  Allows my finger to caress
  Your lips' contour and downiness,
Provided it supply a glove.

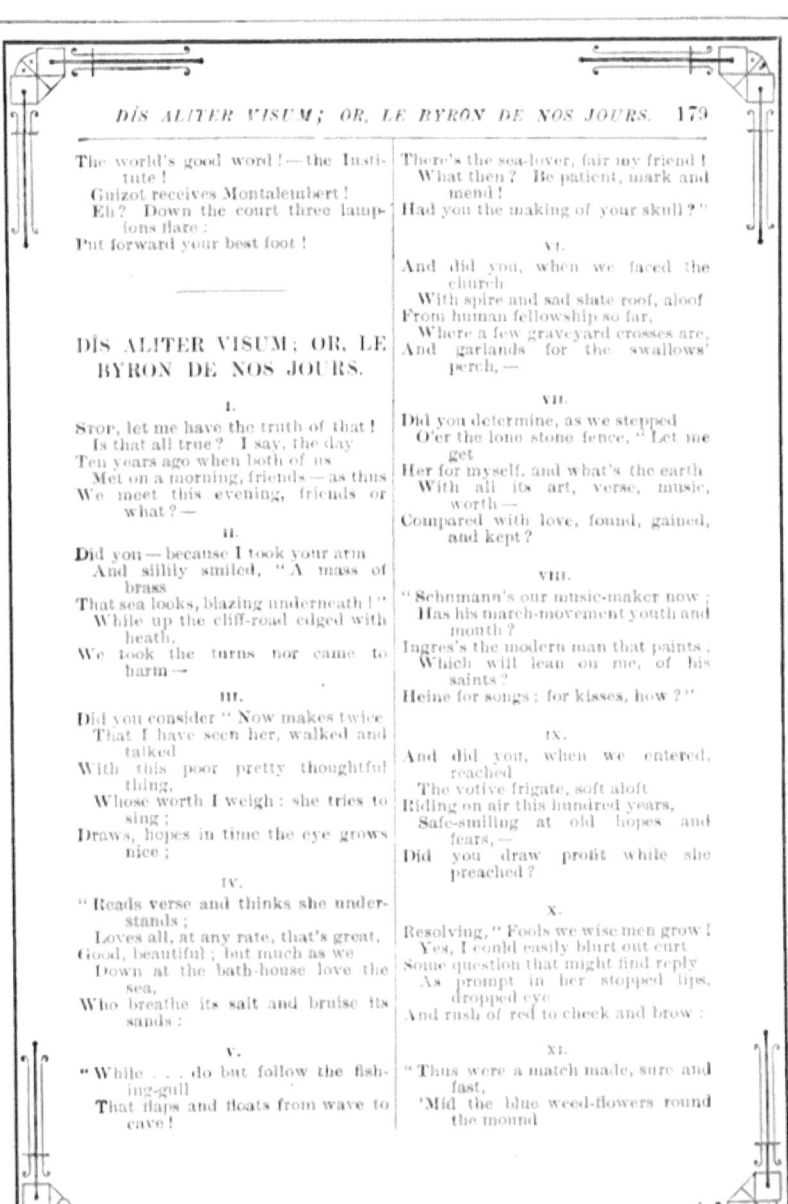

The world's good word!—the Insti-
tute!
Guizot receives Montalembert!
Eh? Down the court three lamp-
ions flare:
Put forward your best foot!

DÍS ALITER VISUM; OR, LE BYRON DE NOS JOURS.

I.

STOP, let me have the truth of that!
  Is that all true? I say, the day
Ten years ago when both of us
Met on a morning, friends—as thus
  We meet this evening, friends or
    what?—

II.

Did you—because I took your arm
  And sillily smiled, "A mass of
    brass
That sea looks, blazing underneath!"
While up the cliff-road edged with
    heath,
  We took the turns nor came to
    harm—

III.

Did you consider "Now makes twice
  That I have seen her, walked and
    talked
With this poor pretty thoughtful
    thing,
  Whose worth I weigh: she tries to
    sing;
Draws, hopes in time the eye grows
    nice;

IV.

"Reads verse and thinks she under-
    stands;
  Loves all, at any rate, that's great,
Good, beautiful; but much as we
  Down at the bath-house love the
    sea,
Who breathe its salt and bruise its
    sands:

V.

"While .... do but follow the fish-
    ing-gull
  That flaps and floats from wave to
    cave!

There's the sea-lover, fair my friend!
  What then? Be patient, mark and
    mend!
Had you the making of your skull?"

VI.

And did you, when we faced the
    church
  With spire and sad slate roof, aloof
From human fellowship so far,
  Where a few graveyard crosses are,
And garlands for the swallows'
    perch,—

VII.

Did you determine, as we stepped
  O'er the lone stone fence, "Let me
    get
Her for myself, and what's the earth
  With all its art, verse, music,
    worth—
Compared with love, found, gained,
    and kept?

VIII.

"Schumann's our music-maker now;
  Has his march-movement youth and
    mouth?
Ingres's the modern man that paints;
  Which will lean on me, of his
    saints?
Heine for songs; for kisses, how?"

IX.

And did you, when we entered,
    reached
  The votive frigate, soft aloft
Riding on air this hundred years,
  Safe-smiling at old hopes and
    fears,—
Did you draw profit while she
    preached?

X.

Resolving, "Fools we wise men grow!
  Yes, I could easily blurt out curt
Some question that might find reply
  As prompt in her stopped lips,
    dropped eye,
And rush of red to cheek and brow:

XI.

"Thus were a match made, sure and
    fast,
  'Mid the blue weed-flowers round
    the mound

Where, issuing, we shall stand and
stay
  For one more look at baths and bay,
Sands, sea-gulls, and the old church
last —

XII.

" A match 'twixt me, bent, wigged,
and lamed,
Famous, however, for verse and
worse,
Sure of the Fortieth spare Arm-chair
  When gout and glory seat me there,
So, one whose love-freaks pass un-
blamed, —

XIII.

" And this young beauty, round and
sound
  As a mountain-apple, youth and
truth
With loves and doves, at all events
  With money in the Three per Cents;
Whose choice of me would seem pro-
found : —

XIV.

" She might take me as I take her.
  Perfect the hour would pass, alas !
Climb high, love high, what matter ?
  Still,
Feet, feelings, must descend the
hill :
  An hour's perfection can't recur.

XV.

" Then follows Paris and full time
  For both to reason : 'Thus with
us,'
She'll sigh, 'Thus girls give body and
soul
  At first word, think they gain the
goal,
When 'tis the starting-place they
climb !

XVI.

" ' My friend makes verse and gets
renown ;
  Have they all fifty years, his peers ?
He knows the world, firm, quiet, and
gay ;
  Boys will become as much one
day :
They're fools ; he cheats, with beard-
less brown.

XVII.

" ' For boys say, *Love me or I die !*
  He did not say, *The truth is, youth
I want, who am old and know too much ;
  I'd catch youth : lend me sight and
touch !*
*Drop heart's blood where life's wheels
grate dry !* '

XVIII.

" While I should make rejoinder " —
  (then
It was, no doubt, you ceased that
least
Light pressure of my arm in yours)
  " ' I can conceive of cheaper cures
For a yawning-fit o'er books and
men.

XIX.

" ' What ? All I am, was, and might
be,
  All, books taught, art brought, life's
whole strife,
Painful results since precious, just
  Were fitly exchanged, in wise dis-
gust,
For two cheeks freshened by youth
and sea ?

XX.

" ' All for a nosegay ! — what came
first ;
  With fields in flower, untried each
side ;
I rally, need my books and men,
  And find a nosegay : ' drop it, then,
No match yet made for best or
worst ! "

XXI.

That ended me. You judged the porch
  We left by, Norman ; took our look
At sea and sky ; wondered so few
  Find out the place for air and view ;
Remarked the sun began to scorch ;

XXII.

Descended, soon regained the baths,
  And then, good-by ! Years ten
since then :
Ten years ! We meet : you tell me,
now,
  By a window-seat for that cliff-
brow,
On carpet - stripes for those sand-
paths.

XXIII.

Now I may speak : you fool, for all
  Your lore ! WHO made things plain
    in vain ?
What was the sea for ? What, the
  gray
Sad church, that solitary day,
Crosses and graves and swallows'
  call ?

XXIV.

Was there naught better than to en-
  joy ?
  No feat which, done, would make
    time break,
And let us pent-up creatures through
Into eternity, our due ?
No forcing earth teach heaven's em-
  ploy ?

XXV.

No wise beginning, here and now,
  What cannot grow complete (earth's
    feat)
And heaven must finish, there and
  then ?
  No tasting earth's true food for
    men,
Its sweet in sad, its sad in sweet ?

XXVI.

No grasping at love, gaining a share
  O' the sole spark from God's life at
    strife
With death, so, sure of range above
  The limits here ? For us and love,
Failure ; but, when God fails, de-
  spair.

XXVII.

This you call wisdom ? Thus you
  add
  Good unto good again, in vain ?
You loved, with body worn and
  weak ;
I loved, with faculties to seek :
Were both loves worthless since ill-
  clad ?

XXVIII.

Let the mere star-fish in his vault
  Crawl in a wash of weed, indeed,
Rose-jacynth to the finger-tips :
  He, whole in body and soul, out-
    strips
Man, found with either in default.

XXIX.

But what's whole, can increase no
  more,
  Is dwarfed and dies, since here's its
    sphere.
The Devil laughed at you in his
  sleeve !
  You knew not ? That I well be-
    lieve ;
Or you had saved two souls : nay,
  four.

XXX.

For Stephanie sprained last night her
  wrist,
  Ankle or something. " Pooh," cry
    you ?
At any rate she danced, all say,
  Vilely : her vogue has had its day.
Here comes my husband from his
  whist.

CONFESSIONS.

I.

WHAT is he buzzing in my ears ?
  " Now that I come to die,
Do I view the world as a vale of
  tears ? "
  Ah, reverend sir, not I !

II.

What I viewed there once, what I
  view again
  Where the physic bottles stand
On the table's edge,—is a suburb
  lane,
  With a wall to my bedside hand.

III.

That lane sloped, much as the bottles
  do,
  From a house you could descry
O'er the garden-wall : is the curtain
  blue
  Or green to a healthy eye ?

IV.

To mine, it serves for the old June
  weather
  Blue above lane and wall ;
And that farthest bottle labelled
  " Ether "
  Is the house o'er-topping all.

v.

At a terrace, somewhat near the stop-
    per,
  There watched for me, one June,
A girl: I know, sir, it's improper,
  My poor mind's out of tune.

vi.

Only, there was a way . . . you crept
  Close by the side, to dodge
Eyes in the house, two eyes except:
  They styled their house "The
    Lodge."

vii.

What right had a lounger up their
  lane?
But, by creeping very close,
With the good wall's help,—their
  eyes might strain
  And stretch themselves to Oes,

viii.

Yet never catch her and me together,
  As she left the attic, there,
By the rim of the bottle labelled
  "Ether,"
  And stole from stair to stair,

ix.

And stood by the rose-wreathed gate.
  Alas,
We loved, sir—used to meet:
How sad and bad and mad it was—
  But then, how it was sweet!

THE HOUSEHOLDER.

i.

Savage I was sitting in my house,
  late, lone:
  Dreary, weary with the long day's
    work:
Head of me, heart of me, stupid as a
  stone:
  Tongue-tied now, now blasphem-
    ing like a Turk;
When, in a moment, just a knock,
  call, cry,
  Half a pang and all a rapture, there
    again were we!—

"What, and is it really you again?"
  quoth I:
"I again, what else did you ex-
  pect?" quoth She.

ii.

"Never mind, hie away from this old
  house—
Every crumbling brick embrowned
  with sin and shame!
Quick, in its corners ere certain
  shapes arouse!
Let them—every devil of the
  night—lay claim,
Make and mend, or rap and rend, for
  me! Good-by!
God be their guard from disturbance
  at their glee,
Till, crash, comes down the carcass in
  a heap!" quoth I:
"Nay, but there's a decency re-
  quired!" quoth She.

iii.

"Ah, but if you knew how time has
  dragged, days, nights!
All the neighbor-talk with man and
  maid—such men!
All the fuss and trouble of street-
  sounds, window-sights:
All the worry of flapping door and
  echoing roof; and then,
All the fancies . . . Who were they
  had leave, dared try
Darker arts that almost struck de-
  spair in me?
If you knew but how I dwelt down
  here!" quoth I:
"And was I so better off up there?"
  quoth She.

iv.

"Help and get it over! *Re-united to
  his wife*
(How draw up the paper lets the
  parish-people know!)
*Lies M. or N., departed from this life,
Day the this or that, month and year
  the so and so,*
What i' the way of final flourish?
  Prose, verse? Try!
Affliction sore, long time he bore, or,
  what is it to be?
Till God did please to grant him ease.
  Do end!" quoth I:
"I end with—Love is all and
  Death is naught!" quoth She.

TRAY.

SING me a hero! Quench my thirst
Of soul, ye bards!
      Quoth Bard the first:
" Sir Olaf, the good knight, did don
His helm and eke his habergeon " . . .
Sir Olaf and his bard ! —

" That sin-scathed brow " (quoth
    Bard the second),
" That eye wide ope as though Fate
    beckoned
My hero to some steep, beneath
Which precipice smiled tempting
    Death " . . .
You too without your host have reck-
    oned !

" A beggar-child " (let's hear this
    third !)
" Sat on a quay's edge : like a bird
Sang to herself at careless play,
And fell into the stream. ' Dismay !
Help, you the standers-by ! ' None
    stirred.

" By-standers reason, think of wives
And children ere they risk their lives.
Over the balustrade has bounced
A mere instinctive dog, and pounced
Plumb on the prize. ' How well he
    dives !

" ' Up he comes with the child, see,
    tight
In mouth, alive too, clutched from
    quite
A depth of ten feet — twelve, I bet !
Good dog ! What, off again ? There's
    yet
Another child to save ? All right !

" ' How strange we saw no other fall !
It's instinct in the animal.
Good dog ! But he's a long while
    under :
If he got drowned I should not won-
    der —
Strong current, that against the wall !

" ' Here he comes, holds in mouth
    this time
— What may the thing be ? Well,
    that's prime !
Now, did you ever ? Reason reigns
In man alone, since all Tray's pains
Have fished — the child's doll from
    the slime ! '

" And so, amid the laughter gay,
Trotted my hero off, — old Tray, —
Till somebody, prerogatived
With reason, reasoned : ' Why he
    dived,
His brain would show us, I should
    say.

" ' John, go and catch — or, if needs
    be,
Purchase that animal for me !
By vivisection, at expense
Of half-an-hour and eighteen pence,
How brain secretes dog's soul, we'll
    see ! ' "

CAVALIER TUNES.

I.

MARCHING ALONG.

1.

KENTISH Sir Byng stood for his King,
Bidding the crop-headed Parliament
    swing :
And, pressing a troop unable to stoop
And see the rogues flourish and hon-
    est folk droop,
Marched them along, fifty-score
    strong,
Great-hearted gentlemen, singing this
    song.

II.

God for King Charles ! Pym and
    such carles
To the Devil that prompts 'em their
    treasonous parles !
Cavaliers, up ! Lips from the cup,
Hands from the pasty, nor bite take
    nor sup
Till you're —
    (*Chorus*) *Marching along, fifty-score
      strong,
      Great - hearted gentlemen,
      singing this song.*

III.

Hampden to hell, and his obsequies'
    knell.
Serve Hazelrig, Fiennes, and young
    Harry as well !

England, good cheer! Rupert is
  near!
Kentish and loyalists, keep we not
  here
  (*Chorus*) *Marching along, fifty-score*
    strong,
    Great - hearted   gentlemen,
    singing this song.

IV.

Then, God for King Charles! Pym
  and his snarls
To the Devil that pricks on such pes-
  tilent carles !
Hold by the right, you double your
  might :
So, onward to Nottingham, fresh for
  the fight,
  (*Chorus*) *March we along, fifty-score*
    strong,
    Great - hearted   gentlemen,
    singing this song.

II.

GIVE A ROUSE.

I.

KING CHARLES, and who'll do him
  right now ?
King Charles, and who's ripe for fight
  now ?
Give a rouse : here's, in hell's despite
  now,
King Charles !

II.

Who gave me the goods that went
  since ?
Who raised me the house that sank
  once ?
Who helped me to gold I spent since ?
Who found me in wine you drank
  once ?
  (*Chorus*) *King   Charles,   and   who'll*
    do him right now ?
    King   Charles,   and   who's
    ripe for fight now ?
    Give   a   rouse: here's,   in
    hell's despite now,
    King Charles!

III.

To whom used my boy George quaff
  else,
By the old fool's side that begot him ?
For whom did he cheer and laugh else,
While Noll's damned troopers shot
  him ?
  (*Chorus*) *King   Charles,   and   who'll*
    do him right now ?
    King   Charles,   and   who's
    ripe for fight now ?
    Give   a   rouse :   here's,   in
    hell's despite now,
    King Charles !

III.

BOOT AND SADDLE.

I.

BOOT, saddle, to horse, and away !
Rescue my castle before the hot day
Brightens to blue from its silvery
  gray,
  (*Chorus*) *Boot, saddle, to horse, and*
    away !

II.

Ride past the suburbs, asleep as you'd
  say ;
Many's the friend there, will listen
  and pray,
"God's luck to gallants that strike up
  the lay —
  (*Chorus*) *Boot, saddle, to horse, and*
    away !"

III.

Forty miles off, like a roebuck at bay,
Flouts Castle Brancepeth the Round-
  heads' array ;
Who laughs, "Good fellows ere this,
  by my fay,
  (*Chorus*) *Boot, saddle, to horse, and*
    away ?"

IV.

Who ? My wife Gertrude ; that, hon-
  est and gay,
Laughs when you talk of surrender-
  ing, "Nay !
I've better counsellors ; what coun-
  sel they ?
  (*Chorus*) *Boot, saddle, to horse, and*
    away !"

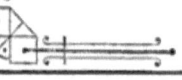

After. — Page 18;.

BEFORE.

I.

Let them fight it out, friend! things
  have gone too far.
God must judge the couple: leave
  them as they are
— Whichever one's the guiltless, to
  his glory,
And whichever one the guilt's with,
  to my story!

II.

Why, you would not bid men, sunk
  in such a slough,
Strike no arm out farther, stick and
  stink as now,
Leaving right and wrong to settle the
  embroilment,
Heaven with snaky hell, in torture
  and entoilment?

III.

Who's the culprit of them? How
  must he conceive
God — the queen he caps to, laughing
  in his sleeve,
" 'Tis but decent to profess one's self
  beneath her:
Still, one must not be too much in
  earnest, either!"

IV.

Better sin the whole sin, sure that
  God observes;
Then go live his life out! Life will
  try his nerves,
When the sky, which noticed all,
  makes no disclosure,
And the earth keeps up her terrible
  composure.

V.

Let him pace at pleasure, past the
  walls of rose,
Pluck their fruits when grape-trees
  graze him as he goes!
For he 'gins to guess the purpose of
  the garden,
With the sly mute thing, beside there,
  for a warden.

VI.

What's the leopard-dog-thing, con-
  stant at his side,
A leer and lie in every eye of its ob-
  sequious hide?

When will come an end to all the
  mock obeisance,
And the price appear that pays for
  the misfeasance?

VII.

So much for the culprit. Who's the
  martyred man?
Let him bear one stroke more, for be
  sure he can!
He that strove thus evil's lump with
  good to leaven,
Let him give his blood at last and get
  his heaven!

VIII.

All or nothing, stake it! Trusts he
  God or no?
Thus far and no farther? farther? be
  it so!
Now, enough of your chicane of pru-
  dent pauses,
Sage provisos, sub-intents, and saving-
  clauses!

IX.

Ah, "forgive" you bid him? While
  God's champion lives,
Wrong shall be resisted: dead, why,
  he forgives,
But you must not end my friend ere
  you begin him:
Evil stands not crowned on earth,
  while breath is in him.

X.

Once more — Will the wronger, at
  this last of all,
Dare to say, "I did wrong," rising in
  his fall?
No? — Let go, then! Both the fight-
  ers to their places!
While I count three, step you back as
  many paces!

AFTER.

Take the cloak from his face, and at
  first
Let the corpse do its worst!

How he lies in his rights of a man.
Death has done all death can.
And, absorbed in the new life he
  leads,
He recks not, he heeds

Nor his wrong nor my vengeance:
  both strike
On his senses alike,
And are lost in the solemn and
  strange
Surprise of the change.

Ha, what avails death to erase
  His offence, my disgrace?
I would we were boys as of old
  In the field, by the fold:
His outrage, God's patience, man's
  scorn
Were so easily borne!

I stand here now, he lies in his place:
  Cover the face!

HERVÉ RIEL.

I.

On the sea and at the Hogue, sixteen
  hundred ninety-two,
  Did the English fight the French, —
    woe to France!
And, the thirty-first of May, helter-
  skelter through the blue,
Like a crowd of frightened porpoises
  a shoal of sharks pursue,
  Came crowding ship on ship to St.
    Malo on the Rance,
With the English fleet in view.

II

'Twas the squadron that escaped, with
  the victor in full chase;
  First and foremost of the drove, in
    his great ship, Damfreville;
  Close on him fled, great and small,
    Twenty-two good ships in all;
And they signalled to the place
" Help the winners of a race!
  Get us guidance, give us harbor,
    take us quick — or, quicker still,
  Here's the English can and will!"

III

Then the pilots of the place put out
  brisk and leapt on board;
  ' Why, what hope or chance have
    ships like these to pass?"
  laughed they:
' Rocks to starboard, rocks to port, all
  the passage scarred and scored,

Shall the ' Formidable ' here with her
  twelve and eighty guns
  Think to make the river-mouth by
    the single narrow way,
Trust to enter where 'tis ticklish for a
  craft of twenty tons,
  And with flow at full beside?
  Now, 'tis slackest ebb of tide.
Reach the mooring? Rather say,
While rock stands or water runs,
Not a ship will leave the bay!"

IV.

Then was called a council straight.
Brief and bitter the debate:
" Here's the English at our heels;
  would you have them take in
    tow
All that's left us of the fleet, linked
  together stern and bow,
For a prize to Plymouth Sound?
Better run the ships aground!"
  (Ended Damfreville his speech.)
" Not a minute more to wait!
Let the Captains all and each
Shove ashore, then blow up, burn
  the vessels on the beach!
France must undergo her fate.

V.

" Give the word!' But no such
  word
Was ever spoke or heard;
  For up stood, for out stepped, for in
    struck amid all these
—A Captain? A Lieutenant? A
  Mate — first, second, third?
No such man of mark, and meet
  With his betters to compete!
But a simple Breton sailor pressed
  by Tourville for the fleet,
A poor coasting-pilot he, Hervé Riel
  the Croisickese.

VI.

And, " What mockery or malice have
  we here?" cries Hervé Riel:
" Are you mad, you Malouins? Are
  you cowards, fools, or rogues?
Talk to me of rocks and shoals, me
  who took the soundings, tell
On my fingers every bank, every shal-
  low, every swell
'Twixt the offing here and Grève
  where the river disembogues?
Are you bought by English gold? Is
  it love the lying's for?
  Morn and eve, night and day,

Have I piloted your bay,
Entered free and anchored fast at the
    foot of Solidor.
Burn the fleet and ruin France?
    That were worse than fifty
    Hogues!
    Sirs, they know I speak the truth!
    Sirs, believe me there's a way!
Only let me lead the line,
Have the biggest ship to steer,
Get this ' Formidable ' clear,
Make the others follow mine,
And I lead them, most and least, by a
    passage I know well,
Right to Solidor past Grève,
    And there lay them safe and
    sound ;
And if one ship misbehave,
    — Keel so much as grate the
    ground,
Why, I've nothing but my life, —
    here's my head!" cries Hervé
    Riel.

VII.

Not a minute more to wait.
" Steer us in, then, small and great!
Take the helm, lead the line, save
    the squadron!" cried its chief.
Captains, give the sailor place!
He is Admiral, in brief.
Still the north-wind, by God's grace!
See the noble fellow's face
As the big ship, with a bound,
Clears the entry like a hound,
Keeps the passage as its inch of way
    were the wide sea's profound!
See, safe through shoal and rock,
How they follow in a flock,
Not a ship that misbehaves, not a
    keel that grates the ground,
Not a spar that comes to grief!
The peril, see, is past.
All are harbored to the last.
And just as Hervé Riel hollas " An-
    chor!" — sure as fate,
Up the English come, too late!

VIII.

So, the storm subsides to calm :
    They see the green trees wave
On the heights o'erlooking Grève.
Hearts that bled are stanched with
    balm.
" Just our rapture to enhance,
Let the English rake the bay,
Gnash their teeth and glare askance
    As they cannonade away!

'Neath rampired Solidor pleasant rid-
    ing on the Rance!"
How hope succeeds despair on each
    Captain's countenance!
Out burst all with one accord,
    " This is Paradise for Hell!
    Let France, let France's King
Thank the man that did the
    thing!"
What a shout, and all one word,
    " Hervé Riel!"
As he stepped in front once more.
    Not a symptom of surprise
    In the frank blue Breton eyes,
Just the same man as before.

IX.

Then said Damfreville, " My friend,
I must speak out at the end,
Though I find the speaking hard.
Praise is deeper than the lips :
You have saved the King his ships,
    You must name your own reward.
'Faith, our sun was near eclipse!
Demand whate'er you will,
France remains your debtor still.
Ask to heart's content and have! or
    my name's not Damfreville."

X.

Then a beam of fun outbroke
On the bearded mouth that spoke,
As the honest heart laughed through
Those frank eyes of Breton blue :
" Since I needs must say my say,
    Since on board the duty's done,
    And from Malo Roads to Croisic
    Point, what is it but a run? —
Since 'tis ask and have, I may —
    Since the others go ashore —
Come! A good whole holiday!
    Leave to go and see my wife, whom
    I call the Belle Aurore!"
That he asked and that he got, —
    nothing more.

XI.

Name and deed alike are lost :
Not a pillar nor a post
    In his Croisic keeps alive the feat as
    it befell ;
Not a head in white and black
On a single fishing-smack,
In memory of the man but for whom
    had gone to wrack
    All that France saved from the
    fight whence England bore the
    bell.

Go to Paris : rank on rank
   Search the heroes flung pell-mell
On the Louvre, face and flank !
   You shall look long enough ere you
      come to Hervé Riel.

So, for better and for worse,
Hervé Riel, accept my verse !
In my verse, Hervé Riel, do thou once
   more
Save the squadron, honor France,
   love thy wife the Belle Aurore !

IN A BALCONY.

CONSTANCE *and* NORBERT.

Nor. Now !
Con.   Not now !
Nor.   Give me them again, those hands —
Put them upon my forehead, how it throbs !
Press them before my eyes, the fire comes through !
You cruellest, you dearest in the world,
Let me ! The Queen must grant whate'er I ask —
How can I gain you and not ask the Queen ?
There she stays waiting for me, here stand you ;
Some time or other this was to be asked ,
Now is the one time — what I ask, I gain :
Let me ask now, Love !
   Con.   Do, and ruin us !
   Nor. Let it be now, Love ! All my soul breaks forth.
How I do love you ! Give my love its way !
A man can have but one life and one death,
One heaven, one hell. Let me fulfil my fate —
Grant me my heaven now ! Let me know you mine,
Prove you mine, write my name upon your brow,
Hold you and have you, and then die away,
If God please, with completion in my soul !
   Con. I am not yours then ? How content this man !
I am not his — who change into himself,
Have passed into his heart and beat its beats,
Who give my hands to him, my eyes, my hair,
Give all that was of me away to him —
So well, that now, my spirit turned his own,
Takes part with him against the woman here,
Bids him not stumble at so mere a straw
As caring that the world be cognizant
How he loves her and how she worships him.
You have this woman, not as yet that world.
Go on, I bid, nor stop to care for me
By saving what I cease to care about,
The courtly name and pride of circumstance —
The name you'll pick up and be cumbered with
Just for the poor parade's sake, nothing more ;
Just that the world may slip from under you —
Just that the world may cry " So much for him —
The man predestined to the heap of crowns :
There goes his chance of winning one, at least ! "
   Nor. The world !
   Con.   You love it ! Love me quite as well,
And see if I shall pray for this in vain !
Why must you ponder what it knows or thinks ?

Nor. You pray for — what, in vain?

Con.   Oh my heart's heart,
How I do love you, Norbert ! That is right :
But listen, or I take my hands away !
You say, " Let it be now :" you would go now
And tell the Queen, perhaps six steps from us,
You love me — so you do, thank God !

Nor.   Thank God !

Con.   Yes, Norbert, — but you fain would tell your love,
And, what succeeds the telling, ask of her
My hand. Now take this rose and look at it,
Listening to me. You are the minister,
The Queen's first favorite, nor without a cause.
To-night completes your wonderful year's-work
(This palace-feast is held to celebrate)
Made memorable by her life's success,
The junction of two crowns, on her sole head,
Her house had only dreamed of anciently :
That this mere dream is grown a stable truth,
To-night's feast makes authentic. Whose the praise?
Whose genius, patience, energy, achieved
What turned the many heads and broke the hearts?
You are the fate, your minute's in the heaven.
Next comes the Queen's turn. " Name your own reward !"
With leave to clinch the past, chain the to-come,
Put out an arm and touch and take the sun
And fix it ever full-faced on your earth,
Possess yourself supremely of her life, —
You choose the single thing she will not grant ;
Nay, very declaration of which choice
Will turn the scale and neutralize your work :
At best she will forgive you, if she can.
You think I'll let you choose — her cousin's hand?

Nor.   Wait. First, do you retain your old belief
The Queen is generous, — nay, is just ?

Con.   There, there,
So men make women love them, while they know
No more of women's hearts than . . . look you here,
You that are just and generous beside,
Make it your own case ! For example now,
I'll say — I let you kiss me, hold my hands —
Why ? do you know why ? I'll instruct you, then —
The kiss, because you have a name at court,
This hand and this, that you may shut in each
A jewel, if you please to pick up such.
That's horrible ? Apply it to the Queen —
Suppose I am the Queen to whom you speak.
" I was a nameless man ; you needed me :
Why did I proffer you my aid ? there stood
A certain pretty cousin at your side.
Why did I make such common cause with you?
Access to her had not been easy else.
You give my labors here abundant praise?
'Faith, labor, which she overlooked, grew play.
How shall your gratitude discharge itself?
Give me her hand !"

Nor.   And still I urge the same.
Is the Queen just ? just — generous or no !

Con. Yes, just. You love a rose ; no harm in that :

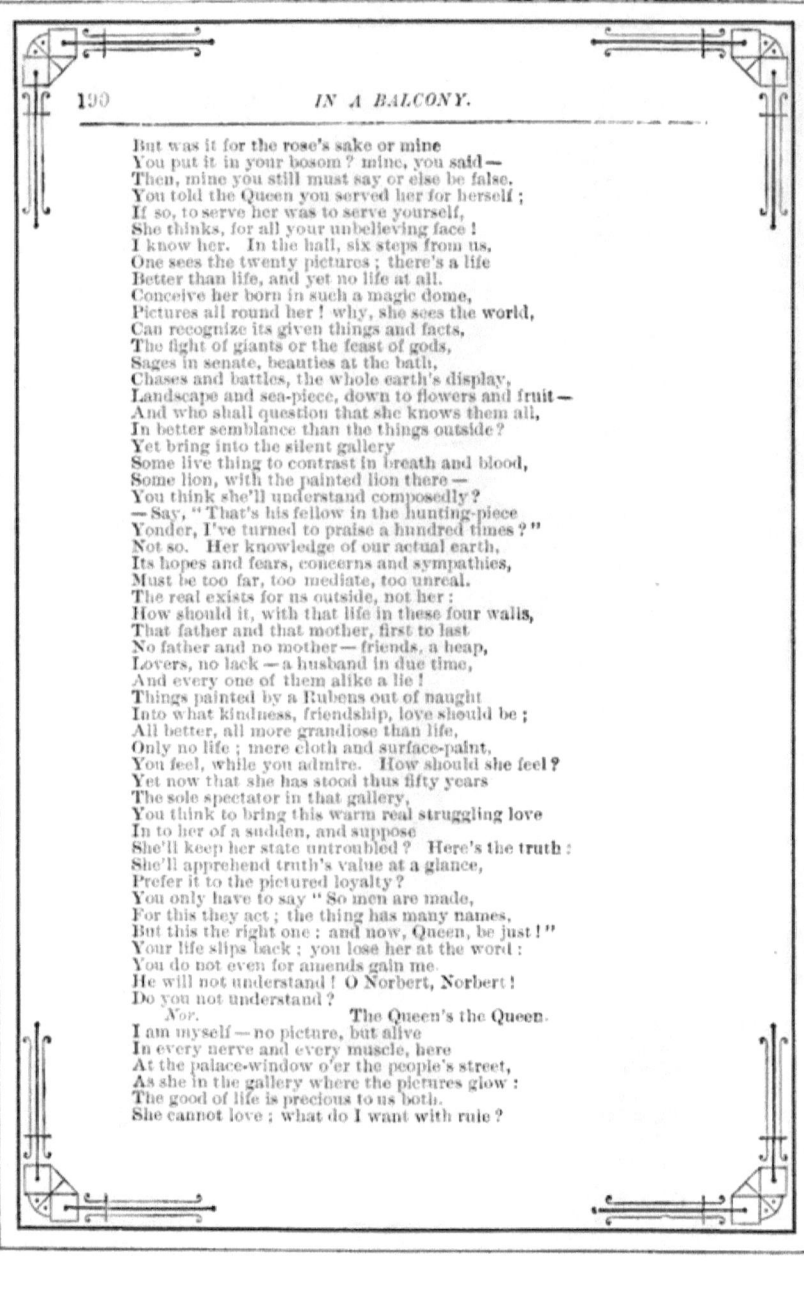

But was it for the rose's sake or mine
You put it in your bosom? mine, you said—
Then, mine you still must say or else be false.
You told the Queen you served her for herself;
If so, to serve her was to serve yourself,
She thinks, for all your unbelieving face!
I know her. In the hall, six steps from us,
One sees the twenty pictures; there's a life
Better than life, and yet no life at all.
Conceive her born in such a magic dome,
Pictures all round her! why, she sees the world,
Can recognize its given things and facts,
The fight of giants or the feast of gods,
Sages in senate, beauties at the bath,
Chases and battles, the whole earth's display,
Landscape and sea-piece, down to flowers and fruit—
And who shall question that she knows them all,
In better semblance than the things outside?
Yet bring into the silent gallery
Some live thing to contrast in breath and blood,
Some lion, with the painted lion there—
You think she'll understand composedly?
—Say, "That's his fellow in the hunting-piece
Yonder, I've turned to praise a hundred times?"
Not so. Her knowledge of our actual earth,
Its hopes and fears, concerns and sympathies,
Must be too far, too mediate, too unreal.
The real exists for us outside, not her:
How should it, with that life in these four walls,
That father and that mother, first to last
No father and no mother—friends, a heap,
Lovers, no lack—a husband in due time,
And every one of them alike a lie!
Things painted by a Rubens out of naught
Into what kindness, friendship, love should be;
All better, all more grandiose than life,
Only no life; mere cloth and surface-paint,
You feel, while you admire. How should she feel?
Yet now that she has stood thus fifty years
The sole spectator in that gallery,
You think to bring this warm real struggling love
In to her of a sudden, and suppose
She'll keep her state untroubled? Here's the truth:
She'll apprehend truth's value at a glance,
Prefer it to the pictured loyalty?
You only have to say "So men are made,
For this they act; the thing has many names,
But this the right one; and now, Queen, be just!"
Your life slips back; you lose her at the word:
You do not even for amends gain me.
He will not understand! O Norbert, Norbert!
Do you not understand?
            Nor.   The Queen's the Queen.
I am myself—no picture, but alive
In every nerve and every muscle, here
At the palace-window o'er the people's street,
As she in the gallery where the pictures glow:
The good of life is precious to us both.
She cannot love; what do I want with rule?

When first I saw your face a year ago
I knew my life's good, my soul heard one voice—
" The woman yonder, there's no use of life
But just to obtain her ! heap earth's woes in one
And bear them — make a pile of all earth's joys
And spurn them, as they help or help not this ;
Only, obtain her !" — how was it to be ?
I found you were the cousin of the Queen ;
I must then serve the Queen to get to you.
No other way. Suppose there had been one,
And I, by saying prayers to some white star
With promise of my body and my soul,
Might gain you, — should I pray the star or no ?
Instead, there was the Queen to serve ! I served,
Helped, did what other servants failed to do.
Neither she sought nor I declared my end.
Her good is hers, my recompense be mine,
I therefore name you as that recompense.
She dreamed that such a thing could never be ?
Let her wake now. She thinks there was more cause
In love of power, high fame, pure loyalty ?
Perhaps she fancies men wear out their lives
Chasing such shades. Then, I've a fancy too ;
I worked because I want you with my soul :
I therefore ask your hand. Let it be now !

    Con. Had I not loved you from the very first,
Were I not yours, could we not steal out thus
So wickedly, so wildly, and so well,
You might become impatient. What's conceived
Of us without here, by the folks within ?
Where are you now ? immersed in cares of state
Where am I now ? — intent on festal robes —
We two, embracing under death's spread hand !
What was this thought for, what that scruple of yours
Which broke the council up ? — to bring about
One minute's meeting in the corridor !
And then the sudden sleights, strange secrecies,
Complots inscrutable, deep telegraphs,
Long-planned chance-meetings, hazards of a look,
" Does she know ? does she not know ? saved, or lost ? "
A year of this compression's ecstasy
All goes for nothing ! you would give this up
For the old way, the open way, the world's,
His way who beats, and his who sells his wife !
What tempts you ? — their notorious happiness,
That you are ashamed of ours ? The best you'll gain
Will be — the Queen grants all that you require,
Concedes the cousin, rids herself of you
And me at once, and gives us ample leave
To live like our five hundred happy friends
The world will show us with officious hand
Our chamber-entry and stand sentinel,
Where we so oft have stolen across its traps !
Get the world's warrant, ring the falcons' feet,
And make it duty to be bold and swift,
Which long ago was nature. Have it so !
We never hawked by rights till flung from fist ?
Oh, the man's thought ! no woman's such a fool.

    Nor. Yes, the man's thought and my thought, which is more—

One made to love you, let the world take note !
Have I done worthy work ? be love's the praise,
Though hampered by restrictions, barred against
By set forms, blinded by forced secrecies !
Set free my love, and see what love can do
Shown in my life — what work will spring from that !
The world is used to have its business done
On other grounds, find great effects produced
For power's sake, fame's sake, motives in men's month.
So, good : but let my low ground shame their high !
Truth is the strong thing. Let man's life be true !
And love's the truth of mine. Time prove the rest !
I choose to wear you stamped all over me,
Your name upon my forehead and my breast,
You, from the sword's blade to the ribbon's edge,
That men may see, all over, you in me —
That pale loves may die out of their pretence
In face of mine, shames thrown on love fall off.
Permit this, Constance ! Love has been so long
Subdued in me, eating me through and through,
That now 'tis all of me and must have way.
Think of my work, that chaos of intrigues,
Those hopes and fears, surprises and delays,
That long endeavor, earnest, patient, slow,
Trembling at last to its assured result —
Then think of this revulsion ! I resume
Life after death (it is no less than life,
After such long unlovely laboring days),
And liberate to beauty life's great need
O' the beautiful, which, while it prompted work,
Suppressed itself erewhile. This eve's the time,
This eve intense with yon first trembling star
We seem to pant and reach ; scarce aught between
The earth that rises and the heaven that bends :
All nature self-abandoned, every tree
Flung as it will, pursuing its own thoughts
And fixed so, every flower and every weed.
No pride, no shame, no victory, no defeat ;
All under God, each measured by itself.
These statues round us stand abrupt, distinct,
The strong in strength, the weak in weakness fixed,
The Muse forever wedded to her lyre,
The Nymph to her fawn, the Silence to her rose :
See God's approval on his universe !
Let us do so — aspire to live as these
In harmony with truth, ourselves being true !
Take the first way, and let the second come !
My first is to possess myself of you ;
The music sets the march-step — forward, then !
And there's the Queen, I go to claim you of,
The world to witness, wonder, and applaud.
Our flower of life breaks open. No delay !
     Con. And so shall we be ruined, both of us.
Norbert, I know her to the skin and bone :
You do not know her, were not born to it,
To feel what she can see or cannot see.
Love, she is generous, — ay, despite your smile,
Generous as you are : for, in that thin frame
Pain-twisted, punctured through and through with cares,

There lived a lavish soul until it starved,
Debarred all healthy food. Look to the soul —
Pity that, stoop to that, ere you begin
(The true man's-way) on justice and your rights,
Exactions and acquittance of the past!
Begin so — see what justice she will deal!
We women hate a debt as men a gift.
Suppose her some poor keeper of a school
Whose business is to sit through summer months
And dole out children leave to go and play,
Herself superior to such lightness — she
In the arm-chair's state and pedagogic pomp,
To the life, the laughter, sun and youth outside:
We wonder such a face looks black on us?
I do not bid you wake her tenderness
(That were vain truly — none is left to wake),
But, let her think her justice is engaged
To take the shape of tenderness, and mark
If she'll not coldly pay its warmest debt!
Does she love me, I ask you? not a whit:
Yet, thinking that her justice was engaged
To help a kinswoman, she took me up —
Did more on that bare ground than other loves
Would do on greater argument. For me,
I have no equivalent of such cold kind
To pay her with, but love alone to give
If I give any thing. I give her love:
I feel I ought to help her, and I will.
So, for her sake, as yours, I tell you twice
That women hate a debt as men a gift.
If I were you, I could obtain this grace —
Could lay the whole I did to love's account,
Nor yet be very false as courtiers go —
Declaring my success was recompense;
It would be so, in fact: what were it else?
And then, once loose her generosity, —
Oh, how I see it! then, were I but you
To turn it, let it seem to move itself,
And make it offer what I really take,
Accepting just, in the poor cousin's hand,
Her value as the next thing to the Queen's —
Since none love Queens directly, none dare that,
And a thing's shadow or a name's mere echo
Suffices those who miss the name and thing!
You pick up just a ribbon she has worn,
To keep in proof how near her breath you came.
Say, I'm so near I seem a piece of her —
Ask for me that way — (oh, you understand)
You'd find the same gift yielded with a grace,
Which, if you make the least show to extort . . .
— You'll see! and when you have ruined both of us,
Dissertate on the Queen's ingratitude!
   Nor. Then, if I turn it that way, you consent?
'Tis not my way; I have more hope in truth:
Still, if you won't have truth — why, this indeed,
Were scarcely false, as I'd express the sense.
Will you remain here?
   Con.   O best heart of mine,
How I have loved you! then, you take my way?

Are mine as you have been her minister,
Work out my thought, give it effect for me,
Paint plain my poor conceit and make it serve?
I owe that withered woman every thing —
Life, fortune, you, remember!   Take my part —
Help me to pay her!   Stand upon your rights?
You, with my rose, my hands, my heart on you?
Your rights are mine — you have no rights but mine.
   Nor.   Remain here.   How you know me!
   Con.   Ah, but still —
       [*He breaks from her: she remains.   Dance-music from within*

                  Enter the QUEEN.

   Queen.   Constance?   She is here as he said.   Speak quick!
Is it so?   Is it true or false?   One word?
   Con.   True.
   Queen.   Mercifullest Mother, thanks to thee!
   Con.   Madam?
   Queen.   I love you, Constance, from my soul.
Now say once more, with any words you will,
'Tis true, all true, as true as that I speak.
   Con.   Why should you doubt it?
   Queen.   Ah, why doubt? why doubt?
Dear, make me see it!   Do you see it so?
None see themselves; another sees them best.
You say, " Why doubt it? " — you see him and me
It is because the Mother has such grace
That if we had but faith — wherein we fail —
Whate'er we yearn for would be granted us;
Howbeit we let our whims prescribe despair,
Our very fancies thwart and cramp our will,
And so, accepting life, abjure ourselves.
Constance, I had abjured the hope of love
And being loved, as truly as yon palm
The hope of seeing Egypt from that plot.
   Con.   Heaven!
   Queen.   But it was so, Constance, it was so!
Men say — or do men say it? fancies say —
" Stop here, your life is set, you are grown old.
Too late — no love for you, too late for love —
Leave love to girls.   Be queen: let Constance love!"
One takes the hint — half meets it like a child,
Ashamed at any feelings that oppose.
"O love, true, never think of love again!
I am a queen: I rule, not love, indeed."
So it goes on; so a face grows like this,
Hair like this hair, poor arms as lean as these,
Till, — nay, it does not end so, I thank God!
   Con.   I cannot understand —
   Queen.   The happier you!
Constance, I know not how it is with men:
For women (I am a woman now like you)
There is no good of life but love — but love!
What else looks good, is some shade flung from love;
Love gilds it, gives it worth.   Be warned by me,
Never you cheat yourself one instant!   Love,
Give love, ask only love, and leave the rest!
O Constance, how I love you!

Con.   I love you.
Queen. I do believe that all is come through you.
I took you to my heart to keep it warm
When the last chance of love seemed dead in me ;
I thought your fresh youth warmed my withered heart.
Oh, I am very old now, am I not ?
Not so ! it is true and it shall be true !
    Con. Tell it me : let me judge if true or false.
    Queen. Ah, but I fear you ! you will look at me
And say, " She's old, she's grown unlovely quite
Who ne'er was beauteous : men want beauty still."
Well, so I feared — the curse ! so I felt sure !
    Con. Be calm. And now you feel not sure, you say ?
    Queen. Constance, he came, — the coming was not strange—
Do not I stand and see men come and go ?
I turned a half-look from my pedestal
Where I grow marble — " one young man the more !
He will love some one ; that is naught to me "
What would he with my marble stateliness ? "
Yet this seemed somewhat worse than heretofore ;
The man more gracious, youthful, like a god,
And I still older, with less flesh to change —
We two those dear extremes that long to touch.
It seemed still harder when he first began
Absorbed to labor at the state-affairs
The old way for the old end — interest.
Oh, to live with a thousand beating hearts
Around you, swift eyes, serviceable hands,
Professing they've no care but for your cause,
Thought but to help you, love but for yourself,
And you the marble statue all the time
They praise and point at as preferred to life,
Yet leave for the first breathing woman's cheek,
First dancer's, gypsy's, or street baladine's !
Why, how I have ground my teeth to hear men's speech
Stifled for fear it should alarm my ear,
Their gait subdued lest step should startle me,
Their eyes declined, such queendom to respect,
Their hands alert, such treasure to preserve,
While not a man of them broke rank and spoke,
Or wrote me a vulgar letter all of love,
Or caught my hand and pressed it like a hand !
There have been moments, if the sentinel
Lowering his halbert to salute the queen,
Had flung it brutally and clasped my knees,
I would have stooped and kissed him with my soul.
    Con. Who could have comprehended ?
    Queen.   Ay, who — who ?
Why, no one, Constance, but this one who did.
Nor they, not you, not I. Even now perhaps
It comes too late — would you but tell the truth.
    Con. I wait to tell it.
    Queen.   Well, you see, he came,
Outfaced the others, did a work this year
Exceeds in value all was ever done,
You know — it is not I who say it — all
Say it. And so (a second pang and worse)
I grew aware not only of what he did,
But why so wondrously. Oh, never work

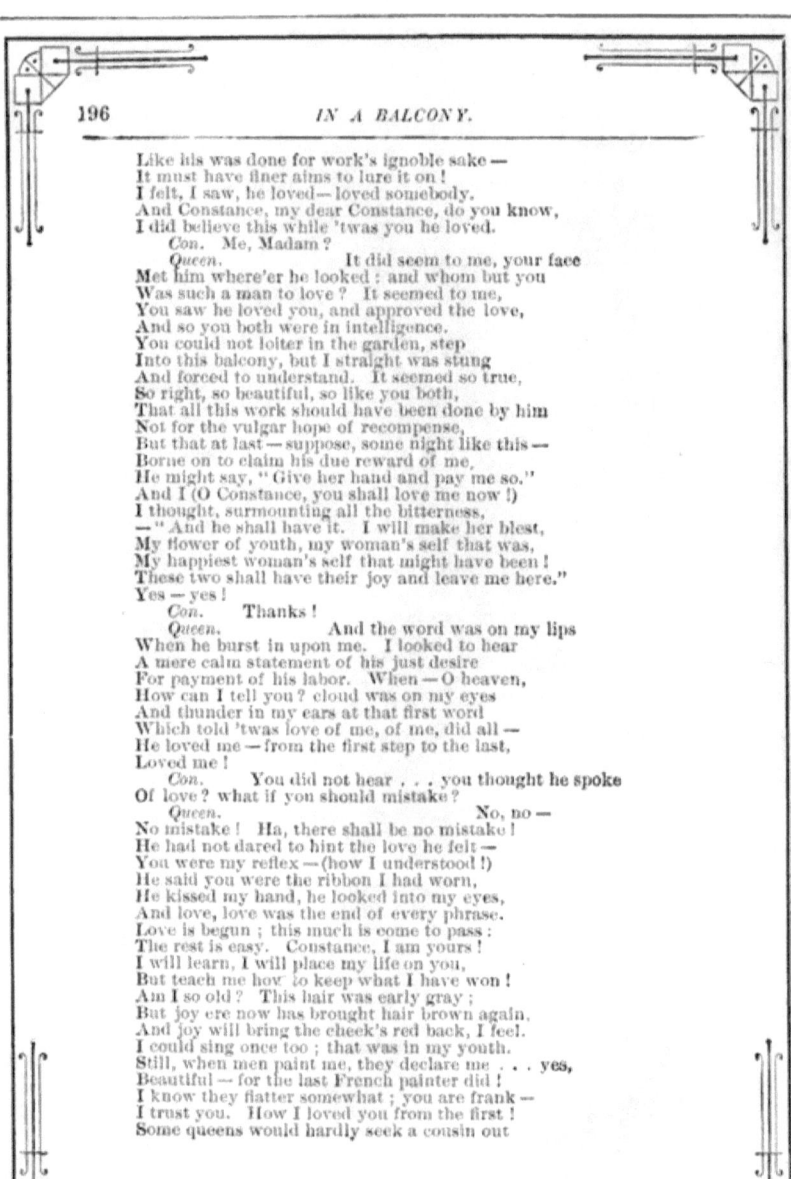

Like his was done for work's ignoble sake —
It must have finer aims to lure it on !
I felt, I saw, he loved — loved somebody.
And Constance, my dear Constance, do you know,
I did believe this while 'twas you he loved.

    Con.   Me, Madam ?

    Queen.   It did seem to me, your face
Met him where'er he looked : and whom but you
Was such a man to love ? It seemed to me,
You saw he loved you, and approved the love,
And so you both were in intelligence.
You could not loiter in the garden, step
Into this balcony, but I straight was stung
And forced to understand. It seemed so true,
So right, so beautiful, so like you both,
That all this work should have been done by him
Not for the vulgar hope of recompense,
But that at last — suppose, some night like this —
Borne on to claim his due reward of me,
He might say, " Give her hand and pay me so."
And I (O Constance, you shall love me now !)
I thought, surmounting all the bitterness,
— " And he shall have it. I will make her blest,
My flower of youth, my woman's self that was,
My happiest woman's self that might have been !
These two shall have their joy and leave me here."
Yes — yes !

    Con.   Thanks !

    Queen.   And the word was on my lips
When he burst in upon me. I looked to hear
A mere calm statement of his just desire
For payment of his labor. When — O heaven,
How can I tell you ? cloud was on my eyes
And thunder in my ears at that first word
Which told 'twas love of me, of me, did all —
He loved me — from the first step to the last,
Loved me !

    Con.   You did not hear . . . you thought he spoke
Of love ? what if you should mistake ?

    Queen.   No, no —
No mistake ! Ha, there shall be no mistake !
He had not dared to hint the love he felt —
You were my reflex — (how I understood !)
He said you were the ribbon I had worn,
He kissed my hand, he looked into my eyes,
And love, love was the end of every phrase.
Love is begun ; this much is come to pass :
The rest is easy. Constance, I am yours !
I will learn, I will place my life on you,
But teach me how to keep what I have won !
Am I so old ? This hair was early gray ;
But joy ere now has brought hair brown again,
And joy will bring the cheek's red back, I feel.
I could sing once too ; that was in my youth.
Still, when men paint me, they declare me . . . yes,
Beautiful — for the last French painter did !
I know they flatter somewhat ; you are frank —
I trust you. How I loved you from the first !
Some queens would hardly seek a cousin out

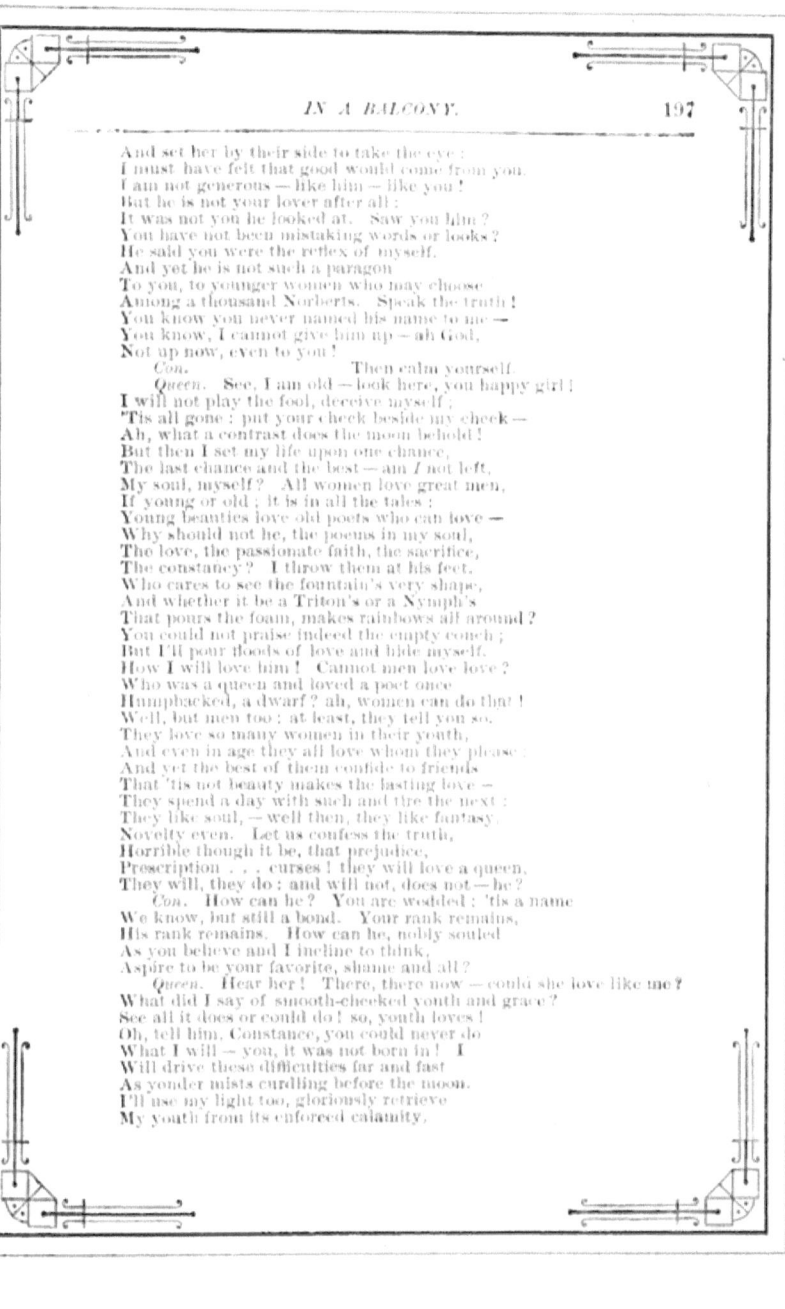

And set her by their side to take the eye :
I must have felt that good would come from you.
I am not generous — like him — like you !
But he is not your lover after all :
It was not you he looked at. Saw you him ?
You have not been mistaking words or looks ?
He said you were the reflex of myself.
And yet he is not such a paragon
To you, to younger women who may choose
Among a thousand Norberts. Speak the truth !
You know you never named his name to me —
You know, I cannot give him up – ah God,
Not up now, even to you !
     Con.   Then calm yourself.
     Queen. See, I am old — look here, you happy girl !
I will not play the fool, deceive myself ;
'Tis all gone : put your cheek beside my cheek —
Ah, what a contrast does the moon behold !
But then I set my life upon one chance,
The last chance and the best — am I not left,
My soul, myself ? All women love great men,
If young or old ; it is in all the tales :
Young beauties love old poets who can love —
Why should not he, the poems in my soul,
The love, the passionate faith, the sacrifice,
The constancy ? I throw them at his feet.
Who cares to see the fountain's very shape,
And whether it be a Triton's or a Nymph's
That pours the foam, makes rainbows all around ?
You could not praise indeed the empty conch ;
But I'll pour floods of love and hide myself.
How I will love him ! Cannot men love love ?
Who was a queen and loved a poet once
Humpbacked, a dwarf ? ah, women can do that !
Well, but men too : at least, they tell you so.
They love so many women in their youth,
And even in age they all love whom they please :
And yet the best of them confide to friends
That 'tis not beauty makes the lasting love —
They spend a day with such and tire the next :
They like soul, — well then, they like fantasy,
Novelty even. Let us confess the truth,
Horrible though it be, that prejudice,
Prescription . . . curses ! they will love a queen.
They will, they do : and will not, does not — he ?
     Con. How can he ? You are wedded ; 'tis a name
We know, but still a bond. Your rank remains,
His rank remains. How can he, nobly souled
As you believe and I incline to think,
Aspire to be your favorite, shame and all ?
     Queen. Hear her ! There, there now — could she love like me ?
What did I say of smooth-cheeked youth and grace ?
See all it does or could do ! so, youth loves !
Oh, tell him, Constance, you could never do
What I will — you, it was not born in ! I
Will drive these difficulties far and fast
As yonder mists curdling before the moon.
I'll use my light too, gloriously retrieve
My youth from its enforced calamity.

Dissolve that hateful marriage, and be his,
His own in the eyes alike of God and man.
    Con. You will do—dare do . . . pause on what you say!
    Queen. Hear her! I thank you, sweet, for that surprise.
You have the fair face: for the soul, see mine!
I have the strong soul: let me teach you, here.
I think I have borne enough and long enough,
And patiently enough, the world remarks,
To have my own way now, unblamed by all.
It does so happen (I rejoice for it)
This most unhoped-for issue cuts the knot.
There's not a better way of settling claims
Than this: God sends the accident express:
And were it for my subjects' good, no more,
'Twere best thus ordered. I am thankful now,
Mute, passive, acquiescent. I receive,
And bless God simply, or should almost fear
To walk so smoothly to my ends at last.
Why, how I baffle obstacles, spurn fate!
How strong I am! Could Norbert see me now!
    Con. Let me consider! It is all too strange.
    Queen. You, Constance, learn of me; do you, like me!
You are young, beautiful: my own, best girl,
You will have many lovers, and love one—
Light hair, not hair like Norbert's, to suit yours,
And taller than he is, for yourself are tall.
Love him, like me! Give all away to him;
Think never of yourself; throw by your pride,
Hope, fear,—your own good as you saw it once,
And love him simply for his very self.
Remember, I (and what am I to you?)
Would give up all for one, leave throne, lose life,
Do all but just unlove him! He loves me.
    Con. He shall.
    Queen.   You, step inside my inmost heart!
Give me your own heart: let us have one heart!
I'll come to you for counsel; "this he says,
This he does; what should this amount to, pray?
Beseech you, change it into current coin!
Is that worth kisses? Shall I please him there?"
And then we'll speak in turn of you—what else?
Your love, according to your beauty's worth,
For you shall have some noble love, all gold:
Whom choose you? we will get him at your choice.
—Constance, I leave you. Just a minute since,
I felt as I must die or be alone
Breathing my soul into an ear like yours:
Now, I would face the world with my new life,
With my new crown. I'll walk around the rooms,
And then come back and tell you how it feels.
How soon a smile of God can change the world!
How we are made for happiness—how work
Grows play, adversity a winning fight!
True I have lost so many years: what then?
Many remain: God has been very good.
You, stay here! 'Tis as different from dreams,
From the mind's cold calm estimate of bliss,
As these stone statues from the flesh and blood.
The comfort thou hast caused mankind, God's moon!
      [*She goes out, leaving* CONSTANCE. *Dance-music from within.*]

NORBERT *enters.*

Nor. Well? we have but one minute and one word!

Con. I am yours, Norbert!

Nor. Yes, mine.

Con. Not till now!

You were mine. Now I give myself to you.

Nor. Constance?

Con. Your own! I know the thriftier way
Of giving — haply, 'tis the wiser way.
Meaning to give a treasure, I might dole
Coin after coin out (each, as that were all,
With a new largess still at each despair),
And force you keep in sight the deed, preserve
Exhaustless to the end my part and yours,
My giving and your taking; both our joys
Dying together. Is it the wiser way?
I choose the simpler: I give all at once.
Know what you have to trust to, trade upon!
Use it, abuse it, — any thing but think
Hereafter, "Had I known she loved me so,
And what my means, I might have thriven with it."
This is your means. I give you all myself.

Nor. I take you and thank God.

Con. Look on through years!
We cannot kiss, a second day like this;
Else were this earth, no earth.

Nor. With this day's heat
We shall go on through years of cold.

Con. So, best!
— I try to see those years, — I think I see.
You walk quick and new warmth comes; you look back
And lay all to the first glow — not sit down
Forever brooding on a day like this
While seeing the embers whiten and love die.
Yes, love lives best in its effect; and mine,
Full in its own life, yearns to live in yours.

Nor. Just so. I take and know you all at once.
Your soul is disengaged so easily,
Your face is there, I know you; give me time,
Let me be proud and think you shall know me.
My soul is slower: in a life I roll
The minute out whereto you condense yours —
The whole slow circle round you I must move,
To be just you. I look to a long life
To decompose this minute, prove its worth.
'Tis th' sparks' long succession one by one
Shall show you, in the end, what fire was crammed
In that mere stone you struck: how could you know,
If it lay ever unproved in your sight,
As now my heart lies? your own warmth would hide
Its coldness, were it cold.

Con. But how prove, how?

Nor. Prove in my life, you ask?

Con. Quick, Norbert — how?

Nor. That's easy told. I count life just a stuff
To try the soul's strength on, educe the man.
Who keeps one end in view makes all things serve.
As with the body — he who hurls a lance

Or heaps up stone on stone, shows strength alike,
So I will seize and use all means to prove
And show this soul of mine, you crown as yours,
And justify us both.

　　Con.　　　　　　Could you write books,
Paint pictures! One sits down in poverty
And writes or paints, with pity for the rich.

　　Nor.　　And loves one's painting and one's writing, then,
And not one's mistress! All is best, believe,
And we best as no other than we are.
We live, and they experiment on life —
Those poets, painters, all who stand aloof
To overlook the farther. Let us be
The thing they look at! I might take your face
And write of it, and paint it, — to what end?
For whom? what pale dictatress in the air
Feeds, smiling sadly, her fine ghost-like form
With earth's real blood and breath, the beauteous life
She makes despised forever? You are mine,
Made for me, not for others in the world,
Nor yet for that which I should call my art,
The cold calm power to see how fair you look.
I come to you; I leave you not, to write
Or paint. You are, I am: let Rubens there
Paint us!

　　Con.　　So, best!

　　Nor.　　　　　I understand your soul.
You live, and rightly sympathize with life,
With action, power, success. This way is straight;
And time were short beside, to let me change
The craft my childhood learnt: my craft shall serve.
Men set me here to subjugate, enclose,
Manure their barren lives, and force the fruit
First for themselves, and afterward for me
In the due tithe; the task of some one man,
Through ways of work appointed by themselves.
I am not bid create, — they see no star
Transfiguring my brow to warrant that, —
But bind in one and carry out their wills.
So I began: to-night sees how I end.
What if it see, too, my first outbreak here
Amid the warmth, surprise, and sympathy,
And instincts of the heart that teach the head?
What if the people have discerned at length
The dawn of the next nature, the new man
Whose will they venture in the place of theirs,
And who, they trust, shall find them out new ways
To heights as new which yet he only sees?
I felt it when you kissed me. See this Queen,
This people, — in our phrase, this mass of men, —
See how the mass lies passive to my hand
And how my hand is plastic, and you by
To make the muscles iron! Oh, an end
Shall crown this issue as this crowns the first!
My will be on this people! then, the strain,
The grappling of the potter with his clay,
The long, uncertain struggle, — the success
And consummation of the spirit-work,
Some vase shaped to the curl of the god's lip,

While rounded fair for lower men to see
The Graces in a dance all recognize
With turbulent applause and laughs of heart!
So triumph ever shall renew itself;
Ever shall end in efforts higher yet,
Ever begin . . .

   Con.   I ever helping?

   Nor.   Thus!

           [*As he embraces her, the* QUEEN *enters.*]

   Con. Hist, madam! So I have performed my part.
You see your gratitude's true decency,
Norbert? A little slow in seeing it!
Begin to end the sooner! What's a kiss?

   Nor. Constance?

   Con.   Why, must I teach it you again?
You want a witness to your dulness, sir?
What was I saying these ten minutes long?
Then I repeat, — when some young, handsome man
Like you has acted out a part like yours,
Is pleased to fall in love with one beyond,
So very far beyond him, as he says, —
So hopelessly in love that but to speak
Would prove him mad, — he thinks judiciously,
And makes some insignificant good soul,
Like me, his friend, adviser, confidant,
And very stalking-horse to cover him
In following after what he dares not face —
When his end's gained — (sir, do you understand?)
When she, he dares not face, has loved him first,
— May I not say so, madam? — tops his hope,
And overpasses so his wildest dream,
With glad consent of all, and most of her
The confidant who brought the same about —
Why, in the moment when such joy explodes,
I do hold that the merest gentleman
Will not start rudely from the stalking-horse,
Dismiss it with a "There, enough of you!"
Forget it, show his back unmannerly;
But like a liberal heart will rather turn
And say, "A tingling time of hope was ours;
Betwixt the fears and falterings, we two lived
A chanceful time in waiting for the prize:
The confidant, the Constance, served not ill.
And though I shall forget her in due time,
Her use being answered now, as reason bids,
Nay as herself bids from her heart of hearts, —
Still, she has rights, the first thanks go to her.
The first good praise goes to the prosperous tool,
And the first — which is the last — rewarding kiss."

   Nor. Constance, it is a dream — ah, see, you smile!

   Con. So, now his part being properly performed,
Madam, I turn to you and finish mine
As duly: I do justice in my turn.
Yes, madam, he has loved you — long and well;
He could not hope to tell you so — 'twas I
Who served to prove your soul accessible,
I led his thoughts on, drew them to their place
When else they had wandered out into despair,
And kept love constant toward its natural aim.

Enough, my part is played ; you stoop half-way
And meet us royally and spare our fears :
'Tis like yourself. He thanks you, so do I
Take him — with my full heart ! my work is praised
By what comes of it. Be you happy, both !
Yourself — the only one on earth who can —
Do all for him, much more than a mere heart
Which though warm is not useful in its warmth
As the silk vesture of a queen ! fold that
Around him gently, tenderly. For him —
For him, — he knows his own part !
    Nor.   Have you done?
I take the jest at last. Should I speak now ?
Was yours the wager, Constance, foolish child,
Or did you but accept it ? Well — at least
You lose by it.
    Con.   Nay, madam, 'tis your turn !
Restrain him still from speech a little more,
And make him happier and more confident !
Pity him, madam, he is timid yet !
Mark, Norbert ! Do not shrink now ! Here I yield
My whole right in you to the Queen, observe !
With her go put in practice the great schemes
You teem with, follow the career else closed —
Be all you cannot be except by her !
Behold her ! — Madam, say for pity's sake
Any thing — frankly say you love him ! Else
He 'll not believe it : there 's more earnest in
His fear than you conceive : I know the man !
    Nor. I know the woman somewhat, and confess
I thought she had jested better : she begins
To overcharge her part. I gravely wait
Your pleasure, madam : where is my reward ?
    Queen. Norbert, this wild girl (whom I recognize
Scarce more than you do, in her fancy-fit,
Eccentric speech, and variable mirth,
Not very wise perhaps and somewhat bold,
Yet suitable, the whole night's work being strange)
— May still be right : I may do well to speak
And make authentic what appears a dream
To even myself. For what she says is truth.
Yes, Norbert — what you spoke just now of love,
Devotion, stirred no novel sense in me,
But justified a warmth felt long before.
Yes, from the first — I loved you, I shall say :
Strange ! but I do grow stronger, now 'tis said.
Your courage helps mine : you did well to speak
To-night, the night that crowns your twelvemonths' toil :
But still I had not waited to discern
Your heart so long, believe me ! From the first
The source of so much zeal was almost plain,
In absence even of your own words just now
Which opened out the truth. 'Tis very strange,
But takes a happy ending — in your love
Which mine meets : be it so ! as you choose me,
So I choose you
    Nor.   And worthily you choose.
I will not be unworthy your esteem.
No, madam. I do love you ; I will meet

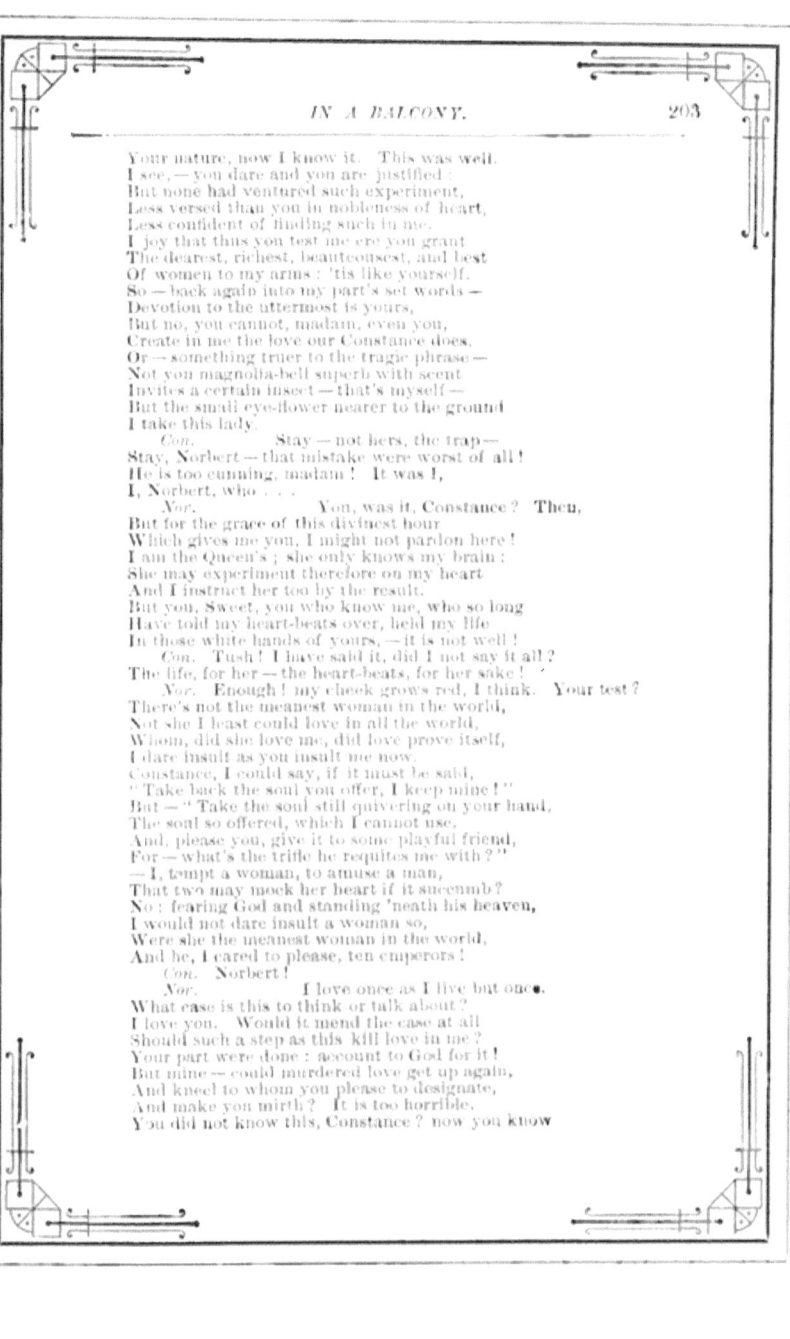

Your nature, now I know it. This was well.
I see,—you dare and you are justified:
But none had ventured such experiment,
Less versed than you in nobleness of heart,
Less confident of finding such in me.
I joy that thus you test me ere you grant
The dearest, richest, beauteousest, and best
Of women to my arms: 'tis like yourself.
So—back again into my part's set words—
Devotion to the uttermost is yours,
But no, you cannot, madam, even you,
Create in me the love our Constance does.
Or—something truer to the tragic phrase—
Not you magnolia-bell superb with scent
Invites a certain insect—that's myself—
But the small eye-flower nearer to the ground
I take this lady.
    Con.   Stay—not hers, the trap—
Stay, Norbert—that mistake were worst of all!
He is too cunning, madam! It was I,
I, Norbert, who . . .
    Nor.   You, was it, Constance? Then,
But for the grace of this divinest hour
Which gives me you, I might not pardon here!
I am the Queen's; she only knows my brain:
She may experiment therefore on my heart
And I instruct her too by the result.
But you, Sweet, you who know me, who so long
Have told my heart-beats over, held my life
In those white hands of yours,—it is not well!
    Con. Tush! I have said it, did I not say it all?
The life, for her—the heart-beats, for her sake!
    Nor. Enough! my cheek grows red, I think. Your test?
There's not the meanest woman in the world,
Not she I least could love in all the world,
Whom, did she love me, did love prove itself,
I dare insult as you insult me now.
Constance, I could say, if it must be said,
"Take back the soul you offer, I keep mine!"
But—"Take the soul still quivering on your hand,
The soul so offered, which I cannot use,
And, please you, give it to some playful friend,
For—what's the trifle he requites me with?"
—I, tempt a woman, to amuse a man,
That two may mock her heart if it succumb?
No: fearing God and standing 'neath his heaven,
I would not dare insult a woman so,
Were she the meanest woman in the world,
And he, I cared to please, ten emperors!
    Con. Norbert!
    Nor.   I love once as I live but once.
What ease is this to think or talk about?
I love you. Would it mend the case at all
Should such a step as this kill love in me?
Your part were done: account to God for it!
But mine—could murdered love get up again,
And kneel to whom you please to designate,
And make you mirth? It is too horrible.
You did not know this, Constance? now you know

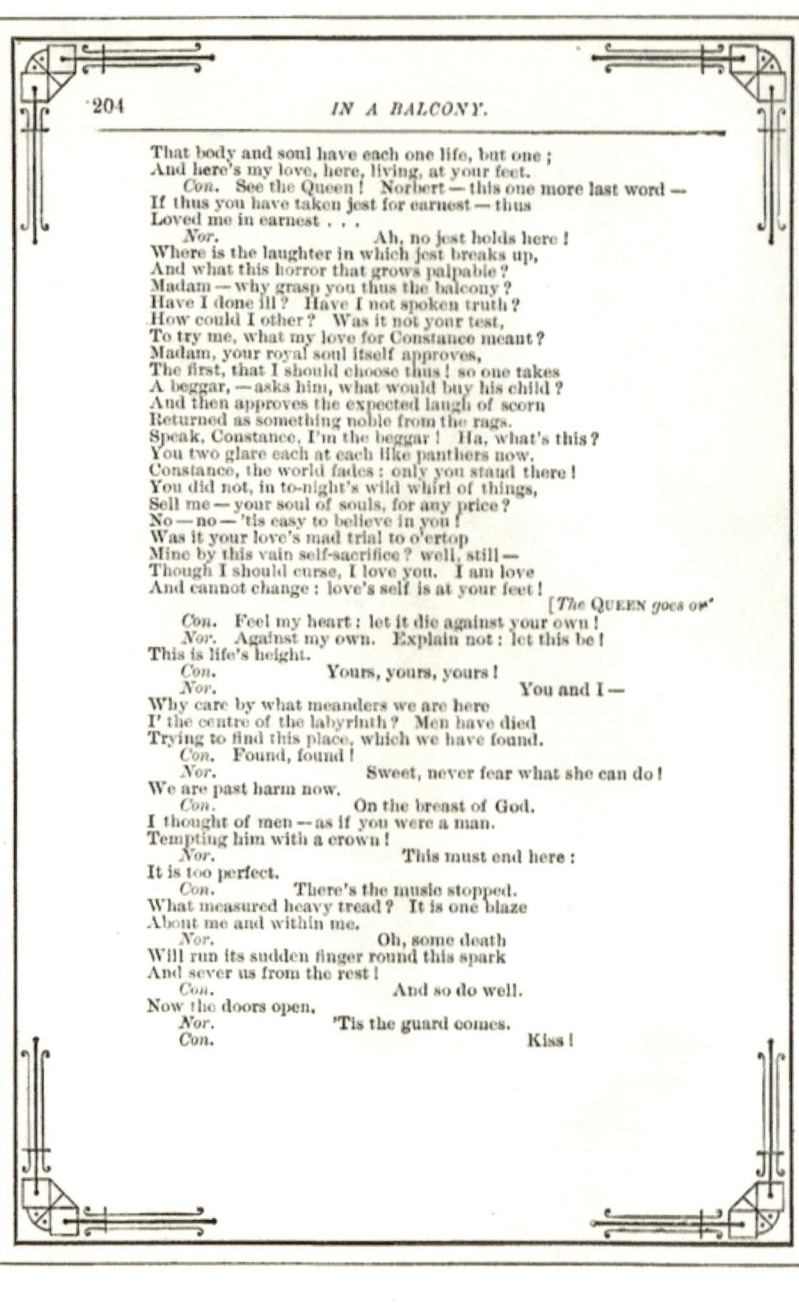

That body and soul have each one life, but one ;
And here's my love, here, living, at your feet.
    Con. See the Queen ! Norbert — this one more last word —
If thus you have taken jest for earnest — thus
Loved me in earnest . . .
    Nor.   Ah, no jest holds here !
Where is the laughter in which jest breaks up,
And what this horror that grows palpable ?
Madam — why grasp you thus the balcony ?
Have I done ill ? Have I not spoken truth ?
How could I other ? Was it not your test,
To try me, what my love for Constance meant ?
Madam, your royal soul itself approves,
The first, that I should choose thus ! so one takes
A beggar, — asks him, what would buy his child ?
And then approves the expected laugh of scorn
Returned as something noble from the rags.
Speak, Constance, I'm the beggar ! Ha, what's this ?
You two glare each at each like panthers now.
Constance, the world fades : only you stand there !
You did not, in to-night's wild whirl of things,
Sell me — your soul of souls, for any price ?
No — no — 'tis easy to believe in you !
Was it your love's mad trial to o'ertop
Mine by this vain self-sacrifice ? well, still —
Though I should curse, I love you. I am love
And cannot change : love's self is at your feet !
                          [*The* QUEEN *goes on*
    Con. Feel my heart : let it die against your own !
    Nor. Against my own. Explain not : let this be !
This is life's height.
    Con.   Yours, yours, yours !
    Nor.   You and I —
Why care by what meanders we are here
I' the centre of the labyrinth ? Men have died
Trying to find this place, which we have found.
    Con. Found, found !
    Nor.   Sweet, never fear what she can do !
We are past harm now.
    Con.   On the breast of God.
I thought of men — as if you were a man.
Tempting him with a crown !
    Nor.   This must end here :
It is too perfect.
    Con.   There's the music stopped.
What measured heavy tread ? It is one blaze
About me and within me.
    Nor.   Oh, some death
Will run its sudden finger round this spark
And sever us from the rest !
    Con.   And so do well.
Now the doors open,
    Nor.   'Tis the guard comes.
    Con.   Kiss !

"And washed by the morning water-gold,
Florence lay out on the mountain side." — Page 205.

OLD PICTURES IN FLORENCE.

I.

THE morn when first it thunders in
  March,
  The eel in the pond gives a leap,
    they say,
As I leaned and looked over the aloed
  arch
  Of the villa-gate this warm March
    day,
No flash snapped, no dumb thunder
  rolled
  In the valley beneath where, white
    and wide
And washed by the morning water-
  gold,
  Florence lay out on the mountain-
    side.

II.

River and bridge and street and
  square
  Lay mine, as much at my beck and
    call,
Through the live translucent bath of
  air,
  As the sights in a magic crystal-ball.
And of all I saw and of all I praised,
  The most to praise and the best to
    see
Was the startling bell-tower Giotto
  raised:
  But why did it more than startle
    me?

III.

Giotto, how, with that soul of yours,
  Could you play me false who loved
    you so?
Some slights if a certain heart en-
  dures
  Yet it feels, I would have your fel-
    lows know!
U' faith, I perceive not why I should
  care
  To break a silence that suits them
    best,
But the thing grows somewhat hard
  to bear
  When I find a Giotto join the rest.

IV.

On the arch where olives overhead
  Print the blue sky with twig and
    leaf
(That sharp-curled leaf which they
  never shed),
  'Twixt the aloes, I used to learn in
    chief,
And mark through the winter after-
  noons,
  By a gift God grants me now and
    then,
In the mild decline of those suns like
  moons,
  Who walked in Florence, besides her
    men.

V.

They might chirp and chaffer, come
  and go
  For pleasure or profit, her men
    alive —
My business was hardly with them, I
  trow,
  But with empty cells of the human
    hive;
— With the chapter-room, the cloister-
  porch,
  The church's apsis, aisle or nave,
Its crypt, one fingers along with a
  torch,
  Its face set full for the sun to shave.

VI.

Wherever a fresco peels and drops,
  Wherever an outline weakens and
    wanes
Till the latest life in the painting
  stops,
  Stands One whom each fainter pulse-
    tick pains:
One, wishful each scrap should clutch
  the brick,
  Each tinge not wholly escape the
    plaster,
— A lion who dies of an ass's kick,
  The wronged great soul of an an-
    cient Master.

VII.

For oh, this world and the wrong it
  does!
  They are safe in heaven with their
    backs to it,
The Michaels and Rafaels, you hum
  and buzz
  Round the works of, you of the little
    wit!
Do their eyes contract to the earth's
  old scope,
  Now that they see God face to face,

And have all attained to be poets, I
    hope?
    'Tis their holiday now, in any
    case.

VIII.

Much they reck of your praise and
    you!
    But the wronged great souls — can
    they be quit
Of a world where their work is all to
    do,
    Where you style them, you of the
    little wit,
Old Master This and Early the Other,
    Not dreaming that Old and New are
    fellows:
A younger succeeds to an elder
    brother,
    Da Vincis derive in good time from
    Dellos.

IX.

And here where your praise might
    yield returns,
    And a handsome word or two give
    help,
Here, after your kind, the mastiff
    girns,
    And the puppy pack of poodles
    yelp.
What, not a word for Stefano there,
    Of brow once prominent and starry,
Called Nature's Ape and the world's
    despair
    For his peerless painting? (see Va-
    sari.)

X.

There stands the Master. Study, my
    friends,
    What a man's work comes to! So
    he plans it,
Performs it, perfects it, makes amends
    For the toiling and moiling, and
    then, *sic transit!*
Happier the thrifty blind-folk labor,
    With upturned eye while the hand
    is busy,
Not sidling a glance at the coin of
    their neighbor!
    'Tis looking downward makes one
    dizzy.

XI.

" If you knew their work you would
    deal your dole."
    May I take upon me to instruct
    you?

When Greek Art ran and reached the
    goal,
    Thus much had the world to boast
    in fructu —
The Truth of Man, as by God first
    spoken,
    Which the actual generations gar-
    ble,
Was re-uttered, and Soul (which
    Limbs betoken)
    And Limbs (Soul informs) made
    new in marble.

XII.

So, you saw yourself as you wished
    you were,
    As you might have been, as you
    cannot be;
Earth here, rebuked by Olympus
    there:
    And grew content in your poor de-
    gree
With your little power, by those
    statues' godhead,
    And your little scope, by their eyes'
    full sway,
And your little grace, by their grace
    embodied,
    And your little date, by their forms
    that stay.

XIII.

You would fain be kinglier, say, than
    I am?
    Even so, you will not sit like The-
    seus.
You would prove a model? The Son
    of Priam
    Has yet the advantage in arms' and
    knees' use.
You're wroth — can you slay your
    snake like Apollo?
    You're grieved -- still Niobe's the
    grander!
You live — there's the Racers' frieze
    to follow:
    You die — there's the dying Alex-
    ander.

XIV.

So, testing your weakness by their
    strength,
    Your meagre charms by their
    rounded beauty,
Measured by Art in your breadth and
    length,
    You learned — to submit is a mor-
    tal's duty.

— When I say " you," 'tis the common
  soul,
  The collective, I mean : the race of
  Man
That receives life in parts to live in a
  whole,
  And grow here according to God's
  clear plan.

XV.

Growth came when, looking your last
  on them all,
  You turned your eyes inwardly one
  fine day
And cried with a start — What if we
  so small
  Be greater and grander the while
  than they ?
Are they perfect of lineament, per-
  fect of stature ?
In both, of such lower types are we
Precisely because of our wider nature;
  For time, theirs — ours, for eternity.

XVI.

To-day's brief passion limits their
  range ;
  It seethes with the morrow for us
  and more.
They are perfect — how else ? they
  shall never change :
  We are faulty — why not ? we have
  time in store.
The Artificer's hand is not arrested
  With us ; we are rough-hewn, no-
  wise polished.
They stand for our copy, and, once
  invested
  With all they can teach, we shall
  see them abolished.

XVII.

'Tis a life-long toil till our lump be
  leaven —
  The better ! What's come to per-
  fection perishes.
Things learned on earth, we shall
  practise in heaven :
  Works done least rapidly, Art most
  cherishes.
Thyself shalt afford the example,
  Giotto !
  Thy one work, not to decrease or
  diminish,
Done at a stroke, was just (was it
  not ?) " O "
  Thy great Campanile is still to fin-
  ish.

XVIII.

Is it true that we are now, and shall
  be hereafter,
  But what and where depend on
  life's minute ?
Hails heavenly cheer or infernal
  laughter
  Our first step out of the gulf or in
  it ?
Shall Man, such step within his en-
  deavor,
  Man's face, have no more play and
  action
Than joy which is crystallized forever,
  Or grief, an eternal petrifaction ?

XIX.

On which I conclude, that the early
  painters,
  To cries of " Greek Art and what
  more wish you ? " —
Replied, " To become now self-ac-
  quainters,
  And paint man, man, whatever the
  issue !
Make new hopes shine through the
  flesh they fray,
  New fears aggrandize the rags and
  tatters :
To bring the invisible full into play,
  Let the visible go to the dogs —
  what matters ? "

XX.

Give these, I exhort you, their guer-
  don and glory
  For daring so much, before they
  well did it.
The first of the new, in our race's
  story,
  Beats the last of the old ; 'tis no
  idle quiddit.
The worthies began a revolution,
  Which if on earth you intend to
  acknowledge,
Why, honor them now ! (ends my al-
  locution)
  Nor confer your degree when the
  folks leave college.

XXI.

There's a fancy some lean to and
  others hate —
  That, when this life is ended, begins
New work for the soul in another
  state,
  Where it strives and gets weary,
  loses and wins :

Where the strong and the weak, this
    world's congeries,
    Repeat in large what they practised
        in small,
Through life after life in unlimited
    series ;
    Only the scale's to be changed,
        that's all.

XXII.

Yet I hardly know. When a soul has
    seen
    By the means of Evil that Good is
        best,
And, through earth and its noise,
    what is heaven's serene, —
When our faith in the same has
    stood the test—
Why, the child grown man, you burn
    the rod,
The uses of labor are surely done ;
There remaineth a rest for the people
    of God :
    And I have had troubles enough,
        for one.

XXIII.

But at any rate I have loved the sea-
    son
    Of Art's spring-birth so dim and
        dewy ;
My sculptor is Nicolo the Pisan,
    My painter — who but Cimabue ?
Nor even was man of them all in-
    deed,
    From these to Ghiberti and Ghir-
        landajo,
Could say that he missed my critic-
    meed.
    So, now to my special grievance—
        heigh-ho !

XXIV.

Their ghosts still stand, as I said be-
    fore,
    Watching each fresco flaked and
        rasped,
Blocked up, knocked out, or white-
    washed o'er :
    — No getting again what the Church
        has grasped !
The works on the wall must take
    their chance ;
    "Works never conceded to Eng-
        land's thick clime ! "
(I hope they prefer their inheritance
    Of a bucketful of Italian quick-
        lime.)

XXV.

When they go at length, with such a
    shaking
    Of heads o'er the old delusion, sadly
Each master his way through the
    black streets taking,
    Where many a lost work breathes
        though badly —
Why don't they bethink them of who
    has merited ?
Why not reveal, while their pic-
    tures dree
Such doom, how a captive might be
    out-ferreted ?
Why is it they never remember me ?

XXVI.

Not that I expect the great Bigordi,
    Nor Sandro to hear me, chivalric,
        bellicose ;
Nor the wronged Lippino ; and not a
    word I
Say of a scrap of Frà Angelico's :
But are you too fine, Taddeo Gaddi,
    To grant me a taste of your intonaco,
Some Jerome that seeks the heaven
    with a sad eye ?
Not a churlish saint, Lorenzo Mo-
    naco ?

XXVII.

Could not the ghost with the close red
    cap,
    My Pollajolo, the twice a crafts-
        man,
Save me a sample, give me the hap
    Of a muscular Christ that shows
        the draughtsman ?
No Virgin by him the somewhat petty,
    Of finical touch and tempera
        crumbly —
Could not Alesso Baldovinetti
    Contribute so much, I ask him
        humbly ?

XXVIII.

Margheritone of Arezzo,
    With the grave-clothes garb and
        swaddling barret
(Why purse up mouth and beak in a
    pet so,
    You bald old saturnine poll-clawed
        parrot ?)
Not a poor glimmering Crucifixion,
    Where in the foreground kneels the
        donor ?
If such remain, as is my conviction,
    The hoarding it does you but little
        honor.

XXIX.

They pass ; for them the panels may
    thrill,
  The tempera grow alive and tin-
    glish :
Their pictures are left to the mercies
    still
  Of dealers and stealers, Jews and
    the English,
Who, seeing mere money's worth in
    their prize,
  Will sell it to somebody calm as
    Zeno
At naked High Art, and in ecstasies
  Before some clay-cold vile Carlino !

XXX.

No matter for these ! But Giotto,
    you,
  Have you allowed, as the town-
    tongues babble it —
Oh, never ! it shall not be counted
    true —
  That a certain precious little tablet
Which Buonarroti eyed like a lover,
  Was buried so long in oblivion's
    womb
And, left for another than I to dis-
    cover,
  Turns up at last ! and to whom ? —
    to whom ?

XXXI.

I, that have haunted the dim San
    Spirito,
  (Or was it rather the Ognissanti ?)
Patient on altar-step planting a weary
    toe !
  Nay, I shall have it yet ! *Detur
    amanti !*
My Koh-i-noor — or (if that's a plati-
    tude)
  Jewel of Giamschid, the Persian
    Sofi's eye ;
So, in anticipative gratitude,
  What if I take up my hope and
    prophesy ?

XXXII.

When the hour grows ripe, and a cer-
    tain dotard
  Is pitched, no parcel that needs in-
    voicing,
To the worst side of the Mont St.
    Gothard,
  We shall begin by way of rejoicing ;

None of that shooting the sky (blank
    cartridge),
  Nor a civic guard, all plumes and
    lacquer,
Hunting Radetzky's soul like a par-
    tridge
  Over Morello with squib and crack-
    er.

XXXIII.

This time we'll shoot better game and
    bag 'em hot :
  No mere display at the stone of
    Dante,
But a kind of sober Witanagemot
  (Ex : "Casa Guidi," *quod videas
    ante*)
Shall ponder, once Freedom restored
    to Florence,
  How Art may return that departed
    with her.
Go, hated house, go each trace of the
    Loraine's,
  And bring us the days of Orgagna
    hither !

XXXIV.

How we shall prologuize, how we
    shall perorate,
  Utter fit things upon art and history,
Feel truth at blood-heat and falsehood
    at zero rate,
  Make of the want of the age no
    mystery ;
Contrast the fructuous and sterile
    eras,
  Show — monarchy ever its uncouth
    cub licks
Out of the bear's shape into Chimæ-
    ra's,
  While Pure Art's birth is still the
    republic's !

XXXV.

Then one shall propose in a speech
    (curt Tuscan,
  Expurgate and sober, with scarcely
    an "*issimo*"),
To end now our half-told tale of Cam-
    buscan,
  And turn the bell-tower's *alt* to
    altissimo :
And, fine as the beak of a young
    beccaccia,
  The Campanile, the Duomo's fit
    ally,
Shall soar up in gold full fifty braccia,
  Completing Florence, as Florence,
    Italy.

XXXVI.

Shall I be alive that morning the scaffold
  Is broken away, and the long-pent fire,
Like the golden hope of the world, unbaffled
  Springs from its sleep, and up goes the spire,
While, "God and the People" plain for its motto,
  Thence the new tricolor flaps at the sky?
At least to foresee that glory of Giotto
  And Florence together, the first am I!

NOTE.—The space left here tempts to a word on the line about Apollo the snake-slayer, which my friend Professor Colvin condemns, believing that the God of the Belvedere grasps no bow, but the Ægis, as described in the 15th Iliad. Surely the text represents that portentous object (θοῦριν, δεινήν, ἀμφιδάσειαν, ἀριπρεπέ' —μαρμαρέην) as "shaken violently" or "held immovably" by both hands, not a single one, and that the left hand :—

ἀλλὰ συ γ᾽ ἐν χείρεσσι λάβ᾽ αἰγίδα θυσανόεσσαν

τὴν μάλ᾽ ἐπισσείων φοβέειν ἥρωας Ἀχαιούς.

and so on, τὴν ἄρ᾽ ὅ γ᾽ ἐν χείρεσσιν ἔχων —χερσὶν ἔχ᾽ ἀτρέμα, κ. τ. λ. Moreover, while he shook it he "shouted enormously," σεῖσ᾽, ἐπὶ δ᾽ αὐτὸς αὖσε μάλα μέγα, which the statue does not. Presently when Teukros, on the other side, plies the bow, it is τόξον ἔχων ἐν χειρὶ παλίντονον. Besides, by the act of discharging an arrow, the right arm and hand are thrown back as we see,—a quite gratuitous and theatrical display in the case supposed. The conjecture of Flaxman that the statue was suggested by the bronze Apollo Alexikakos of Kalamis, mentioned by Pausanias, remains probable; though the "hardness" which Cicero considers to distinguish the artist's workmanship from that of Muron is not by any means apparent in our marble copy, if it be one.— Feb. 16, 1880.

BISHOP BLOUGRAM'S APOLOGY.

No more wine? then we'll push back chairs and talk.
A final glass for me, though: cool, i' faith!
We ought to have our Abbey back, you see.
It's different, preaching in basilicas,
And doing duty in some masterpiece
Like this of brother Pugin's, bless his heart!
I doubt if they're half baked, those chalk rosettes,
Ciphers and stucco-twiddlings everywhere;
It's just like breathing in a lime-kiln: eh?
These hot, long ceremonies of our Church
Cost us a little — oh, they pay the price,
You take me — amply pay it! Now we'll talk.

So, you despise me, Mr. Gigadibs.
No deprecation, — nay, I beg you, sir!
Beside 'tis our engagement: don't you know,
I promised, if you'd watch a dinner out,
We'd see truth dawn together? — truth that peeps
Over the glass's edge when dinner's done,
And body gets its sop and holds its noise,
And leaves soul free a little. Now's the time:
'Tis break of day! You do despise me then.
And if I say, "despise me," — never fear!
I know you do not in a certain sense —
Not in my arm-chair, for example: here.
I will imagine you respect my place
(Status, entourage, worldly circumstance)

Bishop Blougram's Apology. — Page 216.

Quite to its value — very much indeed ;
— Are up to the protesting eyes of you
In pride at being seated here for once —
You'll turn it to such capital account !
When somebody, through years and years to come,
Hints of the bishop, — names me — that's enough :
"Blougram ? I knew him" — (into it you slide)
"Dined with him once, a Corpus Christi Day,
All alone, we two ; he's a clever man :
And after dinner, — why, the wine you know, —
Oh, there was wine, and good ! — what with the wine . .
'Faith, we began upon all sorts of talk !
He's no bad fellow, Blougram ; he had seen
Something of mine he relished, some review :
He's quite above their humbug in his heart,
Half said as much, indeed — the thing's his trade.
I warrant, Blougram's sceptical at times :
How otherwise ? I like him, I confess !"
Che che, my dear sir, as we say at Rome,
Don't you protest now ! It's fair give and take ;
You have had your turn, and spoken your home-truths :
The hand's mine now, and here you follow suit.

Thus much conceded, still the first fact stays —
You do despise me ; your ideal of life
Is not the bishop's ; you would not be I.
You would like better to be Goethe, now,
Or Buonaparte, or, bless me, lower still,
Count D'Orsay, — so you did what you preferred,
Spoke as you thought, and, as you cannot help,
Believed or disbelieved, no matter what,
So long as on that point, whate'er it was,
You loosed your mind, were whole and sole yourself
— That, my ideal never can include,
Upon that element of truth and worth
Never be based ! for say they make me Pope
(They can't — suppose it for our argument),
Why, there I'm at my tether's end, I've reached
My height, and not a height which pleases you :
An unbelieving Pope won't do, you say.
It's like those eerie stories nurses tell,
Of how some actor played Death on a stage,
With pasteboard crown, sham orb, and tinselled dart,
And called himself the monarch of the world ;
Then, going in the tire-room afterward,
Because the play was done, to shift himself,
Got touched upon the sleeve familiarly,
The moment he had shut the closet door,
By Death himself. Thus God might touch a Pope
At unawares, ask what his baubles mean,
And whose part he presumed to play just now ?
Best be yourself, imperial, plain, and true !

So, drawing comfortable breath again,
You weigh and find, whatever more or less
I boast of my ideal realized,
Is nothing in the balance when opposed
To your ideal, your grand simple life,
Of which you will not realize one jot.

I am much, you are nothing ; you would be all,
I would be merely much : you beat me there.

No, friend, you do not beat me : hearken why !
The common problem, yours, mine, every one's,
Is — not to fancy what were fair in life
Provided it could be, — but, finding first
What may be, then find how to make it fair
Up to our means : a very different thing !
No abstract intellectual plan of life
Quite irrespective of life's plainest laws,
But one, a man, who is man and nothing more,
May lead within a world which (by your leave)
Is Rome or London, not Fool's-paradise.
Embellish Rome, idealize away,
Make paradise of London if you can,
You're welcome, nay, you're wise.

                     A simile !
We mortals cross the ocean of this world
Each in his average cabin of a life ;
The best's not big, the worst yields elbow-room.
Now for our six months' voyage — how prepare ?
You come on shipboard with a landsman's list
Of things he calls convenient : so they are !
An India screen is pretty furniture,
A piano-forte is a fine resource,
All Balzac's novels occupy one shelf,
The new edition fifty volumes long ;
And little Greek books, with the funny type
They get up well at Leipsic, fill the next :
Go on ! slabbed marble, what a bath it makes !
And Parma's pride, the Jerome, let us add !
'Twere pleasant could Correggio's fleeting glow
Hang full in face of one where'er one roams,
Since he more than the others brings with him
Italy's self, — the marvellous Modenese ! —
Yet was not on your list before, perhaps
— Alas, friend ! here's the agent . . . is't the name ?
The captain, or whoever's master here —
You see him screw his face up ; what's his cry
Ere you set foot on shipboard ?   " Six feet square ! "
If you won't understand what six feet mean,
Compute and purchase stores accordingly —
And if, in pique because he overhauls
Your Jerome, piano and bath, you come on board
Bare — why, you cut a figure at the first
While sympathetic landsmen see you off ;
Not afterward, when long ere half seas over,
You peep up from your utterly naked boards
Into some snug and well-appointed berth,
Like mine for instance (try the cooler jug —
Put back the other, but don't jog the ice !)
And mortified you mutter " Well and good ;
He sits enjoying his sea-furniture ;
'Tis stout and proper, and there's store of it :
Though I've the better notion, all agree,
Of fitting rooms up.   Hang the carpenter,
Neat ship-shape fixings and contrivances —

I would have brought my Jerome, frame and all!"
And meantime you bring nothing : never mind —
You've proved your artist-nature : what you don't
You might bring, so despise me, as I say.

Now come, let's backward to the starting-place.
See my way : we're two college friends, suppose.
Prepare together for our voyage, then ;
Each note and check the other in his work, —
Here's mine, a bishop's outfit ; criticise !
What's wrong ? why won't you be a bishop too ?

Why first, you don't believe, you don't and can't
(Not statedly, that is, and fixedly
And absolutely and exclusively),
In any revelation called divine.
No dogmas nail your faith ; and what remains
But say so, like the honest man you are ?
First, therefore, overhaul theology !
Nay, I too, not a fool, you please to think,
Must find believing every whit as hard :
And if I do not frankly say as much,
The ugly consequence is clear enough.

Now wait, my friend : well, I do not believe —
If you'll accept no faith that is not fixed,
Absolute and exclusive, as you say.
You're wrong — I mean to prove it in due time.
Meanwhile, I know where difficulties lie
I could not, cannot solve, nor ever shall,
So give up hope accordingly to solve —
(To you, and over the wine). Our dogmas then
With both of us, though in unlike degree,
Missing full credence — overboard with them !
I mean to meet you on your own premise :
Good, there go mine in company with yours !

And now what are we ? unbelievers both,
Calm and complete, determinately fixed
To-day, to-morrow, and forever, pray ?
You'll guarantee me that ? Not so, I think !
In no wise ! all we've gained is, that belief,
As unbelief before, shakes us by fits,
Confounds us like its predecessor. Where's
The gain ? how can we guard our unbelief,
Make it bear fruit to us ? — the problem here.
Just when we are safest, there's a sunset-touch,
A fancy from a flower-bell, some one's death,
A chorus-ending from Euripides, —
And that's enough for fifty hopes and fears
As old and new at once as nature's self,
To rap and knock and enter in our soul,
Take hands and dance there, a fantastic ring,
Round the ancient idol, on his base again, —
The grand Perhaps ! We look on helplessly.
There the old misgivings, crooked questions are —
This good God, — what he could do, if he would,
Would, if he could — then must have done long since :
If so, when, where, and how ? some way must be, —

Once feel about, and soon or late you hit
Some sense, in which it might be, after all.
Why not " The Way, the Truth, the Life "?

That way
Over the mountain, which who stands upon
Is apt to doubt if it be indeed a road ;
While if he views it from the waste itself,
Up goes the line there, plain from base to brow,
Not vague, mistakable ! what's a break or two
Seen from the unbroken desert either side ?
And then (to bring in fresh philosophy)
What if the breaks themselves should prove at last
The most consummate of contrivances
To train a man's eye, teach him what is faith ?
And so we stumble at truth's very test !
All we have gained then by our unbelief
Is a life of doubt diversified by faith,
For one of faith diversified by doubt :
We called the chess-board white,—we call it black.

" Well," you rejoin, " the end's no worse, at least ;
We've reason for both colors on the board :
Why not confess then, where I drop the faith
And you the doubt, that I'm as right as you ?"

Because, friend, in the next place, this being so,
And both things even,—faith and unbelief
Left to a man's choice,—we'll proceed a step,
Returning to our image, which I like.

A man's choice, yes—but a cabin passenger's—
The man made for the special life o' the world—
Do you forget him ? I remember though !
Consult our ship's conditions and you find
One and but one choice suitable to all ;
The choice, that you unluckily prefer,
Turning things topsy-turvy—they or it
Going to the ground. Belief or unbelief
Bears upon life, determines its whole course,
Begins at its beginning. See the world
Such as it is,—you made it not, nor I ;
I mean to take it as it is,—and you,
Not so you'll take it,—though you get naught else.
I know the special kind of life I like,
What suits the most my idiosyncrasy,
Brings out the best of me and bears me fruit
In power, peace, pleasantness, and length of days.
I find that positive belief does this
For me, and unbelief, no whit of this.
—For you, it does, however ?—that, we'll try !
'Tis clear, I cannot lead my life, at least,
Induce the world to let me peaceably,
Without declaring at the outset, " Friends,
I absolutely and peremptorily
Believe !"—I say, faith is my waking life :
One sleeps, indeed, and dreams at intervals,
We know, but waking's the main point with us,
And my provision's for life's waking part.

Accordingly, I use heart, head, and hand
All day, I build, scheme, study, and make friends;
And when night overtakes me, down I lie,
Sleep, dream a little, and get done with it,
The sooner the better, to begin afresh.
What's midnight doubt before the dayspring's faith?
You, the philosopher, that disbelieve,
That recognize the night, give dreams their weight —
To be consistent you should keep your bed,
Abstain from healthy acts that prove you man,
For fear you drowse perhaps at unawares!
And certainly at night you'll sleep and dream,
Live through the day and bustle as you please.
And so you live to sleep as I to wake,
To unbelieve as I to still believe?
Well, and the common sense o' the world calls you
Bed-ridden, — and its good things come to me.
Its estimation, which is half the fight,
That's the first-cabin comfort I secure:
The next . . . but you perceive with half an eye!
Come, come, it's best believing, if we may;
You can't but own that!

                Next, concede again
If once we choose belief, on all accounts
We can't be too decisive in our faith,
Conclusive and exclusive in its terms,
To suit the world which gives us the good things.
In every man's career are certain points
Whereon he dares not be indifferent:
The world detects him clearly, if he dare,
As baffled at the game, and losing life.
He may care little or he may care much
For riches, honor, pleasure, work, repose,
Since various theories of life and life's
Success are extant which might easily
Comport with either estimate of these;
And whoso chooses wealth or poverty,
Labor or quiet, is not judged a fool
Because his fellow would choose otherwise:
We let him choose upon his own account
So long as he's consistent with his choice.
But certain points, left wholly to himself,
When once a man has arbitrated on,
We say he must succeed there or go hang.
Thus, he should wed the woman he loves most
Or needs most, whatsoe'er the love or need —
For he can't wed twice. Then, he must avouch,
Or follow, at the least, sufficiently,
The form of faith his conscience holds the best,
Whate'er the process of conviction was:
For nothing can compensate his mistake
On such a point, the man himself being judge:
He cannot wed twice, nor twice lose his soul.

    Well now, there's one great form of Christian faith
I happened to be born in — which to teach
Was given me as I grew up, on all hands,
As best and readiest means of living by;

The same on examination being proved
The most pronounced moreover, fixed, precise
And absolute form of faith in the whole world —
Accordingly, most potent of all forms
For working on the world. Observe, my friend!
Such as you know me, I am free to say,
In these hard latter days which hamper one,
Myself — by no immoderate exercise
Of intellect and learning, but the tact
To let external forces work for me,
— Bid the street's stones be bread and they are bread;
Bid Peter's creed, or rather, Hildebrand's,
Exalt me o'er my fellows in the world
And make my life an ease and joy and pride:
It does so, — which for me's a great point gained,
Who have a soul and body that exact
A comfortable care in many ways.
There's power in me and will to dominate
Which I must exercise, they hurt me else:
In many ways I need mankind's respect,
Obedience, and the love that's born of fear:
While at the same time, there's a taste I have,
A toy of soul, a titillating thing,
Refuses to digest these dainties crude.
The naked life is gross till clothed upon:
I must take what men offer, with a grace
As though I would not, could I help it, take!
An uniform I wear though over-rich —
Something imposed on me, no choice of mine;
No fancy-dress worn for pure fancy's sake
And despicable therefore! now folks kneel
And kiss my hand — of course the Church's hand.
Thus I am made, thus life is best for me,
And thus that it should be I have procured;
And thus it could not be another way,
I venture to imagine.

　　　　　　　You'll reply,
So far my choice, no doubt, is a success;
But were I made of better elements,
With nobler instincts, purer tastes, like you,
I hardly would account the thing success
Though it did all for me I say.

　　　　　　　But, friend,
We speak of what is; not of what might be,
And how 'twere better if 'twere otherwise
I am the man you see here plain enough:
Grant I'm a beast, why, beasts must lead beasts' lives!
Suppose I own at once to tail and claws;
The tailless man exceeds me: but being tailed
I'll lash out lion fashion, and leave apes
To dock their stump and dress their haunches up.
My business is not to remake myself,
But make the absolute best of what God made.
Or — our first simile — though you prove me doomed
To a viler berth still, to the steerage-hole,
The sheep-pen or the pig-sty, I should strive
To make what use of each were possible;

And as this cabin gets upholstery,
That hutch should rustle with sufficient straw.

But, friend, I don't acknowledge quite so fast
I fail of all your manhood's lofty tastes
Enumerated so complacently,
On the mere ground that you forsooth can find
In this particular life I choose to lead
No fit provision for them. Can you not?
Say you, my fault is I address myself
To grosser estimators than should judge?
And that's no way of holding up the soul,
Which, nobler, needs men's praise perhaps, yet knows
One wise man's verdict outweighs all the fools' —
Would like the two, but, forced to choose, takes that.
I pine among my million imbeciles
(You think) aware some dozen men of sense
Eye me and know me, whether I believe
In the last winking Virgin, as I vow,
And am a fool, or disbelieve in her
And am a knave, — approve in neither case,
Withhold their voices though I look their way:
Like Verdi when, at his worst opera's end
(The thing they gave at Florence — what's its name?)
While the mad houseful's plaudits near out-bang
His orchestra of salt-box, tongs, and bones,
He looks through all the roaring and the wreaths
Where sits Rossini patient in his stall.

Nay, friend, I meet you with an answer here —
That even your prime men who appraise their kind
Are men still, catch a wheel within a wheel,
See more in a truth than the truth's simple self,
Confuse themselves. You see lads walk the street
Sixty the minute; what's to note in that?
You see one lad o'erstride a chimney-stack;
Him you must watch — he's sure to fall, yet stands!
Our interest's on the dangerous edge of things.
The honest thief, the tender murderer,
The superstitious atheist, demirep
That loves and saves her soul in new French books —
We watch while these in equilibrium keep
The giddy line midway: one step aside,
They're classed and done with. I, then, keep the line
Before your sages, — just the men to shrink
From the gross weights, coarse scales, and labels broad
You offer their refinement. Fool, or knave?
Why needs a bishop be a fool or knave
When there's a thousand diamond weights between?
So, I enlist them. Your picked twelve, you'll find,
Profess themselves indignant, scandalized
At thus being held unable to explain
How a superior man who disbelieves
May not believe as well: that's Schelling's way!
It's through my coming in the tail of time,
Nicking the minute with a happy tact.
Had I been born three hundred years ago
They'd say, "What's strange? Blougram of course believes;"
And, seventy years since, "disbelieves of course."

But now, "He may believe; and yet, and yet
How can he?"   All eyes turn with interest.
Whereas, step off the line on either side —
You, for example, clever to a fault,
The rough and ready man who write apace,
Read somewhat seldomer, think perhaps even less —
You disbelieve!   Who wonders and who cares?
Lord So-and-so — his coat bedropped with wax,
All Peter's chains about his waist, his back
Brave with the needlework of Noodledom —
Believes!   Again, who wonders and who cares?
But I, the man of sense and learning too,
The able to think yet act, the this, the that,
I, to believe at this late time of day!
Enough; you see, I need not fear contempt.
  — Except it's yours!   Admire me as these may,
You don't.   But whom at least do you admire?
Present your own perfection, your Ideal,
Your pattern man for a minute — oh, make haste!
Is it Napoleon you would have us grow?
Concede the means; allow his head and hand
(A large concession, clever as you are),
Good!   In our common primal element
Of unbelief (we can't believe, you know —
We're still at that admission, recollect!)
Where do you find — apart from, towering o'er
The secondary temporary aims
Which satisfy the gross taste you despise —
Where do you find his star? — his crazy trust
God knows through what or in what? it's alive
And shines and leads him, and that's all we want.
Have we aught in our sober night shall point
Such ends as his were, and direct the means
Of working out our purpose straight as his,
Nor bring a moment's trouble on success
With after-care to justify the same?
— Be a Napoleon and yet disbelieve —
Why, the man's mad, friend, take his light away!
What's the vague good o' the world, for which you dare
With comfort to yourself blow millions up?
We neither of us see it! we do see
The blown-up millions — spatter of their brains
And writhing of their bowels and so forth,
In that bewildering entanglement
Of horrible eventualities
Past calculation to the end of time!
Can I mistake for some clear word of God
(Which were my ample warrant for it all)
His puff of hazy instinct, idle talk,
"The State, that's I," quack-nonsense about crowns,
And (when one beats the man to his last hold)
A vague idea of setting things to rights,
Policing people efficaciously,
More to their profit, most of all to his own;
The whole to end that dismallest of ends
By an Austrian marriage, cant to us the Church,
And resurrection of the old *régime*?
Would I, who hope to live a dozen years,
Fight Austerlitz for reasons such and such?

No : for, concede me but the merest chance
Doubt may be wrong — there's judgment, life to come !
With just that chance, I dare not.   Doubt proves right ?
This present life is all ? — you offer me
Its dozen noisy years, without a chance
That wedding an arch-duchess, wearing lace,
And getting called by divers new-coined names,
Will drive off ugly thoughts and let me dine,
Sleep, read, and chat in quiet as I like !
Therefore I will not.

                    Take another case,
Fit up the cabin yet another way.
What say you to the poets ? shall we write
Hamlet, Othello — make the world our own,
Without a risk to run of either sort ?
I can't ! — to put the strongest reason first,
" But try," you urge, " the trying shall suffice ;
The aim, if reached or not, makes great the life :
Try to be Shakspeare, leave the rest to fate ! "
Spare my self-knowledge — there's no fooling me !
If I prefer remaining my poor self,
I say so not in self-dispraise but praise.
If I'm a Shakspeare, let the well alone ;
Why should I try to be what now I am ?
If I'm no Shakspeare, as too probable, —
His power and consciousness and self-delight
And all we want in common, shall I find —
Trying forever ? while on points of taste
Wherewith, to speak it humbly, he and I
Are dowered alike — I'll ask you, I or he,
Which in our two lives realizes most ?
Much, he imagined : somewhat, I possess.
He had the imagination ; stick to that !
Let him say, " In the face of my soul's works
Your world is worthless and I touch it not
Lest I should wrong them " — I'll withdraw my plea.
But does he say so ? look upon his life !
Himself, who only can, gives judgment there.
He leaves his towers and gorgeous palaces
To build the trimmest house in Stratford town ;
Saves money, spends it, owns the worth of things,
Giulio Romano's pictures, Dowland's lute ;
Enjoys a show, respects the puppets too,
And none more, had he seen its entry once,
Than ' Pandulph, of fair Milan cardinal."
Why then should I who play that personage,
The very Pandulph Shakspeare's fancy made,
Be told that had the poet chanced to start
From where I stand now (some degree like mine
Being just the goal he ran his race to reach)
He would have run the whole race back, forsooth,
And left being Pandulph, to begin write plays ?
Ah, the earth's best can be but the earth's best !
Did Shakspeare live, he could but sit at home
And get himself in dreams the Vatican,
Greek busts, Venetian paintings, Roman walls,
And English books, none equal to his own,
Which I read, bound in gold (he never did).

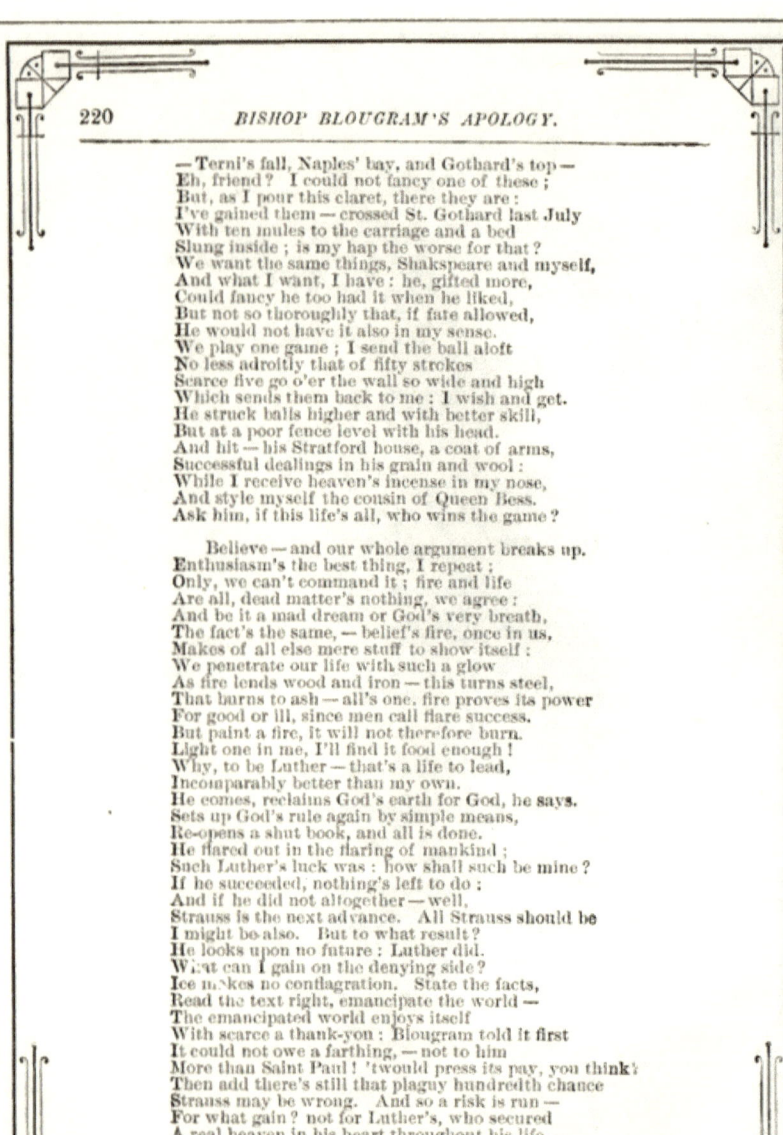

— Terni's fall, Naples' bay, and Gothard's top —
Eh, friend? I could not fancy one of these;
But, as I pour this claret, there they are:
I've gained them — crossed St. Gothard last July
With ten mules to the carriage and a bed
Slung inside; is my hap the worse for that?
We want the same things, Shakspeare and myself,
And what I want, I have: he, gifted more,
Could fancy he too had it when he liked,
But not so thoroughly that, if fate allowed,
He would not have it also in my sense.
We play one game; I send the ball aloft
No less adroitly that of fifty strokes
Scarce five go o'er the wall so wide and high
Which sends them back to me: I wish and get.
He struck balls higher and with better skill,
But at a poor fence level with his head.
And hit — his Stratford house, a coat of arms,
Successful dealings in his grain and wool:
While I receive heaven's incense in my nose,
And style myself the cousin of Queen Bess.
Ask him, if this life's all, who wins the game?

Believe — and our whole argument breaks up.
Enthusiasm's the best thing, I repeat;
Only, we can't command it; fire and life
Are all, dead matter's nothing, we agree:
And be it a mad dream or God's very breath,
The fact's the same, — belief's fire, once in us,
Makes of all else mere stuff to show itself:
We penetrate our life with such a glow
As fire lends wood and iron — this turns steel,
That burns to ash — all's one. fire proves its power
For good or ill, since men call flare success.
But paint a fire, it will not therefore burn.
Light one in me, I'll find it food enough!
Why, to be Luther — that's a life to lead,
Incomparably better than my own.
He comes, reclaims God's earth for God, he says.
Sets up God's rule again by simple means,
Re-opens a shut book, and all is done.
He flared out in the flaring of mankind;
Such Luther's luck was: how shall such be mine?
If he succeeded, nothing's left to do:
And if he did not altogether — well,
Strauss is the next advance. All Strauss should be
I might be also. But to what result?
He looks upon no future: Luther did.
What can I gain on the denying side?
Ice makes no conflagration. State the facts,
Read the text right, emancipate the world —
The emancipated world enjoys itself
With scarce a thank-you: Blougram told it first
It could not owe a farthing, — not to him
More than Saint Paul! 'twould press its pay, you think?
Then add there's still that plaguy hundredth chance
Strauss may be wrong. And so a risk is run —
For what gain? not for Luther's, who secured
A real heaven in his heart throughout his life..
Supposing death a little altered things.

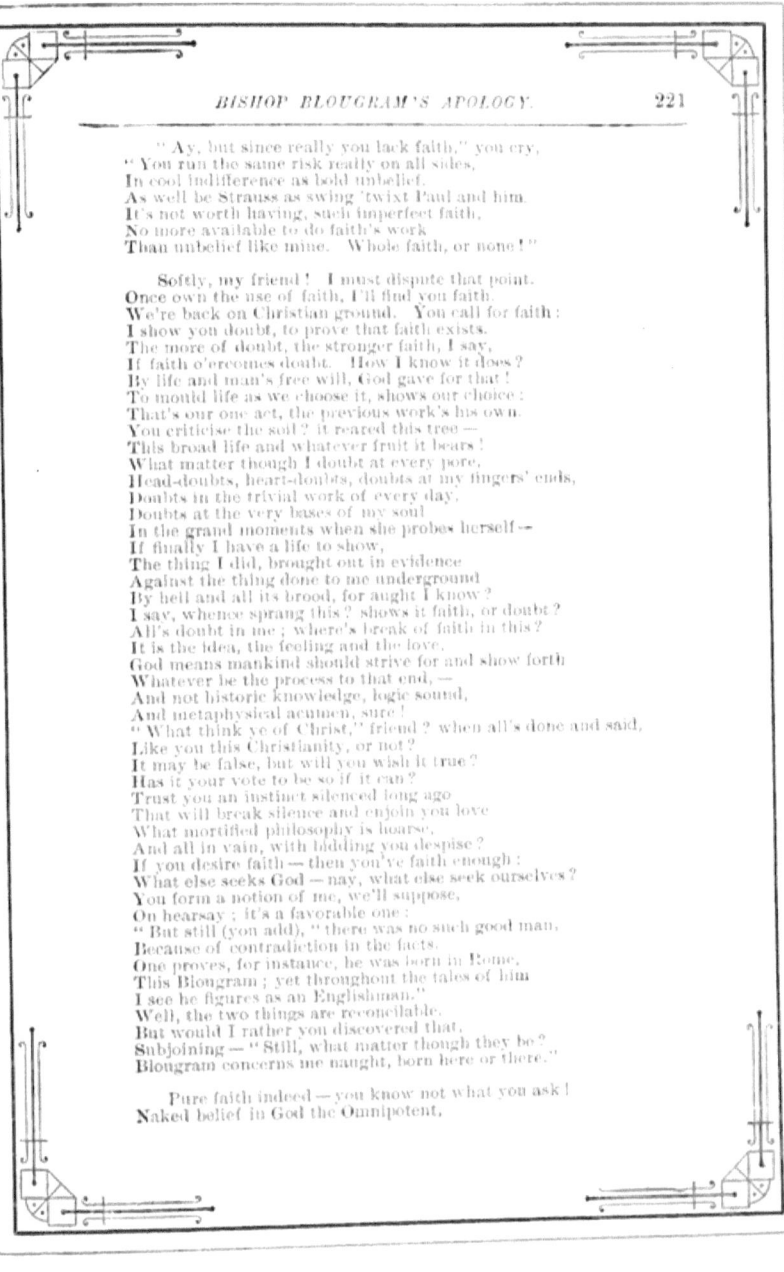

" Ay, but since really you lack faith," you cry,
" You run the same risk really on all sides,
In cool indifference as bold unbelief.
As well be Strauss as swing 'twixt Paul and him.
It's not worth having, such imperfect faith,
No more available to do faith's work
Than unbelief like mine. Whole faith, or none!"

Softly, my friend! I must dispute that point.
Once own the use of faith, I'll find you faith.
We're back on Christian ground. You call for faith:
I show you doubt, to prove that faith exists.
The more of doubt, the stronger faith, I say,
If faith o'ercomes doubt. How I know it does?
By life and man's free will, God gave for that!
To mould life as we choose it, shows our choice:
That's our one act, the previous work's his own.
You criticise the soil? it reared this tree —
This broad life and whatever fruit it bears!
What matter though I doubt at every pore,
Head-doubts, heart-doubts, doubts at my fingers' ends,
Doubts in the trivial work of every day,
Doubts at the very bases of my soul
In the grand moments when she probes herself—
If finally I have a life to show,
The thing I did, brought out in evidence
Against the thing done to me underground
By hell and all its brood, for aught I know?
I say, whence sprang this? shows it faith, or doubt?
All's doubt in me; where's break of faith in this?
It is the idea, the feeling and the love,
God means mankind should strive for and show forth
Whatever be the process to that end, —
And not historic knowledge, logic sound,
And metaphysical acumen, sure!
" What think ye of Christ," friend? when all's done and said,
Like you this Christianity, or not?
It may be false, but will you wish it true?
Has it your vote to be so if it can?
Trust you an instinct silenced long ago
That will break silence and enjoin you love
What mortified philosophy is hoarse,
And all in vain, with bidding you despise?
If you desire faith — then you've faith enough:
What else seeks God — nay, what else seek ourselves?
You form a notion of me, we'll suppose,
On hearsay; it's a favorable one:
" But still (you add), " there was no such good man,
Because of contradiction in the facts.
One proves, for instance, he was born in Rome,
This Blougram; yet throughout the tales of him
I see he figures as an Englishman."
Well, the two things are reconcilable.
But would I rather you discovered that,
Subjoining — " Still, what matter though they be?
Blougram concerns me naught, born here or there."

Pure faith indeed — you know not what you ask!
Naked belief in God the Omnipotent,

Omniscient, Omnipresent, sears too much
The sense of conscious creatures to be borne.
It were the seeing him, no flesh shall dare.
Some think, Creation's meant to show him forth:
I say it's meant to hide him all it can,
And that's what all the blessed evil's for.
Its use in Time is to environ us,
Our breath, our drop of dew, with shield enough
Against that sight till we can bear its stress
Under a vertical sun, the exposed brain
And lidless eye and disemprisoned heart
Less certainly would wither up at once
Than mind, confronted with the truth of him.
But time and earth case-harden us to live.
The feeblest sense is trusted most; the child
Feels God a moment, ichors o'er the place,
Plays on, and grows to be a man like us
With me, faith means perpetual unbelief
Kept quiet like the snake 'neath Michael's foot
Who stands calm just because he feels it writhe.
Or, if that's too ambitious, — here's my box —
I need the excitation of a pinch
Threatening the torpor of the inside-nose
Nigh on the imminent sneeze that never comes.
"Leave it in peace!" advise the simple folk:
Make it aware of peace by itching-fits,
Say I — let doubt occasion still more faith!

You'll say, once all believed, man, woman, child,
In that dear middle-age these noodles praise.
How you'd exult if I could put you back
Six hundred years, blot out cosmogony,
Geology, ethnology, what not
(Greek endings, each the little passing-bell
That signifies some faith's about to die).
And set you square with Genesis again!
When such a traveller told you his last news,
He saw the ark a-top of Ararat
But did not climb there since 'twas getting dusk
And robber-bands infest the mountain's foot!
How should you feel, I ask, in such an age,
How act? As other people felt and did.
With soul more blank than this decanter's knob,
Believe — and yet lie, kill, rob, fornicate
Full in belief's face, like the beast you'd be!

No, when the fight begins within himself,
A man's worth something. God stoops o'er his head,
Satan looks up between his feet — both tug —
He's left, himself, i' the middle: the soul wakes
And grows. Prolong that battle through his life!
Never leave growing till the life to come!
Here we've got callous to the Virgin's winks
That used to puzzle people wholesomely:
Men have outgrown the shame of being fools.
What are the laws of nature, not to bend
If the Church bid them? — brother Newman asks.
Up with the Immaculate Conception, then —
On to the rack with faith! — is my advice.

Will not that hurry us upon our knees,
Knocking our breasts, "It can't be — yet it shall!
Who am I, the worm, to argue with my Pope?
Low things confound the high things!" and so forth.
That's better than acquitting God with grace,
As some folks do. He's tried — no case is proved,
Philosophy is lenient — He may go!

You'll say, the old system's not so obsolete
But men believe still : ay, but who and where?
King Bomba's lazzaroni foster yet
The sacred flame, so Antonelli writes ;
But even of these, what ragamuffin-saint
Believes God watches him continually,
As he believes in fire that it will burn,
Or rain that it will drench him? Break fire's law,
Sin against rain, although the penalty
Be just a singe or soaking? "No," he smiles ;
"Those laws are laws that can enforce themselves."

The sum of all is — yes, my doubt is great,
My faith's still greater, then my faith's enough.
I have read much, thought much, experienced much,
Yet would die rather than avow my fear
The Naples' liquefaction may be false,
When set to happen by the palace-clock
According to the clouds or dinner-time,
I hear you recommend, I might at least
Eliminate, decrassify my faith
Since I adopt it ; keeping what I must
And leaving what I can — such points as this.
I won't — that is, I can't throw one away.
Supposing there's no truth in what I hold
About the need of trial to man's faith,
Still, when you bid me purify the same,
To such a process I discern no end.
Clearing off one excrescence to see two,
There's ever a next in size, now grown as big,
That meets the knife : I cut and cut again!
First cut the Liquefaction, what comes last
But Fichte's clever cut at God himself?
Experimentalize on sacred things!
I trust nor hand nor eye nor heart nor brain
To stop betimes : they all get drunk alike.
The first step, I am master not to take.

You'd find the cutting-process to your taste
As much as leaving growths of lies unpruned,
Nor see more danger in it, — you retort.
Your taste's worth mine ; but my taste proves more **wise**
When we consider that the steadfast hold
On the extreme end of the chain of faith
Gives all the advantage, makes the difference
With the rough purblind mass we seek to rule :
We are their lords, or they are free of us,
Just as we tighten or relax our hold.
So, other matters equal, we'll revert
To the first problem — which, if solved my way
And thrown into the balance, turns the scale —

How we may lead a comfortable life,
How suit our luggage to the cabin's size.

Of course you are remarking all this time
How narrowly and grossly I view life,
Respect the creature-comforts, care to rule
The masses, and regard complacently
" The cabin," in our old phrase. Well, I do.
I act for, talk for, live for this world now,
As this world prizes action, life, and talk :
No prejudice to what next world may prove,
Whose new laws and requirements, my best pledge
To observe then, is that I observe these now,
Shall do hereafter what I do meanwhile.
Let us concede (gratuitously though)
Next life relieves the soul of body, yields
Pure spiritual enjoyment : well, my friend,
Why lose this life i' the mean time, since its use
May be to make the next life more intense ?

Do you know, I have often had a dream
(Work it up in your next month's article)
Of man's poor spirit in its progress, still
Losing true life forever and a day
Through ever trying to be and ever being —
In the evolution of successive spheres —
Before its actual sphere and place of life,
Half way into the next, which having reached,
It shoots with corresponding foolery
Half way into the next still, on and off !
As when a traveller, bound from North to South,
Scouts fur in Russia ; what's its use in France ?
In France spurns flannel ; where's its need in Spain ?
In Spain drops cloth, too cumbrous for Algiers !
Linen goes next, and last the skin itself,
A superfluity at Timbuctoo.
When, through his journey, was the fool at ease ?
I'm at ease now, friend ; worldly in this world,
I take and like its way of life ; I think
My brothers, who administer the means,
Live better for my comfort — that's good too ;
And God, if he pronounce upon such life,
Approves my service, which is better still.
If he keep silence, — why, for you or me
Or that brute-beast pulled-up in to-day's " Times,"
What odds is't, save to ourselves, what life we lead ?

You meet me at this issue ; you declare, —
All special-pleading done with, truth is truth,
And justifies itself by undreamed ways.
You don't fear but it's better, if we doubt,
To say so, act up to our truth perceived
However feebly. Do then, — act away !
'Tis there I'm on the watch for you. How one acts
Is, both of us agree, our chief concern :
And how you'll act is what I fain would see
If, like the candid person you appear,
You dare to make the most of your life's scheme
As I of mine, live up to its full law

Since there's no higher law that counterchecks,
Put natural religion to the test
You've just demolished the revealed with — quick,
Down to the root of all that checks your will,
All prohibition to lie, kill, and thieve,
Or even to be an atheistic priest !
Suppose a pricking to incontinence —
Philosophers deduce you chastity
Or shame, from just the fact that at the first
Whoso embraced a woman in the field,
Threw club down and forewent his brains beside,
So, stood a ready victim in the reach
Of any brother-savage, club in hand ;
Hence saw the use of going out of sight
In wood or cave to prosecute his loves :
I read this in a French book t'other day.
Does law so analyzed coerce you much ?
Oh, men spin clouds of fuzz where matters end,
But you who reach where the first thread begins,
You'll soon cut that ! — which means you can, but won't
Through certain instincts, blind, unreasoned-out,
You dare not set aside, you can't tell why,
But there they are, and so you let them rule.
Then, friend, you seem as much a slave as I,
A liar, conscious coward and hypocrite,
Without the good the slave expects to get,
In case he has a master after all !
You own your instincts ? why, what else do I,
Who want, am made for, and must have a God
Ere I can be aught, do aught ? — no mere name
Want, but the true thing with what proves its truth,
To wit, a relation from that thing to me,
Touching from head to foot — which touch I feel,
And with it take the rest, this life of ours !
I live my life here : yours you dare not live.

— Not as I state it, who (you please subjoin)
Disfigure such a life and call it names,
While, to your mind, remains another way
For simple men ; knowledge and power have rights,
But ignorance and weakness have rights too.
There needs no crucial effort to find truth
If here or there or anywhere about :
We ought to turn each side, try hard and see,
And if we can't, be glad we've earned at least
The right, by one laborious proof the more,
To graze in peace earth's pleasant pasturage.
Men are not angels, neither are they brutes :
Something we may see, all we cannot see.
What need of lying ? I say, I see all.
And swear to each detail the most minute
In what I think a Pan's face — you, mere cloud :
I swear I hear him speak and see him wink,
For fear, if once I drop the emphasis,
Mankind may doubt there's any cloud at all.
You take the simple life — ready to see,
Willing to see (for no cloud's worth a face)—
And leaving quiet what no strength can move,
And which, who bids you move ? who has the right ?

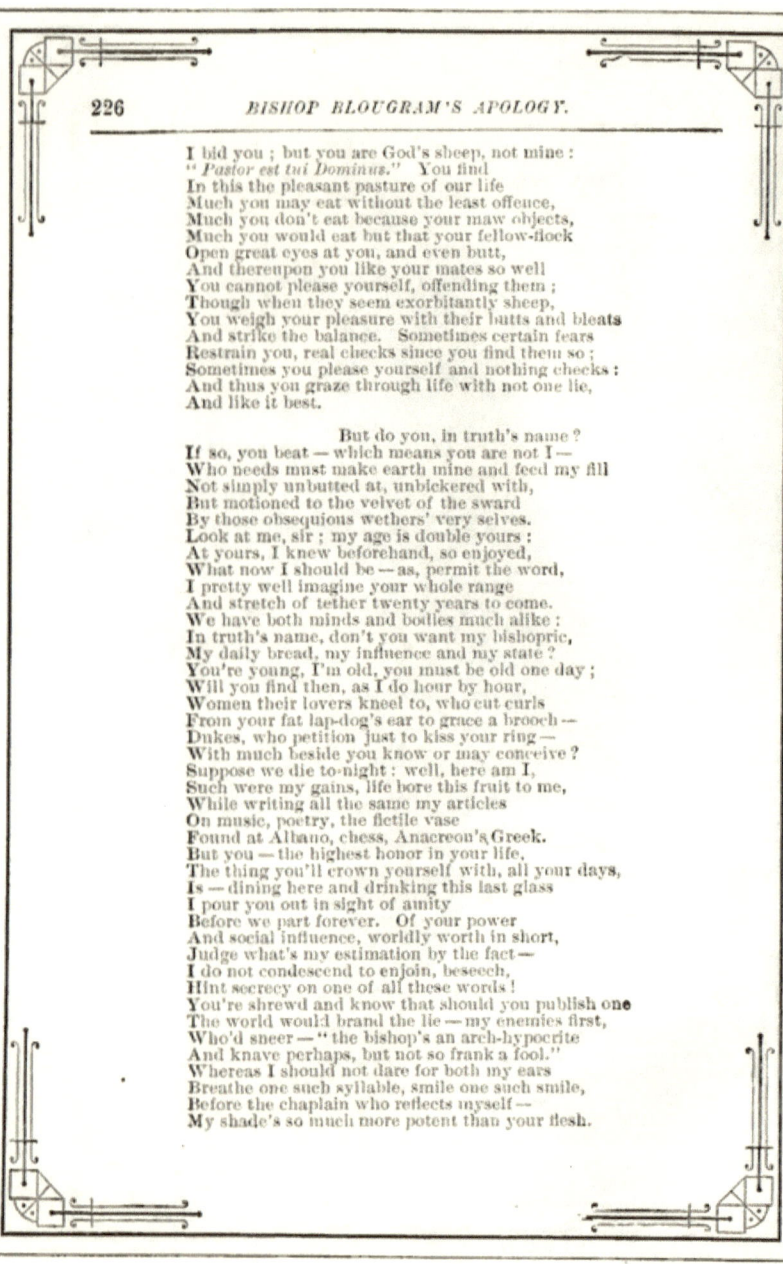

I bid you ; but you are God's sheep, not mine :
"*Pastor est tui Dominus.*" You find
In this the pleasant pasture of our life
Much you may eat without the least offence,
Much you don't eat because your maw objects,
Much you would eat but that your fellow-flock
Open great eyes at you, and even butt,
And thereupon you like your mates so well
You cannot please yourself, offending them ;
Though when they seem exorbitantly sheep,
You weigh your pleasure with their butts and bleats
And strike the balance. Sometimes certain fears
Restrain you, real checks since you find them so ;
Sometimes you please yourself and nothing checks :
And thus you graze through life with not one lie,
And like it best.

            But do you, in truth's name ?
If so, you beat — which means you are not I —
Who needs must make earth mine and feed my fill
Not simply unbutted at, unbickered with,
But motioned to the velvet of the sward
By those obsequious wethers' very selves.
Look at me, sir ; my age is double yours :
At yours, I knew beforehand, so enjoyed,
What now I should be — as, permit the word,
I pretty well imagine your whole range
And stretch of tether twenty years to come.
We have both minds and bodies much alike :
In truth's name, don't you want my bishopric,
My daily bread, my influence and my state ?
You're young, I'm old, you must be old one day ;
Will you find then, as I do hour by hour,
Women their lovers kneel to, who cut curls
From your fat lap-dog's ear to grace a brooch —
Dukes, who petition just to kiss your ring —
With much beside you know or may conceive ?
Suppose we die to-night : well, here am I,
Such were my gains, life bore this fruit to me,
While writing all the same my articles
On music, poetry, the fictile vase
Found at Albano, chess, Anacreon's Greek.
But you — the highest honor in your life,
The thing you'll crown yourself with, all your days,
Is — dining here and drinking this last glass
I pour you out in sight of amity
Before we part forever. Of your power
And social influence, worldly worth in short,
Judge what's my estimation by the fact —
I do not condescend to enjoin, beseech,
Hint secrecy on one of all these words !
You're shrewd and know that should you publish one
The world would brand the lie — my enemies first,
Who'd sneer — " the bishop's an arch-hypocrite
And knave perhaps, but not so frank a fool."
Whereas I should not dare for both my ears
Breathe one such syllable, smile one such smile,
Before the chaplain who reflects myself —
My shade's so much more potent than your flesh.

What's your reward, self-abnegating friend?
Stood you confessed of those exceptional
And privileged great natures that dwarf mine —
A zealot with a mad ideal in reach,
A poet just about to print his ode,
A statesman with a scheme to stop this war,
An artist whose religion is his art —
I should have nothing to object : such men
Carry the fire, all things grow warm to them,
Their drugget's worth my purple, they beat me.
But you — you're just as little those as I —
You, Gigadibs, who, thirty years of age,
Write statedly for Blackwood's Magazine,
Believe you see two points in Hamlet's soul
Unseized by the Germans yet — which view you'll print —
Meantime the best you have to show being still
That lively lightsome article we took
Almost for the true Dickens, — what's its name?
" The Slum and Cellar, or Whitechapel life
Limned after dark ! " it made me laugh, I know,
And pleased a month, and brought you in ten pounds.
— Success I recognize and compliment,
And therefore give you, if you choose, three words
(The card and pencil-scratch is quite enough)
Which whether here, in Dublin or New York,
Will get you, prompt as at my eyebrow's wink,
Such terms as never you aspired to get
In all our own reviews and some not ours.
Go write your lively sketches ! be the first
" Blougram, or the Eccentric Confidence " —
Or better simply say, " The Outward-bound."
Why, men as soon would throw it in my teeth
As copy and quote the infamy chalked broad
About me on the church-door opposite.
You will not wait for that experience though,
I fancy, howsoever you decide,
To discontinue — not detesting, not
Defaming, but at least — despising me !

Over his wine so smiled and talked his hour
Sylvester Blougram, styled *in partibus*
Episcopus, nec non — (the deuce knows what
It's changed to by our novel hierarchy)
With Gigadibs the literary man,
Who played with spoons, explored his plate's design,
And ranged the olive-stones about its edge,
While the great bishop rolled him out a mind
Long rumpled, till creased consciousness lay smooth.

For Blougram, he believed, say, half he spoke.
The other portion, as he shaped it thus
For argumentatory purposes,
He felt his foe was foolish to dispute.
Some arbitrary accidental thoughts
That crossed his mind, amusing because new,
He chose to represent as fixtures there,
Invariable convictions (such they seemed

Beside his interlocutor's loose cards
Flung daily down, and not the same way twice)
While certain hell-deep instincts, man's weak tongue
Is never bold to utter in their truth
Because styled hell-deep ('tis an old mistake
To place hell at the bottom of the earth)
He ignored these, — not having in readiness
Their nomenclature and philosophy :
He said true things, but called them by wrong names.
"On the whole," he thought, "I justify myself
On every point where cavillers like this
Oppugn my life : he tries one kind of fence,
I close, he's worsted, that's enough for him.
He's on the ground : if ground should break away
I take my stand on, there's a firmer yet
Beneath it, both of us may sink and reach.
His ground was over mine and broke the first :
So, let him sit with me this many a year !"

He did not sit five minutes. Just a week
Sufficed his sudden healthy vehemence.
Something had struck him in the "Ontward-bound"
Another way than Blougram's purpose was :
And having bought, not cabin-furniture
But settler's implements (enough for three)
And started for Australia — there, I hope,
By this time he has tested his first plough,
And studied his last chapter of Saint John.

MR. SLUDGE, "THE MEDIUM."

Now, don't, sir ! Don't expose me ! Just this once !
This was the first and only time, I'll swear, —
Look at me, — see, I kneel, — the only time,
I swear, I ever cheated, — yes, by the soul
Of Her who hears — (your sainted mother, sir !)
All, except this last accident, was truth —
This little kind of slip ! — and even this,
It was your own wine, sir, the good champagne
(I took it for Catawba, you're so kind),
Which put the folly in my head !

                              "Get up ?"
You still inflict on me that terrible face ?
You show no mercy ? — Not for Her dear sake,
The sainted spirit's, whose soft breath even now
Blows on my cheek — (don't you feel something, sir ?)
You'll tell ?

              Go tell, then ! Who the Devil cares
What such a rowdy chooses to . . .
                        Aie — aie — aie !
Please, sir ! your thumbs are through my windpipe, sir !
Ch — ch !

Mr. Sludge, "The Medium." — Page 228.

Well, sir, I hope you've done it now!
O Lord! I little thought, sir, yesterday,
When your departed mother spoke those words
Of peace through me, and moved you, sir, so much,
You gave me — (very kind it was of you)
These shirt-studs — (better take them back again,
Please, sir) — yes, little did I think so soon
A trifle of trick, all through a glass too much
Of his own champagne, would change my best of friends
Into an angry gentleman!

                    Though, 'twas wrong.
I don't contest the point; your anger's just:
Whatever put such folly in my head,
I know 'twas wicked of me. There's a thick
Dusk undeveloped spirit (I've observed)
Owes me a grudge — a negro's, I should say,
Or else an Irish emigrant's; yourself
Explained the case so well last Sunday, sir,
When we had summoned Franklin to clear up
A point about those shares i' the telegraph:
Ay, and he swore . . . or might it be Tom Paine? . . .
Thumping the table close by where I crouched,
He'd do me soon a mischief: that's come true!
Why, now your face clears! I was sure it would!
Then, this one time . . . don't take your hand away,
Through yours I surely kiss your mother's hand . . .
You'll promise to forgive me? — or, at least,
Tell nobody of this? Consider, sir!
What harm can mercy do? Would but the shade
Of the venerable dead-one just vouchsafe
A rap or tip! What bit of paper's here?
Suppose we take a pencil, let her write,
Make the least sign, she urges on her child
Forgiveness? There now! Eh? Oh! 'Twas your foot,
And not a natural creak, sir?

                    Answer, then!
Once, twice, thrice . . . see, I'm waiting to say "thrice!"
All to no use? No sort of hope for me?
It's all to post to Greeley's newspaper?

What? If I told you all about the tricks?
Upon my soul! — the whole truth, and naught else,
And how there's been some falsehood — for your part,
Will you engage to pay my passage out,
And hold your tongue until I'm safe on board?
England's the place, not Boston — no offence!
I see what makes you hesitate: don't fear!
I mean to change my trade and cheat no more,
Yes, this time really it's upon my soul!
Be my salvation! — under heaven, of course.
I'll tell some queer things. Sixty Vs must do.
A trifle, though, to start with! We'll refer
The question to this table?

                    How you're changed!
Then split the difference; thirty more, we'll say.
Ay, but you leave my presents! Else I'll swear

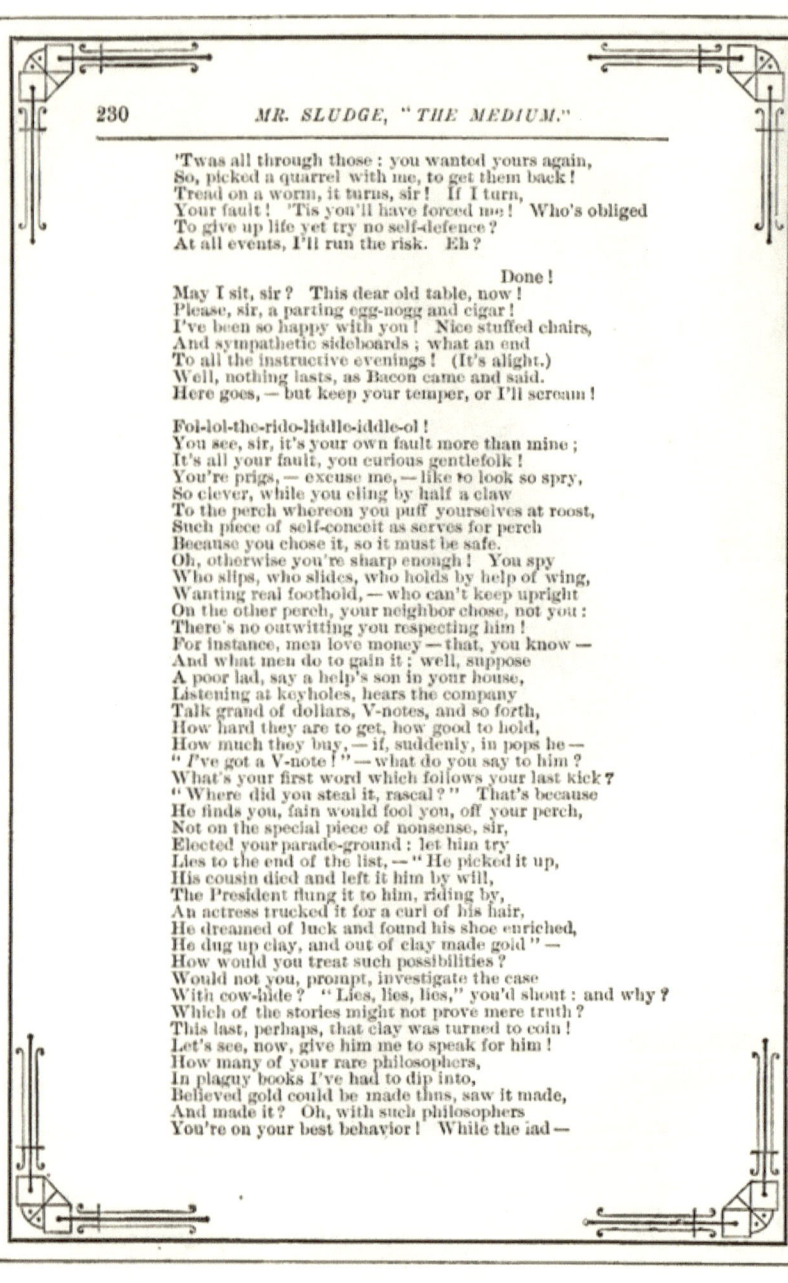

'Twas all through those : you wanted yours again,
So, picked a quarrel with me, to get them back!
Tread on a worm, it turns, sir! If I turn,
Your fault! 'Tis you'll have forced me! Who's obliged
To give up life yet try no self-defence?
At all events, I'll run the risk. Eh?

                          Done!

May I sit, sir? This dear old table, now!
Please, sir, a parting egg-nogg and cigar!
I've been so happy with you! Nice stuffed chairs,
And sympathetic sideboards ; what an end
To all the instructive evenings! (It's alight.)
Well, nothing lasts, as Bacon came and said.
Here goes, — but keep your temper, or I'll scream!

Fol-lol-the-rido-liddle-iddle-ol!
You see, sir, it's your own fault more than mine ;
It's all your fault, you curious gentlefolk!
You're prigs, — excuse me, — like to look so spry,
So clever, while you cling by half a claw
To the perch whereon you puff yourselves at roost,
Such piece of self-conceit as serves for perch
Because you chose it, so it must be safe.
Oh, otherwise you're sharp enough! You spy
Who slips, who slides, who holds by help of wing,
Wanting real foothold, — who can't keep upright
On the other perch, your neighbor chose, not you :
There's no outwitting you respecting him!
For instance, men love money — that, you know —
And what men do to gain it : well, suppose
A poor lad, say a help's son in your house,
Listening at keyholes, hears the company
Talk grand of dollars, V-notes, and so forth,
How hard they are to get, how good to hold,
How much they buy, — if, suddenly, in pops he —
" I've got a V-note!"— what do you say to him?
What's your first word which follows your last kick?
" Where did you steal it, rascal?" That's because
He finds you, fain would fool you, off your perch,
Not on the special piece of nonsense, sir,
Elected your parade-ground : let him try
Lies to the end of the list, — " He picked it up,
His cousin died and left it him by will,
The President flung it to him, riding by,
An actress trucked it for a curl of his hair,
He dreamed of luck and found his shoe enriched,
He dug up clay, and out of clay made gold" —
How would you treat such possibilities?
Would not you, prompt, investigate the case
With cow-hide? " Lies, lies, lies," you'd shout : and why?
Which of the stories might not prove mere truth?
This last, perhaps, that clay was turned to coin!
Let's see, now, give him me to speak for him!
How many of your rare philosophers,
In plaguy books I've had to dip into,
Believed gold could be made thus, saw it made,
And made it? Oh, with such philosophers
You're on your best behavior! While the lad —

With him, in a trice, you settle likelihoods,
Nor doubt a moment how he got his prize :
In his case, you hear, judge, and execute,
All in a breath : so would most men of sense.

But let the same lad hear you talk as grand
At the same keyhole, you and company,
Of signs and wonders, the invisible world ;
How wisdom scouts our vulgar unbelief
More than our vulgarest credulity ;
How good men have desired to see a ghost,
What Johnson used to say, what Wesley did,
Mother Goose thought, and fiddle-diddle-dee : —
If he then break in with, "Sir, *I* saw a ghost !"
Ah, the ways change ! He finds you perched and prim ;
It's a conceit of yours that ghosts may be :
There's no talk now of cow-hide. "Tell it out !
Don't fear us ! Take your time and recollect !
Sit down first ; try a glass of wine, my boy !
And, David, (is not that your Christian name ?)
Of all things, should this happen twice, — it may, —
Be sure, while fresh in mind, you let us know !"
Does the boy blunder, blurt out this, blab that,
Break down in the other, as beginners will ?
All's candor, all's considerateness, — "No haste !
Pause and collect yourself ! We understand !
That's the bad memory, or the natural shock,
Or the unexplained *phenomena !*"

                              Egad,
The boy takes heart of grace ; finds, never fear,
The readiest way to ope your own heart wide,
Show — what I call your peacock-perch, pet post
To strut, and spread the tail, and squawk upon !
"Just as you thought, much as you might expect !
There be more things in heaven and earth, Horatio," . . .
And so on. Shall not David take the hint,
Grow bolder, stroke you down at quickened rate ?
If he ruffle a feather, it's "Gently, patiently !
Manifestations are so weak at first !
Doubting, moreover, kills them, cuts all short,
Cures with a vengeance !"

                      There, sir, that's your style !
You and your boy — such pains bestowed on him,
Or any headpiece of the average worth,
To teach, say, Greek, would perfect him apace,
Make him a Person ("Parson ?" thank you, sir !)
Much more, proficient in the art of lies
You never leave the lesson ! Fire alight,
Catch you permitting it to die ! You've friends ;
There's no withholding knowledge, — least from those
Apt to look elsewhere for their soul's supply :
Why should not you parade your lawful prize ?
Who finds a picture, digs a medal up,
Hits on a first edition, — he henceforth
Gives it his name, grows notable : how much more
Who ferrets out a "medium" ? "David's yours,
You highly favored man ? Then, pity souls

Less privileged! Allow us share your luck!"
So, David holds the circle, rules the roast,
Narrates the vision, peeps in the glass ball,
Sets-to the spirit-writing, hears the raps,
As the case may be.

         Now mark! To be precise,—
Though I say, "lies" all these, at this first stage,
'Tis just for science' sake: I call such grubs
By the name of what they'll turn to, dragonflies.
Strictly, it's what good people style untruth;
But yet, so far, not quite the full-grown thing:
It's fancying, fable-making, nonsense-work,—
What never meant to be so very bad,—
The knack of story-telling, brightening up
Each dull old bit of fact that drops its shine.
One does see somewhat when one shuts one's eyes,
If only spots and streaks; tables do tip
In the oddest way of themselves: and pens, good Lord,
Who knows if you drive them or they drive you?
'Tis but a foot in the water and out again;
Not that duck-under which decides your dive.
Note this, for it's important: listen why.

I'll prove, you push on David till he dives
And ends the shivering. Here's your circle, now:
Two-thirds of them, with heads like you their host,
Turn up their eyes, and cry, as you expect,
"Lord, who'd have thought it!" But there's always one
Looks wise, compassionately smiles, submits
"Of your veracity no kind of doubt,
But—do you feel so certain of that boy's?
Really, I wonder! I confess myself
More chary of my faith!" That's galling, sir!
What! he the investigator, he the sage,
When all's done? Then, you just have shut your eyes,
Opened your mouth, and gulped down David whole,
You! Terrible were such catastrophe!
So, evidence is redoubled, doubled again,
And doubled besides; once more, "He heard, we heard,
You and they heard, your mother and your wife,
Your children and the stranger in your gates:
Did they, or did they not?" So much for him,
The black sheep, guest without the wedding-garb,
And doubting Thomas! Now's your turn to crow:
"He's kind to think you such a fool: Sludge cheats?
Leave you alone to take precautions!"
         Straight
The rest join chorus. Thomas stands abashed,
Sips silent some such beverage as this,
Considers if it be harder, shutting eyes
And gulping David in good fellowship,
Than going elsewhere, getting, in exchange,
With no egg-nogg to lubricate the food,
Some just as tough a morsel. Over the way,
Holds Captain Sparks his court: is it better there?
Have not you hunting-stories, scalping-scenes,
And Mexican War exploits to swallow plump
If you'd be free o' the stove-side, rocking-chair,
And trio of affable daughters?

Doubt succumbs!
Victory !   All your circle's yours again !
Out of the clubbing of submissive wits,
David's performance rounds, each chink gets patched,
Every protrusion of a point's filed fine,
All's fit to set a-rolling round the world,
And then return to David finally,
Lies seven-feet thick about his first half-inch.
Here's a choice birth o' the supernatural,
Poor David's pledged to !   You've employed no too!
That laws exclaim at, save the Devil's own,
Yet screwed him into henceforth gulling you
To the top o' your bent, — all out of one half-lie !

You hold, if there's one half or a hundredth part
Of a lie, that's his fault, — his be the penalty !
I dare say !   You'd prove firmer in his place ?
You'd find the courage, — that first flurry over,
That mild bit of romancing-work at end, —
To interpose with " It gets serious, this ;
Must stop here.   Sir, I saw no ghost at all.
Inform your friends I made . . . well, fools of them,
And found you ready made.   I've lived in clover
These three weeks : take it out in kicks of me ! "
I doubt it.   Ask your conscience !   Let me know,
Twelve months hence, with how few embellishments
You've told almighty Boston of this passage
Of arms between us, your first taste o' the foil
From Sludge who could not fence, sir !   Sludge, your boy !
I lied, sir, — there !   I got up from my gorge
On offal in the gutter, and preferred
Your canvas-backs : I took their carver's size,
Measured his modicum of intelligence,
Tickled him on the cockles of his heart
With a raven feather, and next week found myself
Sweet and clean, dining daintily, dizened smart,
Set on a stool buttressed by ladies' knees,
Every soft smiler calling me her pet,
Encouraging my story to uncoil
And creep out from its hole, inch after inch,
" How last night, I no sooner snug in bed,
Tucked up, just as they left me, — than came raps !
While a light whisked " . . . " Shaped somewhat like a star ? " —
" Well, like some sort of stars, ma'am," — " So we thought !
And any voice ?   Not yet ?   Try hard next time,
If you can't hear a voice ; we think you may :
At least, the Pennsylvanian ' mediums ' did."
Oh, next time comes the voice !   " Just as we hoped ! "
Are not the hopers proud now, pleased, profuse
O' the natural acknowledgment ?

Of course !
So, off we push, illy-oh-yo, trim the boat,
On we sweep with a cataract ahead,
We're midway to the Horse-shoe : stop, who can,
The dance of bubbles gay about our prow !
Experiences become worth waiting for,
Spirits now speak up, tell their inmost mind,
And compliment the " medium " properly,

Concern themselves about his Sunday coat,
See rings on his hand with pleasure. Ask yourself
How you'd receive a course of treats like these !
Why, take the quietest hack and stall him up,
Cram him with corn a month, then out with him
Among his mates on a bright April morn,
With the turf to tread ; see if you find or no
A caper in him, if he bucks or bolts !
Much more a youth whose fancies sprout as rank
As toadstool-clump from melon-bed. 'Tis soon,
" Sirrah, you spirit, come, go, fetch and carry,
Read, write, rap, rub-a-dub, and hang yourself ! "
I'm spared all further trouble ; all's arranged ;
Your circle does my business ; I may rave
Like an epileptic dervish in the books,
Foam, fling myself flat, rend my clothes to shreds ;
No matter : lovers, friends, and countrymen
Will lay down spiritual laws, read wrong things right
By the rule o' reverse. If Francis Verulam
Styles himself Bacon, spells the name beside
With a *y* and a *k*, says he drew breath in York,
Gave up the ghost in Wales when Cromwell reigned
(As, sir, we somewhat fear he was apt to say,
Before I found the useful book that knows),
Why, what harm's done ? The circle smiles apace,
" It was not Bacon, after all, do you see !
We understand ; the trick's but natural ;
Such spirits' individuality
Is hard to put in evidence : they incline
To gibe and jeer, these undeveloped sorts.
You see, their world's much like a jail broke loose,
While this of ours remains shut, bolted, barred,
With a single window to it. Sludge, our friend,
Serves as this window, whether thin or thick,
Or stained or stainless ; he's the medium-pane
Through which, to see us and be seen, they peep :
They crowd each other, hustle for a chance,
Tread on their neighbor's kibes, play tricks enough !
Does Bacon, tired of waiting, swerve aside ?
Up in his place jumps Barnum — ' I'm your man,
I'll answer you for Bacon ! ' Try once more ! "

Or else it's — " What's a ' medium ? ' He's a means,
Good, bad, indifferent, still the only means
Spirits can speak by ; he may misconceive,
Stutter, and stammer, — he's their Sludge and drudge.
Take him or leave him ; they must hold their peace,
Or else, put up with having knowledge strained
To half-expression through his ignorance.
Suppose, the spirit Beethoven wants to shed
New music he's brimful of ; why, he turns
The handle of this organ, grinds with Sludge,
And what he poured in at the mouth o' the mill
As a Thirty-third Sonata, (fancy now !)
Comes from the hopper as brand-new Sludge, naught else,
The Shakers' Hymn in G, with a natural F,
Or the ' Stars and Stripes ' set to consecutive fourths."

Sir, where's the scrape you did not help me through,

You that are wise? And for the fools, the folk
Who came to see, — the guests, (observe that word!)
Pray do you find guests criticise your wine,
Your furniture, your grammar, or your nose?
Then, why your " medium "? What's the difference?
Prove your Madeira red-ink and gamboge, —
Your Sludge, a cheat — then somebody's a goose
For vaunting both as genuine. "Guests!" Don't fear!
They'll make a wry face, not too much of that,
And leave you in your glory.

                " No, sometimes
They doubt and say as much!" Ay, doubt they do!
And what's the consequence? "Of course they doubt" —
(You triumph) " that explains the hitch at once!
Doubt posed our ' medium,' puddled his pure mind;
He gave them back their rubbish; pitch chaff in,
Could flour come out o' the honest mill?" So, prompt
Applaud the faithful: cases flock in point,
" How, when a mocker willed a ' medium ' once
Should name a spirit James whose name was George,
' James ' cried the ' medium,' — 'twas the test of truth!"
In short, a hit proves much, a miss proves more.
Does this convince? The better: does it fail?
Time for the double-shotted broadside, then —
The grand means, last resource. Look black and big!
" You style us idiots, therefore — why stop short?
Accomplices in rascality: this we hear
In our own house, from our invited guest
Found brave enough to outrage a poor boy
Exposed by our good faith! Have you been heard?
Now, then, hear us; one man's not quite worth twelve.
You see a cheat? Here's some twelve see an ass;
Excuse me if I calculate: good day!"
Out slinks the sceptic, all the laughs explode,
Sludge waves his hat in triumph!

                Or — he don't.
There's something in real truth (explain who can!)
One casts a wistful eye at, like the horse
Who mopes beneath stuffed hay-racks and won't munch
Because he spies a corn-bag: hang that truth,
It spoils all dainties proffered in its place!
I've felt at times when, cockered, cossetted,
And coddled by the aforesaid company,
Bidden enjoy their bullying — never fear,
But o'er their shoulders spit at the flying man, —
I've felt a child; only, a fractious child
That, dandled soft by nurse, aunt, grandmother,
Who keep him from the kennel, sun, and wind,
Good fun and wholesome mud, — enjoined be sweet,
And comely and superior, — eyes askance
The ragged sons o' the gutter at their game,
Fain would be down with them i' the thick o' the filth,
Making dirt-pies, laughing free, speaking plain,
And calling granny the gray old cat she is.
I've felt a spite, I say, at you, at them,
Huggings and humbug — gnashed my teeth to mark
A decent dog pass! It's too bad, I say,
Ruining a soul so!

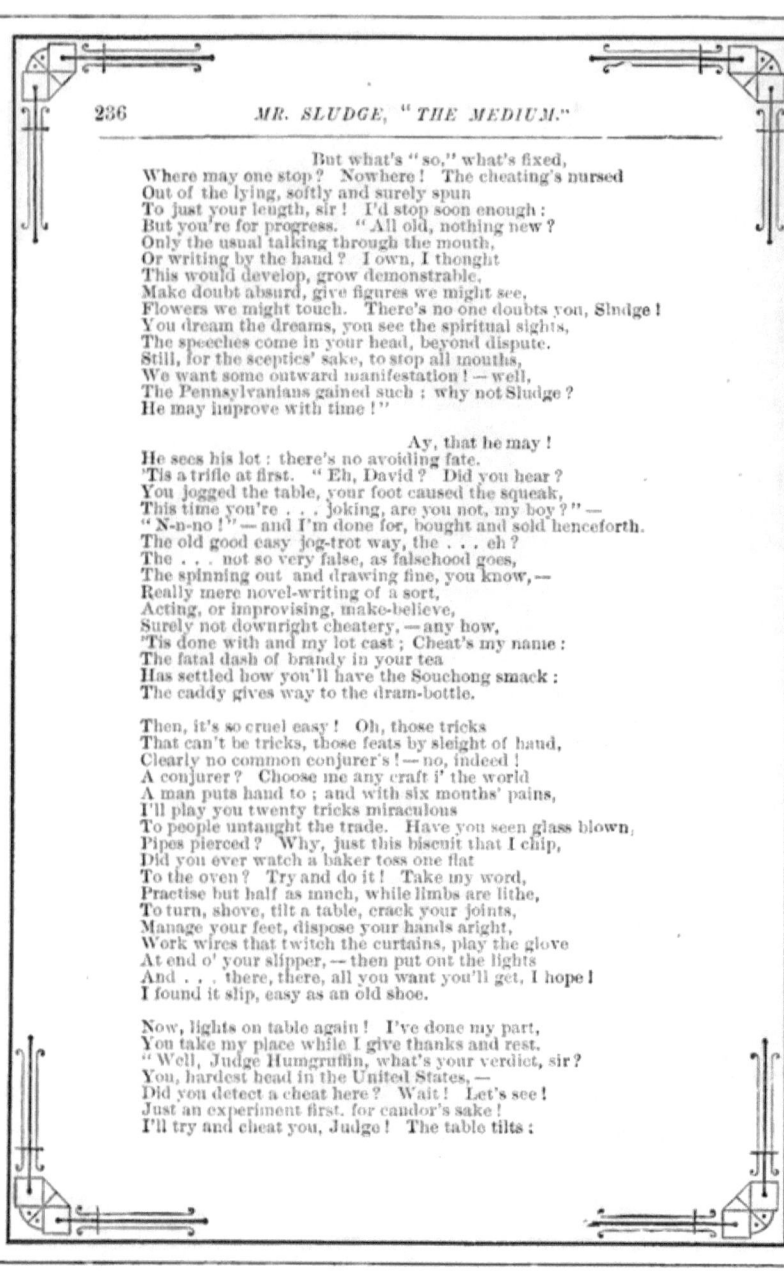

But what's "so," what's fixed,
Where may one stop? Nowhere! The cheating's nursed
Out of the lying, softly and surely spun
To just your length, sir! I'd stop soon enough:
But you're for progress. "All old, nothing new?
Only the usual talking through the mouth,
Or writing by the hand? I own, I thought
This would develop, grow demonstrable,
Make doubt absurd, give figures we might see,
Flowers we might touch. There's no one doubts you, Sludge!
You dream the dreams, you see the spiritual sights,
The speeches come in your head, beyond dispute.
Still, for the sceptics' sake, to stop all mouths,
We want some outward manifestation! — well,
The Pennsylvanians gained such; why not Sludge?
He may improve with time!"

                      Ay, that he may!
He sees his lot: there's no avoiding fate.
'Tis a trifle at first. "Eh, David? Did you hear?
You jogged the table, your foot caused the squeak,
This time you're . . . joking, are you not, my boy?" —
"N-n-no!" — and I'm done for, bought and sold henceforth.
The old good easy jog-trot way, the . . . eh?
The . . . not so very false, as falsehood goes,
The spinning out and drawing fine, you know, —
Really mere novel-writing of a sort,
Acting, or improvising, make-believe,
Surely not downright cheatery, — any how,
'Tis done with and my lot cast; Cheat's my name:
The fatal dash of brandy in your tea
Has settled how you'll have the Souchong smack:
The caddy gives way to the dram-bottle.

Then, it's so cruel easy! Oh, those tricks
That can't be tricks, those feats by sleight of hand,
Clearly no common conjurer's! — no, indeed!
A conjurer? Choose me any craft i' the world
A man puts hand to; and with six months' pains,
I'll play you twenty tricks miraculous
To people untaught the trade. Have you seen glass blown,
Pipes pierced? Why, just this biscuit that I chip,
Did you ever watch a baker toss one flat
To the oven? Try and do it! Take my word,
Practise but half as much, while limbs are lithe,
To turn, shove, tilt a table, crack your joints,
Manage your feet, dispose your hands aright,
Work wires that twitch the curtains, play the glove
At end o' your slipper, — then put out the lights
And . . . there, there, all you want you'll get, I hope!
I found it slip, easy as an old shoe.

Now, lights on table again! I've done my part,
You take my place while I give thanks and rest.
"Well, Judge Humgruffin, what's your verdict, sir?
You, hardest head in the United States, —
Did you detect a cheat here? Wait! Let's see!
Just an experiment first, for candor's sake!
I'll try and cheat you, Judge! The table tilts:

Is it I that move it? Write! I'll press your hand:
Cry when I push, or guide your pencil, Judge!"
Sludge still triumphant! "That a rap, indeed?
That the real writing? Very like a whale!
Then, if, sir, you — a most distinguished man,
And, were the Judge not here, I'd say, ... no matter!
Well, sir, if you fail, you can't take us in, —
There's little fear that Sludge will!"

                              Won't he, ma'am?

But what if our distinguished host, like Sludge,
Bade God bear witness that he played no trick,
While you believed that what produced the raps
Was just a certain child who died, you know,
And whose last breath you thought your lips had felt?
Eh? That's a capital point, ma'am: Sludge begins
At your entreaty with your dearest dead,
The little voice set lisping once again,
The tiny hand made feel for yours once more,
The poor lost image brought back, plain as dreams.
Which image, if a word had chanced recall,
The customary cloud would cross your eyes,
Your heart return the old tick, pay its pang!
A right mood for investigation, this!
One's at one's ease with Saul and Jonathan,
Pompey and Cæsar: but one's own lost child . .
I wonder, when you heard the first clod drop
From the spadeful at the grave, did you feel free
To investigate who twitched your funeral scarf,
Or brushed your flounces? Then, it came of course
You should be stunned and stupid; then (how else?)
Your breath stopped with your blood, your brain struck work
But now, such causes fail of such effects,
All's changed, — the little voice begins afresh,
Yet you, calm, consequent, can test and try
And touch the truth. "Tests? Didn't the creature tell
Its nurse's name, and say it lived six years,
And rode a rocking-horse? Enough of tests!
Sludge never could learn that!"

                              He could not, eh?

You compliment him "Could not?" Speak for yourself!
I'd like to know the man I ever saw
Once, — never mind where, how, why, when, — once saw,
Of whom I do not keep some matter treasured
He'd swear I "could not" know, sagacious soul!
What? Do you live in this world's blow of blacks,
Palaver, gossipry, a single hour
Nor find one smut has settled on your nose,
Of a smut's worth, no more, no less? — one fact
Out of the drift of facts, whereby you learn
What some one was, somewhere, somewhen, somewhy?
You don't tell folk — "See what has stuck to me!
Judge Humgraffin, our most distinguished man,
Your uncle was a tailor, and your wife
Thought to have married Miggs, missed him, hit you!" —
Do you, sir, though you see him twice a week?
"No," you reply, "what use retailing it?
Why should I?" But, you see, one day you *should*.

Because one day there's much use, — when this **fact**
Brings you the Judge upon both gouty knees
Before the supernatural ; proves that Sludge
Knows, as you say, a thing he "could not" know :
Will not Sludge thenceforth keep an outstretched face
The way the wind drives ?

                     "Could not !" Look **you now**.
I'll tell you a story ! There's a whiskered chap,
A foreigner, that teaches music here
And gets his bread, — knowing no better way.
He says, the fellow who informed of him
And made him fly his country and fall West,
Was a hunchback cobbler, sat, stitched soles, and sang,
In some outlandish place, the city Rome,
In a cellar by their Broadway, all day long ;
Never asked questions, stopped to listen or look,
Nor lifted nose from lapstone ; let the world
Roll round his three-legged stool, and news run in
The ears he hardly seemed to keep pricked up.
Well, that man went on Sundays, touched his pay,
And took his praise from government, you see ;
For something like two dollars every week,
He'd engage tell you some one little thing
Of some one man, which led to many more
(Because one truth leads right to the world's end),
And make you that man's master — when he dined
And on what dish, where walked to keep his health,
And to what street. His trade was, throwing thus
His sense out, like an anteater's long tongue,
Soft, innocent, warm, moist, impassible,
And when 'twas crusted o'er with creatures — slick,
Their juice enriched his palate. "Could not Sludge !"
I'll go yet a step farther, and maintain,
Once the imposture plunged its proper depth
I' the rotten of your natures, all of you —
(If one's not mad nor drunk, and hardly then),
It's impossible to cheat —that's, be found out !
Go tell your brotherhood this first slip of mine,
All to-day's tale, how you detected Sludge,
Behaved unpleasantly, till he was fain confess,
And so has come to grief ! You'll find, I think,
Why Sludge still snaps his fingers in your face.
There now, you've told them ! What's their prompt **reply ?**
" Sir, did that youth confess he had cheated me,
I'd disbelieve him. He may cheat at times ;
That's in the ' medium '-nature, thus they're made,
Vain and vindictive, cowards, prone to scratch.
And so all cats are ; still a cat's the beast
You coax the strange electric sparks from out,
By rubbing back its fur ; not so a dog,
Nor lion, nor lamb : 'tis the cat's nature, sir !
Why not the dog's ? Ask God, who made them **beasts !**
D'ye think the sound, the nicely balanced man
Like me " — (aside) — " like you yourself," — (aloud)
— " He's stuff to make a ' medium ' ? Bless your soul,
'Tis these hysteric, hybrid half-and-halfs,
Equivocal, worthless vermin yield the fire !
We must take such as we find them, 'ware their tricks,

Wanting their service. Sir, Sludge took in you —
How, I can't say, not being there to watch;
He was tried, was tempted by your easiness, —
He did not take in me!"

          Thank you for Sludge!
I'm to be grateful to such patrons, eh,
When what you hear's my best word? 'Tis a challenge;
"Snap at all strangers, half-tamed prairie-dog,
So you cower duly at your keeper's nod!
Cat, show what claws were made for, muffling them
Only to me! Cheat others if you can,
Me, if you dare!" And, my wise sir, I dared —
Did cheat you first, made you cheat others next,
And had the help o' your vaunted manliness
To bully the incredulous. You used me?
Have not I used you, taken full revenge,
Persuaded folk they knew not their own name,
And straight they'd own the error! Who was the fool
When, to an awe-struck wide-eyed open-mouthed
Circle of sages, Sludge would introduce
Milton composing baby-rhymes, and Locke
Reasoning in gibberish, Homer writing Greek
In naughts and crosses, Asaph setting psalms
To crotchet and quaver? I've made a spirit squeak
In sham voice for a minute, then outbroke
Bold in my own, defying the imbeciles —
Have copied some ghost's pothooks, half a page,
Then ended with my own scrawl undisguised.
"All right! The ghost was merely using Sludge,
Suiting itself from his imperfect stock!"
Don't talk of gratitude to me! For what?
For being treated as a showman's ape,
Encouraged to be wicked and make sport,
Fret or sulk, grin or whimper, any mood
So long as the ape be in it and no man —
Because a nut pays every mood alike.
Curse your superior, superintending sort,
Who, since you hate smoke, send up boys that climb
To cure your chimney, bid a "medium" lie
To sweep you truth down! Curse your women too,
Your insolent wives and daughters, that fire up
Or faint away if a male hand squeeze theirs,
Yet, to encourage Sludge, may play with Sludge
As only a "medium," only the kind of thing
They must humor, fondle . . . oh, to misconceive
Were too preposterous! But I've paid them out!
They've had their wish — called for the naked truth,
And in she tripped, sat down, and bade them stare:
They had to blush a little and forgive!
"The fact is, children talk so; in next world
All our conventions are reversed, — perhaps
Made light of: something like old prints, my dear!
The Judge has one, he brought from Italy,
A metropolis in the background, — o'er a bridge,
A team of trotting roadsters, — cheerful groups
Of wayside travellers, peasants at their work,
And, full in front, quite unconcerned, why not?
Three nymphs conversing with a cavalier,

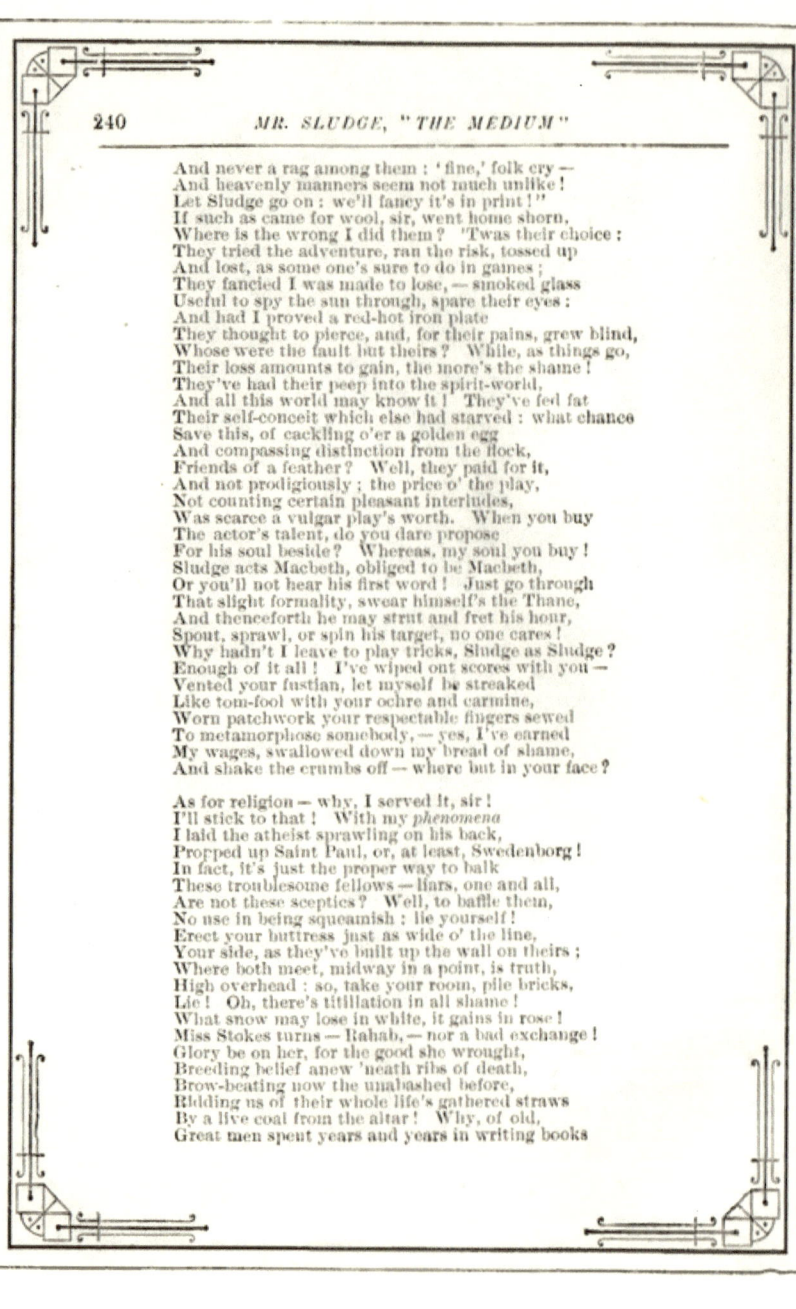

And never a rag among them : ' fine,' folk cry —
And heavenly manners seem not much unlike !
Let Sludge go on : we'll fancy it's in print !"
If such as came for wool, sir, went home shorn,
Where is the wrong I did them ? 'Twas their choice :
They tried the adventure, ran the risk, tossed up
And lost, as some one's sure to do in games ;
They fancied I was made to lose, — smoked glass
Useful to spy the sun through, spare their eyes :
And had I proved a red-hot iron plate
They thought to pierce, and, for their pains, grew blind,
Whose were the fault but theirs ? While, as things go,
Their loss amounts to gain, the more's the shame !
They've had their peep into the spirit-world,
And all this world may know it ! They've fed fat
Their self-conceit which else had starved : what chance
Save this, of cackling o'er a golden egg
And compassing distinction from the flock,
Friends of a feather ? Well, they paid for it,
And not prodigiously ; the price o' the play,
Not counting certain pleasant interludes,
Was scarce a vulgar play's worth. When you buy
The actor's talent, do you dare propose
For his soul beside ? Whereas, my soul you buy !
Sludge acts Macbeth, obliged to be Macbeth,
Or you'll not hear his first word ! Just go through
That slight formality, swear himself's the Thane,
And thenceforth he may strut and fret his hour,
Spout, sprawl, or spin his target, no one cares !
Why hadn't I leave to play tricks, Sludge as Sludge ?
Enough of it all ! I've wiped out scores with you —
Vented your fustian, let myself be streaked
Like tom-fool with your ochre and carmine,
Worn patchwork your respectable fingers sewed
To metamorphose somebody, — yes, I've earned
My wages, swallowed down my bread of shame,
And shake the crumbs off — where but in your face ?

As for religion — why, I served it, sir !
I'll stick to that ! With my *phenomena*
I laid the atheist sprawling on his back,
Propped up Saint Paul, or, at least, Swedenborg !
In fact, it's just the proper way to balk
These troublesome fellows — liars, one and all,
Are not these sceptics ? Well, to baffle them,
No use in being squeamish : lie yourself !
Erect your buttress just as wide o' the line,
Your side, as they've built up the wall on theirs ;
Where both meet, midway in a point, is truth,
High overhead : so, take your room, pile bricks,
Lie ! Oh, there's titillation in all shame !
What snow may lose in white, it gains in rose !
Miss Stokes turns — Rahab, — nor a bad exchange !
Glory be on her, for the good she wrought,
Breeding belief anew 'neath ribs of death,
Brow-beating now the unabashed before,
Ridding us of their whole life's gathered straws
By a live coal from the altar ! Why, of old,
Great men spent years and years in writing books

To prove we've souls, and hardly proved it then :
Miss Stokes with her live coal, for you and me !
Surely, to this good issue, all was fair —
Not only fondling Sludge, but, even suppose
He let escape some spice of knavery, — well,
In wisely being blind to it ! Don't you praise
Nelson for setting spy-glass to blind eye
And saying . . . what was it — that he could not see
The signal he was bothered with ? Ay, indeed !

I'll go beyond : there's a real love of a lie,
Liars find ready-made for lies they make,
As hand for glove, or tongue for sugar-plum.
At best, 'tis never pure and full belief ;
Those farthest in the quagmire, — don't suppose
They strayed there with no warning, got no chance
Of a filth-speck in their face, which they clinched teeth,
Bent brow against ! Be sure they had their doubts,
And fears, and fairest challenges to try
The floor o' the seeming solid sand ! But no !
Their faith was pledged, acquaintance too apprised,
All but the last step ventured, kerchiefs waved,
And Sludge called " jet : " 'twas easier marching on
To the promised land : join those who, Thursday next,
Meant to meet Shakspeare ; better follow Sludge —
Prudent, oh sure ! — on the alert, how else ?
But making for the mid-bog, all the same !
To hear your outcries, one would think I caught
Miss Stokes by the scruff o' the neck, and pitched her flat,
Foolish-face-foremost ! Hear these simpletons,
That's all I beg, before my work's begun,
Before I've touched them with my finger-tip !
Thus they await me (do but listen, now !
It's reasoning, this is, — I can't imitate
The baby voice, though) " In so many tales
Must be some truth, truth though a pin-point big,
Yet, some : a single man's deceived, perhaps —
Hardly, a thousand : to suppose one cheat
Can gull all these, were more miraculous far
Than aught we should confess a miracle " —
And so on. Then the Judge sums up — (it's rare)
Bids you respect the authorities that leap
To the judgment-seat at once, — why, don't you note
The limpid nature, the unblemished life,
The spotless honor, indisputable sense
Of the first upstart with his story ? What —
Outrage a boy on whom you ne'er till now
Set eyes, because he finds raps trouble him ?

Fools, these are : ay, and how of their opposites
Who never did, at bottom of their hearts,
Believe for a moment ? — Men emasculate,
Blank of belief, who played, as eunuchs use,
With superstition safely, — cold of blood,
Who saw what made for them i' the mystery,
Took their occasion, and supported Sludge
— As proselytes ? No, thank you, far too shrewd !
— But promisers of fair play, encouragers
O' the claimant ; who in candor needs must hoist

Sludge up on Mars' Hill, get speech out of Sludge
To carry off, criticise, and cant about!
Didn't Athens treat Saint Paul so?—at any rate,
It's "a new thing," philosophy fumbles at.
Then there's the other picker out of pearl
From dung-heaps,—ay, your literary man,
Who draws on his kid gloves to deal with Sludge
Daintily and discreetly,—shakes a dust
O' the doctrine, flavors thence, he well knows how,
The narrative or the novel,—half-believes,
All for the book's sake, and the public's stare,
And the cash that's God's sole solid in this world!
Look at him! Try to be too bold, too gross
For the master! Not you! He's the man for muck;
Shovel it forth, full-splash, he'll smooth your brown
Into artistic richness, never fear!
Find him the crude stuff; when you recognize
Your lie again, you'll doff your hat to it,
Dressed out for company! "For company,"
I say, since there's the relish of success:
Let all pay due respect, call the lie truth,
Save the soft, silent, smirking gentleman
Who ushered in the stranger: you must sigh
"How melancholy, he, the only one
Fails to perceive the bearing of the truth
Himself gave birth to!"— There's the triumph's smack!
That man would choose to see the whole world roll
I' the slime o' the slough, so he might touch the tip
Of his brush with what I call the best of browns—
Tint ghost-tales, spirit-stories, past the power
Of the outworn umber and bistre!

                                    Yet I think
There's a more hateful form of foolery—
The social sage's, Solomon of saloons
And philosophic diner-out, the fribble
Who wants a doctrine for a chopping-block
To try the edge of his faculty upon,
Prove how much common sense he'll hack and hew
I' the critical minute 'twixt the soup and fish!
These were my patrons: these, and the like of them
Who, rising in my soul now, sicken it,—
These I have injured! Gratitude to these?
The gratitude, forsooth, of a prostitute
To the greenhorn and the bully—friends of hers,
From the wag that wants the queer jokes for his club,
To the snuff-box-decorator, honest man.
Who just was at his wits' end where to find
So genial a Pasiphae! All and each
Pay, compliment, protect from the police,
And how she hates them for their pains, like me!
So much for my remorse at thanklessness
Toward a deserving public!

                                    But, for God?
Ay, that's a question! Well, sir, since you press—
(How you do teaze the whole thing out of me!
I don't mean you, you know, when I say, "them:"
Hate you, indeed! But that Miss Stokes, that Judge!

Enough, enough — with sugar : thank you, sir !)
Now for it then ! Will you believe me, though ?
You've heard what I confess ; I don't unsay
A single word : I cheated when I could,
Rapped with my toe-joints, set sham hands at work,
Wrote down names weak in sympathetic ink,
Rubbed odic lights with ends of phosphor-match,
And all the rest ; believe that ; believe this,
By the same token, though it seem to set
The crooked straight again, unsay the said,
Stick up what I've thrown down , I can't help that,
It's truth ! I somehow vomit truth to-day.
This trade of mine — I don't know, can't be sure
But there was something in it, tricks and all !
Really, I want to light up my own mind.
They were tricks, — true, but what I mean to add
Is also true. First, — don't it strike you, sir ?
Go back to the beginning, — the first fact
We're taught is, there's a world beside this world,
With spirits, not mankind, for tenantry ;
That much within that world once sojourned here,
That all upon this world will visit there,
And therefore that we, bodily here below,
Must have exactly such an interest
In learning what may be the ways o' the world
Above us, as the disembodied folk
Have (by all analogic likelihood)
In watching how things go in the old world
With us, their sons, successors, and what not.
Oh, yes, with added powers probably,
Fit for the novel state, — old loves grown pure,
Old interests understood aright, — they watch !
Eyes to see, ears to hear, and hands to help,
Proportionate to advancement : they're ahead,
That's all — do what we do, but nobler done —
Use plate, whereas we eat our meals off delf
(To use a figure).

         Concede that, and I ask
Next what may be the mode of intercourse
Between us men here, and those once-men there ?
First comes the Bible's speech ; then, history
With the supernatural element, — you know —
All that we sucked in with our mothers' milk,
Grew up with, got inside of us at last,
Till it's found bone of bone and flesh of flesh.
See now, we start with the miraculous,
And know it used to be, at all events :
What's the first step we take, and can't but take,
In arguing from the known to the obscure ?
Why, this : "What was before, may be to-day.
Since Samuel's ghost appeared to Saul, — of course
My brother's spirit may appear to me."
Go tell your teacher that ! What's his reply ?
What brings a shade of doubt for the first time
O'er his brow late so luminous with faith ?
"Such things have been," says he, " and there's no doubt
Such things may be ; but I advise mistrust
Of eyes, ears, stomach, — more than all, of brain,

Unless it be of your great-grandmother,
Whenever they propose a ghost to you!"
The end is, there's a composition struck;
'Tis settled, we've some way of intercourse
Just as in Saul's time; only, different:
How, when, and where, precisely,—find it out!
I want to know, then, what's so natural
As that a person born into this world
And seized on by such teaching, should begin
With firm expectancy and a frank look-out
For his own allotment, his especial share
I' the secret,—his particular ghost, in fine?
I mean, a person born to look that way,
Since natures differ: take the painter-sort,
One man lives fifty years in ignorance
Whether grass be green or red,—"No kind of eye
For color," say you; while another picks
And puts away even pebbles, when a child,
Because of bluish spots and pinky veins—
"Give him forthwith a paint-box!" Just the same
Was I born . . . "medium," you won't let me say,—
Well, seer of the supernatural
Everywhen, everyhow, and everywhere,—
Will that do?

      I and all such boys of course
Started with the same stock of Bible-truth;
Only,—what in the rest you style their sense,
Instinct, blind reasoning but imperative,
This, betimes, taught them the old world had one law
And ours another: "New world, new laws," cried they:
"None but old laws, seen everywhere at work,"
Cried I, and by their help explained my life
The Jews' way, still a working way to me.
Ghosts made the noises, fairies waved the lights,
Or Santa Claus slid down on New-Year's Eve
And stuffed with cakes the stocking at my bed,
Changed the worn shoes, rubbed clean the fingered slate
O' the sum that came to grief the day before.

This could not last long: soon enough I found
Who had worked wonders thus, and to what end:
But did I find all easy, like my mates?
Henceforth no supernatural any more?
Not a whit: what projects the billiard-balls?
"A cue," you answer: "Yes, a cue," said I;
"But what hand, off the cushion, moved the cue?
What unseen agency, outside the world,
Prompted its puppets to do this and that,
Put cakes and shoes and slates into their mind,
These mothers and aunts, nay even schoolmasters?"
Thus high I sprang, and there have settled since.
Just so I reason, in sober earnest still,
About the greater godsends, what you call
The serious gains and losses of my life.
What do I know or care about your world
Which either is or seems to be? This snap
O' my fingers, sir! My care is for myself;
Myself am whole and sole reality

Inside a raree-show and a market-mob
Gathered about it : that's the use of things.
'Tis easy saying they serve vast purposes,
Advantage their grand selves : be it true or false,
Each thing may have two uses. What's a star ?
A world, or a world's sun : doesn't it serve
As taper also, time-piece, weather-glass,
And almanac ? Are stars not set for signs
When we should shear our sheep, sow corn, prune trees ?
The Bible says so.

        Well, I add one use
To all the acknowledged uses, and declare
If I spy Charles's Wain at twelve to-night,
It warns me, " Go, nor lose another day,
And have your hair cut, Sludge ! " You laugh : and why ?
Were such a sign too hard for God to give ?
No : but Sludge seems too little for such grace :
Thank you, sir ! So you think, so does not Sludge !
When you and good men gape at Providence,
Go into history and bid us mark
Not merely powder-plots prevented, crowns
Kept on kings' heads by miracle enough,
But private mercies — oh, you've told me, sir,
Of such interpositions ! How yourself
Once, missing on a memorable day
Your handkerchief — just setting out, you know, —
You must return to fetch it, lost the train,
And saved your precious self from what befell
The thirty-three whom Providence forgot.
You tell, and ask me what I think of this ?
Well, sir, I think, then, since you needs must know,
What matter had you and Boston City to boot
Sailed skyward, like burnt onion-peelings ? Much
To you, no doubt : for me — undoubtedly
The cutting of my hair concerns me more,
Because, however sad the truth may seem,
Sludge is of all-importance to himself.
You set apart that day in every year
For special thanksgiving, were a heathen else :
Well, I who cannot boast the like escape,
Suppose I said " I don't thank Providence
For my part, owing it no gratitude ? " —
" Nay, but you owe as much " — you'd tutor me,
You, every man alive, for blessings gained
In every hour o' the day, could you but know !
I saw my crowning mercy : all have such,
Could they but see ! " Well, sir, why don't they see ?
" Because they won't look, — or perhaps they can't."
Then, sir, suppose I can, and will, and do
Look, microscopically as is right,
Into each hour with its infinitude
Of influences at work to profit Sludge ?
For that's the case : I've sharpened up my sight
To spy a providence in the fire's going out,
The kettle's boiling, the dime's sticking fast
Despite the hole i' the pocket. Call such facts
Fancies, too petty a work for Providence,
And those same thanks which you exact from me,

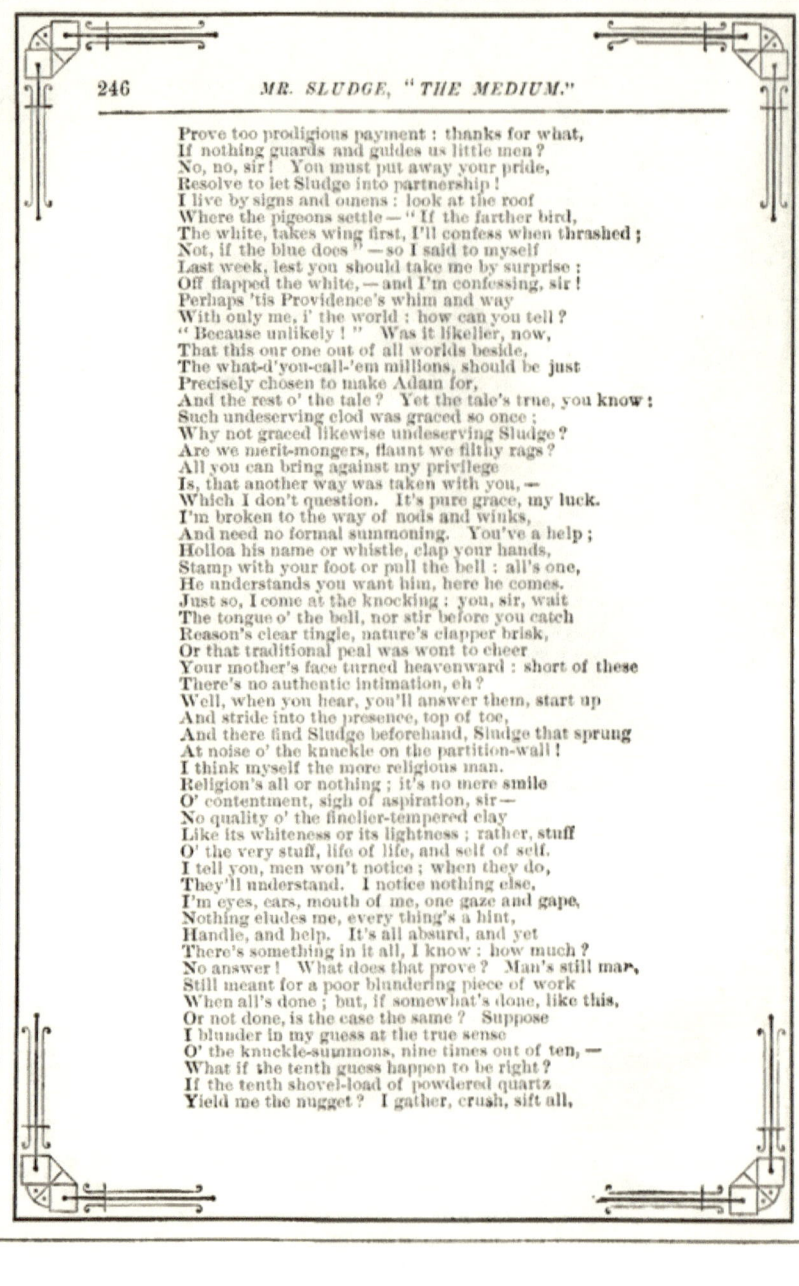

Prove too prodigious payment : thanks for what,
If nothing guards and guides us little men ?
No, no, sir ! You must put away your pride,
Resolve to let Sludge into partnership !
I live by signs and omens : look at the roof
Where the pigeons settle — " If the farther bird,
The white, takes wing first, I'll confess when thrashed ;
Not, if the blue does " — so I said to myself
Last week, lest you should take me by surprise :
Off flapped the white, — and I'm confessing, sir !
Perhaps 'tis Providence's whim and way
With only me, i' the world : how can you tell ?
" Because unlikely ! " Was it likelier, now,
That this our one out of all worlds beside,
The what-d'you-call-'em millions, should be just
Precisely chosen to make Adam for,
And the rest o' the tale ? Yet the tale's true, you know :
Such undeserving clod was graced so once ;
Why not graced likewise undeserving Sludge ?
Are we merit-mongers, flaunt we filthy rags ?
All you can bring against my privilege
Is, that another way was taken with you, —
Which I don't question. It's pure grace, my luck.
I'm broken to the way of nods and winks,
And need no formal summoning. You've a help ;
Holloa his name or whistle, clap your hands,
Stamp with your foot or pull the bell : all's one,
He understands you want him, here he comes.
Just so, I come at the knocking : you, sir, wait
The tongue o' the bell, nor stir before you catch
Reason's clear tingle, nature's clapper brisk,
Or that traditional peal was wont to cheer
Your mother's face turned heavenward : short of these
There's no authentic intimation, eh ?
Well, when you hear, you'll answer them, start up
And stride into the presence, top of toe,
And there find Sludge beforehand, Sludge that sprung
At noise o' the knuckle on the partition-wall !
I think myself the more religious man.
Religion's all or nothing ; it's no mere smile
O' contentment, sigh of aspiration, sir —
No quality o' the finelier-tempered clay
Like its whiteness or its lightness ; rather, stuff
O' the very stuff, life of life, and self of self.
I tell you, men won't notice ; when they do,
They'll understand. I notice nothing else,
I'm eyes, ears, mouth of me, one gaze and gape,
Nothing eludes me, every thing's a hint,
Handle, and help. It's all absurd, and yet
There's something in it all, I know : how much ?
No answer ! What does that prove ? Man's still man,
Still meant for a poor blundering piece of work
When all's done ; but, if somewhat's done, like this,
Or not done, is the case the same ? Suppose
I blunder in my guess at the true sense
O' the knuckle-summons, nine times out of ten, —
What if the tenth guess happen to be right ?
If the tenth shovel-load of powdered quartz
Yield me the nugget ? I gather, crush, sift all,

Pass o'er the failure, pounce on the success.
To give you a notion, now — (let who wins, laugh!)
When first I see a man, what do I first?
Why, count the letters which make up his name,
And as their number chances, even or odd,
Arrive at my conclusion, trim my course:
Hiram H. Horsefall is your honored name,
And haven't I found a patron, sir, in you?
" Shall I cheat this stranger?" I take apple-pips,
Stick one in either *canthus* of my eye,
And if the left drops first — (your left, sir, stuck)
I'm warned, I let the trick alone this time.
You, sir, who smile, superior to such trash,
You judge of character by other rules:
Don't your rules sometimes fail you? Pray, what rule
Have you judged Sludge by hitherto?

                                        Oh, be sure,

You, everybody blunders, just as I,
In simpler things than these by far! For see:
I knew two farmers, — one, a wiseacre
Who studied seasons, rummaged almanacs,
Quoted the dew-point, registered the frost,
And then declared, for outcome of his pains,
Next summer must be dampish: 'twas a drought,
His neighbor prophesied such drought would fall,
Saved hay and corn, made cent per cent thereby,
And proved a sage indeed: how came his lore?
Because one brindled heifer, late in March,
Stiffened her tail of evenings, and somehow
He got into his head that drought was meant!
I don't expect all men can do as much:
Such kissing goes by favor. You must take
A certain turn of mind for this, — a twist
I' the flesh, as well. Be lazily alive,
Open-mouthed, like my friend the anteater,
Letting all nature's loosely guarded motes
Settle and, slick, be swallowed! Think yourself
The one i' the world, the one for whom the world
Was made, expect it tickling at your mouth!
Then will the swarm of busy buzzing flies,
Clouds of coincidence, break eggs-shell, thrive,
Breed, multiply, and bring you food enough.
I can't pretend to mind your smiling, sir!
Oh, what you mean is this! Such intimate way,
Close converse, frank exchange of offices,
Strict sympathy of the immeasurably great
With the infinitely small, betokened here
By a course of signs and omens, raps and sparks, —
How does it suit the dread traditional text
O' the "Great and Terrible Name?" Shall the Heaven of **heavens**
Stoop to such child's play?

                            Please, sir, go with me

A moment, and I'll try to answer you.
The " *Magnum et terribile* " (is that right?)
Well, folk began with this in the early day;
And all the acts they recognized in proof
Were thunders, lightnings, earthquakes, whirlwinds, dealt

Indisputably on men whose death they caused.
There, and there only, folk saw Providence
At work, — and seeing it, 'twas right enough
All heads should tremble, hands wring hands amain,
And knees knock hard together at the breath
O' the Name's first letter ; why, the Jews, I'm told,
Won't write it down, no, to this very hour,
Nor speak aloud : you know best if't be so.
Each ague-fit of fear at end, they crept
(Because somehow people once born must live)
Out of the sound, sight, swing, and sway o' the Name,
Into a corner, the dark rest of the world,
And safe space where as yet no fear had reached :
'Twas there they looked about them, breathed again,
And felt indeed at home, as we might say.
The current o' common things, the daily life,
This had their due contempt ; no Name pursued
Man from the mountain-top where fires abide,
To his particular mouse-hole at its foot
Where he ate, drank, digested, lived in short :
Such was man's vulgar business, far too small
To be worth thunder ; "small," folk kept on, "small,"
With much complacency in those great days !
A mote of sand, you know, a blade of grass —
What was so despicable as mere grass,
Except perhaps the life o' the worm or fly
Which fed there ? These were "small" and men were great.
Well, sir, the old way's altered somewhat since,
And the world wears another aspect now :
Somebody turns our spyglass round, or else
Puts a new lens in it : grass, worm, fly grow big :
We find great things are made of little things,
And little things go lessening till at last
Comes God behind them. Talk of mountains now ?
We talk of mould that heaps the mountain, mites
That throng the mould, and God that makes the mites.
The Name comes close behind a stomach-cyst,
The simplest of creations, just a sac
That's mouth, heart, legs, and belly at once, yet lives
And feels, and could do neither, we conclude,
If simplified still further one degree :
The small becomes the dreadful and immense !
Lightning, forsooth ? No word more upon that ?
A tin-foil bottle, a strip of greasy silk,
With a bit of wire and knob of brass, and there's
Your dollar's worth of lightning ! But the cyst —
The life of the least of the little things ?

        No, no !
Preachers and teachers try another tack,
Come near the truth this time : they put aside
Thunder and lightning : "That's mistake," they cry,
"Thunderbolts fall for neither fright nor sport,
But do appreciable good, like tides,
Changes o' the wind, and other natural facts —
'Good' meaning good to man, his body or soul.
Mediate, immediate, all things minister
To man, — that's settled : be our future text
'We are His children !'" So, they now harangue

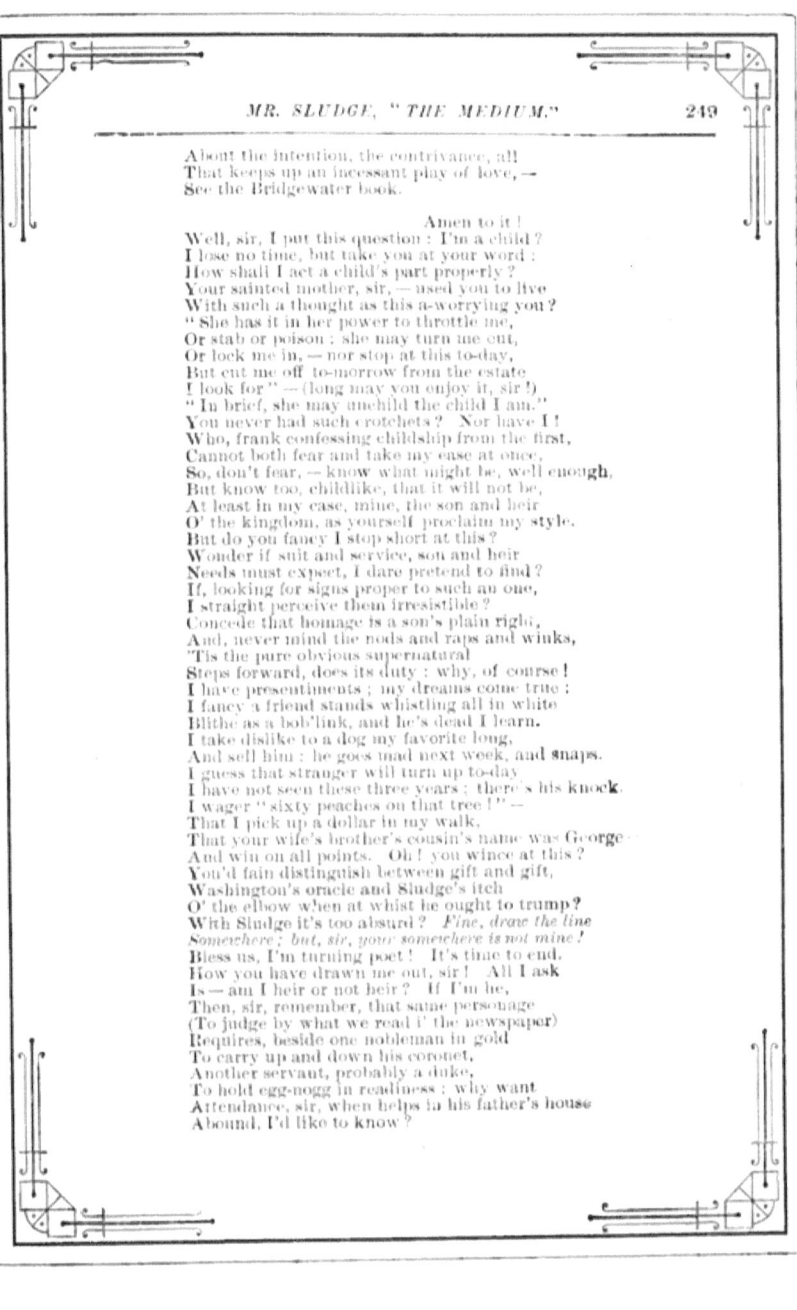

About the intention, the contrivance, all
That keeps up an incessant play of love, —
See the Bridgewater book.

　　　　　　　Amen to it!
Well, sir, I put this question: I'm a child?
I lose no time, but take you at your word:
How shall I act a child's part properly?
Your sainted mother, sir, — used you to live
With such a thought as this a-worrying you?
" She has it in her power to throttle me,
Or stab or poison: she may turn me out,
Or lock me in, — nor stop at this to-day,
But cut me off to-morrow from the estate
I look for " — (long may you enjoy it, sir!)
" In brief, she may unchild the child I am."
You never had such crotchets? Nor have I!
Who, frank confessing childship from the first,
Cannot both fear and take my ease at once,
So, don't fear, — know what might be, well enough,
But know too, childlike, that it will not be,
At least in my case, mine, the son and heir
O' the kingdom, as yourself proclaim my style.
But do you fancy I stop short at this?
Wonder if suit and service, son and heir
Needs must expect, I dare pretend to find?
If, looking for signs proper to such an one,
I straight perceive them irresistible?
Concede that homage is a son's plain right,
And, never mind the nods and raps and winks,
'Tis the pure obvious supernatural
Steps forward, does its duty: why, of course!
I have presentiments; my dreams come true:
I fancy a friend stands whistling all in white
Blithe as a bob'link, and he's dead I learn.
I take dislike to a dog my favorite long,
And sell him: he goes mad next week, and snaps.
I guess that stranger will turn up to-day
I have not seen these three years; there's his knock.
I wager " sixty peaches on that tree! " —
That I pick up a dollar in my walk,
That your wife's brother's cousin's name was George —
And win on all points. Oh! you wince at this?
You'd fain distinguish between gift and gift,
Washington's oracle and Sludge's itch
O' the elbow when at whist he ought to trump?
With Sludge it's too absurd? *Fine, draw the line
Somewhere; but, sir, your somewhere is not mine!*
Bless us, I'm turning poet! It's time to end.
How you have drawn me out, sir! All I ask
Is — am I heir or not heir? If I'm he,
Then, sir, remember, that same personage
(To judge by what we read i' the newspaper)
Requires, beside one nobleman in gold
To carry up and down his coronet,
Another servant, probably a duke,
To hold egg-nogg in readiness; why want
Attendance, sir, when helps in his father's house
Abound, I'd like to know?

Enough of talk !
My fault is that I tell too plain a truth.
Why, which of those who say they disbelieve,
Your clever people, but has dreamed his dream,
Caught his coincidence, stumbled on his fact
He can't explain (he'll tell you smilingly),
Which he's too much of a philosopher
To count as supernatural, indeed,
So calls a puzzle and problem, proud of it :
Bidding you still be on your guard, you know,
Because one fact don't make a system stand,
Nor prove this an occasional escape
Of spirit beneath the matter : that's the way !
Just so wild Indians picked up, piece by piece,
The fact in California, the fine gold
That underlay the gravel — hoarded these,
But never made a system stand, nor dug !
So wise men hold out in each hollowed palm
A handful of experience, sparkling fact
They can't explain ; and since their rest of life
Is all explainable, what proof in this?
Whereas I take the fact, the grain of gold,
And fling away the dirty rest of life,
And add this grain to the grain each fool has found
O' the million other such philosophers, —
Till I see gold, all gold and only gold,
Truth questionless though unexplainable,
And the miraculous proved the commonplace !
The other fools believed in mud, no doubt —
Failed to know gold they saw : was that so strange ?
Are all men born to play Bach's fiddle-fugues,
"Time" with the foil in carte, jump their own height,
Cut the mutton with the broadsword, skate a five,
Make the red hazard with the cue, clip nails
While swimming, in five minutes row a mile,
Pull themselves three feet up with the left arm,
Do sums of fifty figures in their head,
And so on, by the scores of instances?
The Sludge with luck, who sees the spiritual facts,
His fellows strive and fail to see, may rank
With these, and share the advantage.

Ay, but share
The drawback ! Think it over by yourself :
I have not heart, sir, and the fire's gone gray.
Defect somewhere compensates for success,
Every one knows that. Oh, we're equals, sir !
The big-legged fellow has a little arm
And a less brain, though big legs win the race :
Do you suppose I 'scape the common lot ?
Say, I was born with flesh so sensitive,
Soul so alert, that, practice helping both,
I guess what's going on outside the veil,
Just as a prisoned crane feels pairing-time
In the islands where his kind are, so must fall
To capering by himself some shiny night,
As if your back-yard were a plot of spice —
Thus am I 'ware o' the spirit-world : while you,
Blind as a beetle that way, — for amends,

Why, you can double fist and floor me, sir !
Ride that hot hardmouthed horrid horse of yours,
Laugh while it lightens, play with the great dog,
Speak your mind though it vex some friend to hear,
Never brag, never bluster, never blush, —
In short, you've pluck, when I'm a coward — there !
I know it, I can't help it, — folly or no,
I'm paralyzed, my hand's no more a hand,
Nor my head, a head, in danger : you can smile,
And change the pipe in your cheek. Your gift's not mine.
Would you swap for mine ? No ! but you'd add my gift
To yours ; I dare say ! I too sigh at times,
Wish I were stouter, could tell truth nor flinch,
Kept cool when threatened, did not mind so much
Being dressed gayly, making strangers stare,
Eating nice things ; when I'd amuse myself,
I shut my eyes and fancy in my brain,
I'm — now the President, now, Jenny Lind,
Now, Emerson, now, the Benicia Boy —
With all the civilized world a-wondering
And worshipping. I know it's folly and worse ;
I feel such tricks sap, honeycomb the soul :
But I can't cure myself, — despond, despair,
And then, hey, presto, there's a turn o' the wheel,
Under comes uppermost, fate makes full amends ;
Sludge knows and sees and hears a hundred things
You all are blind to, — I've my taste of truth,
Likewise my touch of falsehood, — vice no doubt,
But you've your vices also : I'm content.

What, sir ? You won't shake hands ? "Because I cheat !"
"You've found me out in cheating !" That's enough
To make an apostle swear ! Why, when I cheat,
Mean to cheat, do cheat, and am caught in the act,
Are you, or rather, am I sure o' the fact ?
(There's verse again, but I'm inspired somehow.)
Well then I'm not sure ! I may be, perhaps,
Free as a babe from cheating : how it began,
My gift, — no matter ; what 'tis got to be
In the end now, that's the question : answer that !
Had I seen, perhaps, what hand was holding mine,
Leading me whither, I had died of fright.
So, I was made believe I led myself.
If I should lay a six-inch plank from roof
To roof, you would not cross the street, one step,
Even at your mother's summons : but, being shrewd,
If I paste paper on each side the plank,
And swear 'tis solid pavement, why, you'll cross
Humming a tune the while, in ignorance
Beacon Street stretches a hundred feet below :
I walked thus, took the paper-cheat for stone.
Some impulse made me set a thing o' the move
Which, started once, ran really by itself ;
Beer flows thus, suck the siphon ; toss the kite,
It takes the wind and floats of its own force.
Don't let truth's lump rot stagnant for the lack
Of a timely helpful lie to leaven it !
Put a chalk-egg beneath the clucking hen,
She'll lay a real one, laudably deceived,

Daily for weeks to come. I've told my lie,
And seen truth follow, marvels none of mine ;
All was not cheating, sir, I'm positive !
I don't know if I move your hand sometimes
When the spontaneous writing spreads so far,
If my knee lifts the table all that height,
Why the inkstand don't fall off the desk a-tilt,
Why the accordion plays a prettier waltz
Than I can pick out on the piano-forte,
Why I speak so much more than I intend,
Describe so many things I never saw.
I tell you, sir, in one sense, I believe
Nothing at all, — that everybody can,
Will, and does cheat : but in another sense
I'm ready to believe my very self —
That every cheat's inspired, and every lie
Quick with a germ of truth.

                    You ask perhaps
Why I should condescend to trick at all
If I know a way without it ? This is why !
There's a strange, secret, sweet self-sacrifice
In any desecration of one's soul
To a worthy end, — isn't it Herodotus
(I wish I could read Latin !) who describes
The single gift o' the land's virginity,
Demanded in those old Egyptian rites,
(I've but a hazy notion — help me, sir !)
For one purpose in the world, one day in a life,
One hour in a day — thereafter, purity,
And a veil thrown o'er the past for evermore !
Well now, they understood a many things
Down by Nile city, or wherever it was !
I've always vowed, after the minute's lie,
And the end's gain, — truth should be mine henceforth.
This goes to the root o' the matter, sir, — this plain
Plump fact : accept it, and unlock with it
The wards of many a puzzle !

                    Or, finally,
Why should I set so fine a gloss on things ?
What need I care ? I cheat in self-defence,
And there's my answer to a world of cheats !
Cheat ? To be sure, sir ! What's the world worth else ?
Who takes it as he finds, and thanks his stars ?
Don't it want trimming, turning, furbishing up
And polishing over ? Your so-styled great men,
Do they accept one truth as truth is found,
Or try their skill at tinkering ? What's your world ?
Here are you born, who are, I'll say at once,
Of the luckiest whether as to head and heart,
Body and soul, or all that helps the same.
Well, now, look back : what faculty of yours
Came to its full, had ample justice done
By growing when rain fell, biding its time,
Solidifying growth when earth was dead,
Spiring up, broadening wide, in seasons due ?
Never ! You shot up and frost nipped you off,
Settled to sleep when sunshine bade you sprout ;

One faculty thwarted its fellow : at the end,
All you boast is, " I had proved a topping tree
In other climes " — yet this was the right clime
Had you foreknown the seasons. Young, you've force
Wasted like well-streams : old, — oh, then indeed,
Behold a labyrinth of hydraulic pipes
Through which you'd play off wondrous waterwork ;
Only, no water left to feed their play.
Young, — you've a hope, an aim, a love ; it's tossed
And crossed and lost : you struggle on, some spark
Shut in your heart against the puffs around,
Through cold and pain ; these in due time subside,
Now then for age's triumph, the hoarded light
You mean to loose on the altered face of things, —
Up with it on the tripod ! It's extinct.
Spend your life's remnant asking — which was best,
Light smothered up that never peeped forth once,
Or the cold cresset with full leave to shine ?
Well, accept this too, — seek the fruit of it
Not in enjoyment, proved a dream on earth,
But knowledge, useful for a second chance,
Another life, — you've lost this world, you've gained
Its knowledge for the next. — What knowledge, sir,
Except that you know nothing ? Nay, you doubt
Whether 'twere better have been made man or brute,
If aught is true, if good and evil clash.
No foul, no fair, no inside, no outside,
There's your world !

    Give it me ! I slap it brisk
With harlequin's pasteboard sceptre : what's it now ?
Changed like a rock-flat, rough with rusty weed,
At first wash-over o' the returning wave !
All the dry, dead, impracticable stuff
Starts into life and light again ; this world
Pervaded by the influx from the next.
I cheat, and what's the happy consequence ?
You find full justice straightway dealt you out,
Each want supplied, each ignorance set at ease,
Each folly fooled. No life-long labor now
As the price of worse than nothing ! No more film
Holding you chained in iron, as it seems,
Against the outstretch of your very arms
And legs i' the sunshine moralists forbid !
What would you have ? Just speak and, there, you see !
You're supplemented, made a whole at last :
Bacon advises, Shakspeare writes you songs,
And Mary Queen of Scots embraces you.
Thus it goes on, not quite like life perhaps,
But so near, that the very difference piques,
Shows that e'en better than this best will be —
This passing entertainment in a hut
Whose bare walls take your taste — since, one stage more,
And you arrive at the palace : all half real,
And you, to suit it, less than real beside,
In a dream, lethargic kind of death in life,
That helps the interchange of natures, flesh
Transfused by souls, and such souls ! Oh, 'tis choice !
And if at whiles the bubble, blown too thin,

Seem nigh on bursting, — if you nearly see
The real world through the false, — what *do* you see?
Is the old so ruined?   You find you're in a flock
O' the youthful, earnest, passionate — genius, beauty,
Rank and wealth also, if you care for these,
And all depose their natural rights, hail you
(That's me, sir) as their mate and yoke-fellow.
Participate in Sludgehood — nay, grow mine,
I veritably possess them — banish doubt,
And reticence and modesty alike!
Why, here's the Golden Age, old Paradise,
Or new Eutopia!   Here is life indeed,
And the world well won now, yours for the first time!

And all this might be, may be, and with good help
Of a little lying shall be : so, Sludge lies!
Why, he's at worst your poet who sings how Greeks
That never were, in Troy which never was,
Did this or the other impossible great thing!
He's Lowell — it's a world, you smile and say,
Of his own invention — wondrous Longfellow,
Surprising Hawthorne!   Sludge does more than they,
And acts the books they write : the more his praise!

But why do I mount to poets?   Take plain prose —
Dealers in common sense, set these at work,
What can they do without their helpful lies?
Each states the law and fact and face o' the thing
Just as he'd have them, finds what he thinks fit,
Is blind to what missuits him, just records
What makes his case out, quite ignores the rest.
It's a History of the World, the Lizard Age,
The Early Indians, the Old Country War,
Jerome Napoleon, whatsoever you please,
All as the author wants it.   Such a scribe
You pay and praise for putting life in stones,
Fire into fog, making the past your world.
There's plenty of "How did you contrive to grasp
The thread which led you through this labyrinth?
How build such solid fabric out of air?
How on so slight foundation found this tale,
Biography, narrative?" or, in other words,
"How many lies did it require o make
The portly truth you here present us with?" —
"Oh!" quoth the penman, purring at your praise,
"'Tis fancy all; no particle of fact :
I was poor and threadbare when I wrote that book
'Bliss in the Golden City.'   I, at Thebes?
We writers paint out of our heads, you see!"
— "Ah, the more wonderful the gift in you,
The more creativeness and godlike craft!"
But I, do I present you with my piece,
It's "What, Sludge?   When my sainted mother spoke
The verses Lady Jane Grey last composed
About the rosy bower in the seventh heaven
Where she and Queen Elizabeth keep house, —
You made the raps?   'Twas your invention that?
Cur, slave, and devil!" — eight fingers and two thumbs
Stuck in my throat?

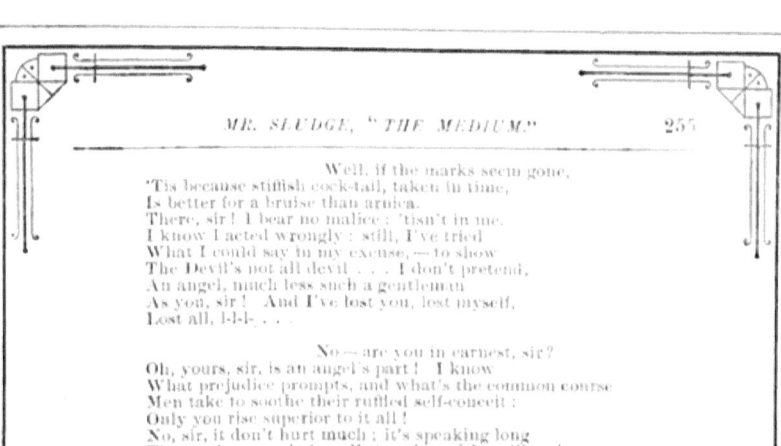

Well, if the marks seem gone,
'Tis because stiffish cock-tail, taken in time,
Is better for a bruise than arnica.
There, sir! I bear no malice: 'tisn't in me.
I know I acted wrongly: still, I've tried
What I could say in my excuse,—to show
The Devil's not all devil . . . I don't pretend,
An angel, much less such a gentleman
As you, sir! And I've lost you, lost myself,
Lost all, l-l-l- . . .

            No—are you in earnest, sir?
Oh, yours, sir, is an angel's part! I know
What prejudice prompts, and what's the common course
Men take to soothe their ruffled self-conceit:
Only you rise superior to it all!
No, sir, it don't hurt much; it's speaking long
That makes me choke a little: the marks will go!
What? Twenty V-notes more, and outfit too,
And not a word to Greeley? One—one kiss
O' the hand that saves me! You'll not let me speak
I well know, and I've lost the right, too true!
But I must say, sir, if She hears (she does)
Your sainted . . . Well, sir,—be it so! That's, I think,
My bed-room candle. Good-night! Bl-l-less you, sir!

––––––––––

R-r-r, you brute-beast and blackguard! Cowardly scamp!
I only wish I dared burn down the house
And spoil your sniggering! Oh! what, you're the man?
You're satisfied at last? You've found out Sludge?
We'll see that presently: my turn, sir, next!
I too can tell my story: brute,—do you hear?—
You throttled your sainted mother, that old hag,
In just such a fit of passion: no, it was . . .
To get this house of hers, and many a note
Like these . . . I'll pocket them, however . . . five,
Ten, fifteen . . . ay, you gave her throat the twist,
Or else you poisoned her! Confound the cuss!
Where was my head? I ought to have prophesied
He'll die in a year and join her; that's the way.
I don't know where my head is: what had I done?
How did it all go? I said he poisoned her,
And hoped he'd have grace given him to repent,
Whereon he picked this quarrel, bullied me,
And called me cheat: I thrashed him,—who could help?
He howled for mercy, prayed me on his knees
To cut and run and save him from disgrace:
I do so, and once off, he slanders me.
An end of him. Begin elsewhere anew!
Boston's a hole, the herring-pond is wide,
V-notes are something, liberty still more.
Beside, is he the only fool in the world?

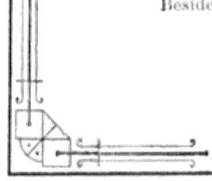

THE BOY AND THE ANGEL.

MORNING, evening, noon, and night,
" Praise God ! " sang Theocrite.

Then to his poor trade he turned,
Whereby the daily meal was earned.

Hard he labored, long and well :
O'er his work the boy's curls fell.

But ever, at each period,
He stopped and sang, " Praise God ! "

Then back again his curls he threw,
And cheerful turned to work anew.

Said Blaise, the listening monk,
" Well done ;
I doubt not thou art heard, my son,

" As well as if thy voice to-day
Were praising God, the Pope's great
way.

" This Easter Day, the Pope at Rome
Praises God from Peter's dome."

Said Theocrite, " Would God that I
Might praise him, that great way, and
die ! "

Night passed, day shone ;
And Theocrite was gone.

With God a day endures alway :
A thousand years are but a day.

God said in heaven, " Nor day nor
night
Now brings the voice of my delight."

Then Gabriel, like a rainbow's birth,
Spread his wings and sank to earth ;

Entered, in flesh, the empty cell,
Lived there, and played the craftsman
well ;

And morning, evening, noon, and
night,
Praised God in place of Theocrite.

And from a boy, to youth he grew ;
The man put off the stripling's hue ;

The man matured and fell away
Into the season of decay ;

And ever o'er the trade he bent,
And ever lived on earth content.

(He did God's will ; to him, all one
If on the earth or in the sun.)

God said, " A praise is in mine ear ;
There is no doubt in it, no fear :

" So sing old worlds, and so
New worlds that from my footstool
go.

" Clearer loves sound other ways :
I miss my little human praise."

Then forth sprang Gabriel's wings, off
fell
The flesh disguise, remained the cell.

'Twas Easter Day : he flew to Rome,
And paused above Saint Peter's dome.

In the tiring-room close by
The great outer gallery,

With his holy vestments dight,
Stood the new Pope, Theocrite :

And all his past career
Came back upon him clear,

Since when, a boy, he plied his trade,
Till on his life the sickness weighed ;

And in his cell, when death drew near,
An angel in a dream brought cheer :

And rising from the sickness drear
He grew a priest, and now stood here.

To the East with praise he turned,
And on his sight the angel burned.

" I bore thee from thy craftsman's cell,
And set thee here : I did not well.

" Vainly I left my angel-sphere,
Vain was thy dream of many a year.

" Thy voice's praise seemed weak : it
dropped —
Creation's chorus stopped !

" Go back and praise again
The early way, while I remain.

" With that weak voice of our disdain
Take up creation's pausing strain.

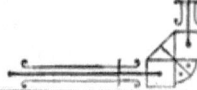

"Said Blaise, the listening monk, ' Well done ;
I doubt not thou art heard, my son.' " — Page 256.

" Back to the cell and poor employ :
Resume the craftsman and the boy !"

Theocrite grew old at home :
A new Pope dwelt in Peter's dome.

One vanished as the other died :
They sought God side by side.

A DEATH IN THE DESERT.

[SUPPOSED of Pamphylax the Antio-
chene :
It is a parchment, of my rolls the
fifth,
Hath three skins glued together, is
all Greek,
And goeth from *Epsilon* down to *Mu* :
Lies second in the surnamed Chosen
Chest,
Stained and conserved with juice of
terebinth,
Covered with cloth of hair, and let-
tered *Xi*,
From Xanthus, my wife's uncle, now
at peace :
Mu and *Epsilon* stand for my own
name,
I may not write it, but I make a cross
To show I wait His coming, with the
rest,
And leave off here : beginneth Pam-
phylax.]

I said, "If one should wet his lips
with wine,
And slip the broadest plantain-leaf
we find,
Or else the lappet of a linen robe,
Into the water-vessel, lay it right,
And cool his forehead just above the
eyes,
The while a brother, kneeling either
side,
Should chafe each hand and try to
make it warm, —
He is not so far gone but he might
speak."

This did not happen in the outer cave,
Nor in the secret chamber of the rock,
Where, sixty days since the decree
was out,
We had him, bedded on a camel-skin,

And waited for his dying all the while;
But in the midmost grotto : since
noon's light
Reached there a little, and we would
not lose
The last of what might happen on
his face.

I at the head, and Xanthus at the
feet,
With Valens and the Boy, had lifted
him,
And brought him from the chamber
in the depths,
And laid him in the light where we
might see :
For certain smiles began about his
mouth,
And his lids moved, presageful of the
end.

Beyond, and half way up the mouth
o' the cave,
The Bactrian convert, having his
desire,
Kept watch, and made pretence to
graze a goat
That gave us milk, on rags of various
herb,
Plantain and quitch, the rocks' shade
keeps alive :
So that if any thief or soldier passed
(Because the persecution was aware),
Yielding the goat up promptly with
his life,
Such man might pass on, joyful at a
prize,
Nor care to pry into the cool o' the
cave.
Outside was all noon and the burning
blue.

" Here is wine," answered Xanthus,
— dropped a drop ;
I stooped and placed the lap of cloth
aright,
Then chafed his right hand, and the
Boy his left :
But Valens had bethought him, and
produced
And broke a ball of nard, and made
perfume.
Only, he did — not so much wake, as
— turn
And smile a little, as a sleeper does
If any dear one call him, touch his
face —
And smiles and loves, but will not be
disturbed.

Then Xanthus said a prayer, but still
   he slept :
It is the Xanthus that escaped to
   Rome,
Was burned, and could not write the
   chronicle.

Then the Boy sprang up from his
   knees, and ran,
Stung by the splendor of a sudden
   thought,
And fetched the seventh plate of
   graven lead
Out of the secret chamber, found a
   place,
Pressing with finger on the deeper
   dints,
And spoke, as 'twere his mouth pro-
   claiming first
" I am the Resurrection and the Life."

Whereat he opened his eyes wide at
   once,
And sat up of himself, and looked at
   us ;
And thenceforth nobody pronounced
   a word :
Only, outside, the Bactrian cried his
   cry
Like the lone desert-bird that wears
   the ruff,
As signal we were safe, from time to
   time.

First he said, " If a friend declared
   to me,
This my son Valens, this my other
   son,
Were James and Peter, — nay, de-
   clared as well
This lad was very John, — I could
   believe !
—Could, for a moment, doubtlessly
   believe :
So is myself withdrawn into my
   depths,
The soul retreated from the perished
   brain
Whence it was wont to feel and use
   the world
Through these dull members, done
   with long ago.
Yet I myself remain ; I feel myself :
And there is nothing lost. Let be,
   a while !"

[This is the doctrine he was wont to
   teach.

How divers persons witness in each
   man,
Three souls which make up one soul :
   first, to wit,
A soul of each and all the bodily
   parts,
Seated therein, which works, and is
   what Does,
And has the use of earth, and ends
   the man
Downward : but, tending upward for
   advice,
Grows into, and again is grown into
By the next soul, which, seated in
   the brain,
Useth the first with its collected use,
And feeleth, thinketh, willeth, — is
   what Knows :
Which, duly tending upward in its
   turn,
Grows into, and again is grown into
By the last soul, that uses both the
   first,
Subsisting whether they assist or no,
And, constituting man's self, is what
   Is —
And leans upon the former, makes
   it play,
As that played off the first : and,
   tending up,
Holds, is upheld by, God, and ends
   the man
Upward in that dread point of inter-
   course,
Nor needs a place, for it returns to
   Him.
What Does, what Knows, what Is ;
   three souls, one man.
I give the glossa of Theotypas.]

And then, " A stick, once fire from
   end to end ;
Now, ashes save the tip that holds a
   spark !
Yet, blow the spark, it runs back,
   spreads itself
A little where the fire was ; thus I
   urge
The soul that served me, till it task
   once more
What ashes of my brain have kept
   their shape,
And these make effort on the last o'
   the flesh,
Trying to taste again the truth of
   things " —
(He smiled) — " their very superficial
   truth ;
As that ye are my sons, that it is long

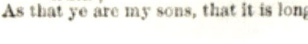

Since James and Peter had release
   by death,
And I am only he, your brother John,
Who saw and heard, and could re-
   member all.
Remember all! It is not much to say.
What if the truth broke on me from
   above
As once and ofttimes? Such might
   hap again;
Doubtlessly He might stand in pres-
   ence here,
With head wool-white, eyes, flame,
   and feet like brass,
The sword and the seven stars, as I
   have seen —
I who now shudder only and surmise
' How did your brother bear that sight
   and live?'

" If I live yet, it is for good, more love
Through me to men: be naught but
   ashes here
That keep a while my semblance, who
   was John,—
Still, when they scatter, there is left
   on earth
No one alive who knew (consider this!)
— Saw with his eyes and handled
   with his hands
That which was from the first, the
   Word of Life.
How will it be when none more saith
   ' I saw'?

" Such ever was love's way: to rise, it
   stoops.
Since I, whom Christ's mouth taught,
   was bidden teach,
I went, for many years, about the
   world,
Saying, ' It was so; so I heard and
   saw,'
Speaking as the case asked: and men
   believed.
Afterward came the message to my-
   self
In Patmos isle; I was not bidden
   teach,
But simply listen, take a book and
   write,
Nor set down other than the given
   word,
With nothing left to my arbitrament
To choose or change: I wrote, and
   men believed.
Then, for my time grew brief, no mes-
   sage more,
No call to write again, I found a way,

And, reasoning from my knowledge,
   merely taught
Men should, for love's sake, in love's
   strength, believe;
Or I would pen a letter to a friend
And urge the same as friend, nor less
   nor more:
Friends said I reasoned rightly, and
   believed.
But at the last, why, I seemed left
   alive
Like a sea-jelly weak on Patmos
   strand,
To tell dry sea-beach gazers how I
   fared
When there was mid-sea, and the
   mighty things;
Left to repeat, ' I saw, I heard, I
   knew,'
And go all over the old ground again,
With Antichrist already in the world.
And many Antichrists, who answered
   prompt
' Am I not Jaspar as thyself art John?
Nay, young, whereas through age thou
   mayest forget:
Wherefore, explain, or how shall we
   believe?'
I never thought to call down fire on
   such,
Or, as in wonderful and early days,
Pick up the scorpion, tread the serpent
   dumb;
But patient stated much of the Lord's
   life
Forgotten or misdelivered, and let it
   work:
Since much that at the first, in deed
   and word,
Lay simply and sufficiently exposed,
Had grown (or else my soul was grown
   to match,
Fed through such years, familiar with
   such light,
Guarded and guided still to see and
   speak)
Of new significance and fresh result;
What first were guessed as points, I
   now knew stars,
And named them in the Gospel I have
   writ.
For men said, ' It is getting long
   ago:'
' Where is the promise of His coming?'
   — asked
These young ones in their strength, as
   loth to wait,
Of me who, when their sires were
   born, was old.

I, for I loved them, answered, joy-
　fully,
Since I was there, and helpful in my
　age ;
And, in the main, I think such men
　believed.
Finally, thus endeavoring, I fell sick,
Ye brought me here, and I supposed
　the end,
And went to sleep with one thought
　that, at least,
Though the whole earth should lie in
　wickedness,
We had the truth, might leave the
　rest to God.
Yet now I wake in such decrepitude
As I had slidden down and fallen
　afar,
Past even the presence of my former
　self,
Grasping the while for stay at facts
　which snap,
Till I am found away from my own
　world.
Feeling for foot-hold through a blank
　profound,
Along with unborn people in strange
　lands,
Who say — I hear said or conceive
　they say —
'Was John at all, and did he say he
　saw ?
Assure us, ere we ask what he might
　see !'

"And how shall I assure them ? Can
　they share
— They, who have flesh, a veil of
　youth and strength
About each spirit, that needs must
　bide its time,
Living and learning still as years
　assist
Which wear the thickness thin, and
　let man see —
With me who hardly am withheld at
　all,
But shudderingly, scarce a shred be-
　tween,
Lie bare to the universal prick of
　light ?
Is it for nothing we grow old and
　weak,
We whom God loves ? When pain
　ends, gain ends too.
To me, that story — ay, that Life and
　Death
Of which I wrote 'it was'—to me, it
　is ;

— Is, here and now : I apprehend
　naught else.
Is not God now i' the world his power
　first made ?
Is not his love at issue still with sin,
Visibly when a wrong is done on
　earth ?
Love, wrong, and pain, what see I else
　around ?
Yea, and the Resurrection and Uprise
To the right hand of the throne — what
　is it beside,
When such truth, breaking bounds,
　o'erfloods my soul,
And, as I saw the sin and death, even
　so
See I the need yet transiency of both,
The good and glory consummated
　thence ?
I saw the Power ; I see the Love, once
　weak,
Resume the Power : and in this word
　' I see,'
Lo, there is recognized the Spirit of
　both
That moving o'er the spirit of man,
　unblinds
His eye and bids him look. These
　are, I see ;
But ye, the children, his beloved ones
　too,
Ye need, — as I should use an optic
　glass
I wondered at erewhile, somewhere i'
　the world,
It had been given a crafty smith to
　make ;
A tube, he turned on objects brought
　too close,
Lying confusedly insubordinate
For the unassisted eye to master
　once :
Look through his tube, at distance
　now they lay,
Become succinct, distinct, so small,
　so clear !
Just thus, ye needs must apprehend
　what truth
I see, reduced to plain historic fact,
Diminished into clearness, proved a
　point
And far away : ye would withdraw
　your sense
From out eternity, strain it upon
　time,
Then stand before that fact, that Life
　and Death,
Stay there at gaze, till it dispart, dis-
　pread,

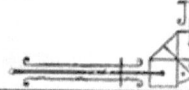

As though a star should open out, all
  sides,
Grow the world on you, as it is my
  world.
" For life, with all it yields of joy and
  woe,
And hope and fear, — believe the aged
  friend, —
Is just our chance o' the prize of
  learning love,
How love might be, hath been in-
  deed, and is ;
And that we hold thenceforth to the
  uttermost
Such prize despite the envy of the
  world,
And, having gained truth, keep truth :
  that is all.
But see the double way wherein we
  are led.
How the soul learns diversely from
  the flesh !
With flesh, that hath so little time to
  stay,
And yields more basement for the
  soul's emprize,
Expect prompt teaching. Helpful
  was the light,
And warmth was cherishing and food
  was choice
To every man's flesh, thousand years
  ago,
As now to yours and mine ; the body
  sprang
At once to the height, and stald :
  but the soul, — no !
Since sages who, this noontide, medi-
  tate
In Rome or Athens, may descry some
  point
Of the eternal power, hid yestereve :
And, as thereby the power's whole
  mass extends,
So much extends the ether floating
  o'er
The love that tops the might, the
  Christ in God.
Then, as new lessons shall be learned
  in these
Till earth's work stop and useless
  time run out,
So duly, daily, needs provision be
For keeping the soul's prowess pos-
  sible,
Building new barriers as the old de-
  cay,
Saving us from evasion of life's
  proof,

Putting the question ever, ' Does God
  love,
And will ye hold that truth against
  the world ? '
Ye know there needs no second proof
  with good
Gained for our flesh from any earthly
  source :
We might go freezing, ages, — give us
  fire,
Thereafter we judge fire at its full
  worth,
And guard it safe through every
  chance, ye know !
That fable of Prometheus and his
  theft,
How mortals gained Jove's fiery
  flower, grows old
(I have been used to hear the pagans
  own)
And out of mind ; but fire, howe'er
  its birth,
Here is it, precious to the sophist now
Who laughs the myth of Æschylus to
  scorn,
As precious to those satyrs of his
  play,
Who touched it in gay wonder at the
  thing.
While were it so with the soul, —
  this gift of truth
Once grasped, were this our soul's
  gain safe, and sure
To prosper as the body's gain is
  wont, —
Why, man's probation would con-
  clude, his earth
Crumble ; for he both reasons and
  decides,
Weighs first, then chooses : will he
  give up fire
For gold or purple once he knows its
  worth ?
Could he give Christ up were His
  worth as plain ?
Therefore, I say, to test man, the
  proofs shift,
Nor may he grasp that fact like other
  fact,
And straightway in his life acknowl-
  edge it,
As, say, the indubitable bliss of fire.
Sigh ye, ' It had been easier once than
  now ? '
To give you answer I am left alive ;
Look at me who was present from the
  first !
Ye know what things I saw ; then
  came a test,

My first, befitting me who so had
 seen :
'Forsake the Christ thou sawest trans-
 figured, Him
Who trod the sea and brought the
 dead to life ?
What should wring this from thee ? '
 — ye laugh and ask.
What wrung it ? Even a torchlight
 and a noise,
The sudden Roman faces, violent
 hands,
And fear of what the Jews might do !
 Just that,
And it is written, 'I forsook and
 fled : '
There was my trial, and it ended
 thus.
Ay, but my soul had gained its truth,
 could grow :
Another year or two, — what little
 child,
What tender woman that had seen no
 least
Of all my sights, but barely heard
 them told,
Who did not clasp the cross with a
 light laugh,
Or wrap the burning robe round,
 thanking God ?
Well, was truth safe forever, then ?
 Not so.
Already had begun the silent work
Whereby truth, deadened of its abso-
 lute blaze,
Might need love's eye to pierce the
 o'erstretched doubt.
Teachers were busy, whispering 'All
 is true
As the aged ones report ; but youth
 can reach
Where age gropes dimly, weak with
 stir and strain,
And the full doctrine slumbers till to-
 day.'
Thus, what the Roman's lowered
 spear was found,
A bar to me who touched and handled
 truth,
Now proved the glozing of some new
 shrewd tongue,
This Ebion, this Cerinthus or their
 mates,
Till imminent was the outcry 'Save
 our Christ !'
Whereon I stated much of the Lord's
 life
Forgotten or misdelivered, and let it
 work.

Such work done, as it will be, what
 comes next ?
What do I hear say, or conceive men
 say,
'Was John at all, and did he say he
 saw ?
Assure us, ere we ask what he might
 see ! '

" Is this indeed a burthen for late
 days,
And may I help to bear it with you
 all,
Using my weakness which becomes
 your strength ?
For if a babe were born inside this
 grot,
Grew to a boy here, heard us praise
 the sun,
Yet had but yon sole glimmer in
 light's place, —
One loving him and wishful he should
 learn,
Would much rejoice himself was
 blinded first
Month by month here, so made to
 understand
How eyes, born darkling, apprehend
 amiss :
I think I could explain to such a
 child
There was more glow outside than
 gleams he caught,
Ay, nor need urge 'I saw it, so be-
 lieve ! '
It is a heavy burthen you shall bear
In latter days, new lands, or old
 grown strange,
Left without me, which must be very
 soon.
What is the doubt, my brothers ?
 Quick with it !
I see you stand conversing, each new
 face,
Either in fields, of yellow summer
 eves,
On islets yet unnamed amid the sea ;
Or pace for shelter 'neath a portico
Out of the crowd in some enormous
 town
Where now the larks sing in a soli-
 tude ;
Or muse upon blank heaps of stone
 and sand
Idly conjectured to be Ephesus :
And no one asks his fellow any
 more
'Where is the promise of His com-
 ing ?' but

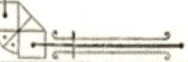
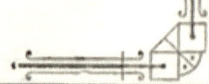

Was He revealed in any of His lives,
As Power, as Love, as Influencing Soul?'

"Quick, for time presses, tell the whole mind out,
And let us ask and answer and be saved!
My book speaks on, because it cannot pass;
One listens quietly, nor scoffs but pleads
'Here is a tale of things done ages since;
What truth was ever told the second day?
Wonders, that would prove doctrine, go for naught.
Remains the doctrine, love; well, we must love,
And what we love most, power and love in one,
Let us acknowledge on the record here,
Accepting these in Christ: must Christ then be?
Has He been? Did not we ourselves make Him?
Our mind receives but what it holds, no more.
First of the love, then; we acknowledge Christ—
A proof we comprehend His love, a proof
We had such love already in ourselves,
Knew first what else we should not recognize.
'Tis mere projection from man's inmost mind,
And, what he loves, thus falls reflected back,
Becomes accounted somewhat out of him;
He throws it up in air, it drops down earth's,
With shape, name, story added, man's old way.
How prove you Christ came otherwise at least?
Next try the power: He made and rules the world:
Certes there is a world once made, now ruled,
Unless things have been ever as we see.
Our sires declared a charioteer's yoked steeds

Brought the sun up the east and down the west,
Which only of itself now rises, sets,
As if a hand impelled it and a will,—
Thus they long thought, they who had will and hands;
But the new question's whisper is distinct,
Wherefore must all force needs be like ourselves?
We have the hands, the will; what made and drives
The sun is force, is law, is named, not known,
While will and love we do know; marks of these,
Eye-witnesses attest, so books declare—
As that, to punish or reward our race,
The sun at undue times arose or set
Or else stood still: what do not men affirm?
But earth requires as urgently reward
Or punishment to-day as years ago,
And none expects the sun will interpose:
Therefore it was mere passion and mistake,
Or erring zeal for right, which changed the truth.
Go back, far, farther, to the birth of things;
Ever the will, the intelligence, the love,
Man's!—which he gives, supposing he but finds,
As late he gave head, body, hands, and feet,
To help these in what forms he called his gods.
First, Jove's brow, Juno's eyes were swept away,
But Jove's wrath, Juno's pride continued long;
As last, will, power, and love discarded these,
So law in turn discards power, love, and will.
What proveth God is otherwise at least?
All else, projection from the mind of man!
Nay, do not give me wine, for I am strong,
But place my gospel where I put my hands.

"I say that man was made to grow, not stop;

That help, he needed once, and needs
  no more,
Having grown but an inch by, is
  withdrawn :
For he hath new needs, and new
  helps to these.
This imports solely, man should
  mount on each
New height in view ; the help where-
  by he mounts,
The ladder-rung his foot has left, may
  fall,
Since all things suffer change save
  God the Truth.
Man apprehends Him newly at each
  stage
Whereat earth's ladder drops, its ser-
  vice done ;
And nothing shall prove twice what
  once was proved.
You stick a garden-plot with ordered
  twigs
To show inside lie germs of herbs
  unborn,
And check the careless step would
  spoil their birth ;
But when herbs wave, the guardian
  twigs may go,
Since should ye doubt of virtues,
  question kinds,
It is no longer for old twigs ye look,
Which proved once underneath lay
  store of seed,
But to the herb's self, by what light
  ye boast,
For what fruit's signs are. This
  book's fruit is plain,
Nor miracles need prove it any more.
Doth the fruit show ? Then miracles
  bade 'ware
At first of root and stem, saved both
  till now
From trampling ox, rough boar, and
  wanton goat.
What ? Was man made a wheelwork
  to wind up,
And be discharged, and straight
  wound up anew ?
No !— grown, his growth lasts ;
  taught, he ne'er forgets :
May learn a thousand things, not
  twice the same.
This might be pagan teaching : now
  hear mine.

"I say, that as the babe, you feed a
  while,
Becomes a boy and fit to feed him-
  self,

So, minds at first must be spoon-fed
  with truth :
When they can eat, babe's nurture is
  withdrawn.
I fed the babe whether it would or
  no :
I bid the boy or feed himself or starve.
I cried once, 'That ye may believe in
  Christ,
Behold this blind man shall receive
  his sight !'
I cry now, 'Urgest thou, *for I am
  shrewd,*
*And smile at stories how John's word
  could cure —*
Repeat that miracle and take my faith?'
I say, that miracle was duly wrought
When, save for it, no faith was possi-
  ble.
Whether a change were wrought i'
  the shows o' the world,
Whether the change came from our
  minds which see
Of shows o' the world so much as
  and no more
Than God wills for His purpose, —
  (what do I
See now, suppose you, there where
  you see rock
Round us ?) — I know not ; such was
  the effect,
So faith grew, making void more
  miracles
Because too much : they would com-
  pel, not help.
I say, the acknowledgment of God in
  Christ
Accepted by thy reason, solves for
  thee
All questions in the earth and out of
  it,
And has so far advanced thee to be
  wise.
Wouldst thou unprove this to re-
  prove the proved?
In life's mere minute, with power to
  use that proof,
Leave knowledge and revert to how
  it sprung?
Thou hast it ; use it and forthwith, or
  die !
For I say, this is death and the sole
  death,
When a man's loss comes to him from
  his gain,
Darkness from light, from knowledge
  ignorance,
And lack of love from love made
  manifest :

A lamp's death when, replete with
   oil, it chokes ;
A stomach's when, surcharged with
   food, it starves.
With ignorance was surety of a cure.
When man, appalled at nature, ques-
   tioned first
'What if there lurk a might behind
   this might?'
He needed satisfaction God could
   give,
And did give, as ye have the written
   word :
But when he finds might still redouble
   might,
Yet asks, 'Since all is might, what
   use of will?'
— Will, the one source of might, — he
   being man
With a man's will and a man's might,
   to teach
In little how the two combine in
   large, —
That man has turned round on him-
   self and stands :
Which in the course of nature is, to
   die.

"And when man questioned, 'What
   if there be love
Behind the will and might, as real as
   they?' —
He needed satisfaction God could
   give,
And did give, as ye have the written
   word :
But when, beholding that love every-
   where,
He reasons, 'Since such love is every-
   where,
And since ourselves can love and
   would be loved,
We ourselves make the love, and
   Christ was not,' —
How shall ye help this man who
   knows himself,
That he must love and would be loved
   again,
Yet, owning his own love that proveth
   Christ,
Rejecteth Christ through very need of
   Him?
The lamp o'erswims with oil, the
   stomach flags
Loaded with nurture, and that man's
   soul dies.

'If he rejoin, 'But this was all the
   while

A trick : the fault was, first of all, in
   thee,
Thy story of the places, names and
   dates,
Where, when, and how the ultimate
   truth had rise,
— Thy prior truth, at last discovered
   none,
Whence now the second suffers detri-
   ment,
What good of giving knowledge if,
   because
O' the manner of the gift, its profit
   fail ?
And why refuse what modicum of
   help
Had stopped the after-doubt, impossi-
   ble
I' the face of truth — truth absolute,
   uniform ?
Why must I hit of this and miss of
   that,
Distinguish just as I be weak or
   strong,
And not ask of thee and have answer
   prompt,
Was this once, was it not once? —
   then and now
And evermore, plain truth from man
   to man.
Is John's procedure just the heathen
   bard's ?
Put question of his famous play again
How for the ephemerals' sake, Jove's
   fire was filched,
And carried in a cane and brought to
   earth :
The fact is in the fable, cry the wise,
*Mortals obtained the boon, so much is
   fact,*
*Though five be spirit and produced on
   earth.*
As with the Titan's, so now with thy
   tale :
Why breed in us perplexity, mistake,
Nor tell the whole truth in the proper
   words ?'

"I answer, Have ye yet to argue out
The very primal thesis, plainest law,
— Man is not God but hath God's end
   to serve,
A master to obey, a course to take,
Somewhat to cast off, somewhat to
   become ?
Grant this, then man must pass from
   old to new,
From vain to real, from mistake to
   fact,

From what once seemed good, to what now proves good,
How could man have progression otherwise?
Before the point was mooted 'What is God?'
No savage man inquired 'What is myself?'
Much less replied, 'First, last, and best of things.'
Man takes that title now if he believes
Might can exist with neither will nor love,
In God's case — what he names now Nature's Law —
While in himself he recognizes love
No less than might and will: and rightly takes.
Since if man prove the sole existent thing
Where these combine, whatever their degree,
However weak the might or will or love,
So they be found there, put in evidence, —
He is as surely higher in the scale
Than any might with neither love nor will,
As life, apparent in the poorest midge
(When the faint dust-speck flits, ye guess its wing),
Is marvellous beyond dead Atlas' self —
Given to the nobler midge for resting-place!
Thus, man proves best and highest — God, in fine,
And thus the victory leads but to defeat,
The gain to loss, best rise to the worst fall,
His life becomes impossible, which is death.

"But if, appealing thence, he cower, avouch
He is mere man, and in humility
Neither may know God nor mistake himself;
I point to the immediate consequence
And say, by such confession straight he falls
Into man's place, a thing nor God nor beast,
Made to know that he can know and not more:
Lower than God who knows all and can all,

Higher than beasts which know and can so far
As each beast's limit, perfect to an end,
Nor conscious that they know, nor craving more;
While man knows partly but conceives beside,
Creeps ever on from fancies to the fact,
And in this striving, this converting air
Into a solid he may grasp and use,
Finds progress, man's distinctive mark alone,
Not God's, and not the beasts': God is, they are,
Man partly is and wholly hopes to be.
Such progress could no more attend his soul
Were all it struggles after found at first
And guesses changed to knowledge absolute,
Than motion wait his body, were all else
Than it the solid earth on every side,
Where now through space he moves from rest to rest.
Man, therefore, thus conditioned, must expect
He could not, what he knows now, know at first;
What he considers that he knows to-day,
Come but to-morrow, he will find mis-known;
Getting increase of knowledge, since he learns
Because he lives, which is to be a man,
Set to instruct himself by his past self:
First, like the brute, obliged by facts to learn,
Next, as man may, obliged by his own mind,
Bent, habit, nature, knowledge turned to law.
God's gift was that man should conceive of truth,
And yearn to gain it, catching at mistake,
As midway help till he reach fact indeed.
The statuary ere he mould a shape
Boasts a like gift, the shape's idea, and next
The aspiration to produce the same

So, taking clay, he calls his shape
    thereout,
Cries ever 'Now I have the thing I
    see;'
Yet all the while goes changing what
    was wrought,
From falsehood like the truth, to
    truth itself.
How were it had he cried 'I see no
    face,
No breast, no feet i' the ineffectual
    clay?'
Rather commend him that he clapped
    his hands,
And laughed 'It is my shape and
    lives again!'
Enjoyed the falsehood, touched it on
    to truth,
Until yourselves applaud the flesh
    indeed
In what is still flesh-imitating clay.
Right in you, right in him, such way
    be man's!
God only makes the live shape at a
    jet.
Will ye renounce this pact of crea-
    tureship?
The pattern on the Mount subsists no
    more,
Seemed a while, then returned to
    nothingness;
But copies, Moses strove to make
    thereby,
Serve still and are replaced as time
    requires:
By these, make newest vessels, reach
    the type!
If ye demur, this judgment on your
    head,
Never to reach the ultimate, angels'
    law,
Indulging every instinct of the soul
There where law, life, joy, impulse
    are one thing!

"Such is the burthen of the latest
    time.
I have survived to hear it with my
    ears,
Answer it with my lips: does this
    suffice?
For if there be a further woe than
    such,
Wherein my brothers struggling need
    a hand,
So long as any pulse is left in mine,
May I be absent even longer yet,
Plucking the blind ones back from
    the abyss,

Though I should tarry a new hun-
    dred years!"

But he was dead: 'twas about noon,
    the day
Somewhat declining: we five buried
    him
That eve, and then, dividing, went
    five ways,
And I, disguised, returned to Ephe-
    sus.

By this, the cave's mouth must be
    filled with sand.
Valens is lost, I know not of his
    trace;
The Bactrian was but a wild childish
    man,
And could not write nor speak, but
    only loved:
So, lest the memory of this go quite,
Seeing that I to-morrow fight the
    beasts,
I tell the same to Phœbas, whom I
    believe!
For many look again to find that face,
Beloved John's to whom I minis-
    tered,
Somewhere in life about the world;
    they err:
Either mistaking what was darkly
    spoke
At ending of his book, as he relates,
Or misconceiving somewhat of this
    speech
Scattered from mouth to mouth, as I
    suppose.
Believe ye will not see him any more
About the world with his divine re-
    gard!
For all was as I say, and now the
    man
Lies as he lay once, breast to breast
    with God.

[Cerinthus read and mused; one
    added this:—

"If Christ, as thou affirmest, be of
    men
Mere man, the first and best but
    nothing more,—
Account Him, for reward of what He
    was,
Now and forever, wretchedest of all.
For see; Himself conceived of life as
    love,

Conceived of love as what must enter in,
Fill up, make one with His each soul He loved :
Thus much for man's joy, all men's joy for Him.
Well, He is gone, thou sayest, to fit reward.
But by this time are many souls set free,
And very many still retained alive :
Nay, should His coming be delayed a while,
Say, ten years longer (twelve years, some compute)
See if, for every finger of thy hands,
There be not found, that day the world shall end,
Hundreds of souls, each holding by Christ's word
That He will grow incorporate with all,
With me as Pamphylax, with him as John,
Groom for each bride! Can a mere man do this?
Yet Christ saith, this He lived and died to do.
Call Christ, then, the illimitable God, Or lost !"

But 'twas Cerinthus that is lost.]

FEARS AND SCRUPLES.

I.

HERE's my case. Of old I used to love him,
　This same unseen friend, before I knew :
Dream there was none like him, none above him, —
　Wake to hope and trust my dream was true.

II.

Loved I not his letters full of beauty?
　Not his actions famous far and wide?
Absent, he would know I vowed him duty ;
　Present, he would find me at his side.

III.

Pleasant fancy ! for I had but letters,
　Only knew of actions by hearsay :
He himself was busied with my betters ; ′
　What of that ? My turn must come some day.

IV.

" Some day " proving — no day !
　Here's the puzzle.
Passed and passed my turn is. Why complain?
He's so busied ! If I could but muzzle
People's foolish mouths that give me pain !

V.

" Letters ?" (hear them !) " You a judge of writing?
　Ask the experts ! How they shake the head
O'er these characters, your friend's inditing —
　Call them forgery from A to Z !

VI.

" Actions? Where's your certain proof" (they bother)
" He, of all you find so great and good,
He, he only, claims this, that, the other
Action — claimed by men, a multitude ?"

VII.

I can simply wish I might refute you,
　Wish my friend would, — by a word, a wink, —
Bid me stop that foolish mouth, — you brute you !
　He keeps absent, — why, I cannot think.

VIII.

Never mind ! Though foolishness may flout me,
　One thing's sure enough : 'tis neither frost,
No, nor fire, shall freeze or burn from out me
　Thanks for truth — though falsehood, gained — though lost.

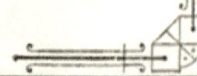

IX.

All my days, I'll go the softlier, sad-
ller,
  For that dream's sake! How for-
get the thrill
Through and through me as I thought
  " The gladlier
Lives my friend because I love him
  still ! "

X.

Ah, but there's a menace some one
  utters !
  " What and if your friend at home
play tricks ?
Peep at hide-and-seek behind the
  shutters ?
Mean your eyes should pierce
  through solid bricks ?

XI.

" What and if he, frowning, wake
  you, dreamy
Lay on you the blame that bricks—
  conceal ?
Say ' *At least I saw who did not see me,
Does see now, and presently shall
feel.*' "

XII.

" Why, that makes your friend a
  monster ! " say you :
Had his house no window ? At
  first nod,
Would you not have hailed him ? "
  Hush, I pray you !
What if this friend happen to be—
  God ?

ARTEMIS PROLOGIZES.

I am a goddess of the ambrosial
  courts,
And save by Here, Queen of Pride,
  surpassed
By none whose temples whiten this
  the world.
Through heaven I roll my lucid moon
  along ;
I shed in hell o'er my pale people
  peace ;
On earth I, caring for the creatures,
  guard
Each pregnant yellow wolf and fox-
  bitch sleek,

And every feathered mother's cal-
  low brood,
And all that love green haunts and
  loneliness.
Of men, the chaste adore me, hang-
  ing crowns
Of poppies red to blackness, bell and
  stem,
Upon my image at Athenai here ;
And this dead Youth, Asclepios bends
  above,
Was dearest to me. He, my bus-
  kined step
To follow through the wild-wood
  leafy ways,
And chase the panting stag, or swift
  with darts
Stop the swift ounce, or lay the leop-
  ard low,
Neglected homage to another god :
Whence Aphrodite, by no midnight
  smoke
Of tapers lulled, in jealousy de-
  spatched
A noisome lust that, as the gadbee
  stings,
Possessed his stepdame Phaidra for
  himself
The son of Theseus her great absent
  spouse.
Hippolutos exclaiming in his rage
Against the fury of the Queen, she
  judged
Life insupportable ; and, pricked at
  heart
An Amazonian stranger's race should
  dare
To scorn her, perished by the murder-
  ous cord :
Yet, ere she perished, blasted in a
  scroll
The fame of him her swerving made
  not swerve.
And Theseus, read, returning, and
  believed,
And exiled, in the blindness of his
  wrath,
The man without a crime who, last as
  first,
Loyal, divulged not to his sire the
  truth.
Now Theseus from Poseidon had ob-
  tained
That of his wishes should be granted
  three,
And one he imprecated straight—
  " Alive
May ne'er Hippolutos reach other
  lands ! "

Poseidon heard, ai ai! And searce
    the prince
Had stepped into the fixed boots of
    the car
That give the feet a stay against the
    strength
Of the Henetian horses, and around
His body flung the rein, and urged
    their speed
Along the rocks and shingles of the
    shore,
When from the gaping wave a mon-
    ster flung
His obscene body in the coursers'
    path.
These, mad with terror, as the sea-
    bull sprawled
Wallowing about their feet, lost care
    of him
That reared them ; and the master-
    chariot-pole
Snapping beneath their plunges like a
    reed,
Hippolutos, whose feet were tram-
    melled fast,
Was yet dragged forward by the
    circling rein
Which either hand directed ; nor they
    quenched
The frenzy of their flight before each
    trace,
Wheel-spoke and splinter of the woe-
    ful car,
Each bowlder-stone, sharp stub, and
    spiny shell,
Huge fish-bone wrecked and wreathed
    amid the sands
On that detested beach, was bright
    with blood
And morsels of his flesh : then fell the
    steeds
Head-foremost, crashing in their
    mooned fronts,
Shivering with sweat, each white eye
    horror-fixed.
His people, who had witnessed all
    afar,
Bore back the ruins of Hippolutos.
But when his sire, too swoln with
    pride, rejoiced
(Indomitable as a man foredoomed)
That vast Poseidon had fulfilled his
    prayer,
I, in a flood of glory visible,
Stood o'er my dying votary, and, deed
By deed, revealed, as all took place,
    the truth.
Then Theseus lay the woefullest of
    men,

And worthily ; but ere the death-veils
    hid
His face, the murdered prince full
    pardon breathed
To his rash sire. Whereat Athenai
    wails.

So I, who ne'er forsake my votaries,
Lest to the cross-way none the honey-
    cake
Should tender, nor pour out the dog's
    hot life ;
Lest at my fane the priests disconso-
    late
Should dress my image with some
    faded poor
Few crowns, made favors of, nor dare
    object
Such slackness to my worshippers who
    turn
Elsewhere the trusting heart and
    loaded hand,
As they had climbed Olumpos to re-
    port
Of Artemis and nowhere found her
    throne—
I interposed : and, this eventful
    night—
(While round the funeral pyre the
    populace
Stood with fierce light on their black
    robes which bound
Each sobbing head, while yet their
    hair they clipped
O'er the dead body of their withered
    prince,
And, in his palace, Theseus prostrated
On the cold hearth, his brow cold as
    the slab
'Twas bruised on, groaned away the
    heavy grief—
As the pyre fell, and down the cross
    logs crashed
Sending a crowd of sparkles through
    the night,
And the gay fire, elate with mastery,
Towered like a serpent o'er the clotted
    jars
Of wine, dissolving oils and frankin-
    cense,
And splendid gums like gold), — my
    potency
Conveyed the perished man to my re-
    treat
In the thrice-venerable forest here.
And this white-bearded sage who
    squeezes now
The berried plant, is Phoibos' son of
    fame,

Asclepios, whom my radiant brother taught
The doctrine of each herb and flower and root,
To know their secret'st virtue and express
The saving soul of all : who so has soothed
With lavers the torn brow and murdered cheeks,
Composed the hair and brought its gloss again,
And called the red bloom to the pale skin back,
And laid the strips and jagged ends of flesh
Even once more, and slacked the sinew's knot
Of every tortured limb — that now he lies

As if mere sleep possessed him underneath
These interwoven oaks and pines.
Oh cheer,
Divine presenter of the healing rod,
Thy snake, with ardent throat and lulling eye,
Twines his lithe spires around ! I say, much cheer !
Proceed thou with thy wisest pharmacies !
And ye, white crowd of woodland sister-nymphs,
Ply, as the sage directs, these buds and leaves
That strew the turf around the twain !
While I
Await, in fitting silence, the event.

PHEIDIPPIDES.

χαίρετε, νικῶμεν.

FIRST I salute this soil of the blessed, river and rock !
Gods of my birthplace, demons and heroes, honor to all !
Then I name thee, claim thee for our patron, co-equal in praise
— Ay, with Zeus the Defender, with Her of the ægis and spear !
Also, ye of the bow and the buskin, praised be your peer,
Now, henceforth, and forever, — O latest to whom I upraise
Hand and heart and voice ! For Athens, leave pasture and flock !
Present to help, potent to save, Pan — patron I call !

Archons of Athens, topped by the tettix, see, I return !
See, 'tis myself here standing alive, no spectre that speaks !
Crowned with the myrtle, did you command me, Athens and you,
" Run, Pheidippides, run and race, reach Sparta for aid !
Persia has come, we are here, where is She ?" Your command I obeyed,
Ran and raced : like stubble, some field which a fire runs through,
Was the space between city and city : two days, two nights did I burn
Over the hills, under the dales, down pits and up peaks.

Into their midst I broke : breath served but for " Persia has come !
Persia bids Athens proffer slaves'-tribute, water and earth ;
Razed to the ground is Eretria — but Athens, shall Athens sink,
Drop into dust and die — the flower of Hellas utterly die,
Die, with the wide world spitting at Sparta, the stupid, the stander-by ?
Answer me quick, what help, what hand do you stretch o'er destruction's brink ?
How, — when ? No care for my limbs ! — there's lightning in all and some —
Fresh and fit your message to bear, once lips give it birth !"

O my Athens — Sparta love thee ? Did Sparta respond ?
Every face of her leered in a furrow of envy, mistrust,

Malice, — each eye of her gave me its glitter of gratified hate!
Gravely they turned to take counsel, to cast for excuses. I stood
Quivering, — the limbs of me fretting as fire frets, an inch from dry wood;
" Persia has come, Athens asks aid, and still they debate?
Thunder, thou Zeus ! Athene, are Spartans a quarry beyond
Swing of thy spear? Phoibos and Artemis, clang them ' Ye must ' ! "

No bolt launched from Olumpos ! Lo, their answer at last !
" Has Persia come, — does Athens ask aid, — may Sparta befriend?
Nowise precipitate judgment — too weighty the issue at stake !
Count we no time lost time which lags through respect to the Gods !
Ponder that precept of old, ' No warfare, whatever the odds
In your favor, so long as the moon, half-orbed, is unable to take
Full-circle her state in the sky ! ' Already she rounds to it fast:
Athens must wait, patient as we — who judgment suspend."

Athens, — except for that sparkle, — thy name, I had mouldered to ash !
That sent a blaze through my blood ; off, off and away was I back,
— Not one word to waste, one look to lose on the false and the vile !
Yet " O Gods of my land ! " I cried, as each hillock and plain,
Wood and stream, I knew, I named, rushing past them again,
" Have ye kept faith, proved mindful of honors we paid you erewhile?
Vain was the filleted victim, the fulsome libation ! Too rash
Love in its choice, paid you so largely service so slack !

" Oak and olive and bay, — I bid you cease to inwreathe
Brows made bold by your leaf ! Fade at the Persian's foot,
You that, our patrons were pledged, should never adorn a slave !
Rather I hail thee, Parnes, — trust to thy wild waste tract !
Treeless, herbless, lifeless mountain ! What matter if slacked
My speed may hardly be, for homage to crag and to cave
No deity deigns to drape with verdure, — at least I can breathe,
Fear in thee no fraud from the blind, no lie from the mute ! "

Such my cry as, rapid, I ran over Parnes' ridge ;
Gully and gap, I clambered and cleared till, sudden, bar
Jutted, a stoppage of stone against me, blocking the way.
Right ! for I minded the hollow to traverse, the fissure across :
" Where I could enter, there I depart by ! Night in the fosse?
Out of the day dive, into the day as bravely arise ! No bridge
Better ! " — when — ha ! what was it I came on, of wonders that are?

There, in the cool of a cleft, sat he — majestical Pan !
Ivy drooped wanton, kissed his head, moss cushioned his hoof :
All the great God was good in the eyes grave-kindly — the curl
Carved on the bearded cheek, amused at a mortal's awe,
As, under the human trunk, the goat-thighs grand I saw.
" Halt, Pheidippides ! " — halt I did, my brain of a whirl :
" Hither to me ! Why pale in my presence ? " he gracious began :
" How is it, — Athens, only in Hellas, holds me aloof !

" Athens, she only, rears me no fane, makes me no feast !
Wherefore ? Than I what godship to Athens more helpful of old ?
Ay, and still, and forever her friend ! Put Pan to the test !
Go, bid Athens take heart, laugh Persia to scorn, have faith
In the temples and tombs ! Go, say to Athens, ' The Goat-God saith :
When Persia — so much as strews not the soil — is cast in the sea,
Then praise Pan who fought in the ranks with your most and least,
Goat-thigh to greaved-thigh, made one cause with the free and the bold ! '

"Say Pan saith : ' Let this, foreshowing the place, be the pledge ! ' "
(Gay, the liberal hand held out this herbage I bear
—Fennel, whatever it bode — I grasped it a-tremble with dew.)
"While, as for thee . . . ." But enough ! He was gone. If I ran hither
        to —
Be sure that, the rest of my journey, I ran no longer, but flew.
Here am I back. Praise Pan, we stand no more on the razor's edge !
Pan for Athens, Pan for me ! myself have a guerdon rare !

Then spoke Miltiades. "And thee, best runner of Greece,
Whose limbs did duty indeed, — what gift is promised thyself ?
Tell it us straightway, — Athens the mother demands of her son !"
Rosily blushed the youth : he paused ; but, lifting at length
His eyes from the ground, it seemed as he gathered the rest of his strength
Into the utterance —" Pan spoke thus : ' For what thou hast done
Count on a worthy reward ! Henceforth be allowed thee release
From the racer's toil, no vulgar reward in praise or in pelf !'

"I am bold to believe, Pan means reward the most to my mind !
Fight I shall, with our foremost, wherever this fennel may grow, —
Pound — Pan helping us — Persia to dust, and, under the deep,
Whelm her away forever ; and then, — no Athens to save, —
Marry a certain maid, I know keeps faith to the brave, —
He to my house and home : and, when my children shall creep
Close to my knees, — recount how the God was awful yet kind,
Promised their sire reward to the full — rewarding him — so !"

Unforeseeing one ! Yes, he fought on the Marathon day :
So, when Persia was dust, all cried "To Akropolis !
Run, Pheidippides, one race more ! the meed is thy due !
'Athens is saved, thank Pan,' go shout !" He flung down his shield,
Ran like fire once more ; and the space 'twixt the Fennel-field
And Athens was stubble again, a field which a fire runs through,
Till in he broke : "Rejoice, we conquer !" Like wine through clay,
Joy in his blood bursting his heart, he died — the bliss !

So, to this day, when friend meets friend, the word of salute
Is still "Rejoice !" — his word which brought rejoicing indeed.
So is Pheidippides happy forever, — the noble strong man
Who could race like a God, bear the face of a God, whom a God loved so
        well
He saw the land saved he had helped to save, and was suffered to tell
Such tidings, yet never decline, but, gloriously as he began,
So to end gloriously — once to shout, thereafter be mute :
"Athens is saved !" — Pheidippides dies in the shout for his meed.

THE PATRIOT.

AN OLD STORY.

I.

IT was roses, roses, all the way,
With myrtle mixed in my path like
    mad:
The house-roofs seemed to heave and
    sway,
The church-spires flamed, such flags
    they had,
A year ago on this very day.

II.

The air broke into a mist with bells,
    The old walls rocked with the crowd
    and cries.
Had I said, "Good folk, mere noise
    repels—
But give me your sun from yonder
    skies!"
They had answered "And afterward,
    what else?"

III.

Alack, it was I who leaped at the sun
To give it my loving friends to
    keep!
Naught man could do, have I left un-
    done:
And you see my harvest, what I
    reap
This very day, now a year is run.

IV.

There's nobody on the house-tops
    now—
Just a palsied few at the windows
    set;
For the best of the sight is, all allow,
At the Shambles' Gate—or, better
    yet,
By the very scaffold's foot, I trow.

V.

I go in the rain, and, more than
    needs,
A rope cuts both my wrists behind;
And I think, by the feel, my forehead
    bleeds,
For they fling, whoever has a mind,
Stones at me for my year's misdeeds.

VI.

Thus I entered, and thus I go!
    In triumphs, people have dropped
    down dead,
"Paid by the world, what dost thou
    owe
    Me?"—God might question; now
    instead,
'Tis God shall repay: I am safer so.

POPULARITY.

I.

STAND still, true poet that you are!
I know you; let me try and draw
    you.
Some night you'll fail us: when afar
You rise, remember one man saw
    you,
Knew you, and named a star!

II.

My star, God's glow-worm! Why
    extend
That loving hand of His which leads
    you,
Yet locks you safe from end to end
    Of this dark world, unless He needs
    you,
Just saves your light to spend?

III.

His clinched hand shall unclose at
    last,
I know, and let out all the beauty:
My poet holds the future fast,
    Accepts the coming ages' duty,
Their present for this past.

IV.

That day, the earth's feast-master's
    brow
    Shall clear, to God the chalice rais-
    ing:
"Others give best at first, but Thou
    Forever set'st our table praising,
Keep'st the good wine till now!"

V.

Meantime, I'll draw you as you stand,
    With few or none to watch and
    wonder:

I'll say — a fisher, on the sand
  By Tyre the old, with ocean-plun-
    der,
A netful, brought to land.

VI.

Who has not heard how Tyrian shells
  Enclosed the blue, that dye of dyes
Whereof one drop worked miracles,
  And colored like Astarte's eyes
Raw silk the merchant sells?

VII.

And each by-stander of them all
  Could criticise, and quote tradition
How depths of blue sublimed some
    pall
  --To get which, pricked a king's
    ambition;
Worth sceptre, crown, and ball.

VIII.

Yet there's the dye, in that rough
    mesh,
  The sea has only just o'er-whis-
    pered!
Live whelks, each lip's beard dripping
    fresh,
  As if they still the water's lisp
    heard
Through foam the rock-weeds thresh.

IX.

Enough to furnish Solomon
  Such hangings for his cedar-house,
That, when gold-robed he took the
    throne
  In that abyss of blue, the Spouse
Might swear his presence shone

X.

Most like the centre-spike of gold
  Which burns deep in the blue-bell's
    womb
What time, with ardors manifold,
  The bee goes singing to her groom,
Drunken and overbold.

XI.

Mere conchs! not fit for warp or
    woof!
  Till cunning come to pound and
    squeeze
And clarify, — refine to proof
  The liquor filtered by degrees,
While the world stands aloof.

XII.

And there's the extract, flasked and
    fine,
  And priced and salable at last!
And Hobbs, Nobbs, Stokes, and Nokes
    combine
  To paint the future from the past,
Put blue into their line.

XIII.

Hobbs hints blue, — straight he turtle
    eats:
  Nobbs prints blue, — claret crowns
    his cup:
Nokes outdares Stokes in azure
    feats, —
  Both gorge. Who fished the murex
    up?
What porridge had John Keats?

PISGAH-SIGHTS. 1.

I.

Over the ball of it,
  Peering and prying,
How I see all of it,
  Life there, outlying!
Roughness and smoothness,
  Shine and defilement,
Grace and uncouthness;
  One reconcilement.

II.

Orbed as appointed,
  Sister with brother
Joins, ne'er disjointed
  One from the other.
All's lend-and-borrow;
  Good, see, wants evil,
Joy demands sorrow,
  Angel weds devil!

III.

"Which things must — *why* be?"
  Vain our endeavor!
So shall things aye be
  As they were ever.
"Such things should *so* be!"
  Sage our desistence!
Rough-smooth let globe be,
  Mixed — man's existence!

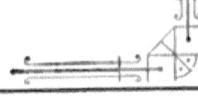

IV.

Man — wise and foolish,
  Lover and scorner,
Docile and mulish —
  Keep each his corner!
Honey yet gall of it!
  There's the life lying,
And I see all of it,
  Only, I'm dying!

PISGAH—SIGHTS. 2.

I.

Could I but live again,
  Twice my life over,
Would I once strive again?
  Would not I cover
Quietly all of it —
  Greed and ambition —
So, from the pall of it,
  Pass to fruition?

II.

"Soft!" I'd say, "Soul mine!
  Threescore and ten years,
Let the blind mole mine
  Digging out deniers!
Let the dazed hawk soar,
  Claim the sun's rights too!
Turf 'tis thy walk's o'er,
  Foliage thy flight's to."

III.

Only a learner,
  Quick one or slow one,
Just a discerner,
  I would teach no one.
I am earth's native:
  No re-arranging it!
I be creative,
  Chopping and changing it?

IV.

March, men, my fellows!
  Those who, above me
(Distance so mellows),
  Fancy you love me:
Those who, below me
  (Distance makes great so),
Free to forego me,
  Fancy you hate so!

V.

Praising, reviling,
  Worst head and best head,
Past me defiling,
  Never arrested,
Wanters, abounders,
  March, in gay mixture,
Men, my surrounders!
  I am the fixture.

VI.

So shall I fear thee,
  Mightiness yonder!
Mock-sun — more near thee,
  What is to wonder?
So shall I love thee,
  Down in the dark, — lest
Glowworm I prove thee,
  Star that now sparklest!

PISGAH—SIGHTS. 3.

I.

Good, to forgive;
  Best, to forget!
Living, we fret;
  Dying, we live.
Fretless and free,
  Soul, clap thy pinion!
Earth have dominion,
  Body, o'er thee!

II.

Wander at will,
  Day after day, —
  Wander away,
Wandering still —
  Soul that canst soar!
Body may slumber:
  Body shall cumber
Soul-flight no more.

III.

Waft of soul's wing!
  What lies above?
Sunshine and Love,
  Skyblue and Spring!
Body hides — where?
  Ferns of all feather,
Mosses and heather,
  Yours be the care!

AT THE "MERMAID."

The figure that thou here seest . . . Tut!
Was it for gentle Shakspeare put?
　　　　B. JONSON. (*Adapted.*)

I.

I—"Next Poet?" No, my hearties,
　I nor am nor fain would be!
Choose your chiefs and pick your
　　parties,
　Not one soul revolt to me!
I, forsooth, sow song-sedition?
　I, a schism in verse provoke?
I, blown up by bard's ambition,
　Burst — your bubble-king? You
　　joke.

II.

Come, be grave! The sherris man-
　　tling
　Still about each mouth, mayhap,
Breeds you insight — just a scant-
　　ling —
　Brings me truth out — just a scrap.
Look and tell me! Written, spoken,
　Here's my life-long work: and
　　where
— Where's your warrant or my token
　I'm the dead king's son and heir?

III.

Here's my work: does work discover
　What was rest from work — my
　　life?
Did I live man's hater, lover?
　Leave the world at peace, at strife?
Call earth ugliness or beauty?
　See things there in large or small?
Use to pay its Lord my duty?
　Use to own a lord at all?

IV.

Blank of such a record, truly,
　Here's the work I hand, this scroll,
Yours to take or leave; as duly,
　Mine remains the unproffered soul.
So much, no whit more, my debtors —
　How should one like me lay claim
To that largess elders, betters
　Sell you cheap their souls for —
　　fame?

V.

Which of you did I enable
Once to slip inside my breast
There to catalogue and label
　What I like least, what love best,

Hope and fear, believe and doubt of,
　Seek and shun, respect — deride?
Who has right to make a rout of
　Rarities he found inside?

VI.

Rarities or, as he'd rather,
　Rubbish such as stocks his own:
Need and greed (oh strange!) the
　　Father
　Fashioned not for him alone!
Whence — the comfort set a-strutting,
　Whence — the outcry "Haste, be-
　　hold!
Bard's breast open wide, past shut-
　　ting,
　Shows what brass we took for
　　gold!"

VII.

Friends, I doubt not he'd display you
　Brass — myself call oreichalch, —
Furnish much amusement; pray you
　Therefore, be content I balk
Him and you, and bar my portal!
　Here's my work outside; opine
What's inside me mean and mortal!
　Take your pleasure, leave me mine!

VIII.

Which is — not to buy your laurel
　As last king did, nothing loth,
Tale adorned and pointed moral
　Gained him praise and pity both,
Out rushed sighs and groans by
　　dozens,
　Forth by scores oaths, curses flew:
Proving you were cater-cousins,
　Kith and kindred, king and you!

IX.

Whereas do I ne'er so little
　(Thanks to sherris) leave ajar
Bosom's gate — no jot nor tittle
　Grow we nearer than we are.
Sinning, sorrowing, despairing,
　Body-ruined, spirit-wrecked, —
Should I give my woes an airing, —
　Where's one plague that claims
　　respect?

X.

Have you found your life distasteful?
　My life did and does smack sweet.
Was your youth of pleasure waste-
　　ful?
　Mine I saved and hold complete.

Do your joys with age diminish?
When mine fail me, I'll complain.
Must in death your daylight finish?
My sun sets to rise again.

XI.

What, like you, he proved — your
   Pilgrim —
This our world a wilderness,
Earth still gray and heaven still
   grim,
Not a hand there his might press,
Not a heart his own might throb to,
Men all rogues and women — say,
Dolls which boys' heads duck and bob
   to,
Grown folk drop or throw away?

XII.

My experience being other,
   How should I contribute verse
Worthy of your king and brother?
   Balaam-like I bless, not curse.
I find earth not gray but rosy,
   Heaven not grim but fair of hue.
Do I stoop? I pluck a posy.
   Do I stand and stare? All's blue.

XIII.

Doubtless I am pushed and shoved
   by
Rogues and fools enough: the more
Good luck mine, I love, am loved by
   Some few honest to the core.
Scan the near high, scout the far low!
   "But the low come close:" what
     then?
Simpletons? My match is Marlowe;
   Sciolists? My mate is Ben.

XIV.

Womankind — "the cat-like nature,
   False and fickle, vain and weak" —
Scarcely this sad nomenclature
   Suits my tongue, if I must speak.
Does the sex invite, repulse so,
   Tempt, betray, by fits and starts?
So becalm but to convulse so,
   Decking heads and breaking hearts?

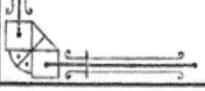

XV.

Well may you blaspheme at fortune!
   I "threw Venus" (Ben, expound!)
Never did I need importune
   Her, of all the Olympian round.

Blessings on my benefactress!
   Cursings suit — for aught I know —
Those who twitched her by the back
     tress,
   Tugged and thought to turn her —
     so!

XVI.

Therefore, since no leg to stand on
   Thus I'm left with, — joy or grief
Be the issue, — I abandon
   Hope or care you name me Chief!
Chief and king and Lord's anointed,
   I? — who never once have wished
Death before the day appointed:
   Lived and liked, not poohed and
     pished!

XVII.

"Ah, but so I shall not enter,
   Scroll in hand, the common heart —
Stopped at surface: since at centre
   Song should reach *Welt-schmerz*,
     world-smart!"
"Enter in the heart?" Its shelly
   Cuirass guard mine, fore and aft!
Such song "enters in the belly
   And is cast out in the draught."

XVIII.

Back then to our sherris-brewage!
   "Kingship" quotha? I shall wait —
Waive the present time: some new
     age . . .
But let fools anticipate!
Meanwhile greet me — "friend, good
     fellow,
   Gentle Will," my merry men!
As for making Envy yellow
   With "Next Poet" — (Manners,
     Ben!)

HOUSE.

I.

Shall I sonnet-sing you about my-
    self?
   Do I live in a house you would like
    to see?
Is it scant of gear, has it store of pelf?
   "Unlock my heart with a sonnet-
    key?"

II.

Invite the world, as my betters have
  done?
  "Take notice: this building re-
    mains on view,
Its suites of reception every one,
  Its private apartment and bedroom
    too;

III.

"For a ticket, apply to the Publish-
  er."
  No: thanking the public, I must
    decline.
A peep through my window, if folks
    prefer;
  But, please you, no foot over thresh-
    old of mine!

IV.

I have mixed with a crowd and heard
    free talk
  In a foreign land where an earth-
    quake chanced
And a house stood gaping, naught to
    balk
  Man's eye wherever he gazed or
    glanced.

V.

The whole of the frontage shaven
    sheer,
  The inside gaped: exposed to day,
Right and wrong and common and
    queer.
  Bare, as the palm of your hand, it
    lay.

VI.

The owner? Oh, he had been crushed,
    no doubt!
  "Odd tables and chairs for a man
    of wealth!
What a parcel of musty old books
    about!
  He smoked,—no wonder he lost
    his health!

VII.

"I doubt if he bathed before he
    dressed.
  A brazier?—the pagan, he burned
    perfumes!
You see it is proved, what the neigh-
    bors guessed:
  His wife and himself had separate
    rooms."

VIII.

Friends, the goodman of the house
    at least
  Kept house to himself till an earth-
    quake came:
'Tis the fall of its frontage permits
    you feast
  On the inside arrangement you
    praise or blame.

IX.

Outside should suffice for evidence:
  And whoso desires to penetrate
Deeper, must dive by the spirit-
    sense—
  No optics like yours, at any rate!

X.

"Hoity toity! A street to explore,
  Your house the exception! 'With
    this same key
Shakspeare unlocked his heart,' once
    more!"
  Did Shakspeare? If so, the less
    Shakspeare he!

SHOP.

I.

So, friend, your shop was all your
    house!
  Its front, astonishing the street,
Invited view from man and mouse
  To what diversity of treat
  Behind its glass—the single sheet!

II.

What gimcracks, genuine Japanese:
  Gape-jaw and goggle-eye, the frog;
Dragons, owls, monkeys, beetles,
    geese;
  Some crush-nosed human-hearted
    dog:
  Queer names, too, such a catalogue!

III.

I thought "And he who owns the
    wealth
  Which blocks the window's vasti-
    tude,
—Ah, could I peep at him by stealth
  Behind his ware, pass shop, intrude
  On house itself, what scenes were
    viewed!

IV.

"If wide and showy thus the shop,
  What must the habitation prove?
The true house with no name a-top —
  The mansion, distant one remove,
Once get him off his traffic-groove!

V.

"Pictures he likes, or books perhaps;
  And as for buying most and best,
Commend me to these city chaps!
  Or else he's social, takes his rest
On Sundays, with a Lord for guest.

VI.

"Some suburb-palace, parked about
  And gated grandly, built last year:
The four-mile walk to keep off gout;
  Or big seat sold by bankrupt peer:
But then he takes the rail, that's
    clear.

VII.

"Or, stop! I wager, taste selects
  Some out o' the way, some all-
    unknown
Retreat: the neighborhood suspects
  Little that he who rambles lone
Makes Rothschild tremble on his
    throne!"

VIII.

Nowise! Nor Mayfair residence
  Fit to receive and entertain, —
Nor Hampstead villa's kind defence
  From noise and crowd, from dust
    and drain, —
Nor country-box was soul's domain!

IX.

Nowise! At back of all that spread
  Of merchandise, woe's me, I find
A hole i' the wall where, heels by
    head,
  The owner couched, his ware be-
    hind,
  — In cupboard suited to his mind.

X.

For, why? He saw no use of life
  But, while he drove a roaring trade,
To chuckle "Customers are rife!"
  To chafe "So much hard cash out-
    laid
Yet zero in my profits made!

XI.

"This novelty costs pains, but—
    takes?
  Cumbers my counter! Stock no
    more!
This article, no such great shakes,
  Fizzes like wild fire? Underscore
The cheap thing — thousands to the
    fore!"

XII.

'Twas lodging best to live most nigh
  (Cramp, coffinlike as crib might be)
Receipt of Custom; ear and eye
  Wanted no outworld: "Hear and
    see
The bustle in the shop!" quoth he.

XIII.

My fancy of a merchant-prince
  Was different. Through his wares
    we groped
Our darkling way to — not to mince
  The matter — no black den where
    moped
The master if we interloped!

XIV.

Shop was shop only: household-
    stuff?
  What did he want with comforts
    there?
"Walls, ceiling, floor, stay blank and
    rough,
So goods on sale show rich and rare!
  'Sell and send home,' be shop's
    affair!"

XV.

What might he deal in? Gems, sup-
    pose!
  Since somehow business must be
    done
At cost of trouble, — see, he throws
  You choice of jewels, every one
Good, better, best, star, moon, and
    sun!

XVI.

Which lies within your power of
    purse?
  This ruby that would tip aright
Solomon's sceptre? Oh, your nurse
  Wants simply coral, the delight
Of teething baby, — stuff to bite!

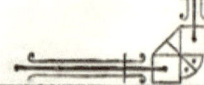

A Tale. — Page 281.

XVII.

Howe'er your choice fell, straight you
    took
  Your purchase, prompt your money
    rang
On counter, — scarce the man forsook
  His study of the "Times," just
    swang
  Till-ward his hand that stopped the
    clang, —

XVIII.

Then off made buyer with a prize,
  Then seller to his "Times" re-
    turned,
And so did day wear, wear, till eyes
  Brightened apace, for rest was
    earned :
  He locked door long ere candle
    burned.

XIX.

And whither went he? Ask him-
    self,
  Not me! To change of scene, I
    think.
Once sold the ware and pursed the
    pelf,
  Chaffer was scarce his meat and
    drink,
  Nor all his music — money-chink.

XX.

Because a man has shop to mind
  In time and place, since flesh must
    live,
Needs spirit lack all life behind,
  All stray thoughts, fancies fugitive,
  All loves except what trade can
    give ?

XXI.

I want to know a butcher paints,
  A baker rhymes for his pursuit,
Candlestick-maker much acquaints
  His soul with song, or, haply mute,
  Blows out his brains upon the flute !

XXII.

But — shop each day and all day long !
  Friend, your good angel slept, your
    star
Suffered eclipse, fate did you wrong !
  From where these sorts of treas-
    ures are,
  There should our hearts be — Christ,
    how far !

A TALE.

I.

WHAT a pretty tale you told me
  Once upon a time
— Said you found it somewhere (scold
    me !)
  Was it prose or was it rhyme,
Greek or Latin? Greek, you said,
While your shoulder propped my
    head.

II.

Anyhow there's no forgetting
  This much if no more,
That a poet (pray, no petting !)
  Yes, a bard, sir, famed of yore,
Went where suchlike used to go,
Singing for a prize, you know.

III.

Well, he had to sing, nor merely
  Sing but play the lyre ;
Playing was important clearly
  Quite as singing : I desire,
Sir, you keep the fact in mind
For a purpose that's behind.

IV.

There stood he, while deep attention
  Held the judges round,
— Judges able, I should mention,
  To detect the slightest sound
Sung or played amiss : such ears
Had old judges, it appears !

V.

None the less he sang out boldly,
  Played in time and tune,
Till the judges, weighing coldly
  Each note's worth, seemed, late or
    soon,
Sure to smile "In vain one tries
Picking faults out : take the prize !"

VI.

When, a mischief ! Were they seven
  Strings the lyre possessed ?
Oh, and afterwards eleven,
  Thank you ! Well, sir, — who had
    guessed
Such ill luck in store ? — it happed
One of those same seven strings
    snapped.

VII.

All was lost, then ! No ! a cricket
 (What "cicada" ? Pooh !)
— Some mad thing that left its thicket
 For mere love of music — flew
With its little heart on fire,
Lighted on the crippled lyre.

VIII.

So that when (Ah joy !) our singer
 For his truant string
Feels with disconcerted finger,
 What does cricket else but fling
Fiery heart forth, sound the note
Wanted by the throbbing throat ?

IX.

Ay and, ever to the ending,
 Cricket chirps at need,
Executes the hand's intending,
 Promptly, perfectly, — indeed
Saves the singer from defeat
With her chirrup low and sweet.

X.

Till, at ending, all the judges
 Cry with one assent
" Take the prize — a prize who grudges
 Such a voice and instrument ?
Why, we took your lyre for harp,
So it shrilled us forth F sharp ! "

XI.

Did the conqueror spurn the creature,
 Once its service done ?
That's no such uncommon feature
 In the case when Music's son
Finds his Lotte's power too spent
For aiding soul-development.

XII.

No ! This other, on returning
 Homeward, prize in hand,
Satisfied his bosom's yearning :
 (Sir, I hope you understand !)
— Said " Some record there must be
Of this cricket's help to me ! "

XIII.

So, he made himself a statue :
 Marble stood, life-size ;

On the lyre, he pointed at you,
 Perched his partner in the prize ;
Never more apart you found
Her, he throned, from him, she
 crowned.

XIV.

That's the tale : its application ?
 Somebody I know
Hopes one day for reputation
 Through his poetry that's — Oh,
All so learned and so wise,
And deserving of a prize !

XV.

If he gains one, will some ticket,
 When his statue's built,
Tell the gazer " 'Twas a cricket
 Helped my crippled lyre, whose lilt
Sweet and low, when strength
  usurped
Softness' place i' the scale, she
 chirped ?

XVI.

" For as victory was nighest,
 While I sang and played, —
With my lyre at lowest, highest,
 Right alike, — one string that made
' Love' sound soft was snapt in twain,
Never to be heard again, —

XVII.

" Had not a kind cricket fluttered,
 Perched upon the place
Vacant left, and duly uttered
 ' Love, Love, Love,' whene'er the
  bass
Asked the treble to atone
For its somewhat sombre drone."

XVIII.

But you don't know music ! Where-
 fore
 Keep on casting pearls
To a — poet ? All I care for
 Is — to tell him that a girl's
" Love" comes aptly in when gruff
Grows his singing. (There, enough !)

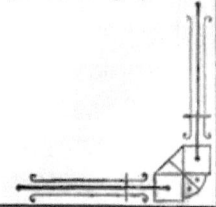